Empires at War

Other Books by the Author

William Ellery: A Rhode Island Politico and Lord of Admiralty

Rebels Under Sail: The American Navy in the Revolution

The American Revolution: Changing Perspectives (coeditor)

The Baron of Beacon Hill: A Biography of John Hancock

Jack Tars and Commodores: The American Navy, 1783–1815

Under Two Flags: The American Navy in the Civil War

Silas Talbot: Captain of Old Ironsides

Samuel Adams Radical Puritan

America and the Sea: A Maritime History (coauthor)

The Seven Years' War and

the Struggle for

North America, 1754–1763

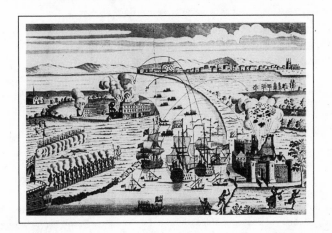

Empires at War

William M. Fowler Jr.

Douglas & McIntyre
Vancouver/Toronto

Douglas & McIntyre Ltd.
2323 Quebec Street, Suite 201
Vancouver, British Columbia
Canada v5t 4s7
www.douglas-mcintyre.com

Originated and published in the U.S. by Walker & Company,
104 Fifth Avenue, New York, New York, 10011.

Art Credits:
Pages 3 (neg. 604), 13 (neg. 4482), 32 (neg. 83497), 76 (neg. 10597), 97 (neg. 27665), 108 (neg.
11235), 112 (neg. 41109), 145 (neg. 96944), 177 (neg. 3916), 185 (neg. 34215), 208 (neg. 100619),
211 (neg. 21457), 212 (neg. 18752), and 253 (neg. 5805) National Archives Canada.
Pages 16, 83, 88, 124, 146, 158, 162, 168, 182, and 187 Massachusetts Historical Society. Pages
19, 247, and 251 Library of Congress, Maps Division. Pages 21, 57, 206, and 234 McCord
Museum of Canadian History. Pages 25, 100, 210, 267, and 286 William L. Clements Library,
University of Michigan. Page 33 John Carter Brown Library, Brown University. Page 43
Washington and Lee University (Washington/Custis/Lee Collection). Page 225 National Portrait
Gallery, London. Page 263 National Maritime Museum, Greenwich.

Library and Archives Canada Cataloguing in Publication
Fowler, William M., 1944–
    Empires at war : the Seven Years' War and the struggle for North America,
    1754-1763 / William Fowler.
    Includes bibliographical references and index.

    ISBN-13: 978-1-55365-181-9 · ISBN-10: 1-55365-181-2

    1. Canada—History—Seven Years' War, 1755-1763. I. Title.
FC384.F68 2005   971.01'88   C2004-907422-9

Cover design by Jessica Sullivan
Cover illustration by Phillips, Fine Art Auctioneers, New York, USA
Interior book design by RLF Design
Printed and bound in Canada by Friesens
Printed on acid-free paper that is forest friendly (100% post-consumer recycled paper)
and has been processed chlorine free.

To my father—

a member of the

"Greatest Generation"

Contents

Acknowledgments

This book began with travel. For many years each summer I have had the opportunity to cruise the shores of eastern Canada, the Saint Lawrence River, and the Great Lakes. It has also been my pleasure in the winter season to visit often in Ottawa. Those trips sparked and then sustained my interest in our northern neighbor and particularly its early connections with New England. That relationship, of course, was often violent, as three peoples—Native Americans, French, and English—competed for land, trade, and influence along the marchlands of North America. In the summer of 1754 an incident in the valley of the Ohio River piled fuel on these smoldering embers and ignited the world's first world war. That war is the focus of this work.

In the course of my travels I talked with many historic-site interpreters, who cheerfully answered my questions. Many of these men and women belong to the staffs of the National Park Service and Parks Canada. Others work for sites held privately. All were invariably helpful. Until 1998 I was a member of the faculty at Northeastern University. To that institution I owe a considerable debt. My colleagues in the Department of History, as well as staff from the Snell Library and university administration, aided my work at every step and created an atmosphere in which scholarship is valued and supported. The same may be said of the Massachusetts Historical Society, to which I moved in 1998. One of the world's great research libraries, the collections of the MHS are, according to the *Harvard Guide to American History*, "the most important collections of American manuscripts outside the Library of Congress." While the collections may be second to the Library of Congress, the staff of the society is second to none! Under the able direction of the librarian Peter Drummey, the staff is invariably amiable and professional. Mary Fabiszewski, the society's chief cataloger, was particularly helpful in finding scarce titles for me. Two neighbors of the society, the Boston Public Library and the Boston Athenaeum, were also gracious. I also extend my thanks to the Huntington Library, San Marino, California, for providing copies of materials from the Loudoun Papers.

In Ottawa the staff at the Library and Archives Canada were exceedingly helpful. During my visits to the Library and Archives materials were made available in a cheerful and timely fashion. The staff, particularly those individuals in the photographic department, also responded quickly to my e-mail and phone inquiries. The same high level of service is characteristic of the National Gallery of Canada. I am also grateful for the kind attention I received from Peter Harrington, curator of the Anne S. K. Brown Military Collection at the Brown University Library, and the staffs at the McCord Museum, Montreal, and the National Maritime Museum, Greenwich.

During the course of my work numerous friends and colleagues were generous with their time, advice, and encouragement. Both Nicholas Westbrook and Ian McCulloch were kind enough to offer their comments. I am particularly thankful to David McCullough, who in the gentlest way often asked me, "So how's the book going?" His queries were a tonic to me. I also thank Linda Smith Rhoads, editor of the *New England Quarterly*, who once again took the time to read and comment. My editor, George Gibson, knew when to stay distant and when to draw close. His keen comments and insight were invaluable, and they were delivered in the most amiable fashion. I also recognize the fine reading given to the manuscript by Arthur Goldwag and the superb copyediting of Vicki Haire. Special thanks go to my dear friend Martin, who for many years offered me his hospitality during my many visits to Ottawa.

Finally, I thank my wife, Marilyn, and our children, Alison and Nathaniel, who patiently endured my absence while writing this book.

Biographical Sketches

Abercromby, James (1706–81), succeeded Lord Loudoun as commander in chief in North America and was defeated at Ticonderoga (1758).

Amherst, Jeffrey (1717–97), was third British commander in chief in North America following Edward Braddock and John Campbell (Lord Loudoun).

Amherst, William (1732–81), the younger brother of Jeffrey Amherst, retook Newfoundland from the French in 1762.

Anson, George (1697–1762), was first lord of the admiralty.

Atkins, Edmund (1697–1761), was superintendent of Indian affairs for the Southern Department.

Attakullakulla, Little Carpenter (1705–80), was a Cherokee chief and British ally known for his skills at diplomacy.

Barré, Isaac (1726–1802), an officer who served with Wolfe, later became an outspoken opponent of taxing America.

Barrin, de la Galissonière, Roland-Michel, Marquis de la Galissonière (1693–1756), was governor of New France from 1746 to 1749.

Boscawen, Edward (1711–61), was a British admiral who commanded the naval force at the siege of Louisbourg in 1758.

Bougainville, Louis-Antoine, Comte de (1729–1811), was a French officer who served with Montcalm and later commanded an exploring expedition into the Pacific Ocean.

Bouquet, Henry (1719–65), was a Swiss officer serving in the British army. He commanded the expedition that relieved Fort Pitt during Pontiac's rebellion.

Bourlamaque, François-Charles de (1716–63), a French officer, accompanied Montcalm to North America and served as an engineer.

Bradstreet, John (1714–74), was born in Nova Scotia and served in North America and captured Fort Frontenac in 1758.

Burton, Ralph (?–1768), was an officer in the forty-eighth Regiment who arrived in America with Braddock and later served with Wolfe at Quebec.

Byng, John (1704–57), British admiral, was executed for failing to relieve the island of Minorca.

Campbell, John, Earl of Loudoun (1705–82), succeeded Edward Braddock as commander in chief in North America.

Céloron de Blainville, Pierre-Joseph (1693–1759), an officer in the Troupes de la Marine, was born in Montreal. He commanded the force sent into the Ohio Valley in 1749. His report of English incursions alarmed the French government.

Chabert de Joncaire, Philippe-Thomas, Nitachinon (1707–66), born in Montreal, was a fur trader, translator, and officer in the Troupes de la Marine. Posted to Venango, Joncaire was responsible for maintaining relations with the Delaware and Shawnee.

Charles III (1716–88), succeeded his brother Ferdinand VI as king of Spain. His foreign policy resulted in Spain's entry into the war with disastrous results.

Chartier de Lotbinière, Michel, Marquis de Lotbinière (1723–98), was a military engineer and officer in the Troupes de la Marine. He was born in Quebec City and worked on the fortifications at Quebec and Fort Ticonderoga.

Chaussegros, de Léry, Gaspard-Joseph (1721–97), born in Quebec City, was an engineer in the Troupes de la Marine. He commanded the attack against Fort Bull on March 27, 1756.

Choiseuil, Etiènne François, duc de (1719–85), was the Minister of Foreign Affairs under Louis XV. He negotiated the Treaty of Paris in 1763.

Clive, Robert (1725–74), was the British governor of Bengal and the victor at the battle of Plassey (1757).

Cook, James (1728–79), master navigator, guided Saunders's fleet up the Saint Lawrence and later explored the Pacific.

Coulon de Villiers de Jumonville, Joseph (1718–54), was born in Vercheres, Quebec. An officer in the Troupes de la Marine, he was killed in an engagement with Washington on May 28, 1754, at the place now known as Jumonville Glen.

Coulon de Villiers, Louis (1710–57), born in Vercheres, Quebec, was an officer in the Troupes de la Marine. He commanded the force that defeated Washington at Fort Necessity. His brother was among those killed at Jumonville Glen.

Croghan, George (?–1782), was a land speculator, fur trader, and a close associate of William Johnson.

D'Arcy, Robert, Earl of Holderness (1718–78), served as secretary of the Southern Department, the office that oversaw colonial affairs.

Dekanahwideh (pre-European contact period), was the legendary founder of the Iroquois Confederation. Born near the Bay of Quinte, he carried a message of peace to the warring Iroquois.

DeLancey, James (1703–60), was lieutenant governor of New York. After the death of the royal governor he served as the chief officer of the colony from 1754 to 1760.

Dieskau, Jean-Armand, Baron de (1701–67), commander of the French regulars, was defeated and captured at the battle of Lake George (1755).

Dinwiddie, Robert (1692–1770), was the lieutenant governor of Virginia who sent Washington on his missions to the West.

Duquesne, De Menneville, Ange, Marquis Duquesne (1700–78), was a naval officer and governor of New France. He ordered the establishment of a fort at the forks of the Ohio River.

Elizabeth II (1709–62), was Empress of Russia and an ally of Austria and France against Frederick the Great. Her death resulted in Russia's temporary withdrawal from the war.

Ferdinand VI (1713–59), was king of Spain. During his reign he resisted joining the French in the war.

Ferdinand, Duke of Prussia (1721–92), was the Prussian general who commanded the allied armies in western Germany.

Forbes, John (1707–59), was the British general who led the expedition that captured Fort Duquesne in 1758.

Fox, Henry (1705–74), was a political leader in the House of Commons. He was often in opposition to William Pitt.

Gage, Thomas (1721–87), an officer in the Forty-Fourth Regiment, arrived with Braddock and remained in America for the entire war.

Gist, Christopher (1706–59), was a land surveyor and speculator. He was involved with the Ohio Company and accompanied Washington on his trip west in 1753.

Glen, James (1701–77), was the royal governor of South Carolina. He established posts within Cherokee country.

Grenville, George (1712–70), a leader in the House of Commons, was among those to propose raising revenue in the American colonies.

Hawke, Edward (1705–81), was the British admiral who defeated the French at the battle of Quiberon Bay (1759).

Hay, Charles Lord (?–1760), was an officer who served under Loudoun while planning the attack against Louisbourg in 1757. Alleged to be "mad" he was arrested and returned to England for a court martial.

Hiawatha (pre-European contact period) was, according to legend, a disciple of Dekanahwideh and journeyed with him to the Iroquois country to preach peace.

Holbourne, Francis (1704–71), was the British admiral who commanded the fleet in the unexecuted attack on Louisbourg in 1757.

Holmes, Charles (1711–61), was a British admiral who served under Saunders and Wolfe at Quebec.

Howe, George Augustus, third Viscount Howe (1725–58), was the oldest of the three Howe brothers. He was killed at Ticonderoga.

Howe, Richard, Earl Howe (1726–99), was the royal naval officer who fired on the French ship *Alcide* before an official declaration of war. He later rose to the rank of admiral and commanded naval forces during the American Revolution.

Howe, William, Viscount Howe (1729–1814), was the younger brother of Richard Howe. He was with Wolfe at Louisbourg and Quebec. He later commanded British forces in the American Revolution.

Hutchinson, Thomas (1711–80), was lieutenant governor of Massachusetts and one of the authors of the Albany Plan of Union.

Johnson, William (1715–74), was Superintendent for Indian Affairs in the Northern Department.

Kaunitz, Count Wenzel von (1711–94), was one of the most able diplomats of eighteenth-century Europe. He served as foreign minister for Empress Maria Theresa of Austria.

Keppel, Augustus, Viscount Keppel (1725–86), was the British admiral who commanded the expedition against Havana in 1761.

Keppel, George, third Earl of Albemarle (1724–72), was the brother of Augustus Keppel and commander of land forces during the Havana expedition.

Legardeur de Saint-Pierre, Jacques, 1701–55, was born in Montreal and was an officer in the Troupes de la Marine. He was commandant at Fort de la Rivière au Boeuf when George Washington visited in 1753.

Le Loutre, Jean Louis (1709–72), a priest and missionary, urged Acadians and Indians in Nova Scotia to harass the British.

Le Marchand de Lignery, François-Marie (1703–59), was born in Montreal and was an officer in the Troupes de la Marine. Lignery commanded Fort Duquesne during Forbes's advance.

Le Moyne de Longueuil, Charles, Baron de Longueuil (1687–1755), was born at Longueuil. He was an officer in the Troupes de la Marine and governor of Montreal. In 1752 he served briefly as governor of New France following the death of governor Jonquière.

Lienard de Beaujeu, Daniel-Hyancinthe-Marie (1711–55), born in Montreal, was an officer in the Troupes de la Marine. He commanded the force sent to attack Braddock and was killed at the opening of the battle July 9, 1755.

Ligonier, John (1680–1770), a British general, succeeded the Duke of Cumberland as commander in chief.

Lyttleton, William Henry (1724–1808), succeeded James Glen as governor of South Carolina in 1755.

Maria Theresa, Empress of Austria (1717–80), was an ally of France against Prussia and England. Her daughter Marie Antoinette married the future king of France Louis XVI.

Marin de La Malgue (La Marque), Paul (1692–1753), born in Montreal, was an officer in the Troupes de la Marine. In 1753 he commanded a large force sent into the Ohio Valley to establish a series of forts.

Mauduit, Israel (1708–87), wrote the influential pamphlet *Considerations on the Present German War* (1760).

Memeskia, also known as Old Briton and La Demoiselle (1695–1752), was a Miami chief who defied the French when they demanded that he cease trading with the English. Subsequently, the French attacked his village, Pickawillany (Piqua, Ohio), on June 21, 1752, killing him and many others.

Moore, John (1718–79), was the royal naval officer who commanded the fleet supporting the capture of Guadeloupe in 1759.

Mordaunt, Charles (1697–1780), was the general in command of the unsuccessful attack against Rochefort in 1757.

Mouet de Langlade, Charles-Michel (1729–1801), was born in Michilimackinac (Mackinaw City). He was an officer in the Troupes de la Marine and led the attack against Pickawillany.

Murray, James (1722–94), was a British officer who served with Wolfe at Quebec and later commanded the city.

Neolin, known as The Delaware Prophet (?–1763), was a religious leader among the Delaware who preached a return to traditional native ways. His message helped inspire Pontiac's rebellion.

Newcastle, Thomas Pelham Hollis, Duke (1693–1768), served almost continuously in high office and as prime minister until his death in 1768.

Oconostota (1712–83), was war leader of the "Overhill" Cherokee. He allied himself with the British and led his people in union with Attakullakulla.

Payen de Noyan et de Chavoy, Pierre-Jacques (1695–1771), was born in Trois-Rivières. He was an officer in the Troupes de la Marine who commanded at both Detroit and Crown Point. On August 27, 1758, he surrendered Fort Frontenac to John Bradstreet.

Pecaudy de Contrecoeur, Claude-Pierre (1705–75), was born in Montreal. He was an officer in the Troupes de la Marine who commanded the force that occupied the forks of the Ohio in April 1755.

Pelham, Henry (1695–1754), served as prime minister until his death and was succeeded by his brother the duke of Newcastle.

Peter III (1728–62), the Czar of Russia, allied himself with Frederick II. His sudden death brought Catherine II, "The Great," to the throne.

Pocock, George (1706–92), commanded the fleet that captured Havana in 1762.

Pompadour, Jeanne Antoinette Poisson le Normant D'Etoiles (1721–64), was mistress to Louis XV and influenced him to oppose Frederick the Great.

Pontiac (1712(?)–69), was the Ottawa chief who led a rebellion that began near Detroit in 1763. As the rebellion spread it took on his name.

Pouchot, Pierre (1712–69), was the French officer who surrendered Fort Niagara in 1759 and delayed Amherst's advance at Fort Levis in 1760.

Rigaud de Vaudreuil, François-Pierre de (1703–79), was born in Montreal. The son of a governor of New France and brother to governor Pierre de Rigaud de Vaudreuil de Cavagnial, he was also a soldier in the Troupes de la Marine.

Rigaud de Vaudreuil de Cavagnial, Pierre de, Marquis de Vaudreuil (1698–1778), was born in Quebec. He was the son of the governor of New France and served as governor of Louisiana and New France.

Rodney, George (1719–92), was a British admiral who served in the West Indies and captured Martinique.

Rogers, Robert (1731–95), born in New Hampshire, organized a group of colonials and trained them in wilderness warfare. The organization became known as Rogers Rangers.

Russell, John, fourth Duke of Bedford (1710–71), was a diplomat and ally of Lord Bute. He negotiated the Treaty of Paris in 1763.

Saunders, Charles (1713–75), commanded the fleet that supported Wolfe at Quebec.

Scarouady (?–1758), was the Oneida chief who succeeded Tanaghrisson as Half King.

Shirley, William (1694–1771), served as governor of Massachusetts and succeeded Braddock as commander in chief in North America.

Stobo, Robert (1727–70?), was an officer in the Virginia militia. He was with Washington at Fort Necessity and stayed with the French as a hostage for the safe return of French prisoners.

Suraj-Ud-Dowlah (?–1757), the nawab of Bengal, was responsible for the "Black Hole of Calcutta."

Taffanel de La Jonquière, Jacques-Pierre de, Marquis de la Jonquière (1685–1752), was the governor of New France from 1749 to 1752.

Tanaghrisson, The Half King (?–1754), was a Seneca chief who led the Iroquois, often referred to as Mingo, in the Ohio Valley. He was with Washington at Fort Necessity.

Teedyuscung (1700–63), was a Delaware leader best known as an orator. A friend to both the English and the French, he was deeply involved in a number of controversial land deals.

Testard de Montigny, Jean-Baptiste-Philippe (1724–86), was born in Montreal. He was an officer in the Troupes de la Marine and was present at Braddock's defeat. He served as second in command during the attack on Fort Bull.

Theyanoguin, Hendrick (1680–1755), was a Christian Mohawk and close friend to William Johnson. Often critical of the English, he worked to keep the Mohawks allied with them. He died at the Battle of Lake George on September 8, 1755.

Townshend, George (1724–1807), was an army officer and politician who served with Wolfe at Quebec.

Vauban, Sebastian le Prestre de (1633–1707), was the masterful architect of fortifications throughout Europe. His style was imitated in North America.

Wall, Richard (1694–1778), was an Irish expatriate who served as foreign minister to King Ferdinand VI of Spain. Wall favored a pro-English policy.

Walpole, Horace (1717–97), was a British author and gadfly whose memoirs and letters are important in understanding eighteenth-century English society and politics.

Webb, Daniel (1700–73), British commander, refused to send assistance to Fort William Henry when it was under attack.

William Augustus, Duke of Cumberland (1721–65), was the son of George II and commander in chief until summarily relieved by his father in 1757.

Winslow, John (1703–74), major general in the Massachusetts militia, was principally responsible for deporting Acadians.

Yorke, Philip, Earl of Hardwicke (1690–1764), was an ally of Newcastle and a noted jurist who rose to become lord chancellor of England.

Chronology

June–July—Albany Congress

July 4—Washington surrenders at Fort Necessity

1755 June 9—Boscawen intercepts French ships

June 16—Fort Beauséjour surrenders to English

June—Vaudreuil arrives as governor of New France

July 9—Braddock is defeated at Monongahela

Summer–Fall—Acadian expulsion

September 8—Battles at Lake George

1756 March 27—Fort Bull falls to French

May 12—Montcalm arrives in Quebec

May 18—England declares war on France

May 20—French defeat Admiral Byng off Minorca

June 20—Suraj ud Dowla captures Calcutta and allegedly confines British prisoners in "Black Hole"

July 23—Lord Loudoun arrives in New York as new commander
in chief

August 14—Oswego surrenders to French

August 29—Prussia invades Saxony

November—Pitt enters government

1757 March 17—French attack Fort William Henry but fail to
capture it

March 23—Clive captures Chandernagor

April 6—Pitt leaves government

April 9—Cumberland leaves to take command in Germany

June—Anson appointed first lord

June 18—Prussia defeated at Battle of Kolin

June 23—Battle of Plassey Grove, British defeat Suraj ud Dowla

June 29—Pitt returns to office

July 26—Battle of Hastenbeck, Cumberland is defeated

August—Loudoun abandons Louisbourg campaign

August 9—Fort William Henry surrenders to French

September 8—Cumberland and Richelieu sign agreement at
convention of Klostersevern

October—British attempt against Rochefort fails

December 1—James Abercromby succeeds Loudoun as
  commander in chief in North America

1758 February 28—Admiral Henry Osbourne defeats French fleet
  off Cartagena

April 24—French surrender Fort St. Louis on Senegal River
  to British

April 29—British (Admiral Pocock) and French (Admiral
  d'Ache) fleets fight indecisive battle off Pondicherry

June 1—General Forbes meets with Cherokee in
  Philadelphia

June 2—French capture Fort St. David

July 8—British fail to capture Fort Ticonderoga

July 27—British capture Louisbourg

August 3—British (Pocock) and French (d'Ache) fleets engage
  in second indecisive battle off Pondicherry

August 3—First British contingents arrive in Germany

August 27—British capture Fort Frontenac

September 14—British force under James Grant is defeated
  near Fort Duquesne

October 7–26—Easton Conference

October 12—Lignery attacks British at Loyal Hannon

November 25—British capture Fort Duquesne

December 13—French besiege Madras

1759 January 19—British fail to capture Martinique

January 23—British land on Guadeloupe

February 17—Siege of Madras is lifted

May 1—Guadeloupe surrenders to British

June 26—British open siege of Quebec

July 26—British capture Fort Niagara

July 31—British are repulsed at Montmorency

August 1—Battle of Minden

August 12—Battle of Kunersdorf

August 18—Boscawen defeats French off Lagos

September 13—British victory at Quebec

September 18—Quebec surrenders

October 4—Rogers Rangers attack St. Francis
November 20—Battle of Quiberon Bay

1760 February 16—Cherokee attack Fort Prince George
      April 28—Battle of Sillery Woods (St. Foy), French fail to re-
          take Quebec
      August 7—Cherokee capture Fort Loudoun
      September 8—Montreal surrenders to Amherst
      September 16—Canadian Iroquois meet with William Johnson
          at Montreal
      October 16—Battle of Kloster Kamp
      October 25—Death of George II

1761 June 7—British capture Dominica
      August 15—Spain and France sign the Family Compact
      September 23—Cherokee sign peace treaty
      October 5—Pitt resigns from cabinet
      November—Spain enters war on side of France

1762 January 5—Death of Czarina Elizabeth of Russia
      February 13—British capture Martinique
      June 18—Conference at Easton with Delaware and Iroquois
      June 24—French capture St. John's, Newfoundland
      August 11—British capture Havana
      September 18—British retake St. John's, Newfoundland
      October 6—British capture Manila

1763 February 10—Treaty of Paris
      April 19—Teedyuscung and his wife die in a mysterious fire

1763–64—Pontiac's rebellion
      May 7, 1763—Pontiac fails to retake Detroit by deception
      May 16—Indians capture Fort Sandusky
      May 25—Indians capture Fort St. Joseph
      May 28—Indians capture Fort Miamis
      June 2—Indians capture Fort Michilimackinac
      August 6—Indians are defeated at Edge Hill
      October 7—King George III issues proclamation setting
          boundaries for new territory in North America

November 17—General Thomas Gage succeeds Amherst as commander in chief in North America; Amherst returns to England

1766 July 23—Pontiac meets with William Johnson at Oswego

1769 April 20—Pontiac assassinated

Empires at War

Prologue

Americans know it as the French and Indian War. Some Canadians, particularly those of French descent, refer to the conflict as the War of the Conquest. In Europe it is called the Seven Years War. None of these titles is fully accurate, for in fact the struggle that raged between 1754 and 1763 (hostilities preceded the formal declarations of war by two years) was the first world war.

The war pitted the world's two superpowers, France and England, against each other in a titanic struggle for imperial domination. This was hardly the first time the French and English had grappled. Ancient enmities going back at least to 1066 had often driven these two nations to conflict, but this time the struggle was not about the usual familial claims to thrones or who should control some petty duchy or principality or even who would dominate the continent of Europe. It was a competition to determine who would dominate the other continents of the world.

At sea, and on battlefields in Europe, North America, the West Indies, Asia, India, and Africa, fleets and armies fought. Every major power in Europe joined the fray. Hundreds of thousands of soldiers, sailors, and civilians died. At the final peace, weary combatants traded territories vaster than all of Europe. England emerged victorious, and its triumph laid the foundation for a global empire from which it would draw the wealth and resources to fuel the industrial revolution and transform the world.

Although the war was fought all over the world, its most decisive battles were in North America. The struggle for this continent among Indians, French, Canadians, British, and British colonials was the hinge upon which the outcome of the war swung. Americans studying their own history commonly describe this war as the prelude to the American Revolution. Aside from being provincial, that interpretation both exaggerates and under-states its real significance. The ideological split between England and its colonies began in earlier generations. Furthermore, the political, eco-nomic, and social forces that drove the colonies toward revolution were in operation long before the war began. The American habit of viewing the French and Indian War backward through the lens of the Revolution masks its true importance as a world-shaping event.

From the very first days of permanent settlement in North America the French and English had been at each other's throats. Competition for trade, uncertain boundaries, and a rambunctious population of frontiers-men kindled violence on both sides. Men in Paris and London knew full well that there was an absence of peace in North America, but minor skir-mishes, a raid here and there, a few homes burned, were petty events hardly worthy of notice when compared to the pageants of Europe. Indeed, on those several occasions in the seventeenth and eighteenth centuries when wars between the great powers came to North America, they arrived as imports from Europe.

In 1689 the War of the League of Augsburg began in Europe. By the time it reached America it was known as King William's War. In 1702 the War of Spanish Succession erupted, to be titled Queen Anne's War when the shooting began in America. The War of the Austrian Succession swept Eu-rope in 1744 and crossed the Atlantic the next year as King George's War. The last and greatest of these struggles, however, followed a very different pattern. The French and Indian War reversed the traditional course of events; beginning in America, it was exported to Europe.

Both England and France had firm footholds in North America by the early eighteenth century. English settlement was ensconced along the At-lantic coast from Maine to Georgia. Tendrils of settlement, particularly in Pennsylvania, Virginia, and the Carolinas, were beginning to creep farther west. The white population of these colonies numbered nearly one million, mostly farmers, nearly all English-speaking Protestants.

Canada was colonized differently. Although the French king claimed a vast territory stretching from the Arctic Circle to the Gulf of Mexico and from the Appalachians across the Mississippi, in fact French settlement was confined to the valley of the St. Lawrence between Quebec and Mon-treal and to the mouth of the Mississippi at New Orleans. Altogether not

Louis XV, king of France

more than sixty thousand French lived in all this territory. From New Orleans and the St. Lawrence Valley a fragile web of control maintained by
peripatetic priests, soldiers, and fur traders extended deep into the interior of North America. Linked by rivers and lakes, and anchored by a series of forts and trading posts in the west (at places like Niagara, Detroit,
and Michilimackinac); in the Ohio region (at Presque Isle, Le Boeuf, and
Venango); and in the south (Fort Toulousse), French dominion was strong
at its center in the St. Lawrence Valley but weak on the edges. It was precisely along these rough edges—in Acadia, along Lake Ontario, and in the
Ohio Valley—where trouble brewed. Everywhere along this jagged edge Indian nations stood between two poles: French and English. Depending

upon shifting circumstances, particularly their own self-interest, native peoples allied with one or the other European rivals. In time of declared war such alliances were open as regular soldiers and colonial militia accompanied their native allies on marches into the enemy homeland. But once the declared war ended—an event marked usually by diplomatic folderol in European capitals, an exchange of territory, regulars sailing home, and the return of French and English settlers to their towns and villages—native allies, parties to the war but not to the peace, continued to be used by the colonial powers as surrogates to bring instability and violence to the frontier.

Neither the British nor the French could properly define the boundaries of Acadia. Lying north of New England, it stretched between present-day eastern New Brunswick and across the Bay of Fundy to the western shore of Nova Scotia. The region was home to the Micmac and Abenaki, Algonquin-speaking Indians. Early in the seventeenth century the French began to settle there. Within a few generations several thousand Acadians were farming along the shores and tidal estuaries of the Bay of Fundy and the Northumberland Strait. But at the conclusion of Queen Anne's War in 1713, France surrendered Acadia to England. As a result, the Acadians found themselves suddenly living in a land called Nova Scotia, subject to an alien culture whose laws, religion, and language were thoroughly unfamiliar to them. Sullenly and silently, the Acadians assented to their fate, while their new British masters looked upon them with disdain and suspicion.[1]

Although the French had ceded Nova Scotia, they still held an important post on the Atlantic coast: the imposing fortress at Louisbourg, on Cape Breton Island. The port flourished as a fishing and trading station as well as a key military post.

To counter French power on Cape Breton Island, in 1748 the British Board of Trade ordered Colonel Edward Cornwallis to lay out a settlement and naval base at Chebucto on the Atlantic shore of Nova Scotia. Christened Halifax in honor of the board's president, it commanded one of the most impressive harbors in North America—spacious enough, according to some local boosters, to accommodate the entire Royal Navy. Barely a two-day sail from Cape Breton Island, Halifax provided the Royal Navy with a powerful base from which it could monitor French activities and prowl the approaches to the Gulf of St. Lawrence.

Many Acadians lived on the western side of Nova Scotia, near the Bay of Fundy, one of the most unusual bodies of water in the world. It is shaped like a huge funnel with its wide mouth facing south, and twice a day its enormous tides, in some places more than forty feet, inundate vast expanses of estuaries and salt marshes. As they ebb, these tides leave a rich and luxuriant soil in their wake. By enclosing these tidal lands with a complex system of dikes and gates, Acadian farmers were able to reclaim and protect large areas of tillable land, among the most fertile in North America. (*Acadie* means "fertile lands" in the native Micmac language.) But these lands were in dispute.

Relations between the English and French were particularly tense along Fundy's north shore approaching the Chignecto Isthmus. Across the isthmus, tying Nova Scotia to the mainland, ran the paths linking Quebec, Cape Breton, Isle St. Jean (Prince Edward Island), and Acadia. The British claimed their sovereignty extended through this area and 150 miles west, as far as Baie des Chaleur. The French set the boundary 150 miles in the opposite direction at the Missaguash River. Within this disputed netherworld roamed Abbé Jean Louis Le Loutre, missionary, agitator, and alleged butcher.

Ordained in Paris in 1737, Le Loutre left almost immediately for missionary work in Acadia, where he took up residence at Shubenacadie near modern-day Truro, Nova Scotia. Driven by a devotion to church and nation that his enemies condemned as fanatical, Abbé Le Loutre preached to the Micmac and Acadians. His gospel text was a long way from the Sermon on the Mount; his objective, to save both the Acadians and his Native American converts from the heresy of English Protestantism. He urged the Acadians who lived under British authority to uproot themselves from their ancient homes and move to the soil of the French king. With the Indians, however, he took a different tack. He saw them as pawns to be used to harass the English and prevent the Anglais from settling west of the Missaguash. Le Loutre informed his superiors, "As we cannot openly oppose the English venture, I think that we cannot do better than to incite the Indians to continue warring on the English." His superiors in Paris were in complete agreement.[2]

To the English, Abbé Le Loutre was the devil incarnate. Cornwallis described him as "a good for nothing scoundrel as ever lived."[3] He was accused of taking up the hatchet into his own hands and leading raids against defenseless farmers, burning homes, and offering a bounty of one hundred livres for each British scalp, women and children included. The British were not the only ones to feel Le Loutre's wrath. He terrified the neutral Acadians, too, warning them that if they swore allegiance to the British heretics, they would forfeit their souls, and that he would personally order the Indians to lay waste to their homes.

To protect themselves in an atmosphere of mounting threats, both the British and French built forts at key locations. Of these posts, none were more critical than a pair that stood barely two miles apart, separated by the Missaquash River: Fort Lawrence and Fort Beauséjour. Peace was brittle in the space between them. On an October evening in 1750 Edward How, an officer at Fort Lawrence, was returning alone from a parley with the French. As he walked the short distance between the two forts, unknown assailants ambushed and murdered him. As usual, the English blamed Le Loutre.

To the west of Acadia lay the vast territory of Canada. Taken together with Louisiana, it represented a huge chunk of North America, dwarfing in size the British colonies hugging the Atlantic coast. Despite its expanse, this territory had only two doors by which to enter and exit: the mouth of the Mississippi and the mouth of the St. Lawrence. Communication within Canada and between Canada and Louisiana was almost wholly dependent upon movement along lakes and rivers. Feeling the heat of British ambitions on the fringes of Acadia, the French grew deeply suspicious when the English began to threaten these vital interior lines. Lake Ontario and the Ohio Valley drew special concern.

Lake Ontario was a key link between the St. Lawrence and all the water routes to the west and south. The French claimed the western shore of the lake and asserted their rights by building a fort at the source of the St.

Lawrence (Fort Frontenac) and another to guard the Niagara portage (Fort Niagara). Ontario's opposite shore was home to the Iroquois Confederation. Since the Iroquois's presence worked to block British occupation, the French supported their claim to the land. Neither the French nor the Iroquois were pleased when British traders built a post at the mouth of the Oswego River in 1727. Much to the anger of the French, English traders at Oswego often diverted Montreal-bound trade, siphoning off large quantities of furs intended for French markets, sending them instead to Albany via the Oswego and Mohawk rivers. The Iroquois were more accommodating, since the English often had better goods for sale than the French and offered them at more reasonable prices. Although the Iroquois Confederation tolerated the British presence, they never regarded these traders as anything more than their guests. The land had been theirs since the days of their legendary founder.

According to Iroquois history, sometime long before Europeans arrived, a virgin Huron living near the Bay of Quinte,* was visited by a heavenly messenger who announced that she would be the mother of a son to be named Dekanahwideh, whose mission would be to bring peace to the warring Mohawk, Onondaga, Cayuga, Seneca, and Oneida nations who lived in the Mohawk Valley between Lake Ontario and the Hudson River. He would do this by planting the "Tree of Peace" at Onondaga.† Under this tree the chiefs of the five nations would meet around a "council fire that never dies."

Upon reaching maturity, Dekanahwideh left his mother and paddled across Lake Ontario in a stone canoe. Following the Great Spirit's vision, he found the place where an Onondaga warrior known for his cruel and evil ways lived. His first test was to bring this violent man to the ways of peace which he did. Once converted, the warrior changed his name to Hiawatha. The two then separated and went about the five nations to preach the message of peace: "The land shall be beautiful, the river shall have no more waves, one may go everywhere without fear." The first tribe to convert were the Mohawk, who resided in the east nearest the Hudson. Soon the other four followed. The Onondaga, who lived midway between the lake

*Near present-day Belleville, Ontario.
†Near present-day Syracuse, New York.

and the river, were named as the keepers of the perpetua council fire, around which the chiefs held their meetings. At the western end, nearest the lake, the Seneca, largest of the five nations, stood paramount. The Oneida and Cayuga dwelled between.

Like all creation stories, the story of Dekanahwideh is a concoction of fact and fiction. What is indisputable is that the Iroquois Confederation, known officially as Kayanerenhkowa (the Great Peace), was the strongest pre-European military alliance in North America. Its strategic position astride the east-west water routes placed it in control of a good part of the fur trade. And its role was strengthened by the arrival of the Europeans, particularly the Dutch in the Hudson River valley, who traded firearms for furs. Armed with such weapons, in the mid–seventeenth century the Iroquois launched a series of wars against their neighbors, especially the Huron, aimed at seizing control of the fur trade.[4]

The Iroquois Confederation, organized to preserve the peace, proved even more successful at waging war. Blessed with superior organization, European technology, and an ample number of warriors, the Five Nations swept to victory, virtually annihilating the Huron. Within a few years the Iroquois dominated all the tribes and territory between the Illinois country in the west, the Hudson Valley in the east, and as far south as the Carolinas, where the powerful Cherokee blocked their expansion.

Eventually, Iroquois ambitions exceeded their power. In the early 1660s they engaged in a series of wars against the French in Canada. Despite some early successes, the French forced them to negotiate a peace in 1667. In the meantime the English had driven the Dutch out of New Netherlands and established themselves in the colony renamed New York. The arrival of the English turned out to be a boon for the Iroquois, for it allowed them to play these two European powers against each other. Oswego was a classic instance of this diplomatic strategy: By allowing the English to remain as tenants at Oswego, the Iroquois reasoned, the French were kept at bay. The British, however, had a very different view. In the Treaty of Utrecht in 1713, the same treaty by which the French surrendered Nova Scotia, they also surrendered their sovereignty over the Iroquois to the English. Swapping sovereignties over native people was something Europeans did easily in all parts of the world. Yet the Iroquois were never consulted; nor were they participants in the treaty. They acknowledged neither empire's rule—they regarded themselves as an independent nation.

Farther east the English and French glowered at each other along the waters of Lake Champlain. Like a giant lizard, Lake Champlain stretches 120 miles on a north-south axis. At its northern end the lake drains down the Richelieu River to the St. Lawrence. Toward the south the lake narrows near the La Chute River where a short portage connects to Lake George, which in turn connects via a twelve-mile portage to the Hudson River. The Lake Champlain/Lake George corridor was a vital waterway and a prime invasion route for armies moving in either direction. In 1731 the French seized the advantage on the lake by building Fort St. Frederic at Crown Point, a promontory standing guard at a place where the lake narrows to barely a mile across. Only ninety miles north of Albany, the fort was a constant threat to the English and, in their minds, at least, a point of trespass by the French.

By far the most menacing specter of British encroachment against the French was west of the Appalachians in the valley of the Ohio River. Here, on a scale larger and more threatening than anything they had encountered in Acadia or on the lakes, the French watched fretfully as the British expanded. From Pennsylvania and Virginia, British fur traders hiked west, tugging at the reins of packhorses heavily laden with trade goods. These Anglo traders found willing customers among Native Americans, who were eager to swap beaver skins for woolen cloth, rum, knives, hatchets, and muskets.

In the competition for trade, the British had the advantage. Bureaucratic restrictions and fees, along with less efficient production in the home country, made French goods more expensive than their British counterparts. Native consumers were well aware of the benefits of having British traders to compete with the men from Montreal and Quebec. It meant, quite simply, that they could sell high and buy low. A Wea chief complained to the French commandant at Miamis:* "You know well, my father, we pay for a wool blanket of 2½ points, 9 beavers; for one of cotton, 5 beavers; a

---

*Near present-day Fort Wayne, Indiana.

pair of mitasses, 3 beavers; a pound of powder, 3 beavers; 2 pounds of lead, a beaver. That is what rebuffs all our young men, and we are no longer able to keep them from going to the English, who give them every thing very cheap."[5] Given an opportunity, even the French traders dealt with the English. French and British officials railed at these scofflaws to no effect.

The competition between the English and French traders was a testy business; nonetheless, had commerce been the only point of friction between them, the rivalry might have smoldered and not exploded. However, when trading conflicts were read against the backdrop of imperial expansion, government ministers in Paris and London interpreted events in the Ohio Valley as sinister proof of the enemy's intent to attack and rob them of their rightful possessions. For generations the French, Indians, and English had been stacking the kindling. It was about to ignite.

(1)

Lining Up Allies

*All I can say is that the natives of these localities are very badly
disposed towards the French, and are entirely devoted to the English.*

—Céloron, "Expedition Down the Ohio"

Among those most aware of the English threat was New France's governor,
the marquis de la Galissonière, an officer in the French navy who arrived
at Quebec in September 1747. During his travels through Canada Peter
Kalm, the Swedish scientist and diarist, met Galissonière and was as-
tounded to discover, deep in the North American wilderness, a man so
well versed in science and philosophy. The governor was equally at ease
bantering in Parisian salons or barking orders from the quarterdeck of a
warship. He brought energy and vision to Canada.

Galissonière was the accidental governor. The marquis de La Jonquière
was the original appointee, but he had the misfortune of being taken prisoner in May 1747 when his vessel was captured by the British off the coast
of Spain. Louis XV sent Galissonière as a stand-in until he could manage
the release of Jonquière from the Tower of London. His instructions reflected both the failure of New France in the eyes of the ministers in Paris
as well as their hope for the colony's future. "Although capable of supporting enterprises both solid and profitable, Canada has made but little
progress in the course of a fair number of years. The first settlers, who
were little concerned with these sorts of enterprises, concerned themselves solely with the fur trade they could manage to carry on with the Indians, and there are still a rather large number of them who, satisfied with
what that trade brings them and attracted still more by the independence

they enjoy in their travels, are not much interested in devoting themselves to farming."[1]

Galissonière embraced the challenge. To strengthen the colony, he supported improvements in agriculture and encouraged the development of manufacturing. Ironically, his superiors at home viewed his work with indifference and sometimes hostility. French mercantilists could not abide the thought that the colonies might compete with the mother country. The comte de Maurepas, minister of marine, to whom Galissonière reported, wrote him that his efforts at improving the economy of New France were not welcomed and that they would "be tolerated only to the extent that they [did] not harm the market in France, and for this reason they must not be allowed to multiply."[2] Although disappointed at Maurepas's comments, Galissonière paid them little heed, for his immediate concerns were less with the colony's economy and more with its defense.

Galissonière appreciated his strategic advantage of interior lines. Despite the huge size of the territory of New France, its vast network of lakes and rivers provided secure routes. As long as Galissonière held these water routes, he had the advantage of mobility, and he could mass his forces to hit decisive points. The French could, in short, move fast and strike hard.

In addition to providing pathways, the water passages served as boundaries and barriers. The Ohio River system marked one of Galissonière's key links. By holding that line, he could block the British advance and secure his communications with the lower Mississippi. Given the length of the line, however, and his limited resources, the only way he could hope to maintain his position was with the aid of Indian allies. Galissonière realized that if the British continued to seep into the west with their cheap goods, which enabled them to woo the Indians to their side, the French were doomed.

From the British point of view, expansion into the west was profitable and legal. By article 15 of the Treaty of Utrecht, France and England had agreed that the Iroquois would be subjects of the British Crown. Since the Iroquois claimed the Ohio Valley, the British, as their sovereign, took it to be theirs as well.

The French rejected the claim and asserted that sovereignty over a mobile people such as the Iroquois could only extend to persons, not to the lands through which they traveled. To prove this point, and to establish his

The Marquis de la Galissonière

king's authority, Galissonière summoned Pierre-Joseph Céloron de Blainville. A native-born Canadian and a grizzled veteran officer in the Troupes de la Marine (regular colonial forces), Céloron had been commandant at both Crown Point as well as in the west at Detroit. Galissonière ordered him to lead an expedition into the Ohio country. His mission was similar to Le Loutre's in Acadia: to remind the Indians of their obligation to the French king and if necessary terrify them into submission.

Both Céloron and the expedition's chaplain, Father Joseph-Pierre de Bonnecamps, kept careful journals. They set off from Lachine on June 15, 1749, with a force of 213 men in twenty-three canoes. After getting past the rapids, where they lost one canoe and one man, they arrived at the mission of La Presentation. Two days later they beached their canoes at Fort Frontenac. From there they made their way along Lake Ontario's north shore to cross the portage at Niagara over to Lake Erie. Hugging the southeastern side of Erie, the expedition beached its canoes at the Chautauqua portage,* where Céloron and his men shouldered their small craft and marched overland to Lake Chautauqua and thence to the headwaters of the Allegheny River. Although the road was "passably good," the portage to the lake took five days.[3]

On June 29 the expedition reached the Allegheny, where the men halted. With great ceremony Céloron ordered the ranks to attention. Father Bon-

*Near present-day Barcelona, New York.

necamps said a few prayers as Céloron buried an engraved lead plate announcing the French king's claim to the territory. Then, with equal dignity, he nailed to a large tree a plaque emblazoned with the king's arms. Céloron and his men continued south to the Ohio. En route they encountered British traders; Céloron told them they were trespassing and ordered them out. On one occasion he gave to a party of Englishmen a letter addressed to the governor of Pennsylvania, warning His Excellency about the perils of trespassing on the French king's lands.

Not surprisingly, burying lead plates and tossing out errant traders had minimal effect. At Logstown on the Ohio the Indians were bold enough to declare to Céloron "that the land was theirs and that while there were any Indians in those Parts they would trade with their Brothers the English."[4] Despite Céloron's bluster and engraved lead plates, the Indians knew that in a few days the French tide would ebb and the British would flow back.

From Logstown the French floated down the Ohio to the Miami River. At the junction of the two rivers Céloron buried his last plate and then turned north. The party stopped at Pickawillany, the village of La Demoiselle, a Miami chief known to the British as Old Briton. Céloron ordered him to leave the area and warned him of the consequences if he continued to do business with the English. Old Briton, true to his name, dismissed Céloron's threats. Five days later the party reached the French post at Fort des Miamis, and from there they traveled overland to Detroit and then via the lakes and St. Lawrence home to Montreal, reaching the city on November 10.

By the time Céloron returned to deliver his alarming reports about British incursions, the imprisoned Jonquière had been released and was in Montreal. Galissonière was already on his way home to France. Jonquière read Céloron's report with grave concern. The old soldier had not minced words. "All I can say," Céloron wrote, "is that the natives of these localities are very badly disposed towards the French, and are entirely devoted to the English. I do not know in what way they could be brought back."[5]

While Jonquière pondered Céloron's gloomy assessment of the French position, Galissonière was halfway across the Atlantic. Governor William Shirley of Massachusetts was at the same time traveling home to London aboard the ship *Boston*. Both governors spent their time at sea preparing reports about affairs in North America. Their views differed in nearly every respect, with one exception. Both men delivered dire warnings that the rivalry in North America was growing more intense and violent. Each urged decisive action against the other.[6]

Shirley argued that Massachusetts and the other colonies would never be secure as long as the French were present in North America. Henry Pelham, the prime minister, and his brother Thomas Pelham Holles (the duke of Newcastle), secretary of the Northern Department, the ministry in charge of diplomatic relations with Protestant Europe and Russia, greeted Shirley's bellicose messages with caution. Others in the government, particularly the imperialist faction led by Henry Dunk (the earl of Halifax), and the duke of Cumberland, applauded Shirley's aggressive stance. Recognizing an ally in Shirley, Halifax and Cumberland engineered a special mission for the governor.

In their rush to end the War of Austrian Succession, the peace negotiators had left a number of critical disputes unresolved, especially the convoluted border issues in North America. These questions were referred to a special Anglo-French commission to which Shirley, thanks to Halifax and Cumberland, was appointed. His fellow commissioners were a lawyer named William Mildmay and the ambassador to France and titular governor of Virginia, the earl of Albemarle. The composition of the commission—Shirley, the bellicose expansionist; Albemarle, the governor of a colony under French threat; and Mildmay, who owed his appointment to Cumberland and Halifax—sent a clear message that the English were not likely to make any concessions. In Shirley's words, the aim was to keep talking until the moment arrived "when it shall be thought proper to reduce 'em."[7] The French commission would be equally unyielding. "Because of the promptness with which he sacrificed his repose, his inclination and personal interests to the pressing needs of the service," the king promoted Galissonière to the rank of rear admiral, placed him in charge of the Hydrographic Office, and appointed him to lead the commission.

On August 31, 1750, the commissioners held their first meeting at Galissonière's private apartments in Paris. The conversation was polite, perfunctory, and pointless. Most of Louis XV's close advisers thought Canada not worth a great deal. Critics outside Versailles shared similar views. Voltaire dismissed Canada contemptuously as a "few acres of snow."[8] But Galissonière argued vehemently that the loss of Canada would bring France's entire overseas empire tumbling down. Without Canada, France's

William Shirley, governor of Massachusetts

fisheries, the source of wealth and sailors, would vanish, leaving the nation's merchant marine and navy in a precarious position unable to defend other parts of its overseas empire.

The marquis understood how far the English had encroached on his king's lands. Virginians had invaded the Ohio Valley; land-hungry New Englanders were pushing at the borders of Acadia; New Yorkers were moving north up the Hudson Valley toward Lac Sacrement (Lake George) and Lake Champlain. On every border there was conflict. Galissonière demanded that the contending parties carve a wide swath of neutral turf between New France and the English colonies to protect both sides from encroachment and violent contact.

Shirley was wary. Galissonière's demands, as he saw them, would deny the English their rightful claims to western lands by raising a Gallic barrier to inland expansion. Deadlocked in their discussions, the two sides stopped meeting face-to-face and fell to exchanging detailed written briefs accompanied by heavily annotated maps, crisscrossed with dozens of lines pretending to be borders. Neither Shirley nor Galissonière was unhappy with the lack of progress. They were partners in a diplomatic dance, playing for time so that each might prepare for the inevitable war to come.[9]

When Shirley returned to London, Halifax welcomed him warmly. The collapse of negotiations served his lordship's expansionist plans. Newcastle and Pelham, on the other hand, were cool. Shirley's truculent attitude had done little to improve relations across the Channel, and his marriage to a French innkeeper's daughter was an embarrassment to the ministry. When Shirley requested the governorship of New York as a reward for his "good work," Newcastle and Pelham ignored him and instead sent him packing back to Boston to resume his post in Massachusetts, a place Shirley had hoped never to see again.[10]

Both Pelham's financial acumen and his obsession with patronage were legendary. Paying off the national debt and finding jobs for friends and relatives were his chief goals. He was appalled at the cost of the War of Austrian Succession and had little appetite for doing anything that might precipitate another major upheaval. Tranquillity suited him. One London wag noted that the years of Pelham's administration were a time when "a bird might have built her nest in the Speaker's chair or in his periwig."[11]

Aside from the continuing rise of parliamentary influence, the most notable feature of Pelham's era was the extraordinary increase in English foreign trade. By the mid–eighteenth century as many as one in five families in Great Britain were directly dependent for their livelihood on foreign commerce. Even more dramatic was the change in direction of trade. While Continental markets grew modestly, colonial markets expanded at an astonishing rate. In the first half of the eighteenth century British exports to North America grew fourfold, those to the West Indies doubled, while East India tea imports increased an incredible forty times. Ninety-five percent of the increase in Britain's commodity exports was sold into protected colonial markets. But the price of prosperity could be high. Continued growth in trade depended upon a relentless expansion of colonial commerce, which inevitably caused conflict as competing nations struggled to protect and enlarge their own overseas interests.[12]

Revenue from levies on trade was key to Pelham's fiscal plan. Should tax receipts from overseas commerce fall, he knew his government would have to raise domestic taxes. And not even Pelham's legendary political skills could save him from the wrath of landed interests should he try to reach deeper into their pockets. From Pelham's perspective peace meant profit, whereas war offered only a painful bill of costs.

Philip Yorke (the earl of Hardwicke), the lord chancellor and Newcastle's and Pelham's longtime ally, agreed. These three formed the center of a moderate coalition within the government willing to negotiate and make concessions. Their challenge was to defend, and if possible expand, overseas trade at the expense of the French and Spanish without unduly alarming those kingdoms. The risk was that colonial conflicts might reverberate in Europe, uncouple alliances, and precipitate war.

Cumberland and Halifax dismissed Pelham's caution as pusillanimous. They believed the Pelhamites exaggerated the risk of war with France because that nation would never hazard a major war in Europe over territorial squabbles abroad. Cumberland and company held blindly to the unrealistic notion that somehow colonial issues could be kept separate from European power politics, that actions in one sphere need not spill into the other. Events were to prove them wrong.

If the American borders were still unsettled, the situation on the Continent was just as unstable. In 1701, in order to ensure a Protestant successor to the English throne, Parliament had passed the Act of Settlement, providing that upon the death of the childless Queen Anne the throne should pass to her cousin George Louis, the Protestant elector of Hanover. Anne died in August 1714, and in accordance with the plan George Louis was proclaimed George I. The "Hanoverian succession" ensured peace within the kingdom. It also, however, dragged England into the quagmire of German politics since George and his successors were simultaneously kings of England and electors of Hanover.

Roughly twice the size of the colony of Massachusetts Bay (excluding Maine), Hanover lies in the northwest corner of Germany. One of several small states making up the long dysfunctional Holy Roman Empire, the electorate was weak, exposed, and vulnerable, conditions its powerful land-hungry neighbors Austria, Russia, and Prussia were eager to exploit. This threat was carefully monitored by the kings of England between 1714 and 1760, George I and George II; Hanoverians by birth and allegiance, they held Hanover's interests as dear as England's. Pelham often sputtered and fumed that familial attachments were tying a great nation's destiny to the coattails of a puny German state, but there was little he could do about it. Any minister who slighted the electorate, either by word or by deed, risked the wrath of the king.

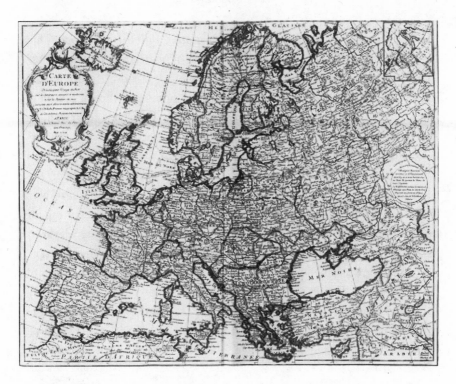

Europe at the time of the Seven Years' War

In the topsy-turvy world of eighteenth-century international politics, the aftermath of war always brought about new diplomatic alignments, and by the early 1750s emissaries were scurrying about the Continent seeking new partners, even as they were abandoning old friends. Where each nation would end up was uncertain except for one immutable fact: England and France would be on opposite sides.

Beyond threats to Hanover, England was concerned over France's lust for the Low Countries. Whoever controlled that coastal region held the best place from which to launch a cross-Channel invasion of England. France could never be allowed to enter the Low Countries. A less serious concern was France's courtship of Spain. Though greatly diminished, the Spanish empire still offered profitable opportunities for trade.

The other major players, Austria, Russia, and Prussia, had no overseas colonial interests. They did, however, covet one another's national territory.

Of the three, Austria was by far the least satisfied with the status quo. That nation had been England's ally during the War of Austrian Succession. England, however, was a fickle friend, and when peace was proposed Pelham's government pressured Austria into surrendering its province of Silesia to France's ally Prussia as the price to end hostilities. Unable to carry on the war without England's support, Austria had no choice but to accept this humiliating condition. The insult festered, and Austria's empress, Maria Theresa, yearned for revenge against both her German neighbor and her untrustworthy ally. In Paris the empress's able envoy, Count Wenzel von Kaunitz, watched closely as England and France fenced. He was waiting for an opening, fully aware that his country's only hope for recovering Silesia lay in abandoning England and forging an alliance with France against Prussia.

Russia too was ruled by an empress—Czarina Elizabeth, the daughter of Peter the Great. She and Maria Theresa shared a distrust for Prussia and a personal hatred for its king, Frederick II. Prussia's support of Russia's traditional Baltic rival Sweden, and its ongoing dalliances with the Ottomans, Russia's enemy in the east, convinced the czarina that Prussia's intentions were hostile.

With enemies on all sides, Frederick faced a daunting challenge. Although he had been France's ally in the war against Austria, and had gained Silesia for his trouble, he distrusted the French. He called them "men made of cotton."[13] To be their ally, he once remarked, was to be their slave. He knew, however, that he could not stand alone. Austria would do everything in its power to retake Silesia, while his other neighbor Russia coveted Prussia's eastern lands.

Prussia's chief business was war, and "Frederick the Great" was its master. One of the most remarkable men of the eighteenth century—and one of the world's greatest military leaders of all times—Frederick had a clear strategic vision. Prussia's central location, and lack of defensible borders, exposed it to attack from several sides. That weakness, however, was also a strength, for it gave the Prussian army the advantage of interior lines of communication. If attacked, Frederick (not unlike the French in Canada) could move his forces rapidly along secure routes in almost any direction of the compass. To take advantage of his position, Frederick fashioned a military machine of incredible efficiency.

Frederick the Great,
king of Prussia

Aside from an occasional ride to visit troops in the field, nearly all eighteenth-century European monarchs were distant armchair commanders. On special occasions, especially their own birthdays, kings and queens might show up to review their splendidly attired troops, but they never deigned to serve with their men in the mud and muck of the field. Not so for Frederick. Both he and his father were generals in the field as well as monarchs in Berlin. During his reign Frederick nearly tripled the size of the Prussian army from thirty thousand to eighty thousand soldiers. Drawing on a country of barely 2.5 million people, this was an astounding accomplishment and simultaneously an incredible national burden. More than three-quarters of the national revenue went to support the army. France, with a population ten times that of Prussia, and a national revenue eight times as great as the German state, struggled to support an army barely twice the size of Prussia's.[14]

At the core of the Prussian military machine was an extraordinarily well-trained and loyal cadre of officers. To fill the officer ranks, Frederick personally selected sons of the landholding Junker class. He brought these young men to Berlin and enrolled them in an elite military academy. The program was rigorous and intense. Out of the ordeal emerged an officer corps of remarkable élan who displayed unwavering loyalty to their king. In return for their devoted service, Frederick granted these officers position and influence above any other rank in the kingdom.

Not only did Frederick's officers meet his high standards, but they drilled the enlisted men to meet similarly exacting criteria. Prussian leaders commanded the best-trained soldiers in Europe. On the battlefield Prussian battalions delivered heavier volumes of fire and maneuvered more adroitly than any other army in Europe; they moved with the precision of a fine clock. In an age when bloody frontal assaults were the norm, Frederick trained his infantry to attack on the oblique, an intricate maneuver that when properly executed confused the enemy and cut their ranks to pieces.

Frederick's neighbors France, Austria, and Russia fielded much larger armies, but they were ponderous, ill equipped, and poorly led.[15] Composed mostly of conscripts, and officered by men who held rank because of birth rather than merit, these clumsy behemoths were awkward, slow, and prone to collapse in the face of a spirited Prussian assault. Still, size does matter in an army. Frederick's greatest enemy was attrition. Prussia might do well at the outset of war, but it lacked the depth of resources, men, and matériel to sustain losses and endure a long struggle. Frederick's best hope was always a quick victory.

Steering England through the dangerous waters of European power politics required skill, and it is to Pelham and Newcastle's credit that they managed the job so well. They did so by keeping in mind certain fundamental points: They never lost sight of the fact that France was the enemy. However much it bedeviled their lives, they understood that the king's attachment to Hanover was permanent, and that England was firmly committed to the electorate's defense. They recognized that the nation's prosperity depended upon an overseas empire linked by a large merchant marine and defended by the Royal Navy.

All of these factors pointed to England's central dilemma: how to contain France in Europe and at the same time defend the empire. Compounding this problem was that England lacked the essential criterion of European Continental power—a large army. Pelham and Newcastle's most serious shortcoming was their failure to fully appreciate the link between the Continent and the colonies. They thought, mistakenly, that these were separate realms. This view found a voice in Parliament and elsewhere in arguments for a "Continental Strategy," while opponents called for a "Blue Water, Colonial" strategy. George II exemplified the former with his gaze fixed on Hanover. The more globally minded, particularly those with close ties to the navy such as Admiral Edward Vernon, dismissed that view and argued that even if France "were mistress of the whole Continent of Europe the Balance of Power" rested in the colonies.[16]

Arguments such as Vernon's carried weight. Grand imperial views struck a resonant chord among numerous factions in the English government. Fear that France might attempt to expand its colonial empire, most notably by sweeping up Spanish possessions, unleashed a flood of jingoistic and paranoid pamphlets and essays that circulated widely in London and the countryside. Hyperbolic writers raised the dark spector of Great Britain under siege; reaching a large and influential audience, their propaganda played a crucial role in shaping policy. Because he appointed ministers and commanded the army and navy, the king ostensibly held the reins over foreign policy, but in fact Parliament and the ministry were at the helm. They controlled the treasury. No one doubted for a moment the wisdom of the old adage "Fare no better, or fare no worse, he rules the roost that carries the purse." It was clear that when "money must be got the House of Commons alone can give it."[17] In English parliamentary politics, public opinion counted, and the public took their opinions from the press.

Unlike in England, where politics belonged to the many and negotiation was the rule, in France ultimate power rested in the throne. Debates on issues centered on divining the pleasure of the king. Louis XV was little different from all the French monarchs who had preceded him. He held firmly to the premise that France was a Continental nation whose territory must be defended and, whenever possible, expanded. Its wealth was in its people and its land. Notwithstanding officers such as Galissonière, who spoke forcefully for expanding the navy and undertaking aggressive overseas expansion, Louis and his chief ministers offered little support for such ambitious goals.

As Europe drifted toward war, Newcastle charted British foreign policy. He was a man of great experience and enormous personal wealth. Educated at Cambridge, he was connected to the kingdom's most influential families. He entered politics in the waning days of Queen Anne, and from that time he had never been absent from government. He was a close associate of Sir Robert Walpole, the masterful leader of Parliament, and from him he learned the intricacies of parliamentary politics. Supported by a coterie of political allies, the most important among them the earl of Holderness, secretary of the Southern Department (the department that oversaw the American colonies as well as Ireland, Wales, and southern Europe), he and his brother led the government.[18]

Newcastle's strategy was to buy enough time to allow him to form alliances that would either dissuade France from any aggressive acts or, if the French dared attack, defeat them. The duke assumed that in the short run nothing important would come of the ongoing conflict in North America. He viewed affairs in that part of the world much like the chronic gout that bedeviled him, that is, distracting and slightly debilitating but not fatal. He believed that neither his king nor the French king thought the wilderness worth a war. In reaction to Halifax's aggressive growls, Newcastle told his friend Hardwicke, that while he understood that the French were "daily encroaching" upon the English, he did not want to do anything precipitous until, he said, "We get our Fleet in order and finish our Defensive Arrangements on the Continent."[19]

Newcastle's "Defensive Arrangements" centered on protecting Hanover and restraining France. To accomplish his goals, he needed a powerful Continental ally to keep both the French and Prussian armies in check. By tradition, that ally was Austria, but its deep distrust of England made it an unlikely friend. Through his spies Newcastle was acutely aware that the French were courting Kaunitz by dangling the promise of Silesia. As for Spain, the other Bourbon power and France's natural ally, Newcastle had done all that he could to cultivate that friendship. Its foreign minister, Richard Wall, was a devoted Anglophile, and Newcastle counted him as much in his pocket as any rotten borough in England.

Stability was Newcastle's goal. For a time he succeeded. He might have been even more successful had he resisted pressure to act precipitously in North America, but his instincts finally failed him. Hectoring voices from

Thomas Pelham Hollis, the duke of Newcastle

Cumberland, Halifax, and other expansionists drowned out moderate advice. In August 1753 Shirley arrived back in Massachusetts and immediately added his voice to those of the other expansionist governors who were bombarding London with alarming, frequently exaggerated accounts of French aggression. Halifax, anxious to believe any evil of the French that might offer an excuse to act, responded to these reports by preparing a detailed indictment of French behavior for cabinet review. At last Holderness, as the secretary of the Southern Department, wrote directly to the North American governors, ordering them "to repel force by force."[20] In the hands of land-hungry men like Governor Shirley, these orders gave them license to do what they had long yearned for: strike at the French.

In January 1754 a letter from William Lithgow, an agent for the Kennebec Proprietors, arrived in Boston with alarming news. According to Lithgow, the French had built a fort deep in the Maine woods at the head of the Kennebec River. If true, this meant that the French controlled the vital overland route between Quebec and northern New England. Lithgow's letter caused a near panic among a number of prominent Bostonians, including some of the governor's in-laws, who were shareholders in the Kennebec Proprietors, a land company formed to sell land in the "invaded" region.[21]

Once he had Holderness's instructions in hand, Shirley called for an expedition to "repel" the French. With unwonted speech the General Court authorized five hundred men, supplies for four months, and ships to carry the small army to Maine. Shirley appointed John Winslow, a popular militia commander from Marshfield, to command. Winslow spent the spring organizing his force, and by late June he and his men were in Falmouth (Portland), Maine.

Leaving his main force behind, Winslow pushed up the Kennebec with a small party to reconnoiter, but after several days of scouting he could not find a single Frenchmen. As Winslow returned downriver, he left groups of men behind. Attracted by generous land offers from the Kennebec company, these men had decided to settle and farm in the river valley. To protect them, Winslow built and garrisoned two forts along the river, Taconnet and Halifax. In the scale of great-power conflict, this "expedition" was of small consequence, but it was emblematic of the colonial land machinations. A cynical view might be that the entire operation was engineered to garner popularity for Shirley, which it did, and land sales for the company, which it also accomplished. Whether or not anyone ever truly believed that the French were there will never be known.

(2)

George Washington
Helps Start a War

*You are to act on the Defensive, but in Case any Attempts are made
to obstruct the Works or interrupt our Settlements by any Persons
whatsoever, You are to restrain all such Offenders, and in Case of
resistance to make Prisoners of or kill and destroy them.*

—Instructions to be observ'd by Maj. Geo. Washington
on the Expeditn to the Ohio

Although Winslow might have had trouble finding the French in the Maine woods, in the Ohio Valley traders from Virginia and Pennsylvania found the enemy easily. Prodded by Galissonière's parting words that he should be fierce in defending his king's lands, Governor Jonquière dispatched men into the Ohio. Unfortunately, as with so many colonial administrators, French and English, Jonquière's devotion to his monarch was matched by his passion to fatten his own purse through illegal trading and bribery. When rumors of his alleged peculations reached Paris, he responded that "there is no one in this country who is not secretly motivated by self-interest."[1] That facile explanation failed to satisfy his superiors, and in the fall of 1751 the king recalled him to answer the charges. But by the time Jonquière received his summons, the St. Lawrence had iced over. The aged governor had to endure one last winter in Canada. Indeed, it was his very last—he died in Montreal on March 17, 1752.

Jonquière's death left New France without a governor but not without an intendant. Louis XIV had created the office of colonial intendant in 1663 as a means to check the power of governors. The office was modeled on the one that had been established in France to monitor provincial administrators. As with the system in France, the lines of authority among the king's officers were not clearly defined, but in general the intendant had charge of the colony's civil administration, including finance, trade, industry, and justice, reporting directly to Paris. The governor acted as commander in chief over the king's forces and was charged with protecting the colony, enforcing the law, and managing relations with Indians. This checks-and-balances system of administration was often clumsy and contentious. Government in Canada swirled about in two different and sometimes colliding orbits, one centered on the governor and the other on the intendant.

Although not of noble birth, François Bigot came from a well-to-do family of Bordeaux. In 1723, at age twenty, he took a post in the Marine Department, where he did well. His skill at fiscal management drew attention from his superiors so that in 1732 he became the resident commissioner of marine at Rochefort. Seven years later he was posted to Louisbourg on Cape Breton Island as financial commissary. After more than a dozen years at Louisbourg, Bigot returned to France, and in 1748 he was appointed intendant of New France.

One of the most controversial figures in the history of French Canada, Bigot is often pictured as an avaricious bureaucrat who presided over a carnival of thieves known as the "Grand Societé." Since corrupt officials rarely keep good records, it is difficult to fully fathom Bigot's administration; nonetheless, even by the loose standards of eighteenth-century France, he seems to have been a particularly clever and imaginative bookkeeper.

A vacant governorship offered the ambitious intendant a chance to advance his own interests. Without waiting for instructions from Paris, Bigot appointed his friend Charles Le Moyne de Longueil, a native Canadian and the colony's senior military officer, to be governor. Le Moyne agreed to serve, but he was chary about Bigot's authority to appoint him, so he asked the king to confirm him in the post.[2] Unknownst to both of them, the king had already appointed a successor, three months before Jonquière's death. To the surprise of many in Canada, particularly Bigot and Le Moyne, on July 1, 1752, the new governor, Ange Duquesne de Menneville, arrived at Quebec.

* * *

A naval officer and the son of an admiral, Duquesne had served at sea with both Jonquière and Galissonière. Indeed it was Galissonière's influence that had secured his appointment.

Duquesne's instructions bore the seal of the minister of marine, Antoine-Louis Rouille, Comte de Jouy, but the language belonged to Galissonière. The new governor was told that no one ought to trifle with the interests of the king for "the river Ohio and the rivers which fall into it unquestionably belong to France. It was discovered by M. de la Salle; since then we have always had trading posts there, and our possession of it has been all the more continuous since it is the most used communication between Canada and Louisiana."[3] Brandishing the king's orders, he summoned the colony's officers to his quarters at the Chateau St. Louis overlooking the St. Lawrence. From them he learned that only a few weeks before his arrival Le Moyne had dispatched an expedition into the Ohio country.

Led by a twenty-one-year-old native Canadian, Charles-Michel Mouet de Langlade, three hundred men, French and Indian, mostly "hard bitten Ottawa" from Michilimackinac, marched toward the Miami village of Pickawillany, home of "Old Briton." When Céloron had visited the village three years earlier, he had left orders with the chief to remove his people from English land to French territory. Old Briton had ignored the command. Langlade's orders were to punish the people of Pickawillany for their disobedience.

At daybreak on the morning of June 21, the French and Ottawa struck without warning. Within minutes fourteen Miami were killed.[4] As the Ottawa scoured the camp for spoils, scalping the dead and wounded, they came upon the body of Old Briton. They dismembered it and tossed the pieces into a boiling pot and feasted. Langlade stood aside, allowing his allies the pleasure of their triumph.

Duquesne welcomed the news from Pickawillany. With obvious pleasure he wrote to his superiors in Paris, "This blow added to the complete pillage suffered by the English on this occasion will discourage them from trading on our lands." The governor offered high praise for young Langlade, accounting him a Canadian with "much bravery, much influence on the minds of the savages, and much zeal when ordered to attack." Langlade's only shortcoming, in the governor's eyes, was that he was a Canadian. With the arrogance of a Parisian snob, Duquesne reported that

Langlade had "married a Savage woman." Duquesne was confident that a paltry pension of two hundred livres would be enough to satisfy this uncouth provincial.[5]

Duquesne understood that the aggressive measures undertaken by his predecessors would provoke a British response. Yet the government in Paris was unlikely to send him any troops to defend the colony against retaliation. For that, he needed Canadian soldiers led by men like Langlade. Not surprisingly, Canadian militia resented being called from their farms and families to serve on active duty. Blithely ignoring their concerns, Duquesne summoned local leaders and announced to them a series of reforms intended to make "real soldiers" out of these reluctant part-time warriors. Duquesne's demands for more drilling, tighter discipline, and longer service were unwelcome. He further antagonized the *habitants* when he announced preparations for a spring offensive into the Ohio.

Duquesne assigned command of the expedition to one of New France's most experienced and well-regarded soldiers: Paul Marin de La Malgue. At sixty-one, Marin was an experienced soldier who had commanded posts in the west, where he negotiated and traded with the Sioux, Fox, and Sauk. He was best known, however, for having led the war party that sacked Saratoga, New York, in 1746 during King George's War and laid waste to the surrounding countryside. He was, according to Duquesne, an officer "endowed with all the talent imaginable and knows no occupation than that of accomplishing the object he is entrusted with."[6]

Marin's orders were clear: protect the king's lands in the Ohio. In the spring of 1753 he marched with two thousand men, the largest French force ever sent into the Ohio. He followed the path laid out four years earlier by Céloron, only this time, instead of burying plates, Marin built and garrisoned forts at critical locations. The first post he erected was at Presque Isle* on the south shore of Lake Erie. There he cut a road south to the headwaters of the Rivière aux Boeuf (French Creek), one of the tributaries to the Allegheny, which led in turn to the Ohio River. To guard this vital point, Marin laid out his second fort: Le Boeuf (present-day Waterford, Pennsylvania).

At first the mission went well. British traders fled to avoid the French.

---

*Near present-day Erie, Pennsylvania.

Local Indians protested, but for the most part they were more interested in trading opportunities than in questions of sovereignty. Matters came to a head, however, on September 3, when Tanaghrisson arrived at Le Boeuf. A longtime friend to the English, Tanaghrisson hated the French because, according to legend, they had boiled and eaten his father. He was chief, "half king," of the Mingo—that is, displaced Iroquois, mostly Seneca and Cayuga, who had migrated into the Ohio country. Although the Iroquois central council claimed sovereignty over the Ohio, the Mingo, Delaware, and other tribes in the region often tried to assert their independence. When Tanaghrisson told Marin, "I shall strike at whoever" invades this country, Marin's response was contemptuous. He told him that the Mingos had "lost their minds."[7]

By then, however, Marin's enterprise had begun to encounter problems more serious than Tanaghrisson's bluster. A shortage of supplies coupled with disease and exhaustion had slowed his advance. Drought had caused streams to fall shallow, which forced additional overland trekking and portaging. Notwithstanding the obstacles, Marin pressed ahead. From his headquarters at Le Boeuf he ordered detachments south to rid the country of English. At Venango,* where French Creek empties into the Allegheny, one of Marin's patrols surprised a party of British traders. The lucky ones scurried away into the woods. The less fortunate were captured and shipped off to Canada in chains.

Marin's vigorous movements alarmed both the Iroquois and the English. Runners set out carrying news of the French invasion. At midnight on April 20, 1753, a party of exhausted Mohawks arrived unannounced at the home of their friend William Johnson.

Johnson, known to the Iroquois as Warraghiygey, "He Who Does Big Business," was an Anglo-Irishman born in County Meath. Having little future in Ireland, Johnson accepted the invitation of his uncle, Admiral Sir Peter Warren, to manage the latter's estates in northern New York. Johnson arrived in 1738 and soon bought his own tract of land along the north side of the Mohawk River. A man of unusual habits in nearly every aspect of his life, Johnson was equally at ease meeting with the royal governor as he was sitting in council with his friends the Mohawk. In 1746 Governor

*Near present-day Venango, Pennsylvania.

William Johnson

George Clinton commissioned him colonel of the Iroquois and later made him colonel of the western New York militia, Johnson built a great home at Mount Johnson near the Mohawk River. Although the royal governor and other colonial officials exploited Johnson's close relationship to the Iroquois, they were generally disdainful of his personal behavior. On occasion Johnson wore Indian garb and dabbed war paint. He took a young Mohawk, Joseph Brant, into his home, and it was alleged that Brant's sister, Molly, was his mistress.

According to Johnson, the Indians were "whooping and hollowing in a frightful manner."[8] They shouted news of Marin's arrival in the Ohio Valley, and they demanded that the English take action to protect their lands from the invaders. In response, Governor Clinton called a hasty June meeting at Albany.

The Iroquois were led by Chief Hendrick (Theyanoguin), a revered figure, over seventy years of age, who had traveled to England twice. In 1710 he and three other chiefs were presented to Queen Anne, an event memorialized by portraits of the "Four Kings" done by John Verelst. More than forty years later Hendrick returned to London, this time to be introduced to King George II. The king gave him a blue coat, trimmed with gold lace, and an impressive cocked hat. A Protestant convert, Hendrick was a close friend of Johnson's.

At the Albany meeting, Hendrick insisted to Clinton that the English

Chief Hendrick (Theyanoguin). This engraving
shows him in old age, scarred and wearing the
coat and hat given him by George II.

abide by their obligations and move against the French. "[You don't care]
what becomes of our nation," he accused the English. "You sit in Peace and
quietness here whilst we are exposed to the enemy." The session was contentious and ended on a frightening note when Hendrick declared that the
Covenant Chain, a term used to describe the long-standing friendly relations between the Iroquois and English, was "broken."[9]

The situation was equally confusing and critical in Virginia. At Williamsburg Lieutenant Governor Robert Dinwiddie read alarming reports of the
French "invasion." His concerns went beyond mere matters of imperial
rivalry. He and a coterie of wealthy friends risked heavy financial losses if
the French made good on their claim to the Ohio. Like Governor Shirley
and his colleagues in Massachusetts, Dinwiddie and other Virginians had
been speculating for years in land and fur trading. In 1749 their machinations resulted in the formation of the Ohio Company. As a result of heavy
lobbying, the king awarded the company a charter granting them huge
tracts of western lands. From the moment of its conception the company
was controversial. Those Virginians left out of the company cried foul,
while Pennsylvanians, who thought the Ohio belonged to them, raised
fiery objections to Virginia's presumptuous claims. Indians, particularly
the Iroquois overlords, feared any European encroachment on their lands

and watched anxiously as land-hungry settlers chopped down forests and planted crops in their homelands.[10]

Dinwiddie was as cynical about the prospects of peace with the French as William Shirley and the imperialists in London. As far as he was concerned, the Ohio belonged to whoever could hold it. So he decided to make a bold move. Using as his excuse the "repell force by force" instructions from Lord Holderness, Dinwiddie preempted his fellow governors by dispatching a twenty-two-year-old militia major named George Washington to deliver a letter to "the Commandant of the French forces on the Ohio," warning him to vacate Virginia's lands.[11]

Washington invited Jacob Van Braam, a Dutchman, who had settled in Virginia a year before and taught French and fencing, to come along as his translator. On October 31 Washington and Van Braam left Williamsburg and rode to the place where Wills Creek* flowed into the north branch of the Potomac River. The Ohio Company had recently erected a small storehouse there, and a few settlers had gathered nearby. Christopher Gist, an employee of the company, had surveyed the Ohio as far south as Great Falls.† He was probably the first Englishman to explore the river, and Washington was eager for him to join his party. Four other "servants" also signed on for the trip.[12]

By November 26, Washington's party reached Logstown, seventeen miles downstream from the forks of the Ohio. Here the young major met Tanaghrisson, who was still smarting from Marin's insulting rebuff. In the face of a powerful French juggernaut that seemed to be advancing everywhere, erecting forts, evicting traders, and intimidating Indians, Governor Dinwiddie's inexperienced emissary, accompanied by a half dozen men, did little to impress the chief. Dismayed at the lack of resolve on the part of his Virginia friends, Tanaghrisson told Washington that he had seen the power of the French at Le Boeuf. He asked the major what he intended to do. Washington's feckless reply did not impress the "half king." He told Tanaghrisson that his mission was to deliver "a Letter to the French Commandant, of very great Importance." Washington then tried to persuade the Indians to provide a powerful escort as a way to im-

*Present-day Cumberland, Maryland.
†Near present-day Louisville, Kentucky.

press the French. All that would muster were Tanaghrisson and three warriors.

Washington's party headed north from Logstown, slogging along trails left muddy by the cold rains of the late fall. About fifty miles north at Venango, the Virginians encountered Philippe-Thomas Chabert de Joncaire. A soldier, trader, and interpreter, Joncaire was at Venango to court the local Delaware and Shawnee, who were traditionally wary of the Iroquois and English. Through the use of bribes, trade, and, most recently, the imposing presence of a sizable French force, Joncaire had succeeded in bringing them over to the French.

At the prospect of a visit with convivial, albeit English, company, Joncaire brought out the best bottles from his frontier wine cellar and invited Washington to dinner. As the evening wore on, loosened tongues wagged and Washington listened. Joncaire predicted that the French would soon have possession of all of the Ohio. He knew, he told Washington, that "the English could raise two Men for their one," but that seeming advantage, he boasted, was more than offset by the ability of the French to strike quickly. French hatchets would fall while the English slept. Late the next morning the major headed north to Le Boeuf.

Paul Marin was indeed a remarkable soldier. In the face of overwhelming obstacles, he had carried out the orders of his king, but in the process he had driven his soldiers and himself to exhaustion. Duquesne ordered him home to recuperate, but it was too late. On October 29, just two days before Washington and his party left Williamsburg, Marin was buried at Le Boeuf. His successor, Jacques Legardeur de Saint-Pierre, another tough Canadian, had been at the fort barely a week when Washington arrived on November 12. He greeted the Virginian and his bedraggled escort with wry amusement. For his part, Washington was impressed, describing Legardeur as "an elderly Gentleman [with] much the Air of a Soldier."[13] Legardeur invited Washington to dine with him. The French claim to the Ohio was absolute, he declared over the wine, and as a soldier of the king he would defend the territory. When Washington presented Legardeur with Dinwiddie's letter demanding that the French withdraw, the commander responded with more courtesy than the situation required. "As to the summons you send me to retire, I do not think myself obliged to obey it." Washington noted Legardeur's succinct reply, bid a cordial farewell, and headed back to Williamsburg.[14]

After a miserable return trip of nearly a month, in which "there was but one Day on which it did not rain or snow incessantly," Washington arrived at the governor's palace in Williamsburg. His report to Dinwiddie presented an alarming but hardly surprising picture. The French, he told the lieutenant governor, were sweeping south. Having built forts at Presque Isle, Le Boeuf, and Venango, they set their sights on the forks of the Ohio. Once they seized that strategic location, Washington said, there was little to prevent them from controlling the entire river to the Mississippi. Dinwiddie considered the major's report carefully, and then, much to the surprise of Washington, he ordered it printed.[15] The lieutenant governor was playing a dangerous game, and Washington was his pawn. By printing the report and circulating it both at home and in London, he was craftily stirring the political pot, hoping to rally support for another bold move he had already undertaken without awaiting permission from London.

While Washington was still returning from his mission to the French, Dinwiddie had sent a small force under Captain William Trent, a former fur trader, to occupy the forks of the Ohio. Trent's detachment of less than fifty men reached the forks in mid-February and built a modest stockade overlooking the spot where the Allegheny and Monongahela join to form the Ohio. Dinwiddie knew that Trent's fort would provoke the French. It was a fatal move. The lieutenant governor had set a dangerous tripwire on the banks of the Ohio.[16]

Thanks to his Indian allies, Legardeur knew about the English incursion, and in his dispatches to Quebec he kept Governor Duquesne informed. In January 1754 the governor recalled Legardeur to Montreal and ordered him to prepare a spring offensive. At the same time he dispatched another veteran Canadian soldier, Claude-Pierre Pecaudy de Contrecoeur, to take command in Ohio. Contrecoeur's orders were unambiguous: expel the English.[17]

With six hundred men and artillery Contrecoeur arrived at Presque Isle in early March. The trek had been long and difficult. Across the ice and snow each of the French soldiers dragged a *traine* behind him. An Indian invention, the *traine* was a long thin wooden sled shaped much like a toboggan, six to nine feet long and about eighteen inches across. The men wore snowshoes and covered their feet and legs with heavy moccasins and Indian-style leggings called *mitlasses*. They protected their hands with thick deerskin mittens. Every soldier also wore a heavy capote, a long wool coat fitted with a hood. After dropping men off to reinforce the garrisons at Niagara and Presque Isle, Contrecoeur continued south and drew near the forks of the Ohio in early April.

Although Trent and his men had been at work on the fort since mid-February, they had not accomplished much. A dreadful winter, made worse by a shortage of provisions, had weakened the men and broken morale. They sought assistance from local Indians, who refused, fearing retribution at the hands of the large French force rumored to be on its way. In desperate straits, Trent left his men under the command of his subordinate and brother-in-law Ensign Edward Ward and struck out on his own to Wills Creek for help.

The French arrived at the forks on April 16. On condition that his men be allowed to return home, Ward quickly surrendered. With the usual show of civility Contrecoeur invited his opponent to dinner. Table conversation ranged over a wide variety of topics, none more important, however, than the disposition of the carpenters' tools in Ward's possession. Contrecoeur offered rations for the tools, and the next morning as the Virginians were leaving, the French were already busy with their newly acquired hammers and saws, building a proper fort to be named Duquesne.[18]

In the same month that Duquesne was organizing his expedition against Trent, Dinwiddie ordered Washington, whom he had recently promoted to lieutenant colonel, to raise a force and proceed "to the Fork of Ohio [and there] finish and compleat the Fort . . . already begun by the Ohio Company."[19] If Dinwiddie, Washington, and other Ohio Company investors were eager to challenge the French to protect their pocketbooks, other Virginians were not so quick to risk their lives. Washington's expedition was delayed for weeks while he tried unsuccessfully to recruit men. Not until Dinwiddie offered two hundred thousand acres of company land as signing bounties did enough men appear. The recruits were a motley group. Washington described them as "loose, Idle Persons. . . . many of them [are] without Shoes, others want Stockings, some are without shirts, and not a few . . . have Scarce a Coat, or Waistcoat to the Backs."[20]

Washington assembled his force at Alexandria on the Potomac River.

On April 2, 1754, he ordered the men to form ranks by company, one under the command of Captain Peter Hogg, a Scotsman from Augusta County, and the other under Captain Jacob Van Braam. Altogether 132 men stood to arms. At the command they marched, with Washington riding at the head of the column. Compared to their colonel, resplendent in his red coat trimmed with white lace cuffs, red vest, breeches, and highly polished black boots, the rest of the men looked curiously casual, dressed as they were in the common attire of Virginia yeomen, buckskin and homespun. Behind the marching men lumbered a line of clumsy wagons packed with camp supplies and ammunition. They had no artillery. Pulling heavy guns over rutted roads would delay the expedition, and Washington was in a hurry. Few, if any, of these men, including their commander, had ever been in combat. Ahead of them was a difficult march of more than two hundred miles along a winding forest trail. They would have to cross a seemingly endless number of streams and follow switchback trails over steep hills that packhorses, let alone wagons, found a daunting challenge.

On its first day out Washington's little army made barely six miles. The next morning they broke camp and moved off on a northwesterly route. They picked up the pace to a brisk eleven miles a day, and in less than a week they had crossed the Blue Ridge Mountains at Vestal Gap and ferried over the Shenandoah River to Winchester. Captain Adam Stephen and his Virginia company were waiting in the town, bringing Washington's force up to 159 men. The three assembled companies represented half of the entire Virginia militia regiment. Two companies under Captain Andrew Lewis and Robert Stobo were still in Alexandria trying to raise men.[21] As soon as the companies were completed, they would march to join Washington. The sixth company was already at the forks of the Ohio under Captain Trent. Additional reinforcements were promised as well. Dinwiddie had beguiled himself into believing that the southern Indians—Catawba, Cherokee, and Chickasaw—would march, and he had assurances from North Carolina, South Carolina, and Maryland that they would commit militia. For a man who was otherwise savvy and cynical, Dinwiddie was credulous to think that his parochial neighbors would help him defend Virginia and the Ohio Company.

Washington decided to strike ahead as quickly as possible and leave the wagon train to catch up with him. He set out for Wills Creek on April 18.

On the nineteenth, only a few miles out of Winchester and still more than fifty miles from Wills Creek, "an Express with Letters from Captain Trent" met the column with alarming news. According to Trent's message, a flotilla of several hundred canoes and bateaux with more than eight hundred French were headed down the Allegheny. He needed reinforcements immediately.[22]

Washington relayed Trent's plea back to his superiors in Williamsburg, appending his own urgent request that reinforcements be sent as soon as possible. Rather than wait, however, Washington, more bold than prudent, decided to advance against the French. At Wills Creek Washington encountered Ensign Ward and his men, who brought him the not unexpected news that the large French force reported by Trent had taken the forks. Ward also carried a message from Tanaghrisson. The half king pledged that he and his warriors remained loyal to the English, and they were anxious to attack their mutual enemy.[23]

Tanaghrisson's constancy was not matched by Trent's men. They decided that their obligation to defend the colony ended when Ensign Ward surrendered to the French. After staying at Wills Creek long enough to complain to Washington about not being paid, the men drifted off for home. The Virginia regiment now numbered only five companies, three at Wills Creek and two still mustering at Alexandria.

On April 23 Washington convened a council of war. He had, he told the officers, about 180 men. Tanaghrisson's message notwithstanding, the number of Indians available was uncertain but in any event would be few. Reliable intelligence put the French at one thousand men with eighteen cannon.

Washington had no doubt about French intentions. His own failed mission the previous year, followed by Contrecoeur's expulsion of Ward, made matters very clear. The French claimed the Ohio, and they were backing up that claim with force. After some discussion the council came to an unusual decision. They agreed that it was "impracticable" to attack the French, but rather than wait for new orders or reinforcements they decided that "being strongly invited by the Indians, and particularly by the Speeches of the Half-King, the President [i.e., Washington] gave his Opinion, that it would be proper to advance as far as Red-Stone Creek, on the Monongahela, about Thirty-seven Miles on this side of the Fort [Fort Duquesne], and there to raise a Fortification, clearing a Road broad enough to pass with all our Artillery and our Baggage, and there to wait fresh Orders."[24]

In retrospect, Washington's decision was rash. He was crossing into disputed territory and exposing his men to attack by an overwhelmingly superior enemy. His chief motivation seems to have been a desire to demonstrate courage to the Indians and protect Ohio Company property.

Redstone Creek* was a company trading post located on the Monongahela River about one hundred miles from Wills Creek. Nemacolin's Path, a primitive trace first laid out by company traders, was the only link between the two posts. Despite the obstacles, Washington decided to improve the path and build a road to Redstone Creek, where he would set up an advance base to support his counterattack against the French.

Construction got under way on April 25. A work party of sixty men went ahead to reconnoiter and survey the route. A few days later Washington marched out with the rest of the men. It was brutal work. Rain punctuated warm spring days as the men sweated and slogged over steep hills and through dense forest, underbrush, and mud. High water in the numerous creeks and rivers made fording and bridge building a nightmare. Progress was maddeningly slow. On average the crews could not clear more than two miles per day. As the men chopped, dug, filled and, bridged, they met English traders fleeing from the French threat. Wild rumors filled the camp about the closeness of the advancing enemy.

By the end of May, after more than a month of grueling roadwork and hard marching, Washington was barely halfway to Redstone Creek. From behind he heard virtually nothing about reinforcements, while ahead the French were steadily advancing. At least a half dozen men had deserted, and the rest were exhausted and growing more fearful when Washington decided to pause at a place called Great Meadows. It was an open area a few hundred yards wide and about two miles long, tucked in a valley between Laurel Ridge on the east and Chestnut Ridge toward the west. The open meadow offered pasturage for his animals and level space for a field camp. Its chief problem was wetness. The land was low, and a shallow stream called Great Meadows Run ran leisurely through the meadow and over its

---

*Near present-day Brownsville, Pennsylvania.

banks. The constant tramping of soldiers' feet could easily turn the soft ground into a muddy mess.

Fifty miles to the west, at the forks, the French were at work. Contrecoeur's engineer, Captain François-Marc-Antoine Le Mercier, laid out a plan for a fort to accommodate a garrison of three hundred men. Mercier's plan followed the style, although not the scale, of Sebastian Vauban's grand fortresses of Europe and was fashioned from wood rather than stone.[25]

For weeks Contrecoeur and Mercier had heard reports of the approaching English. While they moved quickly to prepare for the enemy's arrival, they were not overly concerned. From his scouting reports Contrecoeur knew that the Virginians were few in number, lightly armed, and were more likely en route to parley than to fight. On May 23 Contrecoeur dispatched a thirty-man patrol under the command of Ensign Joseph Coulon de Villiers de Jumonville to gather information about the English and, if possible, meet with them to order them from the king's lands.

Shortly after the Virginians arrived at Great Meadows, Christopher Gist, Washington's companion on his previous western foray, rode into camp. He reported that the day before a party of Frenchmen had been by his house, and that he had seen their tracks not more than a mile from Washington's position. That evening Silverheels, a messenger from Tanaghrisson, arrived. The chief was encamped six miles away, and he, like Gist, warned that French were in the area. Washington, "fearing" that "the French [planned] to attack" his camp, roused his companies, warned the main body to be on guard, and then left with forty men to search out the French.[26] Led by Silverheels, Washington and his men "tumbled" single file into "a night as dark as pitch." A heavy rain fell, making the way treacherous and uncertain. At sunrise they arrived at Tanaghrisson's camp.

The chief had less than a dozen warriors with him, but combined with Washington's forty men the two leaders believed that they were strong enough to challenge the French party, particularly if they took them by surprise. Tanaghrisson and Washington agreed that they would "attack them together." Two scouts went ahead; the rest followed. Wet, tired, and inexperienced, Washington's men moved in the predawn darkness toward the French.

Not far away, Jumonville and his men had made camp in the bowl of a small glen cluttered with rocks and boulders. To keep their weapons dry, several of the French had stacked their arms off to the side in the shelter of a large rock. By seven in the morning the sun was beginning to chase the morning mist away. The French were just rousing. Contrary to good discipline, Jumonville had failed to post sentries. Silently, and without being detected, the English and Indians surrounded them.

In the 250 years since the battle at the place now called Jumonville Glen, historians have debated the sequence of events that followed Washington's arrival.[27] It seems likely that as Washington maneuvered his men into position, a sleepy Frenchman detected them. He called the alarm to his fellows, and they went for their muskets. But before the French could raise and cock their weapons, Washington ordered his men to volley. The French returned fire as best they could, but it was an unequal exchange. Some French ran for cover, only to be intercepted by Tanaghrisson's men. One lucky Frenchman was off in the woods for his morning toilet. He escaped and eventually made his way back to Duquesne with the bad news. The fight was over in fewer than fifteen minutes. Before Washington could get down the slope to the French camp, Tanaghrisson's men rushed in to scalp the dead and wounded. When Washington regained control, Tanaghrisson demanded that he turn over the prisoners to him. Washington refused. Casualties among the Virginians were one man killed and three wounded; among the French, ten dead—Jumonville among them—and twenty-one taken as prisoners. This was Washington's first experience in combat. The young colonel reported to the governor, "I heard the bullets whistle, and, believe me there is something charming in the sound."[28] Fearful that other French might be nearby, Washington left the enemy dead unburied and hurried back to Great Meadows with his prisoners. After a brief interrogation he sent the prisoners to Wills Creek.

In his official report Washington took great care to place blame for the fight on the French. But the small size of the French force, and the fact that the Virginians fired first, belied his words. Moreover, the French survivors claimed that they were on an "embassy." Washington scoffed at the notion and charged that they were spies. As for Tanaghrisson, he explained that the French were of "bad Hearts" and thereby deserving of their fate.[29] It remains an open question why Washington felt compelled

George Washington, some years after
the French and Indian War, painted by
Charles Willson Peale.

to attack a sleeping camp without warning at a time when the two nations
were at peace.

Dinwiddie found Washington's explanation less than persuasive. In a
politic move to evade responsibility, he told his London superiors: "This
little skirmish was by the Half King and the Indians. We were auxiliaries
to them, as my orders to the commander of our forces was to be on the
defensive." The lieutenant governor suspected that, in the words of Sir
Horace Walpole, Washington may well have "set the world on fire."[30]

Expecting that the French would retaliate, Washington decided to fortify the encampment at Great Meadows. Ever the optimist, he reported to
Dinwiddie, "We have, with Nature's assistance, made a good Intrenchment, and, by clearing the Bushes out of these Meadows, prepar'd a
charming field for an Encounter."[31] Washington's "good Intrenchment"
(soon to be christened Fort Necessity) consisted of a round wooden stockade about fifty-three feet in diameter. In the center was a crude storehouse
to protect provisions and powder from the rain and, if need be, to serve as
a hospital. No more than fifty men could fit within such a small palisade.

Outside the palisade Washington laid out a series of trenches and covered sites. He was full of himself and cocky. He told Dinwiddie that he looked forward to "driving [the French] to Montreal."[32]

On June 2 Tanaghrisson arrived at the fort with nearly one hundred warriors accompanied by their wives and children. Washington tried to persuade the chief to send the women and children farther east. He refused, so Washington was saddled with feeding them. Within a few days everyone was on short rations. Hoping to persuade other tribes in the area to rally to the English, Tanaghrisson sent emissaries off to villages, bearing scalps taken from Jumonville's men. Brandishing these icons of victory, Tanaghrisson's messengers asked the local chiefs to meet at Gist's plantation.

A week after Tanaghrisson's arrival, the two companies Washington had left at Alexandria (under Captains Stobo and Lewis) marched in, adding 110 men to Washington's little army. A few days later 100 more men emerged from the wood line and came toward the fort. They were South Carolinians under the command of Captain James Mackay. At first Washington welcomed them, but that good feeling evaporated quickly when Mackay refused to put himself or his men under Virginia's command. The issue was more than simply Virginia's authority versus South Carolina's. Mackay held a royal commission under the king's hand, whereas Washington's authority was from a mere governor. Any officer holding a commission directly from the king, no matter the rank, was superior to any colonial. Mackay was pleasant enough, but it was clear that he would not put himself under Washington's authority. He and his men remained aloof and distant.

Although concerned about the French, Washington was determined to complete the road to Redstone Creek. Leaving his men to work on this road, he rode to Gist's plantation to meet with the Indian delegations summoned by Tanaghrisson. For three days Washington and Tanaghrisson tried to persuade the visitors to join them. It was hopeless. The Six Nations Council at Onondaga had sent word to their Ohio brothers that they should stay neutral in this quarrel between the white men. But even without Onondaga's instructions they were realistic enough to know that, for the moment at least, the French were clearly stronger.

While Washington courted Indians and pushed his road closer to Redstone Creek, Contrecoeur prepared a force to deliver a counterstroke. A few days before this force planned to leave, "300 savages and 50 Frenchmen" commanded by François Coulon de Villiers, Jumonville's older brother, came upriver from Fort Chartres in the Illinois country. When he learned the sad news of his brother's death and the questionable circumstances of the encounter, de Villiers asked Contrecoeur for the honor of commanding the retaliatory expedition. De Villiers left Duquesne at the head of five hundred men on June 28.[33]

A few hours later, Indian runners were on their way to Washington, carrying news of the approaching French force. Hurriedly, Washington called in his road-building crews and prepared his defenses. Exhausted by the incessant work on the roads, and weak from being on short rations, his men required two full days to assemble at Great Meadows. Had they been stronger, it would have made sense for Washington to retreat the fifty miles to Wills Creek. Understanding that a retreat carried out by exhausted, hungry, ill-trained, and frightened men might turn into a rout, a council of war recommended a stand at Great Meadows.

After a four-day march from Duquesne, de Villiers came to the place where his brother had died. Scavengers and the summer heat made the bodies unrecognizable. The stench was overwhelming. The French paused to bury their dead and then continued on their march.

The next morning, July 3, de Villiers stood at the edge of the wood line on the southwest side of the meadow in full view of the stockade. The French outnumbered the English by about two to one. They advanced across the field toward the English position in three columns. Washington and Mackay formed their men in ranks in front of the entrenchments. The French halted, fired a volley, and continued their approach. As they drew nearer, Washington ordered his men to fall back into the prepared trenches. With surprising precision the men followed the colonel's orders. Not wishing to risk a frontal assault against a protected enemy, the French withdrew and set out to invest the fort.[34]

Washington's men held their ground, and soon there was a steady exchange of fire. The French had better cover, and their fire was more telling. Not only did the English have to dodge enemy fire, but their position was uncomfortable in the extreme. While the sick and wounded were within the stockade, most of the men were hunkered down in shallow trenches. For ten hours the French kept up a steady fire on them. Casualties mounted. In the afternoon heavy rains poured down, making everyone miserable. Rising water and mud exhausted the men and fouled their weapons.

At eight in the evening the French called a case-fire and summoned Washington to parley. He answered that no French soldier would be allowed within his fort. The French invited Washington to send someone to their camp, and he agreed. Only two of Washington's officers spoke French, Ensign William La Peyronie and Jacob Van Braam. La Peyronie had been wounded, and he had to be assisted to the French camp by Van Braam. After the customary pleasantries negotiations began. Both sides knew that the Virginians were beaten. De Villiers told the two officers that since England and France were not at war, he was willing to grant generous terms. Washington and his men must surrender their position, but they would be free to return home. He warned them, however, that the Virginians must accept these terms quickly, for should they delay he could not guarantee the good behavior of his Indian allies.

Van Braam and La Peyronie reported de Villiers's offer to Washington, who had little choice but to accept it, insisting only that the terms be put in writing. La Peyronie, too weak from his wounds to return to the French camp, remained with Washington. Van Braam walked through the lines alone. The Dutchman was gone for what many thought to be an unusually long time, but he eventually returned with two sheets of paper. These were the terms, written in duplicate, both copies in French. Washington had to depend upon Van Braam to translate. Neither French nor English was Van Braam's first language, so the work was difficult. Captain Adam Stephen later described the scene: "When Mr. Van Braam returned with the French proposals, we were obliged to take the sense of them by word of mouth: it rained so heavily that he could not give us a written translation of them; we could scarcely keep the candle light to read them; they were wrote in a bad hand, on wet blotted paper so that no person could read them but Van Braam who had heard them from the mouth of the French officer."[35]

The seven articles of the capitulation were unremarkable. They allowed for the Virginians to leave the fort with all their possessions minus any artillery. Washington would be accorded the "honors of war," that is, a ceremonial departure. Since the Virginians had no wagons, the French agreed that they might leave their belongings at the fort to be picked up later. Finally, to ensure that the French soldiers captured at Jumonville Glen and transported east were returned, Captains Stobo and Van Braam would remain with the French as hostages.

Alas, Van Braam was a clumsy translator, and although he paid attention to the actual terms, he gave less notice to the preamble.

> *Capitulation granted by Mons. De Villier, captain of infantry and commander of troops of his most Christian Majesty, to those English troops actually in the fort of Necessity which was built on the lands of the King's dominions July the 3rd, at eight o'clock at night, 1754.*
>
> *As our intention has never been to trouble the peace and good harmony which reigns between the two friendly princes, but only to revenge the assassination [emphasis added] which has been done on one of our officers, bearer of a summons, upon his party, as also to hinder any establishment on the lands of the dominions of the King, my master; upon these considerations, we are willing to grant protection or favor, to all the English that are in the said fort, upon the conditions hereafter mentioned.*

Van Braam carelessly skipped over the word *assassination* and translated it simply as "killing," thus removing the sinister meaning. Washington signed and thereby admitted his "crime."

At daybreak on the fourth of July two ranks of French soldiers came to attention in Great Meadows. To the steady beat of a French drum, Washington and his men marched between the lines. They moved to a far corner of the meadow and looked back as the French, amid a series of salutes, entered the stockade and raised the fleur-de-lis. A few hours later Washington gave the command, and his somber column fell in for the long march east.

Tanaghrisson and his men slipped away quietly to return to their villages. The surrender of Fort Necessity was a stunning blow for them. Tanaghrisson had put his reputation and that of his Iroquois overlords on the line. He had assured Delaware, Shawnee, and other tribes that the English would defeat the French. The capitulation at Great Meadows undermined both English and Iroquois authority. Disgraced, Tanaghrisson returned to the village of Aughwick,* where, a few weeks later, he died.

---

*Near present-day Harrisburg, Pennsylvania.

Never comfortable under Iroquois domination, the western tribes saw the advantage to cozying up to the French. In August, during a hastily called meeting of Delaware and Iroquois representatives, Beaver, a Delaware spokesman, looked directly at the Iroquois delegates and warned them that there was "a high Wind rising."[36]

(3)

Braddock's March

*I have an hundred and ten miles to march through an uninhabitable
wilderness over steep rocky mountains and almost impassable morass.*

—General Edward Braddock to Robert Napier,

Fort Cumberland, June 8, 1755

In the twisted skein of events leading to war, Washington's western disaster was critical, but it was only one thread in a complex tapestry. He, William Shirley, Colonel John Winslow, Lieutenant Governor Dinwiddie, and others were all participants in a rising drama being played out in several parts of the British Empire. The same summer that Washington encamped at Great Meadows and Winslow searched for French along the Kennebec River, representatives from several colonies were gathering at Albany to meet with delegates from the Six Nations.[1] The Lords of Trade, the agency charged with regulating the administration of the colonies, were concerned about the freewheeling style that the colonies had developed in their relations with Indians.[2] Each colony struck its own deals with local tribes, paying scant regard to the interests of the other colonies or the Crown. Nowhere was this more apparent, or annoying, than in the chaos that passed for negotiation among the Iroquois and the northern colonies. Decentralization (a hallmark of British colonial policy in North America) left too much power in the hands of local authorities and gave rise to endless disputes over land and trade. In an attempt to take control, the Lords of Trade had instructed Sir Danvers Osborne, the newly appointed governor of New York, to call the meeting. Albany was chosen as the site for the convenience of the Iroquois. In addition to the Iroquois, Osborne was to

invite representatives from the New England colonies plus Virginia,
Maryland, and Pennsylvania. Osborne left London bearing his instructions, but two days after stepping ashore at New York City he "was found in
the lower part of Mr. Murray's Garden strangled in his Handkerchief." He
had committed suicide. Lieutenant Governor James DeLancey was now in
charge.[3]

Mired in his own western debacle, Dinwiddie refused to send anyone to
Albany. Pennsylvania hemmed and hawed but finally dispatched a delegation led by Benjamin Franklin.[4] On June 19 the delegates, minus Virginia,
took their seats in the Albany Court House, where Governor DeLancey
called them to order.

For the next five weeks the delegates squabbled. The New Yorkers were
jealous that anyone should try to interfere with "their" Iroquois. To ensure
that his colony's interests were served, DeLancey, over the objections of
some delegates, took the chair and then refused to surrender it, claiming it
as his right since he was the only governor present. By a dexterous wielding
of the gavel, DeLancey controlled the agenda and stifled any attempt to
discuss matters, such as crooked land dealings, that might embarrass his
fellow New Yorkers.

The delegates exchanged familiar pleasantries, but there clearly was an
undercurrent of deep distrust. On July 2 Chief Hendrick of the Mohawk
spoke.[5] He noted DeLancey's opening comments about the threat of
French invasion and the British desire for Iroquois help in turning them
back. Hendrick pointedly reprimanded the English for taking the Iroquois
for granted. With a dramatic flare he threw a stick behind his back and told
DeLancey, "You have thus thrown us behind your back, and discarded us,
whereas the French are . . . ever using their utmost endeavours to seduce
and bring our people over to them." Determined to unbalance the English
even farther, Hendrick went to the heart of the matter: "Brethren—The
Governor of Virginia, and the Governor of Canada, are both quarrelling
about lands which belong to us, and such a quarel [sic] as this may end in
our destruction; they fight who shall have the land. The Governor of Virginia and Pensylvania have made paths thro' our Country to Trade and
build houses without acquainting us with it, they should have first asked
our consent." Hendrick closed his speech with an oratorical flourish.
"Look at the French, they are Men, they are fortifying everywhere—but, we

are ashamed to say it, you are all like women, bare and open without any fortifications."

Hendrick's fiery speech failed to shame the Albany delegates. Distant rumblings from the Ohio notwithstanding, they were bent on taking more Iroquois land and cared little for the means. As some delegates parleyed for profits, others, more politically motivated, had a grander scheme in mind. Led by Thomas Hutchinson, lieutenant governor of Massachusetts, and Benjamin Franklin, a committee presented a "Plan For a General Cooperation of the North American Colonies." The plan called for the king to appoint a "president general" who would preside over a "grand council" selected by the local assemblies. The council would control Indian affairs, raise and pay soldiers, and collect taxes. The delegates approved the plan and forwarded it to each of the colonies and London for approval. It went nowhere. Not a single colonial assembly endorsed the plan, fearing a loss of local power. In London the Lords of Trade behaved in a similar fashion. They were loath to approve any proposal that would empower the colonies. The plan died, and few grieved.[6]

In the rising clamor of London politics, reports from Albany were hardly heard. The big news in the capital was that Henry Pelham had died on March 6, having fallen victim to a malady common among the upper class in Georgian London: excessive eating and drinking. Upon hearing the news of Pelham's death, George II exclaimed, "Now I shall have no more peace."[7] The king was right. Political orderliness dissolved as Pelham's older brother the duke of Newcastle, Secretary at War Henry Fox, and William Pitt, paymaster of the forces, vied to see who would inherit political leadership. Thanks in part to a deep purse which gave him enormous patronage, Newcastle won, leaving Fox and Pitt to sputter and scheme.

Like his brother, Newcastle was more interested in money than in war. He focused on maintaining low interest rates and containing the national debt rather than rumors of French aggression in the Ohio or negotiations with the Iroquois.[8] Halifax and Cumberland's increasingly dire warnings about the French menace had little effect on him. The duke believed, as he told Horace Walpole, that "the French court is pacific," and that the troubles in North America would be resolved by "debate and negotiation."[9] Newcastle was accustomed to endless discussion in Parliament and deals struck behind closed doors. Everything in his world was negotiable. That illusion vanished in August when news of the disaster at Great Meadows reached London. Who could doubt now that the French were intent upon seizing the west in order to trap the British between them and the sea? Having thus far resisted consulting with Cumberland, with whom he had deep political differences, Newcastle decided that he needed to visit the duke.

It was the summertime in London, and the posh set had retired to their country homes. Newcastle was at his estate in Epsom, and the other principles, Cumberland, Lord Halifax, Sir Thomas Robinson, secretary of state for the southern department—the post responsible for colonial affairs—and George Anson, first lord of the Admirality, were on holiday. The king too was away. It took weeks to inform these widely dispersed gentlemen of the developments in the west and even longer to get their advice.

Everyone seems to have agreed that troops had to be sent to Virginia. The question was how many and from where should they be taken. The king urged raising men in the Highlands. Cumberland disagreed, arguing that it would take too long to recruit and train new men. He pointed out that two regiments on the Irish establishment, Colonel Thomas Dunbar's Forty-eighth foot and Sir Peter Halkett's Forty-fourth foot, were available and could be moved quickly. He admitted that, as was usually the case with Irish regiments, both were under strength, but he assured his colleagues that the ranks could be filled quickly by drafts from other regiments or with men to be recruited in America.

Newcastle, wary of Cumberland's belligerency, and concerned about unnerving his European partners, still needed coaxing, and so it was not until early October that he approved the plan. The Irish regiments were to be sent, and two new regiments would be raised in America. The king gave overall command of the forces in America to Major General Edward Braddock.[10] Braddock belonged to a distinguished military family.[11] His father had risen to the rank of major general in the elite Coldstream Guards. In the common practice of the day he had purchased a commission for his son in his own regiment. Although the guards saw considerable action in the War of Austrian Succession, the younger Braddock seems not to have participated in any of the battles. Despite his lack of front-line experience, he earned a keen reputation as an administrator and logistician. In February 1753 the king appointed him colonel of the Fifteenth Regiment of Foot and posted him to Gibraltar as governor. In March of the following year he was promoted to major general. Given his background, both personal and professional, Braddock was a logical choice for the American command.

London was abuzz with news of the growing American crisis. Soldiers were gathering in Ireland, warrants for supplies were being issued to the arsenals and supply depots, and the Admiralty was taking up transports for hire and pressing sailors to man them. In Paris the French foreign minister invited Lord Albemarle to explain Braddock's appointment and the purpose of the expedition. Albemarle assured him that England was simply following the French lead and defending its possessions. Albemarle's reply was less than heartening to the French; nonetheless, they saw no reason for immediate alarm. After all, French Canada and the British colonies had long been sniping at each other. That on this occasion French and Englishmen had died at each other's hands rather than by Indian assault was different, but it hardly seemed a cause for general war. Even as war whoops were echoing in the west, Sir Thomas Robinson, and the duke de Mirepoix, the French ambassador in London, were exchanging proposals for peace in America. But it was already too late. While Braddock hurried home from Gibraltar, orders went out from Paris to the naval authorities at Toulon and Brest to prepare ships and men for Canada. What the British could do the French would match.[12]

While the French prepared, the British sailed to North America. On December 22, 1754, HMS *Norwich* and *Centurion* slipped their moorings at Spithead and tacked west for Virginia. Braddock, his secretary William Shirley Jr. (the governor's son), his personal aide Captain William Orme, his body servant Thomas Bishop, and his personal cook Francis Delboux were aboard *Norwich*. Ahead of them plowed *Centurion*, carrying Commodore Augustus Keppel, the commander of the naval escort.

Predictably for the time of year, the crossing was boisterous and miserable. Braddock knew the risks of a winter passage, but he had decided to leave ahead of his regiments, who were still assembling in Cork, in order to arrive in Virginia with enough time to prepare the campaign. Time was his ally. Even if the French managed to assemble reinforcements, Canada's long winter and its ice-clogged ports would prevent them from arriving until early spring. By that time the general planned to be closing in on his objectives.

Braddock's orders were specific. He was to drive the French from the Ohio, take Fort Niagara, seize Crown Point, and destroy Fort Beauséjour. He carried the high-sounding title commander in chief, which meant that he held command over all military units, colonial and regular, in North America.[13] To pay for these forces, Parliament expected the colonies to contribute to a common fund "to be employed for the general service in North America." Privately, the ministry conceded that the colonies were unlikely to raise this money, so in secret instructions they told Braddock that he could forward his bills to the paymaster general in London. True to form, the colonies found a variety of ways to dodge their responsibilities, and Braddock's bills went home. Braddock learned quickly about the realities of politics in America.[14]

Closeted in an aft cabin with Orme and young Shirley, Braddock spent the days at sea formulating his plan.[15] He had seven regular regiments, seven independent companies, and a detachment of royal artillery at his disposal. Of the seven regiments, three were quartered in Nova Scotia and two were to be raised in America. The remaining two were from the Irish establishment. The seven independent companies were part of the permanent garrisons in New York and South Carolina. Since two of the regiments were still being raised and the rest were undermanned, Braddock's force was more impressive on paper than in fact. Only with strong support from colonial authorities would he be able to recruit enough men to bring his anemic force to full strength. Braddock's ambitious agenda was constructed on a pitiful foundation. Cumberland's bellicosity was still a hostage to Newcastle's parsimony.[16]

On February 19 *Norwich* passed the Virginia Capes and came to anchor in Hampton Roads. Three days later *Centurion* joined it. The following morning Braddock and Keppel rode to Williamsburg to meet with Dinwiddie.

It was evening when the general and commodore arrived at the governor's palace. Dinwiddie wasted no time before he launched into a litany of complaints, focused mostly on the "obstinacy" of his fellow governors in neglecting to provide support for Virginia's efforts to defend the king's western territory. The next day Braddock's deputy quartermaster general, Sir John St. Clair, joined them. He had arrived several weeks before Braddock and had been busy trying to secure provisions, medical support, and transportation for the expedition. He had already developed a festering resentment toward the "inhabitants," exclaiming to the general that "their Sloth and Ignorance is not to be described."[17] St. Clair was among the first of Braddock's officers to sense the difficulties ahead, particularly local inertia and the logistical nightmare of crossing the mountains with an army and its support train.

Supply and troop ships began to arrive by early March. The convoy had enjoyed an easy crossing; not a single man was sick, and only one had been lost overboard. On the other hand, the cargo had been stowed in such a careless fashion that off-loading took far longer than anyone expected. The governor supplied recruits, but they were hardly what the general expected; indeed, they resembled the motley crew that had gone west with Washington the year before: idle, drunken fellows, some nearly sixty or seventy years of age. Mixing these men in with his own regulars seemed unwise, so Braddock ordered the new recruits to muster separately as carpenters and rangers. Although this arrangement maintained the integrity of his regular regiments, it did nothing to augment their numbers.

From his temporary headquarters at Williamsburg, Braddock summoned the American governors to meet with him at Annapolis in early April. As a professional soldier, Braddock was accustomed to issuing orders and having them obeyed. Increasingly, however, he realized that in the colonies bickering, prevarication, and petty jealousies were the norm, and obedience was rare. Money promised him never materialized. Wagons and teams that had been slated for transport never appeared. Provisions arrived late and short. Quartermaster St. Clair flew between rage and despondency.

When Braddock traveled to Annapolis, he couldn't meet with the governors because a snowstorm had prevented their arrival.[18] The general, restless and agitated at the delay, returned to Alexandria, where at midmonth the governors finally presented themselves. Aside from Braddock and his staff, Dinwiddie, Horatio Sharpe of Maryland, William Shirley, Robert Hunter Morris of Pennsylvania, and James DeLancey of New York were present at the meeting. Also in attendance were Commodore Keppel and Colonel William Johnson.

The participants believed the meeting was a great success, but that was only because each of them got what he wanted. In reality it was a failure.

Politics rather than good military sense prevailed, creating a preposterous scheme that set the stage for a series of military disasters unparalleled in the history of the empire. Braddock's lack of major command experience, ignorance of geography, and political ineptness told dearly. In accordance with his instructions, he proposed four major campaigns, to be conducted simultaneously. Some of the governors winced at the grand scale of operations, but since each stood to gain from the military operation assigned to his area (e.g., supply contracts, command, patronage), they muffled their concerns and sang like a choir.

Shirley left with orders to assemble at Albany and march against Fort Niagara with the two American-raised regiments. No one seemed to give much thought to the fact that Niagara was more than three hundred miles from Albany via an upstream route that required long portages and overland marches across tough terrain as well as a lake crossing. Even if he could manage the arduous trek, once at Niagara's gates Shirley would face a substantial enemy garrison that enjoyed secure lines to the rear via Lake Ontario and the St. Lawrence River, over which they could resupply or retreat. Shirley, whose own field experience did not go beyond reviewing colonial militia on muster day, faced a logistical nightmare.[19]

Colonel William Johnson, the only man present with experience coping with the French and Indians, took on a mission to his friends the Iroquois. His task was to ensure Iroquois cooperation along the critical northern border. If these warriors stood by their side, the British would be able to move quickly and safely through the wilderness without worrying about their rear areas and logistical lines. After the colonel finished his diplomatic mission, he was to return to Albany and raise a provincial army to move against Crown Point on Lake Champlain. The fort was well manned and formidable. Johnson would need all the help he could get, including aid from his Iroquois brothers.

The third line of attack in this complicated weave belonged to Governor Charles Lawrence of Nova Scotia. Lawrence did not attend the Alexandria meeting, but his interests were well represented by Shirley, for both men shared a lust for Acadian land. Liquidating Fort Beauséjour was part of their plan to expel Acadian farmers from their homes. Although Beauséjour was in pitiful condition and ill manned, the English suspected that the fort was a nest of Acadian and Indian vipers who hid behind its walls by daylight and

Major General Edward Braddock

sortied at night to commit mayhem and murder. Eliminating Beauséjour would give Shirley and Lawrence free reign against the Acadians and their Micmac allies. Beauséjour was, all agreed, a minor operation that Lawrence could handle with forces already at hand in Nova Scotia and Massachusetts. Attacking it would have no bearing on the main theaters in western Pennsylvania and New York.

Braddock took command of the key campaign: the assault on Fort Duquesne.

The four commanders faced an immense challenge as they committed their forces across eastern North America. Yet rivers, dense forests, and mountains seemed to make no impression on them. They refused to consider that campaigns in North America were nothing like those in Europe, where supplies could be bought or pillaged from locals. In North America, once the armies moved a few miles inland, local supplies were nonexistent and the roads quickly trailed off into wilderness paths. The more distant the objective, the longer the supply line, and with every mile the line stretched thinner and became more difficult to maintain.

Even as the governors were meeting, Braddock's army began to move. Advance elements traveled via Frederick and Winchester to establish a forward base at Wills Creek.[20] On April 16 St. Clair arrived at the fort in a foul mood.

He had just ridden over a road that was barely fit for packhorses. Braddock's train included four eight-inch brass howitzers, four light twelve-pound guns, four light six-pound guns, and fifteen small cohorns. By European standards, the artillery train was small for the size of the force; nonetheless, to pull the guns and their support elements, he needed nearly two hundred horses.[21] St. Clair railed about the problems he faced. He vented particular bitterness toward colonial sutlers, whose empty promises of supplies, wagons, and horses left soldiers subsisting on salt pork and hard tack while too few overworked horses labored to haul the guns.

At Frederick, Maryland, George Washington joined Braddock. Washington arrived under special circumstances. Two weeks before, he and the general had enjoyed dinner together at the Raleigh Tavern in Williamsburg. Their conversation had centered on the issue that tormented Washington and every other officer in the colonial militia: rank. As commander in chief, Braddock had the king's authority to grant royal commissions, but only up to captain. The previous October Lieutenant Governor Dinwiddie had increased the Virginia militia to ten companies, but instead of forming them into a regiment with a colonel in command (the post Washington desired), he ordered that they take the field as independent companies, with a captain in command of each. Washington refused his captaincy as beneath his dignity, resigned, and returned to Mount Vernon. At the Raleigh Tavern dinner Braddock could offer him no better deal. Washington reacted to the general as he had to the governor: He withdrew to Mount Vernon.

But Braddock needed Washington. The ex-colonel was one of the few white men who had actually been where Braddock intended to go. His presence would facilitate relations with Indians and local traders who knew the young Virginian from his previous frontier travels. Braddock found a clever answer to Washington's question of rank. He instructed Orme to tell Washington, "The general, having been informed that you expressed some desire to make the campaign, but that you declined it upon some disagreeableness that you thought might arise from the regulation of command [i.e., rank], has ordered me to acquaint you, that he will be very glad of your company in his family, by which all inconveniences of that kind will be obviated."[22] Braddock's offer, giving Washington a place, albeit unofficial, on his staff, mollified him, and so he rode to Frederick to join his new "family."

By the fifth of May, Washington and the general were at Winchester. The army marched for Wills Creek on the seventh and arrived on the tenth. Braddock set his men to building a fort, which he named Cumberland in · honor of his patron.

Four tough weeks had gone by since the army had left Alexandria. It had been a miserable and difficult march. Having spent most of their careers in relatively comfortable garrison duty in Ireland, Scotland, and England, Braddock's soldiers were not prepared for the harsh realities of frontier campaigning. Their officers told them to "soldier on," promising them that at Fort Cumberland they could expect fresh provisions and decent shelter. Unfortunately, when they got to the fort they found neither. Again, promised supplies had not been delivered. Weary of salt pork and sore feet, the men grumbled. Braddock and his officers responded in the traditional manner: They damned the men and punished the miscreants so that they might "be better taught."[23]

Fort Cumberland was the jumping-off point for the final long march to Duquesne. Stuck on a small hill to the far side of Wills Creek, the fort was a crude rectangular wooden palisade 600 feet by 150 feet. It was, according to one of Braddock's company, "the most desolate Place" on earth.[24] With the arrival of the army, however, overnight Cumberland became one of the largest and rowdiest "towns" in America. Nearly three thousand redcoats, colonials, and Indians swarmed around the fort. Scarouady, Tanaghrisson's successor as half king, brought in a contingent of warriors along with their wives and children. Redcoats and warriors eyed each other with fascination and fear. For weeks the soldiers had listened to fantastic tales about these natives. Sutlers and other locals had been taunting the young soldiers with lurid stories about Indian cunning and ferocity—how they scalped their enemies, roasted prisoners, and smashed babies against trees.

In the Indian camp curiosity rather than fear reigned. The warriors were taken aback by the spectacle of this huge clumsy crowd of men trudging west at a snaillike pace. For a people accustomed to moving by stealth and speed, it seemed very strange. One night Scarouady's band put on a theatrical demonstration. Their bodies painted in crimson and black, they danced wildly around a blazing campfire brandishing knives and tomahawks in an ancient ritual intended to boost their own courage and awe their allies.

On the hillside beyond the stockade hundreds of neatly dressed tents marked the bivouac area. In every tent the men groused about the shortage of food. Braddock worried that he might have to turn back. To his relief, on May 20 Benjamin Franklin's son William rode into camp with the welcome news that only a few miles behind him was a train of ninety-one Conestoga wagons and twenty packhorses laden with supplies.[25]

Fresh provisions did much to improve morale, but the men were still restless. Officers did what they could to occupy the attention of these young soldiers—days were spent in endless drilling and fatigue parties. When Braddock discovered that his officers had become "scandalously fond of Squas" who were "bringing" their husbands "money in Plenty which they got from the officers," he immediately prohibited Indian women from entering the camp and further ordered that "no sutler" was to "give any liquor to the Indians on any account." As for his own soldiers, anyone found giving liquor to an Indian was to be summarily punished with 250 lashes, a probable death sentence. Carousing, drunken soldiers were hardly a new phenomenon, but in this howling wilderness so far removed from civilization Braddock feared that the slightest crack in the wall of discipline might lead to a total collapse.

Although Braddock's measures were a bit extreme, his soldiers understood army discipline, and while they grumbled quietly they went about their business of drilling and maintaining camp life. The Indians felt otherwise, Braddock, complained Scarouady, had a "bad heart." "He looked upon us as dogs and would never hear any thing what was said to him." A few weeks before, at least fifty Indians had enlisted with Braddock. Yet within a few days of the general's edicts, only the sullen Scarouady, his son, and six others remained.[26]

On May 29, 1755, an advance party of six hundred men got under way under the command of St. Clair. They were to forge ahead, clearing and widening the narrow path to a width of twelve feet in order to accommodate the passage of wagons and artillery. Wills Mountain was their first challenge, and it undid them. Steep, slippery slopes proved fatal for three wagons that slid backward, careening into a deep ravine. Trying to haul heavy artillery proved an even greater curse. Sweating seamen detailed from Keppel's squadron rigged block and tackle to trees in a failed attempt to heave the heavy tubes up the steep incline. Braddock was beside himself. Harry Gordon, a Scot engineer recommended personally to the general by Cumberland, reported that the path on the other side of the mountain was even worse than the one bedeviling them. For his mounting troubles, the general blamed the colonials, who had failed to supply him with provisions, wagons, or sound advice. Braddock saw "falsehood with every person." Gordon, however, found a solution. On a reconnaissance he discovered a nearly level route around the foot of the mountain. It stretched a few miles longer, but it was passable. Braddock ordered work parties forward to cut a road, and finally on the morning of June 7 the forward element, Halkett's brigade, took the van and began the long march toward Duquesne, following behind St. Clair's road builders who were still struggling to clear a way. It took three days for the rest of the force, made up mostly of Dunbar's regiment and the supply train, to get under way.

The delay gave Braddock time to get off an important dispatch to London in which he provided a gloomy assessment of his situation. He was, he confessed, more than a month behind schedule. The future looked even bleaker. "I have an hundred and ten miles to march through an uninhabitable wilderness over steep rocky mountains and almost impassable morass."[27] Since "good intelligence" depended upon "the Indians whose veracity is no more to be depended upon than that of the borderers here," Braddock knew virtually nothing about the strength and disposition of the enemy. He assumed, however, that Duquesne was weak and that as soon as his powerful army drew near the fort, the French "[would] want their forces to the northward."[28]

The road proved "impassable," at least for Braddock's heavy wagons and some of the artillery. Barely three days out from Cumberland the general ordered the largest wagons, whose slow movement had brought the column to a virtual standstill, to return. Two six-pound howitzers and four cohorns, along with a substantial amount of powder and shot, were also sent back. Horses were a serious problem. The few that remained could not pull sufficient weight. Braddock cursed the colonials who had sold him small and underfed beasts. Even Washington agreed that there had "been vile mismanagement in regard to the horses."[29] Following the command to "push on," and with road-clearing parties working ahead, the long column inched its way through the forest. Because security was a constant concern, Braddock ordered flanking parties out one hundred yards on either side to cover the column, and every two hours, when the column paused to rest, the guard formed up two deep and faced outward.

Braddock's enemy was time. Each dreary day on the march drew down the supplies. Braddock assumed that Duquesne was lightly defended, but he couldn't discount the worrisome rumors floating in from Indians that sizable French reinforcements were on their way from Montreal. The army needed nine days to cover the twenty-four miles to Little Meadows. The hard march and salt provisions were taking a gruesome toll. Numerous soldiers, including Washington, had taken ill, and a few had died. As Braddock came down the side of Meadow Mountain, he could see St. Clair's advance guard preparing a fortified camp for his army's arrival. While the soldiers pitched their tents, Braddock summoned Washington to ask his advice. Washington agreed that unless they picked up the pace the expedition was doomed, and urged the general to deploy ahead with a picked force and seize the forks before enemy reinforcements arrived. Braddock agreed.

"Chosen men" from the Forty-fourth and Forty-eighth regiments made up the core of the flying column. Two companies of rangers, fifty men from Captain Horatio Gates's independent New York company, and a small detachment of light horses also joined. Braddock divided his force into two elements. The first, under St. Clair's command, set off before dawn on June 18. They trailed two cannon and three wagons of tools. A day later Braddock led the second, heavier element out of the camp, accompanied by more than a dozen ammunition wagons and six more cannon. Altogether Braddock marched out of Little Meadows with about half of his entire force, leaving Dunbar with orders to follow along as quickly as possible with the remaining men, wagons, and baggage. Braddock, however, left the unfortunate Dunbar with too few wagons and horses to keep up a quick pace, and each day as the general pushed forward, Dunbar fell farther behind.

Despite his desire to reach Duquesne as quickly as possible, Braddock faced a dilemma. If he dropped more artillery and baggage and gave up road and bridge building, he could reach Duquesne in only a few days. But if the fort had been reinforced or was stronger than he anticipated, he would have to undertake a siege for which he would be unprepared. Braddock's deliberate nature won out. His greatest fear was being cut off in the terrifying wilderness, and so he continued building his road. The general's caution exasperated Washington. Braddock halts, he wrote his brother, "to level every Mold Hill, and to erect Bridges over every Brook."[30]

Signs of lurking French and Indians were everywhere. On June 23 three Mohawk arrived in camp and reported that the French had received reinforcements at Duquesne, but that they were desperately short of provisions. During the night the Mohawk quietly left the camp, taking one of Scarouady's scouts with them, leaving the general with barely a half dozen Indians. Two evenings later three soldiers wandered from camp. At the sound of musket fire, parties were dispatched to search for them. Three scalped bodies were found nearby. Braddock responded by offering five pounds for every Indian scalp delivered to him. Sentries and flanking parties saw the ferocious enemy behind every bush and tree. Musket fire became so common and undisciplined that the general issued orders threatening to arrest any officer who could not control his trigger-happy men. These pricking attacks by the French and Indians were effective. They slowed the advance and unnerved the young soldiers, while supplying time for the French at Duquesne to consider their options.

(4)

French Victory, English Defeat

We have done too much or too little.

—Lord Hardwicke to Newcastle

No secret could be contained in the porous bureaucracies of London and Paris. Almost as soon as Braddock broke the seal to his orders, French secret agents hurried across the channel to Paris with news of his mission. The French took the British move seriously, and with unwonted quickness King Louis XV ordered six battalions to Quebec—three times the size of the force being sent to Virginia.

Through official dispatches from Paris and a deluge of rumors relayed by Indians and fur traders, Governor Duquesne was well informed about the enemy's movements. His problem, however, was that it would take months for the king's regiments to make their way to Canada. In the meantime he was forced to rely on Canadian forces: the Troupes de la Marine and local militia.

Cardinal Richelieu, Louis XIV's minister, had organized Les Compagnies Franches de la Marine, also known as Troupes de la Marine, in 1622 to serve as soldiers aboard the king's ships. Compared to Louis's huge land army, the Troupes de la Marine were a modest-sized force organized into small companies of approximately fifty men, rather than regiments of several hundred soldiers. Since the ministry of marine had responsibility for colonial administration, it was a logical move to assign the mission of defending the colonies to the Troupes de la Marine. In 1674 the first company arrived for duty in the West Indies, and in 1683 three companies landed at Quebec.

Initially, the ranks of the Troupes de la Marine were recruited in France. The lower orders of Paris, the drifting populations of seaport towns, and poor country lads were among those shanghaied into the enlisted ranks bound for the colonies. But since the distance from Paris was inversely proportional to an officer's influence and chances of gaining promotion, Frenchmen of the "better sort" who made up the officer corps had little interest in serving in any of the colonies. Forced to look elsewhere for its officers, the ministry of marine found a ready supply of candidates among Canada's elite landed families, who were anxious to obtain commissions for their sons. Young men entered as cadets, the lowest commissioned rank. Duty was arduous, often requiring long periods away from home, garrisoning distant posts, negotiating with Indians, launching punitive raids, and exploring unknown territory. It was a hard, adventurous life and promotion was slow, but the romance and prestige of serving in the Troupes de la Marine was so popular among Canadians that in order to accommodate the demand for billets, by 1728 the enlistment age was lowered to fifteen. By the mid-eighteenth century almost the entire officer corps was Canadian.

Although the Troupes de la Marine were skilled fighters, they were small in number. Duquesne's entire force numbered not more than one thousand men. Militia were far more numerous but also less reliable. Since local parishes were the principal organizing element of Canada, they became the focus for the militia organization. As in New England towns, each parish sponsored its own militia company, led by officers appointed by the governor. Each parish was incorporated into one of three districts headquartered in either Quebec, or Trois-Rivières, or Montreal. At the head of each district was a colonel supported by a staff. The governor was the supreme commander. All men between the ages of sixteen and sixty were required to bear arms. By 1750, 165 companies comprising nearly twelve thousand men were listed for service, nearly one-fifth of Canada's entire population.

The combination of the hard-bitten Troupes de la Marine and the militia, many of whom were experienced woodsmen, provided Duquesne with a powerful fighting force; nonetheless, their numbers were small compared to the manpower available in the British colonies. Compounding the governor's problem, the Troupes de la Marine were scattered in small detachments across French Canada from Cape Breton to Saskatchewan. For the moment, Duquesne's best hope rested with his Indian allies.

Since Washington's humiliating surrender and retreat at Great Meadows, French relations with the Ohio Indians had improved considerably. Several Indian delegations had appeared at the gates of Fort Duquesne to ask forgiveness for not coming sooner to the assistance of the French against the English invasion. Contrecoeur, savvy in Indian affairs, usually left his visitors waiting for several days. Only after abject apologies and profuse promises to remain loyal to Onontio, their father in Quebec, did the commandant grant them pardon and embrace them as allies. To seal the bond, the Indians smoked and exchanged wampum belts with the French as a sign of friendship.

While Contrecoeur secured support from the Ohio Indians, Duquesne sent messengers across "the ice" into the high country to the west and north of the Great Lakes. For generations these tribes, which included Ottawa, Pottawatomi, Ojibwa, and Menominee, had been drawn to the French as much by their hatred of the Iroquois as by ties of trade and religion. As spring approached, bands of warriors prepared to travel east, eager to savage their old enemies and enjoy the spoils of war.

Although Contrecoeur's clever diplomacy drew Indians to his side, the old commander himself was worn out. For nearly thirty hard years he had served Canada and his king, and he yearned to retire to his estates near Montreal. He had done his best to prepare for the British. His men had chopped, dug, and sweated to throw up a rough wooden stockade overlooking the two rivers. Inside they had built barracks and storehouses. To open fields of fire outside the walls, they had cleared the forest for a quarter mile. Even so, Contrecoeur knew that British cannon could demolish the wooden stockade and send the Indians scattering into the forest. Braddock would have to be stopped on the road. Contrecoeur sent out raiding parties to break the enemy advance, but the British came steadily on, "always marching in battle formation."[1]

On April 20 Governor Duquesne came down to Lachine to see off two hundred reinforcements bound for the Ohio under the command of Captain Daniel-Hyacinthe-Marie Lienard de Beaujeu. Like Contrecoeur, Beaujeu was a veteran soldier. In King George's War he had helped lead an epic 150-mile midwinter march against the English force in Nova Scotia. After the war he commanded Fort Niagara, where he honed his skills dealing with Indians and did all that he could to thwart the rising British presence concentrated across Lake Ontario at Oswego.[2] Beaujeu's long experience with Indians, and his assignments in the west, made him the natural choice to lead the relief force to Duquesne and then remain to command so that the anxious Contrecoeur could at last return home.

Beaujeu and his men took the normal six weeks to reach Niagara. Key to his mission was filling the gaps in the five-hundred-mile supply line from Montreal to Duquesne. Early winters and late springs meant that the water route was ice-free barely half the year, so it was critical to move men and supplies as early and quickly as possible. Aside from the sheer distance, the chief obstacle was the numerous portages. At key links (Niagara, Presque Isle, Rivière aux Boeuf, Venango), the French had established posts. Beaujeu's task was to clear better paths and remove obstructions between them. At the same time, he made sure that local commanders kept sufficient canoes and bateaux ready to carry men and supplies down the route. Beaujeu's party portaged around Niagara Falls and set out on Lake Erie with sixteen boats. Following the Chautauqua route, they pushed on south—overland and by water. On June 17, while Braddock was camped near Little Meadow, they arrived at Fort Le Boeuf. A few more days brought them down the French Creek to Venango, where Beaujeu received an urgent message from Contrecoeur: come quickly. At the end of June, when Beaujeu's men finally pulled their canoes onto the riverbank at Fort Duquesne, Contrecoeur was startled by the sight. In the face of a strong advancing enemy, the governor had sent him only two hundred men and no cannon.

Contrecoeur and Beaujeu agreed that the fort was as good as lost. Their best course of action was to fall back toward Lake Erie in order to cover the approach to Niagara, their most vital fort. With fewer men and inferior weapons they could not defeat the enemy, but with the element of surprise a quick blow might delay him. Beaujeu therefore devised a plan to take all the available troops—about three hundred men—and to lay an ambush for the English, while Contrecoeur remained behind to prepare the evacuation. Neither officer believed that the French could actually stop Braddock. Beaujeu's gallant mission was to buy time, not to win a battle.

On the evening before he planned to march, Captain Beaujeu walked to the nearby Indian encampment. For more than two decades Beaujeu had served and fought with Indians. He knew them well; he likely spoke their languages. He understood that they would never stand and fight within a doomed fort; would they, however, join him in a quick attack?

As he entered the camp, Indians of a dozen nations crowded close about him. "Here were Delawares from the Susquehanna . . . , and Shawanoes from Grave Creek and the Muskingum; scattered warriors of the Six nations; Objiwas and Pottawattamies from the far Michigan; Abenakis and Caughnawageas from Canada; Ottawas from Lake Superior . . . , and Hurons from the falls of Montreal and Lorette."[3] Beaujeu beseeched the chiefs to join him. Their spokesman replied: "What Father do you wish to die and sacrifice us? The English are more than four thousand men, and we are only eight hundred and you wish to go and attack them! You see at once that you have no sense. We must have till tomorrow to decide."[4]

In the morning Beaujeu and his men made their confessions to the post chaplain, Father Deny Baron. At mass Beaujeu knelt before Father Baron and received the sacrament. He was naked to the waist. Only the light color of his skin and an officer's gleaming gorget hanging from his neck distinguished him from the Indians gathered outside the fort. After the final blessing, the captain and his men drew their powder and ball and marched toward the gate. As he passed the Indian encampment, Beaujeu paused to ask if the chiefs had made their decision. "We cannot march," they told him. Beaujeu shouted back, "I am determined to go and meet the enemy. Will you let your Father go alone?" As the Indians murmured among themselves, a runner burst through the crowd and announced breathlessly that the English had forded the Monongahela and were approaching the fort, marching in close formation. Hearing the news, a Delaware called out that they would "shoot um down all one pigeon."[5]

The news stirred the camp. "You see my friends," Beaujeu challenged the excited warriors, "the English are going to throw themselves into the lion's mouth. They are weak sheep who pretend to be ravenous wolves. Those who love their father, follow me! You need only hide yourselves in the ravines which line the road, and when you hear us strike, strike yourselves. The victory is ours!"

Beaujeu judged his audience well. Unlike disciplined European troops who would charge blindly to their own death if ordered by their officers, these fighters needed to be persuaded by rhetoric and leadership that victory was at hand. War whoops sounded. Warriors rushed toward open kegs of flints, powder, and shot and filled their powder horns and bullet pouches. Within minutes nearly 650 Indians joined Beaujeu and his men and headed down the path toward the English. There was no time for a plan. In any case the Indians would never have listened. It was a French and Indian mob.

Beaujeu's intelligence was correct. The British line of march to the fort had crossed the Monongahela twice, first at the upper ford and then again at the lower. The scout had only seen the first crossing. Braddock's light horse crossed first, closely followed by the advance guard made up of grenadiers, a detachment from the Forty-fourth Regiment, and half of the independent New York company commanded by Lieutenant Colonel Thomas Gage.[6] As had been the case during the entire march, the soldiers followed sound tactical doctrine. Flanking parties went out. Once the riverbanks were secured, artillery was brought up to cover the main force. As soon as Gage's men were over the embankment, St. Clair's engineers arrived to slope back the steep riverbank and widen the path for men, wagons, and artillery to pass. While the advance guard pushed ahead, the main body, with Braddock leading, crossed the river. Not far ahead Gage's men secured the lower ford for the second crossing. Thus far, aside from a few sightings of Indians, the enemy was nowhere to be seen. By noon on July 9 the men reached the second ford and waded across. Braddock ordered the colors broken out, and the band struck up the "Grenadiers March." Close to his goal, Braddock told Gage to forge ahead and make camp about three miles from Duquesne. The rest of the column would catch up, bivouac for the night, and then march to the fort in the morning.

As the British made their way through the forest with clocklike precision, Beaujeu and his mixed force hurried toward them. The captain had planned to catch the enemy at the second ford, but the Indian conference at the fort had delayed him, and Braddock was safely across. In the distance Beaujeu could hear the sound of drums and fifes and the noise of axes felling trees. Grenadiers, four abreast, marched steadily forward. Two hundred yards in front of the British column rode a small detachment of horsemen, and on either side flanking parties slashed their way through the undergrowth. Behind the advancing wedge trudged St. Clair's engineers, clearing the road for the main body. A quarter of a mile back from them, Braddock rode with the main column. Harry Gordon was with the engineers, supervising the road clearing. Perhaps it was the midday sun glistening off Beaujeu's gorget that first caught his eye, but in an instant Gordon saw the Frenchman crashing out of the forest with what seemed to be a horde of men cascading behind him. One horseman at the front turned his mount and yelled back to the advance guard, "The Indiens was upon us."[7] Scattered firing broke out, war whoops echoed, and Beaujeu waved his cap in the air, directing his men to move left and right into the underbrush. As quickly as they had appeared, the French and Indians disappeared into the wood.

Gordon and his engineers fell back. An officer ordered the grenadiers to fix bayonets and form up in street-firing ranks. They fell in on a four-man front several ranks deep and began firing ahead. After the front rank volleyed, it stepped aside, and the second and third ranks advanced and fired in turn. For years these men had trained in this tactic, and they behaved instinctively and admirably. On the third volley Beaujeu took a ball in the head and fell dead. Captain Jean-Daniel Dumas took command. Whether by instinct or by order, Dumas's men divided like a tuning fork and came down under cover along the flanks of the grenadiers, felling them one by one.

Gage tried to rally his men and advanced against the hidden enemy. The soldiers fired blindly into the woods, cutting down men in their own flanking parties who were struggling to get back to the road. Within minutes most of Gage's officers were either wounded or dead. Command disintegrated, ranks broke, and soldiers scurried rearward. Those who remained fought with fierce tenacity, "having only death" before them.[8]

Shortly after hearing the fire, Braddock impetuously ordered Colonel Ralph Burton forward with eight hundred men while the convoy escort, about three hundred men, stood in place by the wagons facing outward. At the rear, one hundred men under Sir Peter Halkett fixed bayonets and awaited orders. The road was barely twelve feet wide, and Burton's men had to struggle to maneuver by wagons and artillery. Jittery men and nervous horses collided. As Burton drew close to the firing, engineers and grenadiers came tumbling down the road toward them. Having driven back the flanking parties on the English right, the French had taken nearby high ground and were firing into the English ranks. All was confusion. A wounded St. Clair screamed, "For God's sake [take] the rising ground on our right."[9] Braddock ordered Burton up the hill on the right flank. The colonel waved his grenadiers forward and then fell from his saddle, hit by enemy fire. The men "retreated very fast."[10] Washington, still weak from a bout with dysentery, approached the embattled general and asked permission to take men into the woods to dislodge the attackers. Braddock refused. He would not scatter his force. His men were trained to stand together, deliver fire, and advance with the bayonet. Yet soldiers running back and fresh reserves moving forward met and tangled on the narrow road in a twisted mass of falling redcoats.

Halkett left his men in the rear and rode forward. Officers were special targets, particularly those on horseback. A blizzard of shot swept him off his saddle, and when his son James rode to his father's side, he too died in a hail of fire. Braddock's personal secretary, William Shirley Jr., son of the governor, died on the road. With the exception of Washington, every officer on Braddock's staff went down, either killed or wounded.

Braddock was in the heat of the action the whole time. Miraculously, the general survived. Four horses were shot out from under him. For nearly an hour and a half he rode amid the disintegrating ranks, applying the flat of his sword to the backs of men, ordering them to form up. By midafternoon, with nearly half his force wounded or dead, Braddock gave the order to withdraw. The men needed no encouragement, and as the drums sounded the signal they wasted no time retreating down the road. Braddock was on his fifth mount when a ball tore through his right arm and lodged in his side. The wound was mortal.

When the men of the rear guard saw the look of defeat on the faces of their comrades coming down the road, they tore "the gears from their Horses and galloped quite away."[11] Washington was disgusted at what he saw. "Sheep pursued by dogs" was his description of the British rout.[12] Betraying his own personal biases, Washington praised his fellow Virginians and the gallant British officers but condemned the enlisted men as cowards.

Back they fled, abandoning wagons, artillery, and the dead and wounded. According to one British officer, the French and Indians "pursued us butchering as they came as farr as the other side of ye River; during our crossing, they shot many in the Water, and dyed the stream with their blood, scalping and cutting them in a most barbarous manner."[13] No one paused at the river's edge. They jumped in and splashed for the opposite bank. Dumas and his men did not pursue them. There was no need; victory was complete. Collecting spoils left on the battlefield rather than hunting down frightened soldiers became the focus of their attention.

Hundreds of bodies littered the bloody road. Every fallen British soldier was scalped and his body stripped. Tons of equipment that had been hauled through the wilderness fell to the French. Braddock's defeat delivered more arms, powder, ball, and cannon to Dumas than Governor Duquesne could have sent him in an entire year. Thanks to the booty left on the road, the French could easily arm their Indian allies.

By evening, Dumas and his soldiers were back at the fort, where the strains of a Te Deum could be heard from the chapel. Outside, Indians celebrated by dancing, feasting, and torturing their prisoners. After mass the French officers sat at their mess and examined a special prize: Braddock's dispatch box, which included his secret instructions. The British plans to attack the French posts were laid bare. Within hours Contrecoeur's most trusted men were carrying these documents to Quebec.[14]

On the far side of the Monongahela, exhausted and frightened soldiers began to regain their composure. Relieved that the enemy had not pursued them, the remnants of Braddock's mauled army stopped to rest in scattered groups. Washington reported, "[I] had four Bullets through my Coat, and two Horses shot under me." He was near Braddock when the general fell, and he helped to lift him onto a cart to carry him to safety. Fearing that the worst might not be over, and that the French might continue their advance, the dying general ordered Washington to ride ahead and summon Dunbar. For the moment, Braddock's fear of further attack was groundless. Through the night his tattered army filed down the road so laboriously carved out only a few days before. By evening of the following day, July 10, some soldiers had reached the banks of the Youghiogheny River, nearly forty miles from the scene of the disaster. It had taken Braddock's troops weeks to march to Duquesne in good order, but less than two days to retreat in disorder. Once across the Youghiogheny, they walked another few miles. By dark the tattered remnants, Braddock included, had arrived at the farm of Christopher Gist, where they were greeted with smoldering ruins. But Dunbar was only six miles away. Late the next morning, July 11, relief arrived.[15]

As his life ebbed, survival, not victory, was Braddock's objective. He ordered Dunbar to organize the withdrawal to Fort Cumberland, fifty miles to the east. For the next two days the surgeons tended the wounded while burial parties went about their grim work. Supplies that had been left in Dunbar's care were thrown into bonfires so they would neither delay the retreat nor fall into enemy hands. On the thirteenth Braddock resigned his command to Dunbar. The colonel gave the order to break camp and begin the sad march east. Barely one mile down the road, Braddock died. He was quietly buried under the road that he had built. After a brief service, his men marched solemnly over the grave to obliterate any signs of the burial site.

Dunbar and his troops reached Fort Cumberland on July 21. The retreat did not end there. Leaving a force of provincials to hold the garrison, Dunbar took the remainder of the army and marched to Philadelphia. Braddock's defeat and Dunbar's withdrawal left western Pennsylvania, Virginia, and Maryland at the mercy of the French and Indians. Colonials cursed Braddock and Dunbar with almost as much vehemence as they damned the French and Indians. Officers who had been present at the disaster, including Washington, rushed to defend themselves and heap blame on the dead general. Nearly thirty years later Washington had a different, more judicious view of those events and his commander: "He was brave even to a fault and in regular Service would have done honor to his profession. His attachments were warm, his enmities were strong, and having no disguise about him, both appeared in full force. He was generous and disinterested, but plain and blunt in his manner even to rudeness."[16]

News of Braddock's disaster on the Monongahela arrived in London in mid-August. Those dispatches joined others recently delivered that chronicled another British failure—this one at sea.

On February 12, 1755, Admiral Sir Edward Hawke, commander of the Home Fleet, had hoisted his flag on *Terrible* at Spithead. Two days later, thirty-five ships of the line were ordered to prepare for sea, and a "hot press" swept the streets for seamen. For the moment, however, no attempt was made to blockade the French coast. That costly mistake gave the French a chance to send forces to the West Indies and Canada.[17] As Hawke's captains filled their forecastles and took in stores, spies reported that the French were preparing to sail from Brest. Realizing what delaying the blockade may have cost them, the Admiralty rushed to close the gate, but a French convoy was already at sea. Their only choice was to dispatch a flying squadron in the hopes of intercepting the French. On March 18 the cabinet hurriedly issued secret orders dispatching a naval force to sail "directly to Nova Scotia" to "fall upon" and "prevent French ships from going into or landing any forces on the continent of North America." Admiral Edward Boscawen was in command.[18]

Known below decks as "Wry-necked Dick," a nickname he earned by his habit of cocking his head to one side, Boscawen had been in the king's service for nearly thirty years. Never before, however, had he been in such a delicate situation. His orders were to attack a nation with whom England was ostensibly at peace. Braddock's orders, at least, made the pretense that the general was acting in the name of his king to reclaim land illegally occupied. Knowing that a French convoy was ahead of him carrying troops and supplies for Quebec, Boscawen hoped that his fast warships could overtake it. A tough voyage across the Atlantic drove his squadron to a position several degrees north to a landfall at Cape St. Francis near the entrance to Conception Bay, Newfoundland. Boscawen tacked southward toward the Cabot Strait to scour the approaches to the Gulf of St. Lawrence.

Dunkirk, under the command of Captain Richard Howe, was in the van. On June 7 Howe stopped and questioned an English "banker" hand-lining for cod. The fisherman reported that he had seen a large Frenchman go by crammed with soldiers. Howe reported this to the admiral, and the next day they sighted four large vessels bound west. Howe set out in pursuit, with the rest of the squadron following, but by midday a heavy fog closed in and forced the English to shorten sail. When the fog lifted the next morning, Boscawen spied three Frenchmen to windward. The admiral hoisted French colors, and the three unsuspecting Frenchmen approached him. Light winds kept them from meeting, and as night settled in, Boscawen waited patiently for morning, when he would spring his trap.

At first light on June 9, the closest French vessel signaled Boscawen. Not knowing French codes, the admiral gave the wrong reply, and the French ran for it. Howe gave chase and came within hailing distance of the rearmost French ship, *Alcide*. He ordered the vessel to heave to and await his admiral. *Alcide*'s captain, Toussaint Hocquart, rightly refused to obey the order and then asked if England and France were at peace or war. Howe hollered back "Peace, Peace."

While Howe and Hocquart exchanged pleasantries, Boscawen grew fearful that the quarry might escape, and so in accordance with his orders he signaled *Dunkirk* to "engage the enemy" and it let loose a devastating broadside. *Torbay* joined the fray. Surprised and outgunned, Hocquart fired a leeward gun to signal surrender. As Howe secured *Alcide*, other ships in his squadron gave chase to the remaining two Frenchmen. Within two hours *Lys*, with eight companies of soldiers, was captured. But the third ship, *Royal Dauphin*, escaped.

In public Howe and Boscawen rejoiced at their small victory. In private, however, they admitted that these three ships were simply stragglers. Altogether, sixteen of the eighteen ships that had left Brest arrived at either Louisbourg or Quebec. Only eight of the seventy-eight companies bound for Canada fell into enemy hands. Boscawen confessed to his wife, "What I have done will add fewel to the fire only." When the news arrived in London, Lord Hardwicke, the lord chancellor, put it to Newcastle, "We have done too much or too little."[19]

Boscawen's actions at sea were reminiscent of Washington's attack at Jumonville Glen. Both men initiated an attack against forces with whom their nation was ostensibly at peace. Both claimed to be acting under orders. Boscawen clearly was, but Washington's case is less certain. In both instances, however, British forces had committed acts of war in a time of peace.

Among those safely delivered to Quebec was Canada's new governor, Pierre de Rigaud de Vaudreuil de Cavagnial, the marquis de Vaudreuil. Duquesne had requested and been granted leave to return to France. Vaudreuil, who was born in Quebec in 1698, was returning home. His father was a petty nobleman from Languedoc who had come to New France earlier as an officer in the colonial troops. In 1703 Louis XIV appointed him governor of New France. The marquis secured a commission for his son, and for nearly twenty years the younger Vaudreuil served as an officer in the colony. The family was well respected in Canada and enjoyed excellent connections in Paris. After the elder Vaudreuil died in 1725, his wife stayed in close contact with her friends at Versailles. With his mother's help, Vaudreuil moved up several notches in the colonial administration, eventually securing appointment as governor of Louisiana in 1742. From New Orleans Vaudreuil watched uneasily as British influence grew over the tribes in the Illinois, Ohio, and Carolina country. In his dispatches home he urged the government to take strong measures, and he did all that he could to reinforce the small French posts along the Mississippi and in the Illinois country. He paid close attention to the Indians, gaining valuable experience in the complex negotiations required to keep the tribes faithful.

Louisiana was a backwater, a mere way station on Vaudreuil's route of ambition. His goal was to follow in his father's footsteps to become governor of New France. He lobbied incessantly for the post. Jonquière's death in 1752, he thought, gave him the opening, but Duquesne beat him to it. Vaudreuil toyed with the notion of retiring to a chateau on the ancestral lands in Languedoc, but fortunately for him, Duquesne did not view life in New France with the same fondness that Vaudreuil did, and after less than two years as governor, he was pleased to return to France to resume his career as a naval officer. Finally, Vaudreuil had his chance. The king appointed him

Pierre de Rigaud de Vaudreuil de Cavagnial,
the marquis de Vaudreuil

to be the first Canadian-born governor, and on April 1, 1755, he received his secret instructions: "His Majesty is firmly resolved to maintain his rights and his possessions against pretensions so excessive and so unjust; and whatever his love for peace, will not make for its preservation any sacrifice but those which will accord with the dignity of his Crown and the protection he owes his subjects."[20]

Vaudreuil crossed to Canada in the company of General Jean-Armand Dieskau. A protégé of the renowned Marshal Maurice Saxe, Dieskau had been the military governor of Brest when he was tapped to command the army being sent to Canada. Although he was the senior military officer in Canada, Dieskau was subordinate to Vaudreuil. Neither the governor nor the general wasted any time. Within a few days of their arrival Vaudreuil was rallying the people of Canada, and Dieskau was on his way to Fort Niagara to organize an expedition against the "pretensions" of the English at Oswego.

According to the grand strategy laid out at Alexandria, Governor William Shirley was to march to Oswego with the Fiftieth and Fifty-first regiments, and from there launch an attack across the lake against Niagara. Almost as soon as he left Alexandria, however, the plan faltered. Shirley was too inexperienced a commander to handle the enormous logistical problem confronting him. Between Albany and Oswego lay nearly two hundred miles of rough terrain through which he had to move men and matériel. Within a few weeks the challenge had bogged him down to such a degree that he lost any hope of reaching Niagara for at least a year. In contrast, at the other end of New York the indefatigable William Johnson had already succeeded in gathering a large force of militia and Iroquois, mostly Mohawk, to march against Crown Point. Johnson's threat to Crown Point was far more advanced and organized than Shirley's stumbling march toward Niagara. For the moment at least, Niagara was safe, and so Vaudreuil, concerned about Johnson's advance, recalled Dieskau from the west and dispatched him to meet the threat aimed at Crown Point.

Johnson had returned from Alexandria with a new title, colonel of the Six Nations and "Sole Agent and Superintendent of the said Indians." In his new role Johnson reported to Braddock and drew funds directly from the royal treasury. Johnson's star rose even higher when he obtained a commission as major general in the provincial militia, making him one of the most powerful men in America.[21]

The Iroquois, particularly Johnson's close friends the Mohawk, were key to the colonel's plan, but their support was far from certain. Nearly a year had gone by since the debacle at the Albany conference, but little had changed. The British had offered no new proposals to guarantee the safety of their villages. How, the chiefs asked, would the English protect them from the wrath of the French? Adding to the Mohawk's uneasiness was a long-standing division within their own nation. For generations a signifi-cant number of Catholic Mohawk had lived in Kahnawake near Montreal. Faithful to church and the French king, these Mohawk were important al-lies for the French. Yet because they kept in contact with their New York brethren, they were also suspect. Dieskau doubted their "fidelity."[22] Vau-dreuil, on the other hand, dismissed the general's concerns and assured him that the domiciled Mohawk were reliable. The British too were am-bivalent and uncertain about "their" Mohawk. The Albany leaders accused the local Mohawk of being in league with their Kahnawake cousins. Like Vaudreuil, William Johnson dismissed these concerns, and in June, to confirm their loyalty, he invited the Iroquois to Mount Johnson.

The gathering at Mount Johnson was the largest assemblage of Indians ever seen in New York. By some accounts, more than one thousand men, women, and children camped in the orchards and fields surrounding John-son's home. ("They have spoiled my meadow and destroy every green thing about my estate," he later complained.)[23] For nearly two weeks, from June 21 to July 4, the Iroquois leaders sat with Johnson. Like the convening of Parlia-ment, or muster day in a New England town, the meeting was marked by endless rounds of drinking, eating, dancing, smoking, and debating. Both the English and Indians caucused among themselves and then returned to the public council meeting to lay before the audience opinions and propos-als. A moment of high theater occurred when Johnson stood and told the chiefs, "My war kettle is on the fire, my canoe is ready to put into the water, my gun is loaded, my sword by my side, and my axe sharpened! I desire and expect you will now take up the hatchet and join with us!"[24] Johnson's impas-sioned rhetoric notwithstanding, the nations meeting at Mount Johnson were not yet ready to charge into war. Their natural reluctance to commit themselves ripened to deep skepticism when "the incoherent, unexpected, unintelligible, not to be credited damned bad news" of Braddock's disaster came up the river.[25] In spite of the ill tidings, the elderly Mohawk chief Hendrick (Theyanoguin) remained Johnson's faithful friend.

Probably in his midseventies by then, Hendrick traveled about the Mohawk Valley trying to recruit warriors for Johnson's march against Crown Point. Unfortunately, his influence did not reach into Canada, and there was little he could do to persuade the Kahnawake Mohawk to remain neutral. Hendrick's and Johnson's overtures to them were rebuffed with the following reply: "[By] Religion and Treaties [we are] so united to the French, they [we] must obey their orders."[26]

Johnson's problems recruiting Indians were compounded by the ungenerous behavior of his archrival, Governor Shirley, who detested him. Johnson heartily reciprocated the sentiment, calling him "my inveterate enemy."[27] Their relationship only worsened when Shirley, as a result of Braddock's death, became commander in chief in North America.

Late in July 1755 the colonel left Mount Johnson and established his headquarters at Albany. Captain William Eyre, an experienced engineer who had come to America with Braddock, joined him. It was Eyre's good fortune that Braddock had sent him north to assist Johnson before the general left on his ill-fated march to the Monongahela. Through July and early August, as the New England militia assembled, Johnson laid plans for his march on Crown Point. He planned to move his army in three stages. The first objective was to move up the Hudson forty miles and establish a strong base at the Great Carrying Place (Fort Edward, also known as Fort Lyman). This was the northernmost point of navigation on the Hudson, and the southern terminus of a fourteen-mile portage running northwest to the southern tip of Lac Sacrament (Lake George), where Johnson intended to plant his second base, later to be called Fort William Henry. Once he controlled the lake, Johnson intended to sail to the northern end, build a third base (Ticonderoga), and from there launch his final assault on Crown Point. Like Braddock, he faced the daunting challenge of moving men through a hostile wilderness, albeit over shorter distances, much of them over water.[28]

Fort Edward was the key link in Johnson's logistical chain. To protect the depot and its precious stores, Eyre laid out a large stockade surrounding an array of barracks and warehouses. The main gate faced west toward the river landing, where every day bateaux arrived from Albany delivering men and matériel for the campaign. Not even Eyre's substantial stockade and numerous buildings could accommodate the flood of supplies floated up from Albany. Soldiers and sutlers spilled out beyond the walls and made camp among stacked barrels of provisions, gunpowder, and other stores. The post was fast becoming one of the largest towns in North America.

Meanwhile Johnson's axmen were working their way north, widening the portage path to Lac Sacrament.

On August 14 Johnson joined his men at Fort Edward. He brought fifty Mohawk, including his "brother" Hendrick. Some of the New England militia were stunned by the wild appearance of Johnson's Indian friends, noting that "they had juels in Their noses. Their faces painted with all Colouers."[29] Johnson broke camp at Fort Edward on the morning of August 26 and marched for Lac Sacrament with fifteen hundred militia, mostly New Englanders, and forty Indians. Three days later he pitched his headquarters tent on the shores of the lake, which, in order "to honor His Majesty [and] to ascertain his undoubted dominion here," he promptly renamed Lake George.[30] While his men gathered timber and brush to form a temporary barrier around the camp, Johnson sent Eyre to scout a site for a permanent fortification. The next day two hundred more Indians arrived, and Johnson, fearing that the season was getting late, sent word back to Fort Edward to hurry more supplies ahead, including bateaux to be launched on the lake.

There was an eerie silence along the shores of Lake George. Johnson reported, "We have no Interuption from the Enemy," and then he added boastfully, "I do not dread a Surprise." But where were the French? For the moment, however, Johnson's chief worry was more with his own fractious militia, whose ill discipline and contempt for military routine created a scene of "disorderly management."[31] Ill health and improper hygiene were the immediate enemies. The "bloody flux" (dysentery) was ever present and ravaged Fort Edward. When he arrived at the post, Colonel Ralph Burton, one of the lucky survivors from Braddock's march, reported that "between five and six hundred [are] sick. Bury daily from five to eight men, and officers in proportion."[32] British army standing orders required the men to keep standards of personal hygiene, wash their clothes, and dig latrines at distant spots. Militia, ignorant of the hazards of camp life, dismissed the orders as just more harassment by the regulars. Fort William Henry, according to Burton, was even worse.

* * *

The French were waiting at Crown Point. Ten days before Johnson set out from Fort Edward, Dieskau had left Montreal with seven hundred soldiers from the recently arrived regiments, sixteen hundred Troupes de la Marine and militia, and seven hundred Indians—all three thousand, according to their commander, "panting for the attack." Dieskau, however, was not sure what to attack. For two weeks he remained at Crown Point waiting for the Indians to bring him intelligence about the English. He was sorely disappointed. According to Dieskau, the Kahnawake Mohawk were "spoiled." "Never," he complained on September 7, "was I able to obtain from them a faithful scout."[33] A few days later a Canadian scout reported that three thousand enemy were at Fort Edward. Unaware that Johnson had already moved his force north, Dieskau marched toward Fort Edward to attack. After a few days on the march Dieskau learned that Johnson had arrived at Lake George, leaving barely five hundred men to guard Fort Edward. Dieskau saw a chance to sweep around the English at the lake and strike their base camp. With a picked force, he set out on a rapid four-day march.

Successfully avoiding detection, Dieskau led his force south along the lake's west shore. By the evening of September 7 he was within striking distance of Fort Edward, and he planned a night attack. For this, however, he needed the Kahnawake Mohawk to guide his soldiers along the unfamiliar terrain. Unaccountably, the scouts got lost, and Dieskau spent the night in the forest. Having spoiled any hope of a surprise assault on Fort Edward, the next morning Dieskau's Indian allies announced they had no intention of storming the well-defended stockade. They preferred to move north to attack Johnson's unfortified lake camp, where they believed (wrongly, as it turned out) that the defenses were weak and that there was no artillery. Furious, but restrained, Dieskau had little choice but to agree. He dared not risk moving through the forest without Indian allies. He broke camp and sent scouts ahead to guide him toward the lake.

As the French were stirring from camp, Johnson was at Lake George. His scouts reported the stale information that the French were marching toward Fort Edward. Johnson quickly ordered one thousand militia under the command of Colonel Ephraim Williams to march to the fort's relief.

Rutted and narrow, the road between the lake and Fort Edward twisted and climbed gradually over hills and around ponds and streams. Along the road's edge thick forest crowded close, providing ample cover for any lurking enemy, while the hills and curves limited visibility ahead and to the rear.

About eight in the morning Williams's militia, along with two hundred Mohawk led by Hendrick, headed south toward Fort Edward. Despite his age, Hendrick rode at the very front of Williams's column. Behind him were his warriors, moving quickly in single file.

Dieskau's Mohawk alerted their general that the English were approaching. Hastily, Dieskau prepared an ambush. He ordered the Mohawk to conceal themselves in the woods until the English column passed so they could attack them from the rear. On the flanks of the road he placed his Canadians, whose task would be to pour fire into the enemy ranks as they passed between them. Ahead, across the road hidden by a rise, he marshaled his regulars in line formation to block the advance. It was a neat cul de sac. By the time Hendricks and Williams saw the French regulars, they would be covered on both sides and in the rear.

As the English Mohawk drew near, a French Mohawk, against orders, called out suddenly to Hendrick, "Who goes?" No Mohawk in either camp needed to be told who Hendrick was. The call was a warning to a cousin. Hendrick reined in his horse and turned toward the woods. He called to his Kahnawake brothers that they ought to join him and the English to repel the French invaders. The French officers were dumbstruck. This conversation in the middle of the road upended their entire plan. Dieskau described it as "the moment of treachery."[34] A shot rang out, and Hendrick fell from his saddle. The battle was on.

At first the French held the advantage. Unnerved by their leader's fall, Hendrick's Mohawk fell back as Williams's militia advanced up the road. From the flanks the Canadians poured fire into the English. Several militia fell, including Colonel Ephraim Williams. The French Mohawk, however, failed to close the rear gate, allowing the English to fall back. As soon as Johnson heard shots—"the marks of a warm engagement . . . about three or four miles" away—he sent off three hundred men to reinforce Williams. By this time, however, Williams's men, without their colonel, were retreating back toward the lake.[35]

As the sound of fire drew nearer, Johnson ordered his men to throw up a

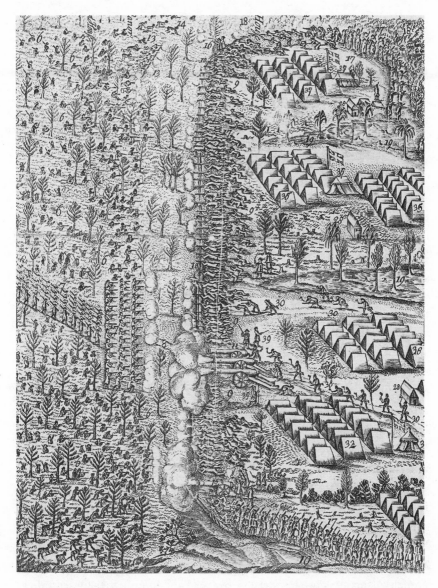

The Battle of Lake George, September 8, 1775. Part of a larger engraving, this shows Dieskau's attack on the fortified camp.

barricade of brush, limbs, barrels, bateaux, wagons, and anything else that could stop a musket ball. Captain Eyre's men hauled cannon into place to cover the hasty defense. Down the road came the militia, running at double time to stay ahead of the French and Indians clamoring at their heels. The provincials barely made it behind the barricade. At half past eleven, nearly two hours after the first shot had been fired on the road, the French regulars came into Johnson's view. In perfect order the soldiers of La Reine and Languedoc drew up on line 150 yards in front of the English position.

Johnson's hasty barricade saved him.[36] His undisciplined militia force would have never stood firm in open formation against French regulars, but the New Englanders proved steady enough behind their barricade. To the perfect cadence of the drum, the French advanced against heavy musket fire. Dieskau was in the lead with his sword raised, ordering his men, "March, let us force the place."[37] From the cover of trees, brush, and wagons Johnson's men volleyed. More devastating than musket balls was the iron storm let loose by Eyre's cannon. The heavy guns caught the French completely by surprise and quickly scattered their Indian allies. As the stunned French fell back, Johnson's Mohawk swept over the barricades, swinging their tomahawks and knives against French bayonets. For several hours fierce hand-to-hand combat raged, during which Johnson suffered a painful wound in the groin. Early in the evening the battered French withdrew. Among the wounded abandoned on the battlefield was Dieskau himself, left propped against a tree. The general had been hit four times.

As the French fell back along the road, a large number of them, mostly Indians and Canadians, stopped a few miles away to rest at Rocky Brook. A contingent of New York and New Hampshire militiamen, led by Captain Maginess from Schenectady, surprised them as they sat by the stream. This was the third encounter of the day and the worst moment for the French. As many as two hundred were killed and their bodies tossed into a nearby pond, which, according to local lore, was stained red for weeks and has been known ever since as "Bloody Pond."[38]

By the end of the day, both sides were bloodied and exhausted. The English gathered their wounded from along the road and withdrew to their camp at Lake George, while the French circled to the west and made their way to the north end of the lake, headed for Crown Point. Although the

English had driven the French back, the battles of September 8, 1755, resulted in a stalemate. Over the next few weeks both sides laid plans to consolidate their positions on the lake. Johnson and Eyre built Fort William Henry on the south shore. On the north, overlooking the portage between Lake George and Lake Champlain, the French drew plans for Fort Carillon, known to the English as Ticonderoga.

Seventeen fifty-five had not been a good year for the British in North America. The exception was Nova Scotia. For decades the English, particularly New England land speculators, had coveted the fertile Acadian lands along the Bay of Fundy and the Minas Basin. The troubles of the 1750s provided them with an opportunity to seize by force what they had been unable to take by persuasion and purchase. In the words of the Boston-born Jonathan Belcher, chief justice of Nova Scotia and Governor William Shirley's protégé, the growing Anglo-French rupture provided "such a juncture as the present may never occur again."[39]

First Fort Beauséjour needed to be taken. On May 26, 1755, a convoy of thirty vessels loaded with Massachusetts militia and supplies left Boston bound for Annapolis Royal on the Bay of Fundy. There the Boston force was joined by regular troops under the command of Lieutenant Colonel Robert Monckton. Two thousand provincials and 250 regulars landed unopposed at the head of the bay covered by the guns of Fort Lawrence. Monckton quickly seized the high ground overlooking Beauséjour, and on June 13 his mortars and artillery commenced fire.[40]

Louis Du Pont Duchambon de Vergor, Beauséjour's commandant, was one of Canada's least impressive officers. His contemporaries alleged that he owed his rise in the Troupes de la Marine to his friendship with the colony's intendant, François Bigot, for whom he acted as a "pimp." The gossipy Sieur de Courville noted that Vergor lacked "sense and education."[41] He did not apparently lack courage. For three days he and his men endured near constant fire from the English lines. Inside the fort Vergor commanded some two hundred soldiers and three hundred uneasy Acadian militia, who, sensing that the British were likely to win this contest, displayed a marked reluctance to join the fray. With morale collapsing on the inside, and mortar shells raining down from outside, on June 16 Vergor surrendered. Beauséjour was quickly renamed Fort Cumberland. Two days later, nearby Fort Gaspereau surrendered without firing a shot.

Within a few weeks the Acadians felt the victor's lash. Firmly in control, and claiming that the Acadians were in league with the French, Governor Lawrence confiscated their property and ordered his troops and New England militia to round up families so that they could be herded aboard waiting ships and expelled from their homeland. The British finally controlled all of Acadia, and they had cut the overland routes to Isle Royale (Cape Breton) and Louisbourg.

"Victory" in Nova Scotia and Acadia was scant comfort for the ministers in London. Braddock was dead, and the valley of the Ohio was in French hands. Shirley was bogged down in northern New York, while Johnson's advance had ground to a halt at the south end of Lake George. In London Newcastle, still a bit befuddled by the onrush of events, consulted with his friend the chief of ordnance, Lieutenant General John Ligonier, about how to defend Nova Scotia against a French counterattack. Ligonier recommended fortifying Annapolis Royal. According to the court insider Horace Walpole, Newcastle, with his characteristic lisp, muttered to the general, "Annapolis, Annapolis, certainly we must defend Annapolis," and then in a whispering aside, queried, "Where is Annapolis?"[42]

By contrast, 1755 had yielded a vintage harvest for the French, and they looked forward to the coming year's campaign. They had more troops in North America than the British. Their native allies were rallying, and spirits were high. Vaudreuil wasted no regrets over the loss of Dieskau. Never short on self-confidence, he wrote to Paris arguing that "war in this country is very different from the wars in Europe." Regular officers were "not acquainted with the country, and Canadians and Indians would not march with the same confidence" under French officers as they would under local commanders.[43] The governor apologized for "flatter[ing] himself," but his message was clear: Vaudreuil was offering to be both governor and commander in chief. He awaited the king's reply.

(5)

Montcalm and Loudoun

*Mercier is a weakling and an ignoramus, Saint-Luc a very
garrulous braggart, Montigny admirable, but a looter.*

—Montcalm to Lévis, August 17, 1756

Braddock's debacle in the Ohio Valley and the Lake George surprise were
major setbacks for the British. Monckton's victories in Nova Scotia and
Boscawen's captures off Newfoundland were poor recompense for these
substantial losses. At sea the British were "vexing" the French "for a little muck."[1] With wanton disregard for the laws of neutrality, the Royal
Navy had taken hundreds of French merchantment. Those illegal
seizures infuriated the French, and by late 1755 Newcastle's spies
brought alarming reports that the French were massing troops and ships
at ports along the Atlantic and Mediterranean. England, Ireland, Scotland, and Minorca were all rumored to be invasion targets. London was
anxious. As regiments were rushed to the coast, the financial markets,
the most reliable barometer of national sentiment, weighed in with their
opinion: Prices of public securities tumbled as interest rates rose, reflecting "near panic in some quarters."[2] Newcastle's problems were
mounting. Not least among them was Sir William Shirley. As the senior
officer in America, Shirley succeeded Braddock to become commander
in chief of the British forces in North America. It was an unfortunate, albeit unavoidable, appointment. Shirley was a petty politician with little
military experience but a passion for self-advancement. The news of his
promotion reached him at his wilderness post near the head of navigation on the Mohawk River, where he had paused en route to Oswego to

organize the attack on Niagara. Instead of returning immediately to Albany to take charge of his much expanded command, Shirley remained with the army, slogging his way through the rough interior to one of the most remote posts in British North America.

Good information had trouble catching up with Shirley's traveling headquarters. Upon learning of Braddock's death, the new commander in chief, completely unaware of the scale of the disaster, dispatched orders to Dunbar to attack Duquesne and then march north to Presque Isle for its "Reduction." Dunbar's reaction to these orders is unrecorded. On August 18, 1755, after nearly a month on the march, Shirley arrived at Oswego. The fort was a mess.[3] Nearly half the garrison was sick, provisions were running low, and dozens of men had deserted. Adding to Shirley's woes was the inept layout of the post. A triptych of "strong points" had been erected on the shore at the point where the Oswego River entered Lake Ontario. The most formidable of the trio stood on a bluff on the north side of the river. The

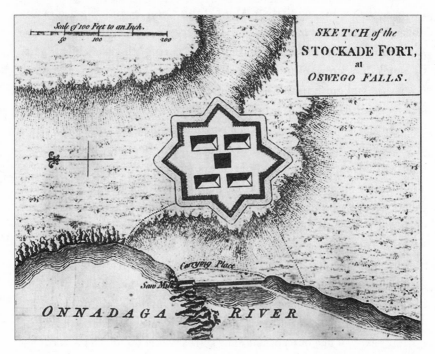

Plan of Fort Oswego

other two posts on the south side were far less impressive. Buildings were crumbling, and the nervous garrison was ready to flee at the first sign of the French and Indians. As best he could, Shirley set to work to repair the defenses and prepare for the attack on Niagara.

Weeks went by. Summer was fading fast and chill winds were sweeping in from across the lake as men deserted and supplies dwindled. Several deserters were caught, and Shirley ordered two of them executed to serve as an example for the rest. In the midst of his professional misery the general learned that his son William was among those who had died with Braddock.[4]

Shirley was, in effect, fighting a war on two fronts: against the French and Indians in front of him and William Johnson to his rear. Shirley had precipitated the unpleasantness with Johnson. When he received the preliminary reports of Johnson's battles at Lake George, instead of biding his time and holding his tongue, Shirley sent off dispatches questioning Johnson's leadership and the courage of his men. Johnson, stung by Shirley's criticisms, found his own way to retaliate against the governor. When Shirley asked him to use his influence to recruit Iroquois for the Niagara campaign, Johnson refused to help, saying that he did not think the commander in chief required "the assistance of any considerable Number of Indians."[5]

Surrounded by failure, overwhelmed by his responsibilities, and having alienated nearly everyone with whom he had had contact, Shirley finally returned to Albany, leaving Oswego with a sizable force he hoped to use for an early spring offensive against Niagara. The garrison had less than a two-month supply of provisions to get them through the harsh winter. It would have to depend upon a supply chain that stretched all the way back to Albany. The most critical and vulnerable link was the portage at the Great Carrying Place,* which connected the Mohawk River and Wood Creek.[6]

As early as 1730, British fur traders had established a small post at the southeastern end of the carry on the Mohawk River. From there, travelers portaged north a short distance to Wood Creek, a shallow, meandering stream that flowed to Oneida Lake. The creek slid between narrow, heavily wooded banks that made navigation extremely difficult. Elkanah Wat-

---

*Near present-day Rome, New York.

son, a land promoter, described it: "In many places the windings are so sudden, and so short, that while the bow of the boat was ploughing in the bank on one side, her stern was rubbing hard against the opposite shore. In some places our men were obliged to drag the boats by main strength; and in others, the boughs and limbs were so closely interwoven, and so low, as to arch the creek completely over, and oblige all hands to lie flat."[7] Once out of the confines of the creek, a quick passage across the lake brought travelers to the headwaters of the Oneida River. A few miles west, that river married the Seneca River to form the Oswego River, which eventually floated the canoes and bateaux to Lake Ontario. In good weather with sufficient water, the trip from Albany to Oswego was likely to take at least two weeks.[8]

To secure the Great Carrying Place, Shirley ordered Captain William Williams to fortify the camp on the Mohawk side, and to lay out a similar post at the other end of the portage near Wood Creek. Williams built two small log houses, and on the Mohawk side of the carry he managed to erect a palisade around the storehouse. Fort Williams, as it came to be called, could accommodate 150 men and four cannon. At the other end of the carry, construction did not go as well. Captain Marcus Petri, the engineer in charge of the workmen at Wood Creek, made every effort to throw up a stockade, but poor weather prevented him from completing the construction. Known officially as Wood Creek Fort but nicknamed by the men Fort Bull after its commander, the half-built fort offered thin protection for the small garrison holed up inside.[9]

Shirley arrived in Albany on December 2.[10] On the twelfth he summoned his staff and presented his plan for the coming year. For the most part he kept to Braddock's strategy, laying out attacks on Niagara, Duquesne, and Crown Point. He also suggested two new targets: an expedition against Fort Frontenac and a thrust up the Kennebec River across the highlands to the Chaudiere River and down to the St. Lawrence. The intent of the latter move was to offer a feint at Quebec City in order to tie down French forces in the north that might otherwise be sent south. Shirley's inclusion of Frontenac and Quebec in his strategic plan hinted at a much more ambitious goal than simply defending the king's territory. But two days of discussion in Albany failed to produce an agreement on strategy. New York's governor, Sir Charles Hardy, resisted any campaign that went beyond Braddock's original defensive orders. An attack on Frontenac, Hardy felt, would provide the French with ample reason to let loose on his colony's frontier. It might also, he feared, set the Iroquois, who claimed the territory around Ontario, to wondering if New York had designs on their lands as well.

Despite his outward confidence and the boastful tone of his letters to officials in London, at heart Shirley was a saddened man. His son William was dead, while another son, Jack, lay near death from dysentery. His operation against Niagara had gone badly. Lake George was still contested, and French power was growing daily. On every side his political enemies, William Johnson chief among them, were swarming. When British agents intercepted four letters written by a high officer in America intended for the French ambassador, rumors circulated that Shirley, who had a French wife, must be the author. In retrospect, such allegations seem preposterous; nonetheless, dark clouds gathered over Shirley as he returned to Boston in late December to complete his plans for the coming year.

Winter was a common enemy in North America, but the English feared it more than the French and Indians. As Shirley sat snug by the fire at his hillside mansion in Roxbury on the outskirts of Boston, enemy raiders swept through the Ohio country. In Montreal Governor Vaudreuil gathered his officers to plan a bold winter attack against Oswego. Lieutenant Jean-Baptiste-Philippe Testard de Montigny had spent several days spying on the English at Oswego. He advised that while it would require troops and cannon to take Oswego, Forts Bull and Williams were more vulnerable. Montigny urged the governor to attack those weak positions. Vaudreuil agreed and summoned Gaspard-Joseph Chaussegros de Léry, an officer in the Troupes de la Marine and the son of Canada's chief engineer, to command the expedition. Montigny joined as second in command.

On the morning of March 12 nearly four hundred men—including one hundred Indians, mostly Mohawk and Abenaki—set off overland on snowshoes and skates, dragging their *traines*. Two weeks out from Montreal, they arrived near the Great Carrying Place in a miserable state. The quartermaster had miscalculated, and for two days the men had marched without food.

Early on the morning of March 27 Léry's Indian scouts brought in two prisoners. When Léry threatened to release them to the Indians, who would "knock their brains out," the prisoners quickly revealed that eight bateaux were loaded at Fort Bull, scheduled to depart for Oswego that same day, and that several sleds laden with supplies were on their way across the portage from Fort Williams.[11] Terrified of being turned over to the Indians, the prisoners went on to tell Léry that Fort Bull had barely 60 men in its garrison and was weakly defended. Fort Williams, on the other hand, had nearly 150 men and cannon. Léry's interrogation was interrupted by the welcome news that the Mohawk and Abenaki had taken the sleds. They had also managed to capture eight Englishmen, but one of the teamsters, a black man, had escaped to Fort Williams. Léry decided to attack Fort Bull before the garrison could be alerted or reinforced. In the meantime, the men feasted on the captured English supplies.

Moving quietly along the creek bank, Léry's men came to within a half mile of the fort undetected. Over the edge of the bank they could see that its gate was open. Nearby six men were loading bateaux. Hoping to rush the gate and take the fort by surprise, Léry ordered his soldiers to fix bayonets. He told the Indians to circle toward the bateauxmen while he moved against the fort. At less than a thousand feet from the gate, Léry and his men were still unnoticed, but off to the other side the Indians, unable to restrain themselves, let loose with a curdling war cry, which sent the bateauxmen running for the open gate while the soldiers inside, equally frightened, rushed to close it. Furious at the ill discipline of his allies, Léry ordered a charge. By the time the unfortunate bateauxmen reached the stockade, their comrades had secured the gate, so they ran for the woods.

Léry divided his assault force into three groups. The main element laid down heavy fire at the men defending the gate. The other two split to the left and right and fired through the wide gaps in the palisade at the flanks of the men defending the gate. Attacking the gate with axes, it took the French less than an hour to chop open a breech, through which they charged, shouting, "Vive le Roi." Within minutes Lieutenant Bull was killed, and most of the garrison was put to the sword. According to the French report, "One woman and a few soldiers only were fortunate enough to escape the fury of our troops."[12] The Mohawk and Abenaki pursued the terrified bateauxmen into the woods to finish them off.

Fort Bull yielded a cornucopia. Between the storehouse, the bateaux, and the piles of supplies within the stockade, Léry took enormous quantities of gunpowder, salt provisions, butter, and bread. Dozens of uniforms and blankets were piled outside and burned, while shot and ammunition were tossed into the creek. Léry's men packed their *traines* with whatever they could carry, and set fire to the rest. A few minutes later a huge explosion tore the stockade and storehouse apart, spewing pieces of debris in every direction, some of them striking and wounding Léry's own men.

Léry's spectacular success set back British plans. Shirley's campaign against Niagara hinged on moving troops and supplies to Oswego as early as possible in the spring before Vaudreuil could send reinforcements up the St. Lawrence. Speed was essential. Any hope of an early campaign went up with the rising smoke at Fort Bull. It would take weeks to replace the lost provisions and munitions. As they huddled behind their walls, fearful of being ambushed by prowling French and Indians, the garrison at Oswego was fast running short on food and hope.

Seemingly ignorant of the geographic and logistical challenges facing him, Shirley proceeded with his plans for the spring. From the comfortable surroundings of Boston's Province House, he sent a torrent of dispatches dunning his own assembly and others, asking them to supply men for the upcoming campaign (3,500 Massachusetts, 2,500 Connecticut, 1,700 New York, 500 New Hampshire, 500 Rhode Island). Expense was no object. At times his pace was almost frenetic—all the while he nervously awaited word from London approving his conduct.

Unlike Shirley, Governor Vaudreuil had a good season. Aside from reverses in Nova Scotia, his forces had been triumphant. Although he had fewer soldiers than his foe (Shirley's manpower requisition from Massachusetts alone exceeded the full strength of the Troupes de la Marine), Vaudreuil's men had proven themselves estimable. Furthermore, his victories enticed the Indians into a closer relationship, bringing added manpower to the French.

In the country of *la belle rivière* (Ohio River), reported Vaudreuil, "the

Delawares and Chouanons, Indians of the Beautiful river, some of whose chiefs have been put to a cruel death by the English, . . . are enraged to an extraordinary degree, and would not take any prisoners were it not for the continual recommendations of the [French] Commandants to commit as few murders as possible." Even the Iroquois, according to the governor, who had previously professed neutrality, had come to the side of the French. With obvious satisfaction he reported that "sixty Indians of the Iroquois Nation have committed frightful ravages." In the west the news was equally encouraging. More than one thousand "Miamis and Outaganons from De-troit and Michilimackinac" as well as Sauteur had spent the winter chanting the war song for Onontio. Vaudreuil looked forward to the spring.[13]

Despite his success, however, Vaudreuil's ambition to become com-mander of France's North American army as well as governor proved anathema to Paris. Only a senior officer of the Troupes de la Terre (regular army) could command the regiments in Canada. For months, though, none had volunteered for service. The French army was notorious for hav-ing a plethora of officers, but it was difficult to find a senior officer who was willing to forego the promise of glory in Europe for the wilderness of Canada. Finally, the king selected Louis-Joseph de Montcalm, marquis de Montcalm, a little-known Languedoc nobleman.[14]

Born in 1712, Montcalm was a minor noble in a nation overrun with petty nobility. He took his commission as ensign in 1721 at age nine but did not begin active duty until 1732. During the War of the Austrian Succession (1744–48) he served in Bohemia and later commanded a regiment in Italy. Always at the front, he was wounded three times during the war. After the peace of Aix la Chapelle he retired to his estates in Languedoc until sum-moned by the king. On March 1, 1756, the king promoted Montcalm to *maréchal de camp* (major general) and presented him with orders to Canada. Despite Montcalm's misgivings, the king instructed the general to place himself under the authority of Governor Vaudreuil in all matters except the discipline and disposition of troops in the colony. This was a modest attempt to placate Vaudreuil and the Canadian officers, who were likely to be miffed at Montcalm's appointment.

Accompanied by his aide-de-camp, Louis-Antoine de Bougainville, Montcalm set out for Brest, where battalions were preparing to board transports for Quebec. Also waiting at the port were his senior staff officers: Brigadier François-Gaston, Chevalier de Lévis, the second in command; and Colonel François-Charles de Bourlamaque, the third in command. Seven years Montcalm's junior, Lévis "entered the army in his teens, merely another poor Gascon cadet."[15] But despite his humble origins, Lévis proved himself a superb soldier. During the War of the Austrian Succession he, like Montcalm, saw considerable service in Bohemia and Italy. His orders to Canada included the proviso that should anything happen to Montcalm, he was to succeed in command. Bourlamaque was the son of an Italian officer in the service of France who was killed at the Battle of Parma in 1732.[16] He entered the king's service in 1739 and fought at the Battles of Fontenoy and Rocourt. Although commissioned in the infantry, Bourlamaque often served as an engineer. Those skills were much needed in Canada, and his sudden promotion from captain to colonel may have been a sweetener to entice him across the Atlantic.

Whereas Montcalm, Lévis, and Bourlamaque were all combat veterans, Bougainville had rarely strayed from his desk. A noted mathematician, he had served as secretary to the French ambassador in London. He enjoyed the distinction of being one of Europe's few eighteenth-century gentlemen elected to both the Royal Society and the Académie des Sciences. Montcalm enjoyed this young philosophe's wit, erudition, and disdain for provincial Canadians.[17]

Montcalm and Bougainville arrived at Quebec on May 12, two days ahead of the main convoy. After being delayed two weeks by spring rains that had washed away the road, the general finally made his way by coach to Montreal, where Vaudreuil offered a restrained welcome. There was little reason for them to like each other, and ample evidence that they did not. Montcalm described the governor as a "good man but . . . somewhat weak." He also derided the men around Vaudreuil, complaining to Lévis that "Mercier is a weakling and an ignoramus, Saint-Luc a garrulous braggart, Montigny admirable, but a looter, Villiers and Lery good, Langy excellent, Marin brave but stupid; the rest are not worth mentioning."[18]

Vaudreuil sneered at Montcalm and his staff as foppish parade-ground soldiers who knew nothing about campaigning in Canada. The governor knew full well that Montcalm and his men were in the colony only because the king had commanded them. Vaudreuil was there because it was his home. Even the fact that he outranked the general gave little comfort to this proud Canadian.

Vaudreuil had not waited for the general's arrival to begin the spring campaign. He informed Montcalm that having successfully severed Oswego's supply line during the winter, he had sent six hundred men under the command of Villiers to further harass and isolate the fort in preparation for a major assault.

Vaudreuil was full of confidence. Ships were arriving daily at Quebec, landing men, munitions, and military supplies. Flotillas of canoes and bateaux were pushing off from Montreal, ferrying soldiers to reinforce the garrisons at Niagara, Frontenac, Crown Point, and Ticonderoga. Impressed by French victories, Indian allies, both the domiciled tribes and those from the west, were eager to attack the English. (To reinforce local alliances, Montcalm traveled to nearby Mohawk and Abenaki settlements, where he sat with the chiefs, smoked the pipe, and exchanged gifts and belts of wampum.)[19] Although he felt slighted by his Parisian superiors, Vaudreuil had kept his post and reputation.

William Shirley would not fare so well. His incessant disputes with William Johnson and a host of other New Yorkers resulted in a flood of letters to London filled with accusations against him. Even his longtime patron, Newcastle, grew weary of the complaints, while Cumberland ranted that the governor ought to be dragged home in chains. Hopelessly muddled financial accounts, stalled expeditions, and a growing list of personal and political enemies made Shirley's recall inevitable.[20] In January 1756 Newcastle and his inner cabinet decided to throw Shirley over the side.[21]

Consensus had it that the post would have to go to an experienced officer who had the ability to command an army and the knack for dealing with squabbling assemblies. The cabinet agreed that the commander be given "every power civil and military."[22] To persuade the fractious colonial assemblies to lend support to the new chief, the cabinet agreed to reimburse the colonies £120,000 for the expenses of 1755. Despite their outward show of support for the Americans, the cabinet members, particularly Cumberland, had little faith in the colonists' ability to fight, and so in addition to cash and

Louis-Joseph de Montcalm,
the marquis de Montcalm

a new commander the ministers decided to send two additional regiments from England and raise a new regiment of four battalions—to be called the Royal Americans—in the colonies. Newcastle groaned at the expense.[23]

Cumberland recommended John Campbell, the fourth earl of Loudoun, to command in America. A high-ranking Scottish peer, and a consistent friend to the ministry and the monarchy, Loudoun was a logical choice. He was a career soldier who had distinguished himself by raising a Highland regiment on behalf of the king to help repress the Scottish rebellion of 1745 led by Charles Stuart, "Bonnie Prince Charlie." His loyalty carried over into politics, where as a sitting Scottish peer he was always reliably in support of the king's interests. In order to ensure an appropriate income and status, Loudoun took the titles of both governor of Virginia and commander in chief, drawing a salary for both. He was also a commissioned colonel of the Royal Americans.[24] Joining him as second in command was Major General James Abercromby, and as third in the chain of command Major General Daniel Webb.[25] Neither Loudoun nor his two senior staff had the campaigning or combat experience of their French counterparts. Abercromby had spent most of his service years as either a peacetime garrison commander or a quartermaster officer. Webb had seen considerable action in the War of the Austrian Succession, but his field reputation was grounded in his well-known skills as an organizer and manager of paperwork. It is likely that Cumberland hoped Webb's talents would be put to use to straighten out Shirley's muddled accounts.[26]

Thus far the war had begun and been carried forward without any official declarations. By spring 1756, however, as military preparations accelerated in France, England, and America, the thin veil of peace fell apart. Since Boscawen's precipitous attack off Newfoundland, the Royal Navy had been waging war on French commerce: Hundreds of French ships had been seized and nearly eight thousand seamen taken. In North America blood—English, French, and Indian—had been shed at numerous locations. Across Europe diplomats were scrambling behind doors to secure allies. The torrent finally reached a crescendo, and England formally declared war against France on May 18, 1756. France returned the favor on June 9.

While Loudoun remained in London attending to final details, his generals left for America. Webb arrived at New York on June 7. Abercromby joined him nine days later. Together they traveled to Albany, where Shirley anxiously awaited them. For at least two months Shirley had known that bad news was coming. On the twenty-fifth Abercromby presented his orders to Shirley commanding him to step aside. Five days later Shirley left Albany for New York City, where he tarried waiting for Loudoun. Shirley and Loudoun met on July 23. It was a cold encounter. Loudoun peppered Shirley with questions about the French, his accounts, Indian affairs, and the status of relations with the various colonies and their militias. In a letter to London dripping with sarcasm, Loudoun described the meeting. He reported that Shirley gave him some papers "of very little use" and then delivered a lecture about strategy in the coming campaign. His career in ruins, the governor returned to Boston. Out of power and out of favor,

Shirley sailed for London in early October to spend the next several years defending his actions in the House of Commons, in the press, and against flocks of political harpies tearing at his reputation.[27]

Shirley's unhappy departure did nothing to improve the precarious situation for the English in North America. In the Carolina borderlands the French continued to intrigue with the Choctaw, Cherokee, and Creek. Across the piedmont regions of Virginia and Pennsylvania, and down through the Shenandoah Valley, French and Indian raiders wrecked havoc, burning and pillaging scattered colonial farms and settlements. Vaudreuil estimated that his Indian allies had "disposed of more than 700 people in the Provinces of Pennsylvania, Virginia and Carolinas."[28] The frontier paths and roads leading from the west were crowded with carts, wagons, and packhorses driven and led by frightened families fleeing their homes to escape fire and tomahawks.

Loudoun paid little heed to pleas for help from the ravaged frontier. He had more serious problems at hand. To his north the French were massing for an invasion. Most of the Lake George–Lake Champlain corridor remained under French control. Like poised daggers, those bodies of water pointed straight at the heart of New York. Having reinforced Crown Point, Vaudreuil sent Michel Chartier de Lotbinière, the son-in-law of his chief engineer, farther south and ordered him to erect a fort near the mouth of La Chute River at the portage between Lake George and Lake Champlain. Named Carillon after the tinkling sound of the nearby rapids, but better known as Ticonderoga, the fort commanded a strategic location. By June 1756, Lotbinière's stone walls were looming over Lake Champlain.[29]

While the walls of Ticonderoga were being built, Loudoun waded through paperwork in Albany. Chosen in part because of his affability, a trait potentially useful in dealing with the less affable provincial assemblies, Loudoun spent his days trying to sort out Shirley's botched accounts and cajoling colonial authorities to send men and supplies, to counter the French buildup to the north. More plodding than aggressive, he was a devil for detail. He drafted every letter personally. John Appy, his hard-pressed secretary, complained bitterly about putting in fifteen-hour days. Loudoun dismissed him as a whiner and suggested that he ought to spend less time

John Campbell, the earl of Loudoun

partying and more time sleeping. In the meantime the commander was the first man up every morning.[31] Loudoun's passion for organization and paperwork was admirable in a logistician, but it was a handicap for a field commander. He seemed more interested in closing in on a report than engaging the enemy. One American noted that the general "was like St. George upon the signposts, always on horseback but never advancing."[31]

As Loudoun struggled to bring order to his command, affairs were dismal at Oswego. Following the March "massacre" at Fort Bull, French and Indian war parties had remained near Wood Creek, making communication and resupply problematic. Determined to hold Oswego, Shirley had ordered his old friend Colonel John Bradstreet to reopen and secure the line to Oswego. Bradstreet cleared a path to Oswego and managed to push a few bateaux through,[32] but security was tenuous. Villiers's men pricked constantly at the line and launched a major ambush on July 3 in which both sides took heavy casualties. The supply stream turned to a trickle. The Oswego garrison, harassed, isolated, and down to half rations, was in a deplorable state. By midsummer Oswego was poised to fall to the French.

Oswego's commander, Colonel John Mercer, pleaded to Albany for help. By this time Shirley was gone and Loudoun had not yet arrived. Abercromby, "a very good second man," refused to make any decision on his own.[33] Instead of acting to relieve the fort, the general remained at Albany, where he pondered, procrastinated, and waited for his superior to arrive.

While Abercromby fretted, Montcalm took bold action. Villiers's harassments against Oswego were only a preliminary to a major attack. To confuse the British about his true intentions, the marquis moved his headquarters to Ticonderoga, suggesting a French move on Lake George. Montcalm's plan was to draw the enemy north while he slipped away and hit them in the west. He made a great show of his arrival at Ticonderoga, and the English took the bait. Indian and ranger reports confirmed that Montcalm was at the fort with a sizable force preparing to lunge toward Lake George. With that information the British commanders had no choice but to concentrate their forces near Albany. Reinforcements could not be spared for Oswego.

As Abercromby dallied in camp awaiting the arrival of his new chief, the French tightened the noose on Oswego. Leaving Lévis in command, Montcalm slipped away from Ticonderoga and was back in Montreal by July 19. Troops and supplies were already on their way up the St. Lawrence. He immediately dispatched Vaudreuil's brother, François-Pierre de Rigaud de Vaudreuil, with a large advance party to reinforce Villiers. Two days later he and Bougainville were on their way to Fort Frontenac. Four days into the journey they paused at La Presentation to meet "forty ambassadors of the Oneidas and Onandagas." An evening of smoking, eating, and inflated rhetoric left the French and Indians in an amiable mood. When the French left in the morning, their Iroquois hosts "sang the war song" and "lined up under arms in the French manner." Two days later they arrived at Frontenac. In the middle of a wilderness the French had assembled an army of twelve hundred regulars, eighteen hundred men of la Marine, and a host of Indians. Hundreds of bateaux and canoes were drawn up on the shore.[34]

Between the edge of the lake and the limestone walls of the fort neat rows of white tents billowed in the breeze. Stacks of muskets dotted the spaces surrounding the tents. Hundreds of soldiers were busily cleaning arms and organizing supplies. Cannon and powder were carefully placed at some distance from the main camp. Around the edges of the bustling camp and at headquarters, smartly uniformed sentries stood guard. Beyond the French encampment warriors from the domiciled settlements and their Iroquois cousins, as well as men from the west, including Nippissing and Menominee, made their camp. The casual arrangement of the Indian camp contrasted sharply with the geometric orderliness of the Europeans.

Thirty miles to the east at the Bay of Niaoure (Sackett's Harbor), Rigaud waited. Combined, the forces of Montcalm, Rigaud, and Villiers represented the largest European army ever to venture into the North American wilderness. On August 4 Montcalm left Frontenac with half his force, including the regiments of La Sarre and Guyenne trailing four pieces of artillery. Two days later he met Rigaud at the bay, where he waited for the remainder of the force, including additional cannon, to join him. There he met with a delegation of domiciled Indians. Their leader told the marquis that they would not fight in the European style. "[Their] custom was never to fight against entrenchments or stockades, but in the forest where they understood war, and where they could find trees for cover." Montcalm listened carefully and then promised that he would "never expose [them] to the fire of artillery and musketry from the forts." He would, he assured them, only call upon them "to watch for reinforcements that might come to the enemy, and to keep a good lookout, while the French fought against the forts."[35]

By then Mercer knew that the French were advancing on him. He split his twelve hundred men among three positions: Forts Ontario, George, and Oswego. The three strongholds stood within cannon shot of one another and were close enough to be mutually supporting. Each, however, by itself was extraordinarily vulnerable. Ontario, the key position, was located on the north bank of the Oswego River on a seventy-foot bluff overlooking the lake. About a quarter mile away, across the river on the south bank, stood Fort Oswego, a trading house defended by a blockhouse surrounded by a crumbling stone wall. In a desperate attempt to fortify it, Mercer ordered two cannon placed on its roof. He abandoned that plan when the recoil of the cannon threatened to collapse the roof. The third point of this fragile trident was Fort George, about eight hundred feet to the northwest of Fort Oswego. It was a poorly constructed palisade with earthworks on two sides. The militia who garrisoned it thought so little of the structure that they dubbed it Fort Rascal.[36]

By August 11 the French were within sight of the British forts. Fort Ontario was their first target. Rigaud's men, along with several Indians, crept toward the walls and sniped at the defenders. Following standard European-style siegecraft, on the night of the twelfth Montcalm's engineers began digging trenches near the fort. By morning the French were within a few hundred feet of the Ontario's walls, ready to open fire with their artillery. Montcalm, however, failed to extend his siege lines fully around the British. While his heavy guns delivered a furious barrage, Mercer took advantage of the gap in the French lines and in a daring daylight operation evacuated his entire garrison across the river to Fort Oswego.

Once he occupied Ontario, Montcalm brought his guns to bear on Fort Oswego. As the bombardment opened, Rigaud (according to his proud brother's account) "plunged" into the river with his men, "some swimming, others in the water up to the waist or neck," and throwing themselves on the opposite shore came around on the southern side of both Fort George and Fort Oswego, cutting both off from any hope of help or escape.[37] In the hail of lead Mercer was killed. Lieutenant Colonel John Littlehales took command and ordered Fort George evacuated. With infantry closing in on three sides, and cannon dropping shot from across the river, Oswego's situation was hopeless. Littlehales surrendered on August 14. Montcalm, despising their pitiful defense, insulted the garrison. He accepted their surrender but refused to offer them the traditional "honors of war"—they would not be allowed to march out of the fort to lay down their arms in a ceremonial fashion.

As the Union Jack came fluttering down less than a hundred miles away, a relief force was struggling up Wood Creek. Loudoun, alarmed at the news from Oswego, had sent General Webb with the Forty-fourth Regiment to relieve Mercer. When news of the surrender reached them, they made a hasty return to Albany.

Montcalm had triumphed at the trifling cost of three men dead and twenty wounded. The booty was impressive: more than 1,000 prisoners (150 men dead), 7 armed vessels, 200 bateaux, 55 cannon, 14 mortars, 5 howitzers, 47 swivels, along with hundreds of barrels of powder and provisions. These were public stores, the sort of prizes deemed legitimate by Europeans. They were not, however, the personal spoils that Montcalm's Indian allies desired. They wanted such items as clothes, watches, and boots, which by European tradition were generally exempt from seizure. When French troops stood between them and the chance to strip prisoners, they grew incensed. Some invaded the hospital, killed the wounded, and took their belongings. Others harassed the prisoners under French guard. Montcalm's dismissal of their claims left them embittered. In his reports to Paris Montcalm was careful to spare his superiors these gruesome details, admitting only to "a little plunder which it was necessary to tolerate" since his troops were not in Europe.[38]

Montcalm understood that permanent occupation of Oswego was unnecessary. It was too far to the south and east to be of any use to the French. Keeping it would only mean stretching his defensive perimeter beyond reasonable bounds. It was best to leave it in the hands of the Iroquois, who in turn were grateful to him for returning to them a place they had long desired. What the French could not carry away they burned. By August 22 Montcalm was leading the regular regiments back to Ticonderoga while "the Canadians went to save their harvests and the Indians returned to their villages, as is their custom when they have struck a blow."[39]

(6)

A Failure and a "Massacre"

I make no doubt that you will soon send us a Reinforcement.

—Lieutenant Colonel George Monro to Major General Daniel Webb,
Fort William Henry, August 3, 1758

From Jumonville Glen to the fall of Oswego affairs had not gone well for the British in North America. An ill wind blew on the other side of the Atlantic as well, where a major war was developing in Europe. After weeks of secret negotiations, in January 1756 England and Prussia signed the Treaty of Westminster, pledging to defend each other's German territory. Maria Theresa howled at the betrayal of Austria by her former ally. English "perfidy" in the form of the Prussian alliance drove the empress into the arms of France, with whom she signed a treaty in May. Meanwhile Frederick readied his Prussian battalions.[1]

The French counted on the Austrian army to check Frederick in Germany, so they turned their attention in the opposite direction. Using as an excuse the British attacks on the merchant marine, the king ordered Admiral Galissonière (formerly governor of New France) to prepare the Toulon fleet for a descent upon the British at Port Mahon on Minorca. On April 18 the French landed an army of fourteen thousand men under the command of the duc de Richelieu. When news of the attack reached the British authorities, they ordered a weak relief force under Admiral John Byng to get under way from Gibraltar. Byng failed to drive Galissonière off, and on May 28 the British garrison surrendered. Thrashing around to find a scapegoat for the defeat, the lords of Admiralty hauled the feckless Byng before a court-martial. The court found him guilty of cowardice and condemned him to be shot on the quarterdeck of his flagship. It was, according to Alexander Pope, an act of judicial murder. In a bit of wry humor Voltaire's *Candide* later remarked that Byng's execution was necessary "pour encourager les autres."

In May and June the pretense of peace collapsed; general war erupted in Europe as well as in North America. By early October Frederick had crossed the border into Saxony and was slicing toward Dresden. Austria, Russia, Sweden, and Saxony mobilized against him. When the Austrians under Marshal Maximilian U. von Browne marched to assist the Saxons, Frederick drove at them with unwonted speed and defeated them at Lobositz. Saxony surrendered. Europe was ablaze. England was in a major world war.[2]

The British government nervously anticipated a French invasion of England. The regular British army was unready, and so deplorable was the state of the militia that Newcastle imported thousands of German mercenaries to defend English soil. The financial cost was huge and the political humiliation even greater. Newcastle's opponents assailed the government for its incompetence and pusillanimity.[3] As the nation "slithered" into war, Newcastle's government slowly broke apart. No one, not even the king or Parliament, had faith in the minister. The duke was groaning under the weight of criticism, and he yearned to be free of his burden. He wrote to his ally Lord Hardwicke, "Pity me; alone as I am in my present distress."[4] But who would replace him? In the hurly-burly world of British politics two candidates stepped forward: Henry Fox and William Pitt.[5]

Although he came from a well-to-do family, William Pitt was not born into England's titled aristocracy. He attended Eton and Trinity College, Oxford, but was forced by ill health to leave before he received a degree. In need of a profession, in 1731 he entered the army as an officer in the cavalry. Four years later in a by-election he ran for Parliament from Old Sarum. Since this was a notorious "rotten borough" in which virtually all the votes were held by Pitt's family, there was no doubt of the outcome. Pitt quickly found he preferred politics over the military. He left the army and devoted himself to Parliament, earning a reputation as a brilliant orator who spoke "very well but very abusively." Pitt could always draw a crowd in the House

of Commons with his acerbic wit and biting satire. In the early 1740s Pitt allied himself with Henry Pelham, and in 1746 he received his reward when
he was appointed to his first important government post: paymaster general. The king was not among Pitt's admirers because the latter was fiercely
opposed to subsidizing Hanover. With his characteristic satire he once exploded in Commons that Hanover was nothing more than "a despicable
electorate." Pitt towered over the other specimens in the garden of Whig
politics. As a faction (*party* is too strong a term), the Whigs sought to limit
royal prerogative, advance their personal ambition, and satisfy their lust for
patronage. By dint of his electric personality, intellect, and an advantageous
marriage into the wealthy and influential Temple family, Pitt came to dominate the Whigs and Commons.

Henry Fox sat in the benches with Pitt. The two had entered politics at almost the same time, and although they agreed on most political points they
were personal rivals. For the most part, however, tension between them remained out of the public eye until early 1755. In that session of Parliament
Pitt stood to attack the duke of Newcastle. He assumed that Fox supported
him and was taken aback when Fox joined Newcastle's government to lead
the duke's forces in Commons. Pitt assailed him mercilessly for crossing
over. In 1756 the "gales of national misfortune" ripped through Newcastle's
administration; Fox resigned in October, and shortly thereafter Newcastle
followed suit. The king summoned Fox and asked him to form a government, begrudgingly admitting that Pitt might have to be in the cabinet. Fox
approached Pitt, only to be rejected. Sensing the moment, however, Pitt,
via the king's mistress, Lady Yarmouth, made it known that while he would
not serve under Fox he would be willing to accept a leadership post in a new
government.[6]

George II would have done nearly anything to keep Pitt out of the government. He and Newcastle "knocked on every door" trying to find someone other than Pitt to lead.[7] No one answered. Finally, in November,
persuaded by Lady Yarmouth and pressed by his political allies to end the
impasse, the king summoned the duke of Devonshire, a middling man of
little weight, unthreatening, and of modest abilities, to form a caretaker
government. Too weak to stand on his own, the duke accepted the post as
first lord of the Treasury and offered Pitt the office of secretary of state for
the Southern Department. Although the duke ostensibly stood at the head

William Pitt

of the government, in fact Pitt led the nation from his seat in Commons. Pitt assured Devonshire, "I can save this country."[8]

While Devonshire and Pitt struggled to form a government from the remnants left by Newcastle and Fox, in America Loudoun, having concentrated his efforts on administration since arriving at his new command, was focusing on campaign plans for 1757. The earl was the highest-ranking peer ever to take station in America. As both a notable lord and commander in chief he expected, as did those who sent him, that the colonials would treat him with deference and unquestioning obedience. This was not to be the case.[9]

North of Albany nearly six thousand provincial troops from New York and New England guarded the frontier. Most of the force was divided between Fort Edward on the Hudson and the newly established Fort William Henry rising at the south end of Lake George. Shirley's friend Major General John Winslow of Massachusetts commanded the provincials under commissions issued to him by the governors of New York, Massachusetts, and Connecticut. In his rush to raise and equip this force, Shirley had failed to make clear to the assemblies that Winslow's army was under his own authority as the king's commander in chief. So some local officials assumed that the northern army was under their authority (although they still expected London to pay for it). When Loudoun took command from Shirley, he had no idea that his authority over these forces was anything but absolute.[10]

Loudoun's views on military authority were at odds with the colonial experience. From the very first days of settlement in Virginia, Massachusetts, and the other colonies, defense had been a local responsibility. With very few exceptions, for more than a century the colonists had taken nearly complete responsibility for their own defense. They raised and paid their own militia, selected their officers, often through elections, and determined how they would be used. Militia mustered periodically (more often in times of war, less so in peace), to drill and exercise their weapons. Unless called to active duty, however, militia units rarely trained more than a few times a year. Since they were formed for local defense, their lack of formal military training was of little consequence. They generally stayed close to home, manning strong points or mounting short-range patrols. Most of the men in the ranks had not seen combat, and they thought of themselves as serving only to protect these people and places close to them. The militia tended to be undisciplined, decentralized, and independent.

Only July 31, 1756, Loudoun had written to Winslow, "inviting" him to meet with him in Albany.[11] The invitation stirred concern among Winslow's officers. They suspected that Loudoun intended to integrate their army into his own. Since royal commissions always ranked over provincial ones, Winslow's officers stood to lose considerable status. The rank and file were also concerned. Militia much preferred to serve under the soft hand of their own officers, many of them friends and neighbors, rather than the brutal discipline likely to be imposed by army regulars. Winslow declined the "invitation."

Loudoun was enraged at Winslow's impertinence. He shot back to him, "As you choose to have the words in direct terms, it is my orders that you repair immediately to Albany."[12] A chastened Winslow hurried to Albany, but even a personal meeting with the commander in chief did not resolve the issue. Winslow was evasive and danced around questions of rank and command. Loudoun's fury rose. The "intractable disposition" of the provincials was beyond his comprehension.[13] The next day, still steaming from the encounter, his lordship wrote to Winslow and "put the question" directly whether Winslow would place himself under his command. A cornered Winslow responded that his forces would "act in conjunction with His Majesty's troops and put themselves under the command of your Lordship who is commander in chief."[14] In the matter of rank Loudoun made a small concession. He permitted provincial generals and field officers (that is, colonels and majors) to hold the rank of senior captain when they served with regulars. The concession was too small to please the proud colonials, and rank in the army remained a festering sore.

Although a good soldier, by temperament and experience Loudoun was ill suited to deal with the hectoring ambiguities of America. When he asked governors for men, they often sent him excuses rather than militia. He had little tolerance for vacillating officials who were more anxious to please obstreperous assemblies than to answer the needs of the commander in chief. "In this country," he wrote Fox, "everything is a matter of dispute."

Loudoun had even less use for his Indian allies. To him they were an expensive nuisance. And while he maintained a cordial relationship with their vocal champion, William Johnson, he never shared the colonel's opinion that the Iroquois were a powerful and reliable ally. Indians "we call friends are no more than Neutrals," he remarked.[15] Whatever reservations the general harbored privately, his official communications with Johnson were always cordial, for he considered anyone who was an enemy of Shirley to be a friend. In September 1756, for example, when he learned that Lieutenant Governor William Denny of Pennsylvania and other governors were striking special deals with the Iroquois and their allies, he made it perfectly clear that Johnson was in charge: "I must tell you once for all; That His Majesty having entirely taken out of the Hands of the Governments and Governors all right to Treat with, Confer or make War or Peace, with the [Iroquois] or any of their Allies or Dependents; and having reposed this Trust wholly and solely in the Hands of Sir William Johnson, his sole agent for these affairs under my direction; I do hereby, for the future, forbid you or your Government from Confering or Treating with these Indians in any shape, or on any account whatsoever."[16]

From his Albany headquarters Loudoun set out to bring order to what he viewed as chaos. Camp hygiene and discipline improved. The water route to Fort Edward was made more secure, and his engineers improved the road to William Henry. His strategy was to hold a strong defensive position, stock his warehouses, and prepare for a spring offensive against Ticonderoga. He was determined to go it alone, placing little reliance on Indians or provincials. As he told his patron, Cumberland, "I am convinced [that we must carry] on the War here, within ourselves."[17]

As winter approached, most of the provincials, according to their enlistment agreement, returned home. Albany, Fort Edward, and William Henry kept sizable garrisons, while elsewhere along the Connecticut River and southern New Hampshire small detachments of fewer than twenty men stood watch in isolated posts.[18] Security against a sudden winter attack was a concern. From bitter experience the British knew that cold, snow, and ice were not impenetrable barriers to the French. The best defense was good reconnaissance, and for that service the general reluctantly relied heavily upon Indians and provincials, though he believed that the Indians lied and the provincials were incompetent. About colonial rangers, however, he was more ambivalent. He told Cumberland, "It is impossible for an Army to Act in this Country without Rangers."[19] By this, he meant rangers under the command of Robert Rogers.

Rogers commanded the first company of the New Hampshire regiment, which had marched with William Johnson in 1755.[20] In September of that year, after the battles at Lake George, Johnson's Indian scouts abandoned him to return home. Desperate for intelligence, he turned to Rogers to lead a reconnaissance. Over the next several weeks Rogers and his New Hampshire men performed admirably. During the winter of 1755–56 Rogers carried out a series of raids against the French and brought back important information. A tireless self-promoter, he lobbied hard for an independent command. In May 1756 Shirley appointed him "Captain of an Independent Company of Rangers."

Loudoun inherited the company, and while he appreciated ranger techniques and tactics, he was less enamored of the men themselves. He described them to Cumberland as "loose-made and indolent [and lacking] Faith or honesty." He also doubted their courage.[21] His faith in them was further shaken in January when Rogers led one hundred of his men into a French ambush while scouting between Ticonderoga and Crown Point.[22]

Robert Rogers

He lost nearly half his force. Harkening back to his determination to go it alone insofar as possible, Loudoun ordered his own officers to patrol with rangers and learn their skills but shun their company.

While the British tucked themselves in for the winter, depending upon the rangers for early warning of any French moves, Vaudreuil planned another daring winter attack. This time his target was ·Fort William Henry. Named for a grandson of George II, the fort stood near the spot at the south end of Lake George where Johnson had repelled Dieskau.[23] Captain William Eyre of the Royal Engineers had laid out the fort, which was in the rough form of a square with diamond-shaped bastions at each corner. The connecting ramparts were mounded earth fifteen feet across faced with pine logs about ten feet high. A five-foot-high log parapet running along the top offered protected firing positions. Both the bastions and ramparts mounted cannon. On the east, west, and south sides a dry ditch thirty feet wide and eight feet deep extended out from the exterior wall.

On the north side facing the lake, a steep rise made any frontal approach difficult. From the rise sentries could scan the lake looking north toward the narrows.

By the standards of military construction in North America, William Henry was a formidable presence. It did, however, have two serious flaws. It lacked outer works or defensive barriers distant from the walls that might prevent an enemy from entrenching close enough to launch an artillery bombardment. And it was too small.[24] Barely five hundred men could be accommodated within the walls. In such cramped quarters camp hygiene became a nightmare.[25] Rather than enlarge the fort, troops fortified an auxiliary camp on high ground to the east.

Had Montcalm been in complete charge, Loudoun's lack of concern about a winter attack would have been justified. Montcalm viewed Vaudreuil's plan to launch a surprise assault on William Henry over snow and ice as a waste of supplies, money, men, and time. Indeed, in January the commissaries were warning of grain shortages. Unlike Loudoun, who floated in a sea of supplies, Montcalm's depots were always on the margin. The general feared that Vaudreuil's reckless plan would gobble up his reserves, which were administered by intendant François Bigot and his bureaucracy. "François Bigot would be as likely a candidate as James Wolfe or William Pitt" to blame for the fall of Canada, wrote one historian.[26] Bigot was corrupt, but his rapaciousness was no worse than that of his peers in Canada and France. However, the effects of his corruption were compounded by scarcity. Canada always lived on the economic edge. During ordinary times there was a sufficient surplus to accommodate a certain amount of cupidity and graft. War reduced the margin.[27]

While Montcalm grumbled over Canadian incompetence and the harsh winter, Vaudreuil and his brother planned the attack. Early in February 1757 the governor dispatched an officer of the Troupes de la Marine to St. Francis "to sing the war song with the Abenakis."[28] Another snowshoed emissary went to recruit the Iroquois at nearby Kahnawake.

In mid-February sixteen hundred attackers gathered at St. Jean on the Richelieu River near Montreal. To avoid detection, Rigaud divided the expedition into four divisions. The first contingent, led by Canadians, got off on February 21. The remaining ones followed over the next few days, with Abenaki and Iroquois closing up the rear.[29] Winter deceived them. Instead of solid ice, the Richelieu and the northern tip of Lake Champlain down to Point a Fer* were open. Rigaud had to send back the sleds and order boats, and the delay cost precious time. After spending two days at Crown Point, Rigaud and his men advanced to Ticonderoga, where he made his final preparations. On the fifteenth they marched from Ticonderoga along the short portage road to the head of Lake George, which was still frozen. Staying close to the western shore, Rigaud's party moved at night in three columns. A few hundred feet ahead of each column one man moved cautiously, carrying a shielded lantern and a pick. At intervals he stopped and poked through the ice, testing its thickness. In the meantime the men behind stared ahead to follow the light.

Rigaud planned to take the fort by surprise, but the sound of the picks and the crunching noise of men walking on ice and snow alerted the garrison. Eyre ordered his men into the fort while the French sacked and burned the outbuildings, including a nearby sawmill, and torched three hundred bateaux and several small-armed vessels beached on the shore. Rigaud and his men made several attempts against the fort itself, but without artillery they found it impossible to breech the walls. On the night of March 21 a blinding snowstorm dropped nearly three feet of snow. The siege had lasted four days when Rigaud ordered his men back to Ticonderoga.

Reactions to the siege were mixed: Montcalm decried the operation. Despite the smoldering ruins outside the fort, the English viewed the French withdrawal as a victory. Vaudreuil crowed that his brother had saved the colony. The Iroquois and Abenaki went home disappointed and resentful, having received nothing for their efforts except frostbite. All in all, Rigaud's venture was another "petty victor[y]" that meant a great deal to Canadians, but much less to the overall strategy of the war since the victors, lacking sufficient logistical support, were unable to follow up their successes and sustain an offensive.[30]

---

*Three miles south of present-day Rouse's Point.

* * *

During the winter Loudoun developed his plan for 1757. He would leave two regular battalions supported by four thousand provincials in northern New York to monitor and threaten the French at Ticonderoga, while with a much larger force, naval and military, he would advance directly against Quebec via the St. Lawrence River.[31] Properly executed, Loudoun's plan would compel Montcalm to defend two major fronts: northern New York and the St. Lawrence. Naval superiority was critical. Halifax was the assembly point where men and supplies from both sides of the Atlantic needed to gather and convoy to Quebec. Loudoun's greatest challenge was the short campaigning season open to him. Arctic breezes began to bite in October, and ice often lingered on the St. Lawrence well into April.[32] At most the general had a twelve- to sixteen-week window of opportunity to assemble and transport a major force to lay siege and conquer the most formidable place in North America.

On May 1 Loudoun received instructions from Pitt upending his plans: "Your Lordship is directed to begin with an Attack upon Louisbough, and to proceed, in the next Place, to Quebeck."[33] Having plotted one course, Loudoun now had to lay out in another direction. Instead of reducing one fortress in a short season, he had to conquer two. Almost nothing went right. Pitt, a naturally secretive politician, knew that Loudoun was in Cumberland's camp, and so he purposely told the commander little that he did not want the duke to know, leaving Loudoun often in the dark about what he might expect in the way of supplies and men for the reshaped campaign.

While Loudoun dangled in uncertainty, Pitt's own political position became increasingly precarious. The bad news from America and the Continent emboldened his domestic rivals, and they hurried to the king's chambers to whisper that Pitt had to go. On April 6, 1757, after much intrigue, the king asked Pitt to resign. His departure came three days before the duke of Cumberland left for Germany to undertake the defense of Hanover. London was in confusion, government offices were left "unfilled," and the "country entered into a period of interministerium."[34]

Loudoun's first problem—tardiness—proved to be his most persistent. The provincial levies were late reporting for duty in New York. The late arrival created a domino effect by delaying the departure of the regulars for

Halifax, where they were expected to assemble for the assault on Louisbourg. In the meantime Loudoun declared an embargo on coastal shipping to prevent news of his movements from reaching the enemy at Louisbourg. He intended the embargo to last only a few weeks, until Admiral Francis Holbourne arrived with his fleet from England. Alas, westerly winds held Holbourne at anchor in England for nearly two months, and he did not sail for Halifax until May 8. Loudoun sailed from New York on June 19 and arrived on the thirtieth. Even more delay piled up when Holbourne, after a slow passage across the Atlantic, was forced to heave to in heavy fog off the Nova Scotia coast. Holbourne's unlucky fleet did not come to anchor inside Halifax Harbor until July 9. The delayed arrival forced Loudoun to prolong the embargo, which was paralyzing American trade at the height of the sailing season, and Americans screamed in protest. The Virginia House of Burgesses refused to vote supplies unless the embargo was lifted. In May Lieutenant Governor Dinwiddie, in open defiance of Loudoun's orders, lifted the embargo in Virginia, and early in June Governor Sharpe of Maryland did the same, undermining Loudoun's authority and endangering his campaign.[35]

While contrary winds and politics delayed the Halifax rendezvous, the French reinforced Louisbourg. Admiral Joseph de Beauffremont arrived on May 31 with four ships of the line. Three weeks later Admiral Du Revest from Toulon eluded British patrols and made port with four more ships, and the next day, Admiral du Bois de la Motte tacked into Louisbourg with nine ships of the line and two frigates. With skill and a good deal of luck, the French admirals had managed to outwit the Royal Navy and assemble a fleet larger than the one gathered at Halifax.

Loudoun's information about Louisbourg was sketchy, so he dispatched fast sloops to reconnoiter Cape Breton. From the reports that came back, Loudoun and his staff slowly put the unhappy picture together. The delays had cost them dearly, and the French were now superior. While Loudoun and his officers debated what to do, the largest combined force ever assembled in America spent its time holystoning decks, conducting mock battles, and "planting . . . cabbages."[36]

Loudoun called a council of war and put the question to his officers: "Was it advisable to proceed against Louisbourg at the late season of the year?" For nine days eight senior officers, four from the navy, four from the army, wrestled with the question. They summoned twenty witnesses to give testimony.[37] As time ticked away, the council proceedings took a bizarre twist. According to Loudoun, during one session Major General Lord Charles Hay left the table abruptly, went to a nearby window, and "laid his legs in it and looked out, then he Asked odd Questions, grinning and Laughing, and using all the Gestures of a Man out of His Senses." Hay, who enjoyed a reputation in the service for extraordinary personal courage, damned his colleagues for their indecision and accused the commander in chief of "keeping the courage of his majesty's troops at bay, and expending the nation's wealth in making sham sieges when he ought to have been fighting." Hay shocked his colleagues by resurrecting the memory of Byng, and he declared that Louisbourg "was another Mediterranean Affair; And that although we did not Fight, there should be blood."[38]

Loudoun portrayed Hay as a madman, but even the insane can stumble upon the truth. The truth was that Loudoun the masterful planner could not make up his mind. Of one thing he was certain: If he attacked Louisbourg and failed, the government would throw him to the wolves. Barely six months before, Admiral Byng had suffered the extreme penalty for failure. Loudoun looked to his council to provide political cover should affairs go awry, and Hay's outbursts were a threat. Loudoun did everything he could to keep the general isolated and silent, even to the point of scheduling secret council meetings and not informing Hay, but Hay continued to speak out. Finally, Loudoun ordered him arrested, confined, and shipped home, where he was summoned before a court-martial. For three weeks the officers heard testimony, much of it from Hay himself. The court made its finding, but then in keeping with this bizarre train of events, the members voted to keep their verdict secret and refer judgment to the king. George II pondered, and for nearly two years the matter remained undecided, while Hay, a broken and sick man, fell seriously ill. To the relief of nearly everyone, the general died on May 1, 1760, sparing the king the necessity of making a decision.[39]

With more than half of the campaigning season over, on the last day of July the council advised proceeding with the attack. On August 4, with a fair tide and a favoring wind, Admiral Holbourne signaled the fleet to get under way. As men scampered aloft to shake out the sails, the schooner *Surprise* hurried into the harbor, bringing new and "exact" information concerning enemy strength: Eighteen ships of the line and five frigates were lying at Louisbourg. Holbourne advised Loudoun that against such a force he saw little probability of success.[40] Loudoun reconvened his council.

Notwithstanding all the effort that had gone into preparing the expedition and the promise of several weeks of good weather still ahead, the council, upon hearing Holbourne's advice, reversed itself and recommended against an attack. Loudoun made preparations to embark seven regiments for New York while leaving five for duty in Nova Scotia and Fundy. The troop transports prepared to sail as Holbourne's warships took on stores for the voyage home. The admiral laid a course north and east to take the fleet past Cape Breton for a peek at Louisbourg, and thence easterly home to England.[41] As the New York–bound transports cleared Halifax, a Boston dispatch boat hailed with stunning news: Fort William Henry had fallen, and the garrison had been massacred. Uncertain as to whether the French tide might already be advancing on Albany, Loudoun immediately recalled two of the Nova Scotia regiments and ordered them aboard the New York–bound transports. The failure to attack Louisbourg was an embarrassment, but the loss of Fort William Henry was a disaster. Loudoun bore responsibility for both.

When Loudoun departed Albany the previous June, he had left General Daniel Webb to command the northern frontier with orders to hold the French army in place. The key post was Fort William Henry, which Webb garrisoned with several hundred provincials, five companies of regulars from the Thirty-fifth Regiment, and two ranger companies. Webb complained that he was short of men and claimed that those he had were inferior. Loudoun, he noted, had taken the best regiments to Halifax. His charge was not wide of the mark. The men of the Thirty-fifth, in Loudoun's own words, were "entirely Raw Officers and Soldiers." Cumberland, who knew the regiment, damned the same soldiers as "ignorant [and] undisciplined." George Monro, lieutenant colonel of this regiment, was in command at the fort.[42] A Scot from near Stirling, he had entered the army in 1718 and had spent almost his entire career on garrison duty in Ireland.

Although Rigaud's winter attack had not caused the walls of William Henry to fall, it certainly left life outside them precarious. Through the spring and early summer war parties of Ottawa, Pottawatomi, and Iroquois from Ticonderoga sortied south toward William Henry. Almost every day reports, some of them wildly exaggerated, arrived at the fort, recounting horrendous tales of nearby kidnappings and scalpings.[43] No one dared venture far beyond the gates. Unable to send out scouts, Monro was starved for information.

On the other hand, Bourlamaque, Ticonderoga's commander, knew a great deal about Monro's desperate situation. Bourlamaque owed his advantage to Indian allies who kept him well informed. The rising tide of French victories—Monongahela, Fort Bull, and Oswego—swept native allies toward Montreal to offer their services to Vaudreuil. Ottawa and Pottawatomi, who had been with the French in 1756, had traveled home, where around winter fires they regaled their kinsmen with stories of great battles and even greater plunder. The following spring, hundreds of warriors from these nations, along with their chiefs, journeyed east to get their share of glory and spoils. Vaudreuil spent endless hours receiving and honoring his Indian friends. He distributed brandy, guns, ammunition, and clothing to warriors, while important chiefs were taken aside and presented with elaborate medals and gorgets as badges of their authority. Montcalm joined Vaudreuil at these elaborate ceremonies to welcome the allies, but unlike the Canadians, he was uneasy embracing these "ferocious people."[44]

Montcalm and Vaudreuil agreed that William Henry was an inviting target. All that stood to oppose them was a mediocre general commanding mediocre troops. Vaudreuil was confident that even in the unlikely event Loudoun captured Louisbourg, he could not do so quickly enough to have sufficient time left in the season to move on Quebec. In any case he was too far away to be of any assistance to William Henry. Thanks to Loudoun, the French were at liberty to concentrate their forces against Webb.[45]

Monro moved slowly to repair the damage left by Rigaud's winter raid. Months after the attack he had done little to rebuild the outbuildings burned in the attack; nor had he made much progress building boats to patrol the lake. When provincial reinforcements arrived at Fort Edward for their seasonal service in June, Webb sent them up to William Henry. Militia from New York, New Jersey, and New Hampshire arrived at the lake and pitched their tents outside the fort. Among the new arrivals were the Jersey Blues under the command of Colonel John Parker. Desperate for information,

Monro decided to risk a reconnaissance in force. He took nearly every boat available and ordered Parker with 350 men down the lake. Monro, an officer with virtually no battle experience, was sending a sizable force into the maw of an enemy about whom he knew almost nothing. Parker and his men would row into a French trap.

Parker set off before dawn on July 21. Barely had the men dipped their oars when French scouts spotted them. The next morning "450 men, almost all Indians," left Ticonderoga under the command of Ensign de Corbière, an officer of the Troupes de la Marine. Parker sent three boats ahead, which the French ambushed, capturing the militiamen. After "questioning" by the Indians, the prisoners told their captors that the colonel planned to land at Sabbath Day Point on the west side of the lake, about twenty miles north of William Henry. At daybreak on the twenty-third Parker's unsuspecting flotilla pulled toward the point. As they drew within sight, they saw three boats and assumed that the men sent out the previous day were on them. The three decoys beckoned Parker to draw near. As soon as Parker's force was within range, French and Indians lying in wait along the shoreline delivered a withering volley. In an instant nearly fifty canoes broke around the point and surrounded Parker's men. According to Bougainville, the Indians "pursued the enemy, hit them, and sank or captured all but two which escaped. The Indians jumped into the water and speared them like fish, and also sinking the barges by seizing them from below and capsizing them. We had only one man slightly wounded. The English terrified by the shooting, the sight, the cries, and the agility of these monsters, surrendered almost without firing a shot."[46] Barely 100 of Parker's men, including the colonel himself, were lucky enough to escape and make their way through heavy brush and thick forest back to William Henry. Nearly 160 militia had been killed or drowned at the point. The remainder were prisoners on their way to Ticonderoga.

As the French and Indian forces paddled north, they sang songs of victory and broke into casks of rum taken from the English boats. At the head of the lake the victors were met by hundreds of Indians gathered at the shore to greet their brothers and their prisoners. Tied with ropes noosed around their necks the Indians pulled the terrified captives up a path to a camp outside the walls of Ticonderoga. According to Father Pierre Roubaud, the rum that the Indians had been drinking nearly all

day "excited their brains, and increased their ferocity." That night,
Roubaud reported, a captive was boiled and eaten. In the morning as the
army prepared to move, Roubaud and two other priests approached Montcalm and "asked if they would be permitted to say mass in a place where
one sacrificed to the devil." The general, a "military casuist," responded
"that it was better to say it there than not to say it at all."[47]

Monro had paid a heavy price to learn that there was a sizable body of
enemy at the other end of the lake. Its intentions, however, remained unclear. On the twenty-sixth Webb arrived at William Henry to assess the situation in person. What distressed him most was the relatively low height of
the walls and their shabby construction. Sand and soft pine logs offered poor
protection against massed artillery.[48] Rigaud had come in winter without
heavy guns; Webb knew that Montcalm would not be so ill equipped. After
consulting with Monro, the general ordered regulars inside the fort while
the militia dug in at the nearby fortified camp on the high ground to the east.
Even though they had no hard information, by now everyone was convinced
that a French attack was imminent. Webb left Monro and hurried back to
Fort Edward. On July 30 he called up the New York militia, and two days later
he sent an additional one thousand provincials, mostly Massachusetts men,
to join Monro.

Montcalm arrived at Ticonderoga on July 18. Awaiting him at the fort
were six battalions of regular troops numbering some 2,600 men. Nearly as
many Troupes de la Marine also mustered, along with a much smaller number of militia. Joining the French and Canadians were almost 2,000 Indians; Abenaki, Iroquois, Huron, and Ottawa made up the majority, but other
tribes were represented as well, including Miami, Sauk, and Fox. It was an
impressive multinational coalition, over which the marquis presided but
did not always "command," since his Indian allies held to their own style of
warfare.

Montcalm divided his force into two bodies. The advance element
under Lévis had the tough task of chopping through the dense forest and
undergrowth along the west shore to envelope Monro's left flank and cut
off the road to Fort Edward. Montcalm pushed off onto Lake George with
his main force, including his Indian allies. Nearly 250 bateaux, including
several rafted together as catamarans to float cannon, made their way
toward William Henry. Neither Lévis on land nor Montcalm on the lake

encountered the slightest opposition. On the morning of August 3 Montcalm's fleet glided into view of William Henry. Although beyond range,
they fired cannon to announce their presence. Busy with last-minute
preparations, the English made no response. The French landed on the
west shore less than half a mile from the fort, and within a few hours the
British could hear the clinking sound of shovels and picks as Montcalm's
engineers prepared entrenchments and approaches. The siege had begun.

Although his own regiment was in the fort, Monro established his headquarters at the militia camp, where the provincials were feverishly throwing up timber-and-brush barricades. The colonel's command presence
was of more use among these untrained soldiers than amid the disciplined
regulars.

Because of the difficulties of travel and distance, Montcalm hadn't had
to worry about enemy reinforcements arriving at Oswego. This time reinforcements, under command of General Webb, were only a few miles down
the road. It was Lévis's mission to cut the Fort Edward road and hold it
against any British attempt to smash through. As was his wont, Lévis
moved quickly and secured the road. If Webb decided to march, he would
have to force his way past Lévis along the same road where two years earlier
the French and Indians had mauled the colonial militia and Mohawk
under Ephraim Williams and Chief Hendrick. Webb appreciated the risk.

Eyre and Monro had collected a considerable supply of arms and munitions in the fort and at the camp. The fort mounted eighteen pieces of cannon, including heavy thirty-two-pounders, three mortars, a howitzer, and
thirteen small swivels. Shot and powder were in ample supply. Although
the fortified camp had more men, it had considerably less artillery—only
six brass guns and four swivels. Bearing over cleared ground around the
fort, these guns enjoyed a wide sweep covering the approaches to William
Henry. An advancing enemy would face a deadly hail of solid and grape
shot. A frontal assault was out of the question. This would be a battle of
cannon and siege.[49]

As he had planned, Montcalm turned the siege operation over to his
"engineer" Bourlamaque, who took advantage of the natural terrain by an-
choring the French left on the lake and securing the right along a deep
ravine. Bourlamaque ordered several battalions to prepare siege materials, while the remainder of the troops pitched tents, unloaded supplies,

positioned guns, and dug latrines. As the soldiers dug, the Indians crept close to the fort, sniping at the British. Well-placed musketry, and a few cannon shot from the ramparts, held them at a distance, but not before they had managed to kill more than one hundred oxen that had been left beyond the gates. By midafternoon Montcalm was ready to open the play. Under a flag of truce he sent a message to Monro, summoning the British to abandon the post which, he claimed, was within the territory of the king of France. Lest Monro spend a long time considering his offer, the marquis warned, "Once our batteries [are] in place and the cannon fired, perhaps there would not be time, nor would it be in our power to restrain the cruelties of a mob of Indians."[50]

Monro declined the invitation to surrender, confident he could hold out long enough for Webb to march from Fort Edward, even though he doubtless recognized that Montcalm's menacing mention of Indian reprisal was a New World version of an Old World custom. In conventional European sieges the defender was expected to put up a good fight, but in the end if defeat seemed certain, the besieged were expected to surrender. Besieged garrisons that stubbornly failed to follow tradition, and thus caused higher casualties, could expect no mercy from the victor. Monro understood the European script. Montcalm shared that convention, but he also understood that his Indian allies had their own customs as well.

The polite encounter between French and English officers within the fort was in contrast to the scene beyond the gates. Outside "an Abenaki warrior speaking bad French but very clearly, shouted 'Ah you won't surrender; well, fire first; my father will then fire his great guns; then take care to defend yourself, for if I capture you, you will get no quarter.' "[51]

Despite the brave front, after dark Monro sent two runners with a message to Webb: "I make no doubt that you will soon send us a Reinforcement."[52]

Montcalm ordered his cannoneers to concentrate their guns on William Henry's northwest bastion. The British returned fire with some effect, dropping several shots into the French camp. Time, however, was on the side of the attacker. William Henry's guns quickly showed signs of fatigue. On the night of August 4 a seven-inch mortar burst. The next day an eighteen-pounder mounted in the northwest bastion exploded, injuring several men. To save his guns, Monro slowed the rate of fire and directed his

A PLAN of
Fort William Henry
and the
English Camps
& Retrenchments
with the
French different Camps
and Attack there upon.

A Scale of this Plan of 200 Yards.

PART OF LAKE GEORGE

I. The Place where they	the main Body of y.ᵉ Army	M. M.ʳ de la Corne with	English Troops Encamped	Retrenchment was made
landed their Artillery	L. M.ʳ de Levi's Camp with	1500 Canadians & Indians	before they was ordered by G.ˡ	O. the bridge over y.ᵉ Morass.
K. M.ʳ Moncalms Camp with	4000 Regulars & Canadians	N. The Ground where the	Webb to the Place where the	P. The English Retrenchment.

The siege of Fort William Henry, August 3–9, 1757

gunners to load reduced charges. He also ordered the wooden roofs over the barracks torn off and any other combustibles within the fort discarded to prevent fire. The Indians, watching the British destroy their own property, complained bitterly to Montcalm that if this continued there would be nothing left for them to take.

By daylight the air around William Henry was filled with the sounds of musket balls whizzing over the parapet, cannon shot smacking into the walls, and mortar shells arcing overhead and dropping into the parade ground. At night French fire let up, and Monro used these moments of respite to tend the wounded and move supplies between the fort and the encampment. From the ramparts British sentries could hear the sounds of digging as the French drew closer.

On the night of August 5 Monro dispatched another runner to Webb, but Lévis's Indians ambushed the bearer somewhere between William Henry and Fort Edward. Ironically, one of Monro's first runners had gotten through, and Webb had read the note on the fourth. Unfortunately for Monro, that same day one of Webb's patrols brought in a Canadian prisoner, who regaled his credulous captors with wild stories of French strength. There were, he told his interrogators, eleven thousand soldiers with Montcalm. Webb, to whom caution was a first instinct, decided to stay at Fort Edward until he could amass a force large enough to challenge Montcalm. This was the sad message he entrusted to three rangers to carry back to William Henry. Neither Webb nor the rangers had counted on Kanectagon.

Kanectagon, a Mohawk scout traveling with Lévis, was lying in wait along the Fort Edward road, hoping to take a prisoner for whom he could claim ransom. He got his wish when he spied Webb's three rangers coming toward him. The first he shot dead; the second one escaped; and the third he captured. After stripping and scalping the dead man, he returned to the French camp with his prisoner. The prisoner was tight-lipped, but among the dead man's possessions a French officer found Webb's reply to Monro's plea for help. Written by the general's aide-de-camp, on now bloodstained paper, the reply was succinct: The general's did "not think it prudent . . . to attempt a junction to assist you."[53] The note concluded coldly that Monro ought to give thought to making the best deal possible. Montcalm read the note and set it on the table. It was not yet the right moment to share it with Colonel Monro.

Near dawn on the sixth the firing resumed. By then the British guns were firing very slowly. Another mortar and four cannon had burst, wounding and killing several soldiers. Monro's cannon posed a greater threat to his own men than to the French.

Early on the seventh Montcalm's artillerymen let loose with a three-hour barrage. Seventeen cannon, two mortars, and two howitzers zeroed in on the fort. At nine, "after a double salvo from the right and left batteries," the French guns fell silent. This was the psychological moment Montcalm had planned. Bougainville was sent forward with a flag of truce and the captured bloodstained letter from Webb to Monro. "I walked out of the trenches," Bougainville later reported, *accompanied by a drummer beating his drum and an escort of fifteen grenadiers. The English cried out to me to halt at the foot of the glacis, an officer and fifteen grenadiers came out to me and asked what I wanted, upon which I said that I had a letter from my general to deliver to the English commander. Two other officers came out from the fort, one of whom remained under guard of my grenadiers, and the other, having blindfolded me, led me first to the fort, and then to the entrenched camp where I handed to the commander the letter of the Marquis de Montcalm and that of General Webb. Much thanks for French politeness, expressions of pleasure at dealing with so generous an enemy. Such is the gist of the reply of Lieutenant Colonel Monro to the Marquis de Montcalm. Then they led me back again, eyes blindfolded all the time, to where they had taken me from, and our batteries started firing again when they judged that the English grenadiers had had time to get back into the fort. I hope that General Webb's letter . . . persuades the English to surrender the sooner.*[54]

Noticeably absent from Bougainville's delegation were representatives of Montcalm's Indian allies. The marquis never consulted them about the terms he might offer to the British. Mohawk, Abenaki, and the others were kept at a distance, from which they could only watch and wonder at the strange ways that Europeans waged war.

Monro's situation was hopeless. Although the fort had survived the bombardment better than anyone might have expected, the garrison was in terrible shape. Stores and munitions were nearly exhausted, and the men according to Monro's aide de camp, Lieutenant George Bartman, were "almost Stupified."[55] At seven in the morning on August 9 the defenders raised a white flag. Montcalm granted to Monro the traditional "honors of war."[56] The officers might depart with side arms and luggage. Persons and personal possessions would be respected. All other arms would be surrendered, except for "one six pound cannon which the marquis de Montcalm granted Colonel Monro and the garrison to witness his esteem for the fine defense they had made." In return, the British gave their word that they would not serve against the French in North America for a period of eighteen months. This treatment was in sharp contrast to the year before, when Montcalm had humiliated the garrison at Oswego and denied them any honor whatsoever.

Montcalm summoned the chiefs of his Indian allies to his tent to announce the terms of surrender. He asked them to promise that "their young men would not commit any disorder"[57]—by which he meant looting, pillaging, and taking captives. But that was precisely what had motivated the Indians in the first place. Unlike Europeans, they cared little for the "honor" of taking a fort, and the folderol that surrounded the surrender ceremony only amused and mystified them. In the great councils at Quebec, Montreal, St. Francis, and Kahnawake, where the French had recruited these warriors, Onontio had always promised booty. More than sixteen hundred unhappy Indians milled about the camp and fort. According to Montcalm's own figures, the number of Indians killed (twenty-one) nearly matched the total of French losses (twenty-nine). By this measure, the Indians had suffered a much higher casualty rate than the French. For their efforts and sacrifices they expected revenge and reward. The most valuable prizes were captives, to be carried home to be killed, adopted, or ransomed.

At noon on the ninth William Henry was turned over to the French. The soldiers in the fort laid down their arms and marched out to the fortified encampment. A number of wounded who were unable to walk were left behind. Within minutes several Indians forced their way past French sentries and into the fort. As the departing troops reached the encampment, they heard screams from behind. Father Roubaud reported that he saw a warrior dash from the building where the wounded had been gathered, carrying a "human head, from which trickled streams of blood."[58] Other warriors burst through the gate and went for the military stores and provisions, including rum. A few French guards tried to restrain them, a move the Indians correctly viewed as a ploy so that the soldiers could take the spoils for themselves. While the Indians and French pillaged the fort, Monro and his men remained in the camp. Montcalm posted sentries to keep the British in and the Indians out. The Indians, however, muscled their way past the French, and all afternoon and into the evening, dozens of drunk and angry Indians marauded among the terrified prisoners, taunting them and stealing their personal goods. Montcalm and his officers attempted to bring order, but with so many different tribes and only a handful of interpreters, their task was nearly impossible.

Montcalm let it be known that he planned to march the prisoners to Fort

Edward in the morning. This was a deception. About midnight two hundred French soldiers were awakened and ordered to fall in near the camp. Montcalm hoped to spirit the British away before the Indians could realize what was happening. It was an ill-conceived plan, and only further antagonized the Indians, who were beginning to view the French and English as partners in league to deny them their spoils. When the warriors woke up, they swarmed toward the encampment. Faced with an angry mob, the French officers hastily countermanded the order to march and returned the prisoners to the encampment. It would, they decided, be safer to leave in daylight.

When Lévis cut the road to Fort Edward, he had posted Indians to guard the route, so dozens of small native campsites dotted the roadside down which the prisoners had to march. At dawn the prisoners—unarmed regulars, militia, civilians, even women and children—left the encampment and made their way toward the road. Montcalm was not at the scene, but several officers of the Troupes de la Marine were on hand. Luc La Corne, a soldier who had spent his entire career with the Indians, Jean Daniel Dumas, the victor over Braddock, and Charles-Michel Mouet de Langlade, the commander who had permitted the massacre at Pickawillany, were all present. These soldiers understood Indians in war better than any of their colleagues. They felt the tension, and they knew what was likely to happen— and in fact did happen. First, the Indians invaded the camp and killed and scalped the wounded who had been left behind. Then they turned to the long column inching its way toward the road. Prisoners were yanked from the line and carried off. The "hell whoop" alarmed Montcalm, and from his tent nearly a mile away he hurried to the scene with his officers. Lévis was already there, desperately trying to regain control. By the time the marquis arrived, most of the harm had been done. For several hours French officers and interpreters scurried about, trying to persuade warriors to surrender their captives. Most refused, and by afternoon hundreds of Indians had disappeared from the scene, taking with them captives and booty.

Webb learned of the formal surrender on the night of August 9. Believing that the standard protocols had been followed, he ordered a five-hundred-man detachment down the road to meet the expected column of prisoners coming under French guard. Instead of an orderly procession, the officer in command of the escort reported that he saw "about 30 of our People coming running down the Hill out of the woods along the Road that comes from

William Henry, mostly stripped to their shirts and Breeches, and many without shirts."[59] How many prisoners were "massacred" at Fort William Henry is difficult to determine. Of the 2,308 who surrendered, at least 69 were killed in the aftermath of chaos at the encampment and along the road, and more than 100 were counted as missing, many of whom were probably captives carried off by the Indians. Although the casualty rate at William Henry pales against the figures for contemporary European battles, what shocked those who heard of the "massacre" was not the toll of death but rather the way people died. The tragedy at William Henry provided emotional fodder for the American and British press, and judging by the number of accounts published, each more lurid than the one before, survivors were eager to share their memories.

Although he was the victor, Montcalm refused to push on to Fort Edward. Having lost his Indian allies, and unsure whether the Canadians would stay with him through the coming harvest season, he opted to level William Henry and return to Ticonderoga. At the same time, he had to explain how the "massacre" had occurred under his command. Naturally, he blamed the sad affair on the Indians and the British. According to the marquis, no harm would have happened if, he alleged, the British soldiers had not given rum to the Indians, and if everyone had followed the orders of the French escort to remain together rather than panicking and running away. In the case of the Indians, Montcalm's explanation rings true. He claimed that he simply could not restrain "3000 Indians of 33 different Nations."[60]

Historians have often painted Montcalm as the villain in this drama, and they have done the same for Webb, whom they often condemn for not marching to the rescue. James Fenimore Cooper's romantic tale *The Last of the Mohicans* (1826) enshrined the view of the brave Monro, a hapless Webb, and a French commander unable to control his allies. Sadly, there was little Webb could have done. He had barely enough troops to defend Fort Edward. They and Monro's beleaguered garrison were the only forces standing between the French and Albany. If Webb had risked a march to William Henry and was defeated, it would have been a disaster. Its sacrifice was a sound and necessary strategic decision.

(7)

Ticonderoga

We must Attack Any Way, and not be losing time
in talking or consulting how.

—William Eyre, quoting General Abercromby,
Robert Napier, July 10, 1758

On June 29, 1757, less than two weeks before the fall of William Henry, William Pitt returned to office in a coalition government led by Newcastle. He faced a deluge of disturbing news not only from America but from Europe as well. It was, he said, "a gloomy scene for this distressed, disgraced country."[1]

Meanwhile, Frederick the Great was in crisis. On June 18 the Austrians had defeated his army at Kolin, thirty-five miles east of Prague. According to Prussian dispatches, the king had lost nearly one-third of his force. Nor was that the total of Frederick's troubles. In the southwest one hundred thousand French were massing to invade Hanover, while on the eastern border an equally large Russian army was advancing through East Prussia.

The previous April King George had sent his son the duke of Cumberland to command the defense of Hanover. Since the monarch was far more concerned with defending his own electorate than with any strategic alliance with Frederick, the duke's orders were not instructions from a king to a commander but rather from a father to a son responsible for protecting the family patrimony. To the duke the king wrote: "The Position and Operations of Our Army must . . . be directed to Our Chief Aim. This is: not to act offensively, neither against the Empress Queen [Austria], nor any other Power, but merely protect our own Dominions, those of the King of Prussia in Westphalia, and those of the Landgrave of Hesse."[2]

Commanding barely forty thousand troops, mostly Germans, Cumberland had to face a French army more than twice the size of his own. Whatever help he might have expected from the Prussians evaporated at Kolin. Cumberland was on his own.

Bridling at his restrictive orders, and desperately in need of additional troops, Cumberland asked London for assistance. Pitt refused to send additional forces, and when asked to dispatch a fleet to hold the Baltic, he refused that request as well. Instead he committed forces to Loudoun and agreed to a diversionary attack on the French naval base at Rochefort. Rudely rebuffed and resigned to his fate, Cumberland wrote to his friend Henry Fox that the men in London "neither heed . . . nor understand."[3] Against overwhelming odds Cumberland retreated before the French. Trapped between the River Elbe and the North Sea, the duke took up a position near the village of Hastenbeck. After three days of battle, on July 26 Cumberland's army withdrew. He told Fox, "We had as brave a handfull of men as ever fought but we had a most numerous enemy."[4]

On August 21 Cumberland wrote to the French commander, the duc de Richelieu, and proposed a "suspense of arms." More than anything else, the duke wanted to preserve his army and prevent it from falling into the hands of the French. This, he assumed, was what his father wanted as well. Richelieu, eager to devote his full attention to Frederick, and fearful that if he did not end the campaign soon winter would sweep in and end any chance for victory, was willing to talk. On September 8 Cumberland and Richelieu signed an agreement at Klosterseven. Cumberland's army would disband and the troops return to their homes. The Hanoverian troops would retire across the River Elbe. Contrary to what Cumberland had assumed, his father was not pleased. The enraged king summoned the duke home and forced him to resign all his offices.[5]

Cumberland's disgrace and ignominious recall served Pitt's domestic political ambitions. The failure in Germany weakened the political influence of the king's friends in Parliament and gave Pitt additional targets at which to hurl his poisoned barbs. Newcastle ostensibly held the reins of government as chancellor of the exchequer, but everyone, including the duke, relied on Pitt, who rose to take charge of foreign affairs and the conduct of the war. The chatty gossips the Earl of Chesterfield and Horace Walpole described the political symbiosis nicely. According to the former, "The Duke of Newcastle and Mr. Pitt jog on like man and wife; that is, seldom agreeing, often quarreling; but by mutual interest upon the whole, not parting." Walpole's views were similar: "Pitt does everything, the Duke of Newcastle gives everything. As long as they can agree in this partition they may do what they will."[6] Newcastle's money and patronage, combined with Pitt's oratory in Commons and astute political sense, forged a potent partnership. Nonetheless, neither leader had any special talents for waging war. Newcastle viewed the conflict as a painful bill of costs, and though Pitt envisioned an end to the struggle and the reduction of the French colonial empire, he was less certain of the means. For advice on the conduct of war, he turned to General John Ligonier and Admiral George Anson, two of the nation's heroes.

Born in 1680, Jean Louis (more commonly called John) Ligonier was a Huguenot refugee who arrived in England and entered military service under Marlborough in 1702. By the time Pitt came to office Ligonier was a living legend. He had fought in twenty-three battles, often at the front with his regiment, and participated in nineteen sieges. Several horses had been shot out from underneath him, and once he had been taken prisoner, but, miraculously, in his entire career he had never been wounded. Cynics like Walpole dismissed him for his "aged brows and approaching coffin," but the people and the king loved him. In October 1757 His Majesty appointed him commander in chief to replace his disgraced son.[7]

George Anson, first lord of the Admiralty, entered the service at age fifteen, was a lieutenant by twenty-one, and had his own command by twenty-seven. Anson's greatest claim to fame was his command of the squadron that had sailed around the world (1740–44), attacking into the far reaches of the Spanish Empire. He left England with five ships and returned with only one: *Centurion*. Nonetheless, during the voyage among other prizes he took *Nuestra Senora de Covadonga*, one of the famed Manila galleons, bound for the Philippines laden with gold and silver. His share of that capture (half a million pounds) had made him a very rich and famous officer. Anson rose quickly in the navy's ranks and in London society, where he enjoyed an evening's entertainment and the company of beautiful women. In 1747 Anson commanded the British fleet off Cape Finisterre, where he managed to defeat the French and further enhance his popular reputation. For that, he was elevated to the peerage as Baron Anson. When his patron, Lord Sandwich, left the Admiralty in 1751, Anson remained, and in June 1757 the king appointed him first lord.[8] Anson was tireless in preparing the navy for a war that he was certain would come and ensuring that the keystone of English naval strategy—controlling the English Channel to prevent any chance of an invasion—was not weakened.[9]

Ligonier and Anson chimed in on strategy, but Pitt dominated the war councils. As usual, he was volatile, abrupt, irascible. As Walpole put it, Pitt "wanted friends for places more than places for friends."[10] Perhaps it was because of his lack of close associates, and his uneasy relationship with a king who made no secret of his distaste for him, that Pitt relied more on talent than friendship for his support. As Pitt drew men to him, what emerged was a crude forerunner of the modern imperial war staff, that is, joint chiefs (Ligonier and Anson) operating within the parameters of a grand strategy laid out by a dynamic prime minister.[11] Pitt's strategy was sound and direct. He was orchestrating a war of conquest. Within the overarching goal of reducing the French overseas empire around the world, priority went to North America. Ligonier's task was to marshal the regiments necessary to accomplish the land mission, while Anson's assignment was to provide transport and protection for the military and at the same time maintain a tight blockade of France to prevent it from moving reinforcements overseas.

Neither chief, however, could permit overseas commitments to imperil the home islands. Ligonier was always careful to keep ready sufficient troops and militia to repel a French landing, and Anson saw to it that the Channel fleet kept a close rendezvous along the southeast coast of England so that Ligonier's regiments would never have to leave their camps. Anson's strategy of protecting home waters provided the double advantage of protecting the island while keeping the fleet within a few days' sail of the enemy's chief ports.

Despite Cumberland's disaster, Pitt made no change in England's German strategy. He would continue to send chests of cash and as few troops as possible to support Frederick. A force composed of British, Hanoverian, and German troops, all in British pay and under the command of Prince Ferdinand of Brunswick-Wolfenbüttel (Frederick's brother-in-law), stood against the French in the west, leaving Frederick to focus on the Austrians

and Russians in the east.[12] Pitt never committed large numbers of British
soldiers to Germany. At the height of the war, he committed far more troops
to North America than to the Continent.[13] As one London wag put it:

> *Our troops they now can plainly see*
> *May Britain guard in Germany;*
> *Hanoverians, Hessians, Prussians,*
> *Are paid t'oppose the French and Russians;*
> *Nor scruple they with truth to say*
> *They're fighting for America.*[14]

British gold (six hundred thousand pounds per year) was a fair substi-
tute for British troops, but Frederick wanted even more. He continued to
urge Pitt to deploy a naval squadron in the Baltic to support his army and
harass the Russians. Anson advised against the venture. Operating in the
Baltic was risky. The only entrance/exit was via narrow straits controlled
by Denmark. Although the Danes, as well as the Swedes on the other side of
the passage, were neutral, they were not well disposed toward the British.
For at least a year they and several other "neutrals" complained that English privateers and warships were illegally seizing their ships.[15] In retaliation for these abuses, the Danes might block passage. Nor would the
troubles be over once the squadron made it into the Baltic, a shallow and
treacherous sea that posed hazardous navigation for deep-draft men-of-
war. Pitt refused to take the risk.

In order to protect the homeland and be ready to sortie against a possible French breakout, Anson had to keep his fleet on a short tether. But
both Frederick's needs, and the requirements for defending the home island, fell into line with a proposal to launch a raid on the port of Rochefort,
which tantalized with the dual attraction of being not only a plump naval
target but also "within the scope and range of the British forces available."[16] A descent on Rochefort would, it was hoped, force the French to
divert forces from Germany to protect the city and defend the coast. In the
joint expedition, Admiral Sir Edward Hawke commanded the sea forces,
while General Sir John Mordaunt led the army. Among Mordaunt's subordinates was the youthful Lieutenant Colonel James Wolfe, acting as quartermaster general. Hawke and Mordaunt were "to attempt as far as should
be found practicable a descent on the coast of France at or near Rochefort,

in order to attack and by vigorous impression force that place, and to burn and destroy to the utmost of their power all such docks, magazines, arsenals, and shipping as shall be found there."[17]

Mordaunt was a poor choice to command. He was, according to Walpole, an old and tired soldier "broken in spirit and constitution" and in a state of "nervous disorder."[18] The general's disorder compounded the problem of finding ships to convoy the force to France. Transports were slow to arrive, delayed by cranky shipowners and bad weather. Not until mid-September 1757, while the ministry was still digesting the news of the fall of William Henry, did the expedition get under way from Portsmouth.[19]

After a few days at sea, Wolfe wrote to his mother complaining about seasickness. "I am," he declared, "the worst mariner in the whole ship."[20] A few days later, on the seventeenth, Wolfe's ship was off the Isle d'Aix, where the young officer reported joyfully to his mother that "the grapes upon the Isle d'Aix are exceedingly delicious—especially to a sea-sick stomach."[21]

For a week the generals and admirals "sat from morning till late at night" debating their course of action. Poor intelligence, faulty charts, and a host of other problems filled them with doubt. Finally, in a stunning decision, the officers decided unanimously "not to attack the place they were ordered to attack," and early in October the force returned to Portsmouth. Wolfe, convinced that if they had attacked immediately, instead of waiting, they could have captured the port in forty-eight hours, took the lesson. In combined operations cooperation between land and sea commanders was essential. During the voyage home Wolfe, ever the romantic and gallant soldier, wrote presciently to his friend William Rickson:

> *Nothing is to be reckoned an obstacle to your undertaking which is not found really so upon trial; that in war something must be allowed to chance and fortune, seeing it is in its nature hazardous, and an option of difficulties; that the greatness of an object should come under consideration opposed to the impediments that lie in the way; that the honour of one's country is to have some weight; and that in particular circumstances and times, the loss of a thousand men is rather an advantage to a nation than otherwise, seeing that gallant attempts raise its reputation and make it respectable; whereas the contrary appearances sink the credit of a country, ruin the troops, and create infinite uneasiness and discontent at home.*[22]

Pitt reeled from reports of the Rochefort follies. In Commons he burst out that he "believed there was a determined resolution, both in the naval and military commanders, against any vigorous exertion of the national power."[23] The phlegmatic minister, preferring to ignore his own culpability for the mess, roared against his pusillanimous admirals and generals. Others put the blame on Pitt. The whole expedition, according to the opposition, was "rash and childish." When poor Mordaunt, by then truly a broken man, was summoned to stand court-martial, tongues wagged that he would likely "suffer a little Bynging." Neither Pitt nor the army, however, had any desire to repeat the public scandal of Admiral Byng, and Mordaunt was acquitted of any wrongdoing.[24]

Sifting through the ruins of 1757, that "last inactive, and unhappy Campaign," Pitt laid plans for the coming year.[25] Frederick would get more money to rebuild his army and regain the offensive; India would be left in the hands of the East India Company with some modest naval support; royal naval squadrons in the West Indies would concentrate on trade protection; and along the West African coast amphibious raids against the French would continue. There could be no doubt, however, that all these theaters were peripheral to the core campaign in North America. There Pitt planned three major operations: against Ticonderoga, Louisbourg, and Duquesne. To achieve his goals in North America, Pitt understood that he needed more support from the colonials. In true Whig parliamentary fashion he came upon a solution: to purchase it. Pitt let the colonial authorities know that henceforth London would pay the war bills. No one in America objected.

After capturing Fort William Henry, Montcalm returned to Quebec with a feeling of unease rather than jubilation. Despite the ferocity of the battle for the fort, all he had accomplished was to snip off a British salient that would soon grow back; in a few months the British advance would continue north again. Furthermore, victory had its cost in terms of human casualties, and Montcalm could ill afford to lose a single soldier. Louix XV, focused on Europe, was not inclined to send more soldiers to defend what Voltaire called a "few acres of snow."[26] Nor could the general look to Canada for succor. The harvests of 1756 and 1757 had been woeful, grain prices were skyrocketing, bread was rationed at a quarter pound per day, and shoes were scarce. An Ursuline at the Quebec convent lamented, "Three plagues have descended on our country, pestilence, famine, and war; but famine is the worst of all."[27] The bread, according to the convent's Mother la Grange, was "as black as [our] robes."[28] Manpower too was in short supply. Montcalm's entire regular force was smaller than the British garrison at Fort Edward, and although the Troupes de la Marine had shown themselves to be able soldiers, there weren't enough of them. As for the militia, they had the same unhappy traits as their counterparts to the south: They were unreliable and undisciplined. Indians were also a concern. After their treatment at William Henry, both the domiciled tribes and those from more distant places returned home angry that Montcalm had denied them their just rewards. Their unhappiness over the division of spoils, however, was about to be eclipsed by an even greater catastrophe.

Smallpox was a frequent visitor to Canada. In most instances the dread virus arrived by ship at Quebec and then spread along the settled parts of the St. Lawrence River valley. Occasionally, fur traders and missionaries carried the plague to the villages far in the interior, but rarely did it reach epidemic proportions among those tribes. In the fall of 1755 the "pox" struck Quebec, undoubtedly brought in by the soldiers newly arrived from France. It swept through the valley, infecting, disfiguring, and killing hundreds of Canadians and domiciled Indians. (Those who were infected and survived—about 80 percent of the sick—developed an immunity.) The disease erupted again in the summer of 1756, and as the weather warmed in 1757, people in Quebec feared a third epidemic. Thankfully, none appeared. Only a few scattered cases were reported, most of them among soldiers. The menace, however, hovered elsewhere.

For several days after the fall of William Henry, the area around the fort was packed with thousands of soldiers—British and French—and as many Indians and civilians. During these hot August days, William Henry was one of the most populous and crowded places in North America. It was also a pest hole and a haven for smallpox. For the time being, however, only a few cases appeared, not enough to cause undue alarm.[29] Once contracted, smallpox takes anywhere from ten to fourteen days to make its deadly presence apparent. That was sufficient time for the Indians at William Henry to become exposed and make their way home before showing serious signs of illness.

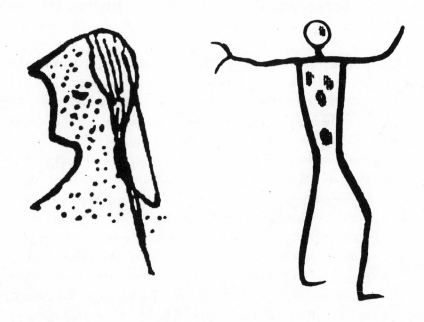

Representations of smallpox among Native Americans

These infected warriors may not have carried spoils home to their families, but they did bring the pox. Through the fall and winter of 1757–58 smallpox ravaged the western tribes. Jean-Nicholas Desandrouins, an engineering officer with Montcalm, noted that the disease "made astonishing ravages," and whole villages were "laid waste."[30] The French blamed the British for the disease. The Indians blamed the nation that invited them east; the French had given them "bad medicine."[31] First cheated of their rightful spoils, then infected by the French, the western tribes simmered as they sickened.

Montcalm ignored the sufferings of both the Indians and Canadians. Early in February 1758 the tone-deaf marquis wrote to his superiors in Paris: "The Canadians, the simple farmer respects and loves me. As to the Indian I believe I have seized their genius and manners." When the marquis addressed the people whose "genius and manners he had seized," to ask them to join him in the coming campaign, they ignored his message.[32]

As spring approached, the western Indians, remembering William Henry and smallpox, remained at home. Montcalm's strategic choice was to play for time. He believed that if his forces could hold the enemy at bay until reinforcements arrived from home (an unlikely event), or until French victories elsewhere in the world forced the British to seek a negotiated peace (much likelier), then France might save Canada by swapping other conquests for its losses in North America. To that end, the general decided to concentrate his forces at Ticonderoga, anticipating that they would eventually fall back to Quebec and Montreal. In this plan the stranded forts in the Ohio and Great Lakes regions, as well as at Louisbourg, could expect no major reinforcements. Their orders were to hold their posts as long as possible in order to block the British drive into the heart of New France.[33]

Vaudreuil, and many other Canadians, accused the general of being a defeatist. For more than one hundred years, with very little direct assistance from regular troops, Canadians had resisted the British. Indeed, the Troupes de la Marine, militia, and Indians had often carried out raids deep into enemy territory. Caught off guard by such sudden violent attacks, the English rarely retaliated. Citing Canada's history, Vaudreuil argued that small units moving aggressively against the British would force them to disperse their army. Montcalm's strategy to pull back and rely on a strong defense was, in the opinion of the governor, badly suited to the Canadian environment. Vaudreuil made his position clear when he wrote to the minister of war reflecting on Montcalm's strategy: "It is in the true and fundamental interest of the colony that I devote my main efforts to defending the soil of our frontiers foot by foot against the enemy, whereas M. de Montcalm and the land troops seek only to preserve their reputation and would like to return to France without having suffered a single defeat."[34]

Montcalm the aristocratic general and Vaudreuil the proud Creole governor grew to despise each other, but on one point they agreed: They both bewailed the lack of support from home. British commanders had a problem of a different sort. They may have been well supported, but they had to operate under the gimlet eye of William Pitt.

Pitt distrusted army officers. He held a whiggish view that the army was

Major General James Abercromby

by its nature an enemy to liberty, and that soldiers must always be held in check by civilian authority. Yet senior officers achieved and held rank at the pleasure of the king. Political differences notwithstanding, Pitt therefore angered His Majesty by questioning the competence of his commanders, especially those in North America. Pitt's friend Sir Charles Hardy, the governor of New York, shared his views with the minister, noting sarcastically that Loudoun's pampered soldiers "can't stir without their curling irons and brown paper; the French make winter expeditions, why can't we?"[35]

Loudoun's liabilities went beyond his military shortcomings. Although he was distressed at what the general had not done to attack the enemy, Pitt was equally concerned about the highhanded methods by which he had managed to antagonize nearly every governor and assembly in America. His incessant and frequently blunt demands for men, matériel, and money threw colonial officials into an uproar that reverberated in London. In December 1757, after covering his political flanks at home, Pitt engineered Loudoun's recall and the appointment of a new chief, Loudoun's second in command, Major General James Abercromby.[36] A Scot like Loudoun, Abercromby was a seasoned soldier, but he had never before held a major independent command. As his friend Loudoun put it delicately, "M.G. Abercromby is a good officer, and a very good second Man any where, whatever he is employed in."[37] The logic of his selection probably rests in the fact that he was already in place and could, at least theoretically, get under way immediately. It may have also been the case that the general was politi-cally safe; that is, his appointment, while not cheered by all, was not likely to raise much opposition.

Pitt's secretaries scrambled to keep up with him. On December 30, 1757, he sent no fewer than nine separate dispatches to America. These included Loudoun's recall, Abercromby's appointment, instructions to governors, and, most important, detailed plans for the campaign of 1758.[38] Unlike Montcalm's superiors in Paris, who gave their commander only the most general instructions, Pitt was detailed and precise. In several densely packed letters he laid out to Abercromby and the governors what he ex-pected to happen in North America during the coming year. The general himself was to concentrate on Ticonderoga and Crown Point. Pitt directed Jeffrey Amherst to take Louisbourg and John Forbes to march against Duquesne. His orders were quite specific, even to the point of insisting that Amherst hire a Mr. Meserve from Portsmouth, New Hampshire, to com-mand eighty carpenters on the Louisbourg expedition. Like Braddock and Loudoun, Abercromby bore the title "Commander in Chief of His Majesty's Forces in North America," but unlike Loudoun, thanks to Pitt's distrust of military commanders and his desire to micromanage, Abercromby really only commanded the forces with him in person, moving against Ticon-deroga and Crown Point. For all intents and purposes, Amherst and Forbes answered directly to Pitt. Abercromby's army had a large number of provin-cial soldiers. To avoid the legacy left by Loudoun of snarling between colo-nials and regulars, Pitt reiterated his promise to provincial authorities that the king would assume the costs of the war. Pitt's largesse delighted the colonial authorities, but even money could not speed up the process of re-cruiting, and as usual the militia arrived late. Slowly, regiments from Mass-achusetts, New Hampshire, New York, Connecticut, Rhode Island, and New Jersey assembled at Fort Edward. By early summer nearly twenty thousand men, regulars and provincials, were encamped.

Not only were the provincials late, but as usual they were ill disciplined and ill trained. Captain Hugh Arnot of the Eightieth Regiment spat out his opinion: "The greater their Numbers, the greater the Evil; for of any sett of people in the Universe they are the worst cut out for war. The most stu-pid and most chicken-hearted sett of Mankind."[39] Unfortunately, the campaign season was already under way, and there was not enough time to train the "chicken-hearted" men. Most of the provincials drilled only a few days at Fort Edward before they were sent off to the assembly point at Lake George.

Abercromby aimed to advance up Lake George, secure a landing site near Ticonderoga, and march against the fort. Over the course of the winter, rangers had gathered intelligence on the French—a good deal of it wrong.[40] Nor could he depend upon Indians. Facing the threat of a French attack from Oswego, and having witnessed the British disasters of the previous season, the Iroquois were wary of their English "brothers" and stayed apart. Not even William Johnson could entice them to join. The only native auxiliaries with Abercromby were from the Stockbridge companies of western Massachusetts and Mohegan of Connecticut.[41] Coralling provincials and gathering intelligence were not Abercromby's only problems. Experienced engineers were in short supply. The ranking engineering officer in the northern theater was the able Colonel James Montresor, but he was ill and unavailable.[42] Next in line was William Eyre. Unfortunately for Abercromby, Eyre was also the senior field officer of the Forty-fourth Regiment. Eyre chose the regiment.[43] By a process of elimination, the engineering duty finally fell on a more junior officer, Lieutenant Matthew Clerk.

Yet whatever skills Abercromby's army might have lacked, it was not short on size. Fifteen thousand men, regulars and provincials, were drawn up on a two-mile front along the southern edge of Lake George. It was the largest and best-equipped army yet to assemble in America. On June 26, 1758, the general rode into the lakeside encampment, where he found his second in command, Lord George Howe, "the very Spirit and Life of the Army," working furiously to prepare the expedition.[44] Captain Joshua Loring of the Royal Navy was in charge of the vast armada of more than one thousand small boats.

George Howe was unusual among officers. He was the third Viscount Howe, the eldest son in a family that produced three distinguished officers. His two younger brothers, Richard and William, would earn fame in the American Revolution. Howe was a gallant soldier-aristocrat. Throwing aside formality and tailored uniforms, he dressed down to a style closer to the look of enlisted troops than his fellow officers, and he often messed and tented with his men in the field, winning their admiration and affection.

With the support of Lieutenant Colonel Thomas Gage, the officer who had commanded Braddock's advance guard and who, as a result, had experienced wilderness fighting firsthand, Howe persuaded Abercromby to order the men to travel light and to shed a good deal of their cumbersome woolen uniforms. By reducing the weight of clothing, the soldiers could better endure July's humidity and heat, and had less to snag them in the undergrowth. Soldiers cut their long coats to jackets and trimmed their wide-brimmed tricornered hats to the size of caps. At the same time, Howe and Gage taught the men new techniques for fire and movement, including shooting and reloading from covered positions. On July 5, as the morning glow became visible over the hills to the east, British drummers beat "The General," the call to fall in, and the regiments marched toward the boats assembled along the shore. First off were Bradstreet's weathered bateauxmen, who formed a skirmish line ahead of the light infantry on the right and rangers on the left. The main body came next, with artillery barges, commissary stores, and hospital boats closing up the rear.[45]

Abercromby made remarkably good time. By late afternoon they were twenty miles down the lake near Sabbath Day Point, the scene of Parker's disaster. Deep in enemy territory the general signaled for the boats to pull toward the western shore. With great display Howe's light infantry scrambled ashore, pitched tents, lit fires, and made as if they were bivouacking for the night, hoping to deceive the French into thinking they would not resume their advance until the morning.

The day before the British set off, Montcalm had dispatched two detachments with orders to set up advance posts on either side of the lake. On the west side 350 men under the command of Captain de Trépezec took an observation post south of Mont Pelee (Rogers Rock) less than ten miles above Sabbath Day Point.[46] On the opposite shore Captain Bernard waited for the British with three hundred men. Well aware that a vastly superior enemy force was coming toward him, Montcalm weighed his options.[47] Ticonderoga was a small fort with serious disadvantages. Within its walls there was barely room to accommodate a single battalion, while outside the fort the terrain to the west was high enough so that if an advancing enemy took those elevated spots it could range artillery on the fort. In addition, Ticonderoga was built on a peninsula from which there was only a single route of escape. Ticonderoga had to be defended by holding the western ground beyond the walls. The general remained at Ticonderoga and awaited news from Trépezec and Bernard. In the meantime he moved some of his regiments toward the lake to cover the landing site and portage road.

At about ten o'clock Abercromby ordered his men back into their boats, and they rowed north on a dark and moonless night. Lead boats with light infantry and rangers displayed shuttered lanterns at their sterns so that those trailing behind could follow and hold their proper position. The boats glided undetected past the French sentries. Just before first light Howe pulled ahead with the rangers and light infantry with orders to secure the landing site. Caught unaware, the main French force was camped too far away to interfere. The few French pickets fled at the approach of the rangers, leaving behind their tents and baggage. By noon the entire British army was ashore.

About a mile to the north of the landing place Bourlamaque guarded a key bridge across the La Chute River. Reluctantly, Bourlamaque ordered the bridge destroyed and withdrew his regiments to join Montcalm at a post a bit farther north. Here Bourlamaque and Montcalm paused long enough to realize their danger. If the British moved quickly enough, they could sweep around the French right, take the ground, and stand between them and the fort. To avoid the trap, Montcalm ordered a late morning withdrawal toward the fort to a place where other troops had already taken up positions.

As the French dug in, Abercromby and Howe debated their options. The most direct route to Ticonderoga was the short portage road, but two river crossings promised to make movement in that direction very costly. They opted for a longer route, swinging around the French right, thereby avoiding the road and river crossings in a maneuver designed to envelop Montcalm. Ahead of the main column Abercromby ordered Rogers and his rangers to sweep west in an arc to dislodge enemy pickets and to secure the fords across Bernetz Brook. Yet heavy rains had filled this otherwise languid brook to the brim, making it a much greater obstacle than anticipated. The unseasonable wetness had also caused the ground cover to grow wild and dense. The rangers had to hack their way through the heavy growth.

Two hours after the rangers left camp, the main force of seven thousand regulars and provincials advanced. On the far right Howe marched closest to the river, playing the role of the pivot element around which the left would eventually swing toward the enemy. Despite the heat and bothersome brush, the army made good time. By midafternoon the main column's advance guard had met up with the rangers, who had paused at a ford.

Lord George Howe

Rogers sent scouts forward to reconnoiter the French position near the sawmill. Danger, however, lurked on his flanks. Earlier in the morning, when Trépezac realized that the British had gotten by him on the lake, he roused his men and led them on a hurried march to rejoin Montcalm and the main body near the sawmill. Abercromby's landing, however, had cut the direct route, and they were forced to swing west to avoid the enemy. As the French made their way through the heavy forest, the men on the point heard movement in the nearby brush. Within seconds firing broke out. Lord Howe rushed to the sound of the guns. The general's brigade major, Captain Alexander Monypenny, described the action.

> *When the firing began on the left part of the column, Lord Howe thinking it would be of the greatest consequence to beat the enemy with the light troops, so as not to stop the march of the main body, went up with them, and had just gained the top of a hill, where the firing was, when he was killed. Never ball had more deadly direction. It entered his breast on the left side, and (as the surgeons say) pierced his lungs, and heart, and shattered his backbone. I was six yards from him, he fell on his back and never moved, only his hands quivered an instant.*[48]

Howe had trained his troops well, preventing a repeat of the battle of the Monongahela, where soldiers either froze or fell into disarray. Instead of falling back, the light infantry and rangers maneuvered forward

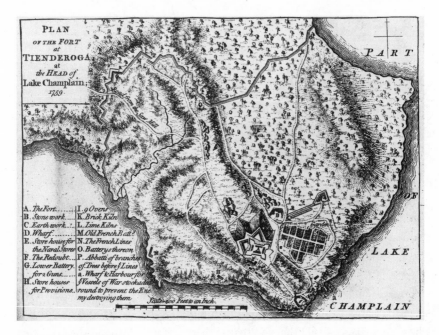

Plan of Fort Ticonderoga

and fanned out to the flanks, their quick response catching the French by surprise. Within minutes the British had nearly surrounded Trépezac's men and were delivering withering fire into their ranks, killing, wounding, or capturing nearly half of them. Fewer than one hundred men managed to escape.

Howe's light infantry set an example that the rest of the army found difficult to follow. News of the brave general's death, and fear of the enemy, "threw our Regulars in to some kind of Consternation," recorded William Eyre.[49] Indeed "Consternation" and confusion were the rules of the afternoon. Abercromby and his officers needed more than three hours to regain control of the army. Even so, as night fell the men heard screams and firing from the woods. With reckless disregard for the safety of their comrades, and their own standing orders, frightened troops fired blindly into the dark. A number of British soldiers were hit by "friendly fire." By morning the entire army was back where it had begun the day before—on the shore of the lake.

The action at Bernetz Brook bought time for Montcalm, and he used it wisely. To avoid envelopment, he withdrew his force closer to Ticonderoga. "At every fifty steps the covering party halted and turned."[50] By dusk all the French regiments were assembled on the heights of Ticonderoga between the fort and the British, and Montcalm put his defensive plan in motion through the services of two skilled military engineers: Nicholas Sarrebource de Pontleroy and Jean-Nicholas Desandrouins.

The two engineers had been anticipating Abercromby's arrival. Work gangs were busy clearing, measuring, and staking out fields of fire around the fort. After letting the men rest for a few hours, at about two in the morning of the seventh Montcalm summoned his officers and led them on a walk along the proposed defensive line. He pointed out each regiment's assigned sector—a one-hundred-yard front. That day enlisted men and officers worked side by side in the July heat, cutting, chopping, and digging. In a single day they managed to throw up an impressive defensive work.

Ticonderoga's newly fashioned outerworks rose on a slope about one thousand yards to the west of the fort. Work parties cut trees and laid them horizontally to provide solid cover behind which infantry could fire with safety. Pontleroy and Desandrouins recognized that the hastily erected barricade was imperfect. The log wall tracked the ground's natural contour, and in some places it slumped into hollows where defenders might be sniped at from adjacent high ground. Nor did the engineers and soldiers have time to lay out the normal zigzags in the line that would allow defenders to deliver angled fire at the approaching enemy. Yet although the line had its weaknesses, it also had an enormous advantage. In front of the formal line stretching west, the soldiers had left a primitive but formidable abatis, a barrier composed of a hodgepodge of upended tree trunks, felled trees, sharp branches, and discarded pieces of timber. The entire approach area was such a tangled mess that from a distance it was difficult to make out the exact line of the fortifications. An advancing enemy would have to make its way through this dangerous ground with little knowledge of the trap that lay ahead of them.[51]

Most worrisome to Montcalm were his exposed flanks. Since there had not been enough time to extend the log barricade out to these wings, both positions were only partially protected. Two volunteer light infantry companies, drawn from Bourlamaque's command, held the extreme left. They dug in on the front face of a steep ravine that fell down to the La Chute. The British having already demonstrated their skill at amphibious operations, Montcalm rightfully worried that they might try to come down the river and stage a landing behind his left flank. On the far right a mixed force of Canadians—Troupes de la Marine and militia—stood ready.

While the French dug, cut, and covered, Abercromby summoned his officers to council. Howe's death had taken the breath out of the army. The strongest voice in council came from the blunt Nova Scotian colonel John Bradstreet, who urged the general to allow him to move ahead on the direct route and seize the river crossing and the high ground behind it. Abercromby hesitated, fearing that if he divided his force the enemy might fall upon him piecemeal, but eventually he agreed, and Bradstreet set out shortly before noon with a strong force of five thousand men. By half past one he had secured the crossing and was asking permission to move rapidly against Ticonderoga. Abercromby wisely held him back.

As Bradstreet waited for the rest of the army to catch up with him, two officers, engineer Matthew Clerk and James Abercromby (no relation to the general), climbed 850 feet to the top of Rattlesnake Mountain* to reconnoiter the French position. Although they could make out the fort and the activity to the front, from more than a mile away the tangle of trees, brush, and cut logs would have looked more like the remnants of a wild windstorm than a well-planned defensive position. By the time the officers returned to the main encampment, the army had settled in for the night. Precisely what they reported is not clear, although given what emerged as the plan of attack, it is highly unlikely that General Abercromby had an accurate picture of the French position. Clerk did see an opportunity for a flanking movement. He advised moving an artillery battery down the La Chute to a place on the south side of the river slightly behind the French lines and within range of the fort. It was, he believed, the perfect spot from which to deliver enfilading fire, and the general agreed.

As Clerk left the general's tent, there was a commotion in the camp. For days Abercromby had been waiting for Johnson and his Mohawk to arrive. According to messages from Johnson, the Mohawk were reluctant to leave

*Present-day Mount Defiance.

their homes, fearing that the French might descend on their villages from Oswego. The indefatigable Johnson invited his brothers to his home, and after days of persuasion, lubricated by enormous quantities of liquor, he finally got the warriors to come east. What Clerk heard were the whoops and hollers from nearly four hundred Mohawk coming into camp, led by Johnson himself, dressed in the garb of a Mohawk chief.

On the morning of the eighth Abercromby made final preparations for the attack. He intended to drive through what he believed to be weak outer defenses and then assault the fort. While his men checked their weapons, he sent Clerk forward for a last-minute look. According to Abercromby, Clerk's report convinced him that there was "no Doubt of the practicality of carrying those works, if attacked before they were finished: it was agreed to storm them that very Day: Accordingly, the Rangers, Light Infantry, and the Right Wing of the Provincials were ordered immediately to march, and post themselves in a Line, out of Cannon Shot of the Intrenchments, their right extending to Lake George [La Chute River], and their left to Lake Champlain, in order that the Regular Troops, destined for the Attack of the Intrenchments might form in their Rear."[52] Officers present, however, remembered less clarity in their instructions. They also mentioned that the meeting was hurried. According to Eyre, the meeting ended abruptly with Abercromby telling his staff, "We must Attack Any Way, and not be losing time in talking or consulting how."[53]

As the provincials and regulars formed up, two Connecticut regiments marched back to the lake encampment to bring up the artillery. Aside from the riverbank battery, Abercromby had made no plan for artillery support, believing that it would take too long to bring up the heavy cannon. As redcoats and provincials prepared for battle, Johnson and the Indians climbed to the top of Rattlesnake Mountain, where they made an ineffectual display of firing off their weapons at an enemy far out of range. At the same time ten whaleboats set off from upriver, towing two rafts with four cannon. This too became a farce. As the whaleboats drew near the landing spot identified by Clerk, they got lost in high reeds and could not find solid ground. French gunners sighted and ranged on them, sinking two boats and forcing the others to beat a hasty retreat.

At about ten, skirmishers emerged from the wood line and advanced. Behind them the provincials and regulars formed up. But within a few steps

the fallen trees and branches broke the advancing rhythm. Men burdened
with heavy packs and weapons stumbled, fell, and struggled to get up. In the
center Colonel William Haviland's regulars were following close behind advancing provincials. Hearing firing on his left, Haviland, who "could not see
what was a doing," mistakenly concluded that the general assault had
begun.[54] He ordered the provincials to make way and "fall down" so that his
brigade might march through and storm the French breastwork by frontal
assault. It was a tragic error; Haviland's men advanced without support and
"fell like pigeons."[55]

All along the front, command and control on the British side collapsed.
Some soldiers stood and advanced, while others cowered behind stumps and
fallen trees. Montcalm had detailed his best marksmen to the front and assigned the less skilled to reload and pass muskets forward. The French
poured a blizzard of shot at the regulars, firing at a rate three to five times
that of the British and with much greater accuracy. In this carnage "no regiment . . . suffered so much as the Highlanders."[56] Recruited out of the
rugged north country of Scotland, the Highlanders were both feared and ad-
mired for their legendary prowess as warriors. With Abercromby was the
senior Highland regiment, the Forty-second "Black Watch." Loudoun had
once remarked that the Black Watch were particularly fearsome; even his
own native allies viewed them, he said, as "a kind of Indians."[57] Abercromby
posted the Forty-second to the left to face the French right, in the sector held
by the regiments of Guyenne and Béarn. Having come into the confused battle late, the Highlanders rushed to take up their position. "We marched up
and attacked the trenches, and got within twenty paces of them and had as
hot a fire for about three hours as possible could be, we all the time seeing
but their hats and the end of their muskets," reported Captain John Murray.
The French defenders were hard-pressed as the "Highlanders returned un-
ceasingly to the attack." Some of the Black Watch leaped onto the top of the
French works, where "they appeared like roaring lions breaking from their
chains."[58] It was a courageous but sad day for the regiment. Like the rest of
Abercromby's army, the Scots were driven back but not before they had
taken devastating losses. By seven in the evening nearly all of the regulars
who could still walk had retreated behind a line held by the provincials.

The French too had suffered heavy casualties but had, nonetheless, won
a glorious victory. Within a few days Montcalm dispatched Bougainville to

Paris with the news. Yet even in jubilation the marquis remained ungenerous toward the Canadians. He disparaged their role in his triumph and condemned them for allegedly cowardly behavior. Weeks later, as he mused
over the situation in Canada, he plunged deeper into gloom. According to
the marquis, the "Grand Society" in which Intendant Bigot was a central
figure "absorbe tout le commerce." The country was in dire straits; "l'agriculture languit, la population diminue, la guerre survient."[59] His close
friend Bougainville summed it up well when he wrote to his wife, "Can we
hope for another miracle to save us? I trust in God; he fought for us on the
8th of July."[60]

Vaudreuil offered a different view. When he received the victorious marquis in Montreal, instead of congratulating him on his victory, the governor
criticized him for not pursuing and destroying Abercromby's army. Taken
aback, Montcalm replied pointedly, "When I went to war I did the best I
could; and . . . when one is not pleased with one's lieutenants, one had better take the field in person." The exchange did not end there. Madame Vaudreuil joined the conversation in support of her husband. This Montcalm
could not abide. "Madame," he told her, "saving due respect, permit me to
have the honour to say that ladies ought not to talk war. . . . if Madame de
Montcalm were here, and heard me talking war with Monsieur le Marquis
de Vaudreuil, she would remain silent."[61]

Although Abercromby's army still outnumbered the French, it was, in the
words of a Rhode Island militia officer, "a confused rabble." As dispirited
and demoralized as his troops, Abercromby was scorned by his own men.
New Englanders called him "Mrs. Nabbycromby," while Johnson's Iroquois
taunted him as "an old Squah that he should wear a petticoat."[62] Abercromby
ordered a general retreat. The day after the debacle the once proud army returned to their boats and rowed dispiritedly back to William Henry.

(8)

Duquesne and Louisbourg

I took possession with my little Army.

—John Forbes to James Abercromby and Jeffrey Amherst,
Fort Duquesne (now Pittsburgh), November 26, 1758

In a letter he wrote to his wife soon after the battle at Ticonderoga, Montcalm told her that he had won "with no Indians and barely any Canadians."[1] Late that summer Montcalm's commissary of wars, André Doreil, sent a lengthy dispatch to the minister of war in Paris, Marshal de Belle Isle, in which he summed up the French position in Canada. Writing with Montcalm's knowledge, he told the minister that "miracles cannot be always expected." English power was overwhelming. The British were "able to furnish more than two hundred thousand men," whereas Canada, could field barely fifteen thousand, and then only if the country abandoned "all sort of work," including the harvest—which could only result in the nation "perishing by hunger." There was no hope. Driven by "frenzy," the English were determined to take Canada "at whatever cost." Awash in pessimism, the commissary advised his Parisian master to "think only of making peace."[2]

Abercromby's thoughts were not about peace. For several days following the withdrawal, the general remained in his headquarters composing his report to Pitt. He gave the minister very little detail of the defeat except to say that in the end he had retreated "with the broken Remains of several Corps."[3] No one wanted to stand on the deck of Abercromby's sinking ship. For officers such as Gage, Bradstreet, and Eyre, saving their own careers was paramount. Gage and James Prevost, colonel of the Sixtieth Regiment, pressured Abercromby (they did it in writing so as to leave a record) to launch a second attack.[4] It was a disingenuous suggestion meant only to display their own initiative, while distancing themselves from the general whom they knew would not agree. Eyre's behavior was even less admirable. He hastened to write to his patron, Adjutant General Robert Napier, describing the disaster and pointing out all the instances where his advice had been ignored.[5] Bradstreet was no less concerned than his fellow officers about the impact of defeat upon his career; however, he alone offered a practical alternative plan: an attack on Fort Frontenac, nearly two hundred miles to the west.

Taking Frontenac was not a new idea. Early in 1758, during the waning days of his command, Loudoun had authorized Bradstreet to strike against Frontenac.[6] Upon assuming command, Abercromby canceled the plan in order to husband forces for the move on Ticonderoga, agreeing that Frontenac would be dealt with as soon as his army "had made an establishment on the north side of Lake George."[7] Bradstreet argued that despite his defeat, Abercromby had ample resources to hold against any (albeit unlikely) French advance and still move against Frontenac. It was, he said, ripe for the plucking.[8]

Although it was a key link in the chain connecting the St. Lawrence with the Ohio, Frontenac was in fact weakly defended. Virtually its entire garrison had been stripped to help defend Ticonderoga. Vaudreuil and Montcalm recognized the risk, but with so few men at their disposal there was little else that they could do. Vaudreuil tried to rally his Indian allies to help fill the gap, but they showed no inclination to help. With a garrison too small to hold against a determined assault, the fort's survival rested on a squadron of nine small vessels moored in the nearby Cataraqui River. Hopefully, their cannon could prevent the British from coming across the lake.

With Abercromby's support Bradstreet gathered 3,600 men at Schenectady on the Mohawk River twenty miles west of Albany. Only 135 were regulars; the rest, provincials from New York, Massachusetts, New Jersey, and Rhode Island. To secure a base of operations and his supply line, he had first to reoccupy Oswego. The long, difficult trek via the Oneida portage took a wasting toll. Aside from a few small French and Indian raiding parties, virtually no one had passed over the Great Carrying Place and down

Wood Creek since the fall of Oswego in 1756. Neglect had not made travel over this route any easier. Fallen trees and branches entangled with heavy brush along the banks made navigation on the creek difficult. As Brad-street's men cut through the mess, they discovered another problem: The creek had silted up, and their deeply laden bateaux ground into the bottom. To reduce their draft and float them over, men were "imployed in Loading and Floating the Battoas." But even reducing the load was not sufficient, and so, to raise water levels, crews built rough dams; "whenever a sufficient quantity of water was gathered, the sluic [was] open'd which convey[ed] them to the next dam."[9] By the time Bradstreet reached the site of the abandoned fort at the mouth of the Oswego River on August 21, nearly six hundred of his men had deserted. Amid the ruins, Bradstreet immediately organized for the final push across the lake, and on the twenty-second several hundred bateaux pulled away from the shore and made their way along the north side of the lake toward Frontenac. Fortune was on the side of the British. The French vessels, which might have raised havoc with Bradstreet's flotilla, failed to detect the oncoming enemy. On the evening of the twenty-fifth the expedition reached a point near the fort and landed without any opposition.[10]

That night Bradstreet's artillerymen laid in their guns, and in the morning they opened a barrage, pounding Frontenac's limestone walls while the engineers dug approaches. The surprise was so complete that the French vessels were trapped at their moorings in the river. The fort's commander, the elderly Pierre-Jacques Payen de Noyan et de Chavoy, had one hundred regulars and a smattering of Indians and Acadians to man the defenses. After a symbolic resistance he surrendered on August 27, 1758, in order to be accorded the traditional "honors of war," which included Bradstreet's permission for the old man to return to Montreal.

Bradstreet had not lost a single man to enemy fire. Inside the fort the English found an incredible storehouse. At least sixty cannon, many of them dismounted, were lying inside the magazines. Ironically, many of the guns bore the mark of George II, spoils taken at the Monongahela and Oswego. Since his mission was to destroy the fort, not occupy it, Bradstreet ordered his soldiers to prepare its destruction. Provincials rolled hundreds of barrels of provisions into the open area, where they stacked and burned them in a grand bonfire. The happy warriors were far more careful with the bundles of valuable furs they discovered awaiting shipment to Montreal. The victors counted and divided the bales among themselves and then stowed them aboard two of the captured French vessels bound for Oswego. In a gesture that gained him huzzahs among his soldiers, Brad-street refused his share of the spoils, insisting that the men divide his por-tion. After throwing what they could not carry into the flames, the English returned to their boats and were back at Oswego on the thirtieth.[11]

Frontenac was a serious loss for the French, for which Vaudreuil assumed the blame. He admitted that he had underestimated the British and told his superiors that he wrongly believed that the English "would not dare to enter the lake [Ontario] on which [the French] had vessels."[12] The governor had not counted on John Bradstreet. In one action, at almost no cost to themselves, the British had made the French position in the west and on the lakes precarious. With their principal depot in ashes, and their lines to the Ohio Valley and the west via the lakes severed, the French could neither reinforce nor supply key positions to the west and south, including Fort Duquesne.[13]

Like Frontenac's garrison, Duquesne's had been sapped to provide men for the defense of Canada. Weak and isolated, Duquesne had seen its strategic importance diminish greatly since the beginning of the war. Nonetheless, the thirst to revenge Braddock's defeat, and the fact that the mere presence of the French at the forks of the Ohio helped incite the Indians, made Duquesne an important British objective. At the same time that Pitt ordered the capture of Louisbourg and Ticonderoga, he also directed an assault against Duquesne. General John Forbes was as-signed the task.[14]

Forbes nominally served under Abercromby; in fact, however, like Amherst he exercised independent command. He too was a Scot, and his fa-ther had been a professional military officer. Forbes, however, began his career as a medical student until, in his midtwenties, he turned to a career in arms. He served with Cumberland and was with the duke at Culloden in 1746. In 1757 he became colonel of the Seventh Regiment and was posted to Nova Scotia. Forbes's skill as an administrator drew Loudoun's attention, and the commander in chief appointed him adjutant general. Forbes had a knack for dealing with "obnoxious" colonials and their fractious assemblies. His organizational and diplomatic skills made him a natural choice to take command in Pennsylvania, where the disorder and acrimony that had helped doom Braddock three years prior still reigned. By mid-April 1758, Forbes was in Philadelphia, preparing his campaign against Duquesne.

Indian assistance would be critical to the campaign. Since Braddock's defeat, the Delaware and other western Indians had inclined to the French. Obtaining help from them seemed unlikely, so Forbes turned to the Cherokee. Still, he worried that the historic rivalry between the Cherokee and the Iroquois, to say nothing of the competition between their white patrons, Edmund Atkins, superintendent of Indian affairs in the south, and his counterpart, William Johnson in New York, would doom any hope of cooperation.[15] Forbes had good reason to be concerned about the Iroquois. Neither he nor Abercromby appreciated Johnson's delicate position. While Johnson held enormous sway in Iroquois councils, he did not dictate policy. For generations the Iroquois had balanced on their pivot point between the French and English with extraordinary deftness. In a war now raging, they realized that the English were gaining the upper hand; nonetheless, they had no desire to sell themselves cheaply. Nor did they wish to see rival tribes, such as the Cherokee, invade their territory. On June 1 a delegation of twelve Cherokee chiefs arrived in Philadelphia to negotiate their support. Pennsylvania's deputy governor, William Denny, and Forbes met with them, and several hundred southern Indians soon joined Forbes. The arrival of the Cherokee proved to be an unmitigated disaster. Their mere presence in territory the Iroquois claimed as their own created tension. And with nothing to do but wait for the general to begin the campaign, the warriors spent their time eating and drinking at British expense. Forbes was beside himself. It seemed to him that either the Indians never came, or they came too early. He aimed his anger directly at Atkins and Johnson, who, understanding their own limited authority, left Forbes and his officers—most of whom knew or cared little about native customs—to deal with these difficult allies themselves. By late May Forbes, who by this time was showing serious signs of the "Cholick" that would soon make him a virtual invalid, wrote, "The Cherokees are now no longer with us."[16]

Left without Indian allies, Forbes pushed ahead with his mixed force of seven thousand regulars and provincials. The regular core consisted of a

battalion of Royal Americans and Colonel Archibald Montgomery's Highlanders, while the provincial levees were mainly Virginia and Pennsylvania regiments.[17] Washington commanded one of the Virginia regiments.
When not dickering with local authorities over men and supplies, Forbes
spent his time pouring over maps and listening to locals, Washington included, advise him about the best route west. For strategic and personal
reasons, Virginians argued for following Braddock's road. Forbes was not
convinced. Flooding streams, lack of forage, and generally rough terrain
made him reluctant to follow on the same cursed road. The more Washington and his Virginia colleagues urged the old route, the more suspicious
Forbes and Henry Bouquet, his able second in command, grew. After a
tense meeting with Washington, Bouquet told Forbes that he "gained no
satisfaction" and that the Virginians were blind to reason in the matter.[18]
Forbes mapped a new northerly route running west through Pennsylvania
from Raystown via Loyal Hannon and thence to Duquesne. Stunned that
Forbes had chosen the Pennsylvania route, an unusually emotional Washington exclaimed, "All is lost. All is lost, by Heavens."[19]

Bouquet went ahead with an advance party while Forbes assembled the
main army at Carlisle. The general was determined not to repeat Braddock's
fatal mistake of pushing forward on too thin a line, too far ahead of support.
Methodical and efficient, Forbes laid out his wilderness march in a textbook
manner, carefully following the doctrine of the "protected advance." At
roughly forty-mile intervals (a two-day march) supply depots were erected
and secured. From these places men and matériel could be hurried forward,
or if misfortune should befall, they could provide refuges to which the army
might withdraw and re-form. Loyal Hannon, the last major post before
Duquesne, was the key staging point. As soon as it was ready to receive
Forbes's men, he planned to concentrate the main army there and then
launch the final attack against Duquesne, about fifty miles distant.[20]

By August, however, Forbes's personal condition had greatly deteriorated. "I eat nothing," he told Richard Peters, secretary to the Pennsylvania council.[21] So incapacitated that he could neither march nor sit on a
horse, the general was carried by his orderlies on a litter, from which he
issued a blizzard of orders attending to the most minute details.

* * *

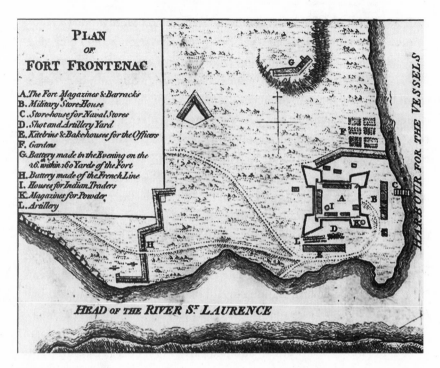

Plan of Fort Frontenac

Forbes would have preferred to have Indian assistance, but since that was not possible, neutralizing them became a priority. In this effort he sought the help of the Quakers. Although they were despised by many in the colony for their dissenting ways and refusal to take up arms, Pennsylvania's Quakers had a long tradition of fair dealing with the Indians. Whether Forbes cared about "fair dealing" is uncertain; nonetheless, he was quite willing to join with the Friends if they could assist him in pacifying the tribes.[22] In June, as his army prepared to march west, Forbes had met with Pennsylvania's deputy governor, William Denny, and others, including Israel Pemberton, a leading Quaker, to make his point that overtures had to be made to the Ohio Indians.[23] With Pemberton's support Forbes got his way, and two messengers—Christian Frederick Post, a Moravian missionary; and Charles Thomson, a Presbyterian schoolmaster—headed west to talk with the legendary Delaware Teedyuscung.

Aging, overweight, and reputed to drink too much, Teedyuscung remained one of the most remarkable men of eighteenth-century America.[24]

No eastern tribe suffered more from European oppression than the Delaware; nor did they escape persecution from their northern neighbors, the Iroquois, who called the Delaware "women" and lusted after their lands. Caught between their own kin and the invading Europeans, the Delaware were pushed constantly about. Teedyuscung experienced all of this turmoil. Born near present-day Trenton, New Jersey, he and his family were pushed west by the expanding settlements. They finally settled at the forks of the Delaware River, where his father led the village of Pocopoco. Near that village Teedyuscung witnessed one of the most outrageous Indian land swindles in American history: the Delaware Walking Purchase.[25]

In 1686 William Penn had negotiated a land cession with the Delaware. The terms were deliberately vague and stipulated that the boundary of the grant was to be the distance a man could walk in a day and a half—about forty miles. More than half a century later, in 1737, Penn's land-hungry successors renegotiated the agreement using the same "one and a half day walk" measure. This time, however, the English purchasers prepared a route and hired a long-distance runner. By the end of the day and a half, he had covered more than sixty-six miles. After a few more "adjustments," the English were able to grab up twelve hundred square miles. When the Delaware protested, the English sought help from the Iroquois, who, in order to curry favor with their allies and enlarge their own empire, obligingly forced their "brothers" off the disputed lands.

Although he styled himself "king of the Delaware," Teedyuscung had no ancestral right to leadership. His skill was in his ability to balance among Delaware, Iroquois, French, and English. Amid a people who valued oratory, Teedyuscung was a star. Like Pitt in Parliament, he could spellbind an audience with his eloquence, passion, wit, and sarcasm. In 1750 Teedyuscung, without abandoning his own roots, delivered himself and his family to be baptized at the Moravian Christian mission at Gnadenhutten. A few years later he made another political shift to broaden his base of friends: He allied himself with the Iroquois. As the French made their move into the Ohio Valley, Teedyuscung sidled up to them as well. In the violent days following Braddock's defeat, he led his people to war against the British, and for several months Teedyuscung and his warriors ravaged the Pennsylvania frontier. But they never forgot that neither the French nor the English held Indian interests dear.

Post's mission to the Indians went well. They listened to their trusted friend and agreed to gather to hear what the English had to say. In October 1758, all the principals met at Easton, Pennsylvania. At least thirteen of the eastern nations, including all the Iroquois, were present, as were Pemberton, Post, and George Croghan, representing William Johnson. Teedyuscung also attended, but in the presence of the powerful Iroquois his influence and future were in grave doubt. By coming to meet with the English, the Indians left no doubt that their French connection was broken. For the moment at least, they sought an accommodation in return for their support. During these negotiations Teedyuscung and the Delaware took the biggest loss. They had hoped their claim to lands in Pennsylvania's Wyoming Valley would be recognized, but neither the Iroquois nor the English were willing to do so. Instead the Iroquois, with English support, lorded it over the Delaware, treating them as tenants on their own land. Riding high, the Iroquois asked the Pennsylvanians to pledge that native lands west of the Alleghenies would remain free from white encroachment, which was agreed.[26]

While messengers were scurrying about the frontier arranging the Easton conference, Forbes continued his advance toward Duquesne. By early September a large advance party of fifteen hundred men under Bouquet had reached Loyal Hannon. Forbes's concern with securing the march, however, had come at a high cost in time. Many in his column, Washington included, feared that it was too late in the season to move on Duquesne and that the army would have to go into winter quarters. Loyal Hannon was the likely spot for the encampment.[27] As Bouquet worked to prepare Loyal Hannon for Forbes's arrival, he discovered the consequences of being without the protection of a screen of Indian scouts. Work parties sent out to gather timber and find forage for the animals came back bloodied by marauding parties of French and Indians, directed from Duquesne. Ambushing work parties in the woods caused a stir in the camp, and led Bouquet to make a serious tactical error. Frustrated at the slowness of the advance and stung by the frequent ambushes, he agreed to a rash proposal from Major James Grant of Montgomery's Highlanders.[28]

Grant offered to take 500 chosen men on a quick march to Duquesne. Bouquet intended it as a reconnaissance in force, but the major, an officer known to have a "thirst for fame," likely had more ambitious plans in mind. Rumors were circulating in camp that the French were weak, and Grant saw an opportunity to grab the glory for capturing Duquesne. Bouquet encouraged Grant's ambition by giving him an additional 250 men.

Duquesne's commander, François-Marie Le Marchand de Lignery, was a battle-hardened, forty-year veteran of la Marine. He had been at Braddock's defeat, and for his valor the king presented him with the cross of St. Louis. When his Indian scouts brought word of Grant's advance, the captain laid plans for an ambush, and Grant played right into his hands. By September 14, after a quick and easy march, Grant was about a mile from the fort. He broke his force into three separate detachments and advanced with bagpipes swirling. Lignery sprang the trap. His native allies and troops swooped down on Grant's men, whose three-pronged attack cracked, "and the Gentlemen were beat by detail."[29] Grant lost three hundred men, more than a third of his force. The rest fled back toward Loyal Hannon. Among the casualties was the major himself, who was taken prisoner and quickly shipped off to Montreal.[30]

Despite his victory, Lignery's situation remained serious. He was running short of provisions, and Bradstreet's capture of Frontenac made it virtually certain that he could expect no new supplies. Desperate to force a decision, and perhaps take the supplies being gathered at Loyal Hannon, Lignery decided to attack. The French struck on October 12.

Bouquet had gone back to the post at Stoney Creek, leaving Colonel James Burd, a Pennsylvania officer, in command. At about eleven in the morning twelve hundred French drew within range of Loyal Hannon's entrenchments and began firing. Over the next four hours they made three unsuccessful assaults. During the night they probed around the edges of the encampment, picking off unwary sentries. By morning, however, they withdrew back toward Duquesne.[31]

Grant's disaster and Lignery's futile attack on Loyal Hannon shocked Forbes, but it did not deter him. On November 2 he arrived at the fort in his litter to take personal command. Ten days later Lignery hit them again, but with no greater success.[32] Approaching winter put Forbes in a difficult situation. Unless he advanced immediately against Duquesne, he knew his army would have to go into winter quarters and wait for spring. Fort Ligonier (Forbes's new name for Loyal Hannon) was crammed with supplies,

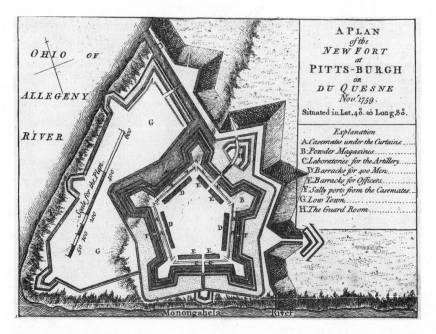

Plan of Fort Duquesne

including artillery.[33] Forbes's logistical triumph was now his tactical burden. When the general asked the post engineer, Captain Harry Gordon, if the fort could withstand an assault, Gordon replied that an enemy with cannon would have little trouble reducing the wooden walls to splinters.[34] Forbes could not risk allowing the huge supply depot to fall into enemy hands. Such a disaster would negate all the advantages secured from the fall of Frontenac. Forbes turned bold and decided to attack.

On November 18, twenty-five hundred picked men, marching without tents or heavy baggage, and trailing only a light train of artillery, set out from Loyal Hannon. Daylight was growing shorter, and even though there were only a few of them the guns and wagons slowed the column. On the twenty-third the column halted a dozen miles east of Duquesne.

Lignery understood that his situation was hopeless. At the news of Forbes's approach, his Indian allies packed their spoils and returned home. The commander's standing orders were to not surrender, but soldiers were too scarce in New France to sacrifice them in a hopeless cause. Lignery prepared to evacuate. He sent one hundred men north to Venango and another one hundred down the Ohio to the Illinois country. The remainder went to work setting demolition charges. On the evening of the twenty-fourth, as Forbes made camp only a few miles away, he heard a dull roar and saw smoke. He sent a light-horse detachment to reconnoiter. They returned with the news that Duquesne was a smoldering ruin and there was no sign of the French. The next morning, as Forbes later reported, "[I] took Possession with my little Army." The British had retaken the forks of the Ohio. In honor of the minister Forbes christened the place Pittsburgh.[35]

Although the French threat was gone, the approaching winter was a worry. The ruined fort could never provide adequate shelter for Forbes's army, so the general decided to leave a few hundred men under Bouquet to garrison and rebuild the post while he led the main body back to Philadelphia. That he had managed to survive the campaign was a miracle. After lingering painfully, Forbes died in Philadelphia on March 11, 1759.

Reports of Forbes's triumph came on the heels of news about the fall of another French bastion. Jeffrey Amherst had taken Louisbourg. Amherst was the well-connected protégé of Lord Ligonier, who referred to him as "my dear pupil." He entered the king's service in 1735 as an ensign in the prestigious First Regiment of Foot guards. During the War of the Austrian Succession Amherst spent most of his time in Germany serving as an aide-de-camp to the duke of Cumberland, ending the war with the rank of lieutenant colonel. In 1756 Amherst returned to Germany as a "commissary" to Hessian troops, handling finance and logistics.[36]

Although Amherst had never commanded a campaign, politics and connections counted for more than experience, and Ligonier persuaded Pitt that his "dear pupil" was the right man to lead the Louisbourg expedition. His youth and inexperience made him suspect to the king, and it took more than one visit to the royal "closet" to persuade His Majesty that an officer barely forty years old and without any battlefield command experience ought to take charge of an army bound against the French forces in Louisbourg. The king finally consented, granting Amherst the rank of major general in North America.

Rarely in any war does a soldier believe that his government has provided enough support for him to win in the field. Those who went to Louisbourg were no exception. In reality, however, Pitt was lavish in providing support for the attack. He assigned three brigadiers to assist Amherst: Charles Lawrence, Edward Whitmore, and James Wolfe. At the time of their appointment Lawrence and Whitmore were veterans already serving in North America, while Wolfe was in London. Command of the sea forces for the expedition was in the hands of "Wry-necked Dick," Admiral Edward Boscawen.[37] Whether by chance, providence, or plan, Pitt had brought together a very able group of commanders.

James Wolfe was the most junior of the brigadiers. The son of Lieutenant General Edward Wolfe, the young colonel knew Amherst and most likely received his new appointment through his friend's influence. He had served with Cumberland, had been at Culloden, and for a time was posted to Germany. Thus far his career had been fairly ordinary, and there was little to elevate him above his peers.[38] During Whitmore's half a century in the army he had seen service in North America, Europe, Scotland, and the West Indies. Wolfe did not like him and described him as a man of "no health nor constitution for such business as we are going on; he never was a soldier."[39] As was often the case with young Wolfe, his opinion was rash and unfounded.

Charles Lawrence was also highly experienced. A career officer, he had been the person most directly responsible for pacifying Nova Scotia since 1749. As part of that effort he had directed the rounding up and deportation of the Acadians. As a reward for his "good work" he was made governor of Nova Scotia in 1756.[40]

Pitt hoped to open this campaign no later than April 20, 1758, but as usual affairs went awry. Spring arrived late, and foul weather delayed the gathering of men, ships, and material at the Halifax rendezvous. On March 19, while Boscawen was still at sea with the main force, Sir Charles Hardy, his second in command, arrived at Halifax with eight ships of the line and two frigates. Hardy understood the absolute necessity of blockading Louisbourg. He turned his squadron around in less than a week and headed northeast to intercept any French vessels bound for Louisbourg.[41]

The appearance of Hardy's ships off Cape Breton offered no surprise to the chevalier de Drucour, governor of Isle Royale and the senior officer at Louisbourg.[42] In the nearly four years he had been at the fortress, Louisbourg had been under a constant threat and intermittent enemy blockade.

Its harbor, once one of the busiest trading centers in North America, was nearly empty save the few warships and transports riding at anchor that had been lucky enough to evade British patrols. Drucour's garrison numbered approximately 3,500 soldiers reinforced by an equal number of sailors and marines impressed from the ships at anchor in the harbor, as well as several hundred Indians and militia. Louisbourg also contained a civilian population of merchants, civil servants, and their families numbering at least 1,000.[43] From its founding Louisbourg's face was set to the sea, and so were its defenses. Even in peace its land connections to the rest of Canada were long and difficult. A simple road ran from the fortress south across the narrow Strait of Canso and westerly to the isthmus at Chignecto. From that point via a variety of rough paths and small streams, travelers made their way over several hundred miles toward the St. Lawrence River. What geography made difficult the British made impossible when they captured Beauséjour and Gaspereau, severing Louisbourg's overland route to the St. Lawrence.

The year before, the presence of the Comte du Bois de la Motte's fleet in the harbor had persuaded Holbourne and Loudoun to abandon their attack. Having once been saved by the navy, Drucour looked again to that quarter for salvation.

But the Admiralty was determined to thwart the French navy. To prevent reinforcements from reaching North America, Anson would keep the French fleet boxed in at home. In the Mediterranean, Admiral Henry Osborne's blockaders kept a careful watch on the French fleet at Toulon. In late February 1758 Duquesne, late governor of Canada, broke out from Toulon and sailed toward Cartagena, hoping to rendezvous with Admiral Sabran La Clue. Once joined, La Clue and Duquesne intended to dash through the Straits of Gibraltar and make for Louisbourg. On the afternoon of February 28 Osborne's squadron caught up with Duquesne, and by evening the squadron was dispersed and the marquis was a prisoner. The remnants of the French Mediterranean squadron scurried to take refuge at Cartagena and Toulon.[44]

The French fared no better in the Atlantic. At the very moment that Osborne was writing dispatches about his victory over Duquesne, Edward Hawke was sailing under orders instructing him to intercept Canada-bound squadrons reported to be assembling at the Atlantic ports of Brest,

Rochefort, and Bordeaux. In early April Hawke found his quarry in Basque Roads near the isle of Aix. Caught unaware, the French made a desperate attempt to escape up the Charente River to Rochefort. All was chaos; ships ran aground as desperate crews hurried to dump stores and cannon overboard, hoping to lighten and refloat their vessels before the British burned them. In the late spring a few lucky French vessels managed to slip past British patrols into Louisbourg, bringing men and supplies, and also news of the unhappy events in the Mediterranean and Basque Roads. From these reports Drucour knew that further help was unlikely to reach him soon.

Drucour prepared for a siege. He called in the small garrisons from the outlying parts of Isle Royale, while Louis Franquet, his chief engineer, did what he could to reinforce the fortress's crumbling walls. In the harbor ten warships mounting nearly five hundred guns were available to aid in the defense. Their commodore, the Marquis des Gouttes, demanded that Drucour allow him to run the British blockade and escape with his squadron to sea. Taken aback, Drucour instead ordered Gouttes to prepare his ships to fight from their moorings.[45]

Boscawen arrived at Halifax on May 19. He waited patiently for Amherst, but aware that he had already fallen more than a full month behind Pitt's schedule, he decided that he could delay no longer. On May 29 he ordered the fleet under way, leaving behind an urgent request for Amherst to hurry and join him. Where was Amherst? Boscawen was mystified. The general had left Portsmouth aboard HMS *Dublin* more than a month ahead of him, and yet there was no sign of him.

Almost as soon as *Dublin* had cleared Portsmouth harbor, it had encountered stiff easterly winds. Its captain, George Rodney, did all he could to tack west, but he was having little luck. When the lookout called out a strange sail to leeward, they were near the coast of France. Rodney took chase of the stranger, which, after pretending to be British, hoisted French colors and identified itself as the French East Indiaman *Monmartel*. It put up a bold fight, but its guns were no match for *Dublin*'s thunderous broadsides. Rodney's prize was bound from Mauritius to Nantes with a rich cargo of coffee and tropical woods. Rodney and his men—not including Amherst and his staff, who were only passengers—stood to reap a tidy fortune provided they could carry *Monmartel* to a safe port for adjudication and sale. Despite the fact that they were already at least two weeks late crossing the Atlantic, and that every day lost was one day less for the campaign in Canada, Rodney ordered *Dublin* to escort *Monmartel* to the Spanish port of Vigo. Two more weeks were needed in Vigo to settle affairs. Finally, *Dublin* laid a course for Halifax.[46] Just as Boscawen was clearing the harbor and rounding on to a northerly course *Dublin* sailed into sight. The admiral hove to long enough to welcome the general aboard his flagship, *Namur*. Amherst apologized for his tardiness, officially laying the blame on "contrary Winds and Fog," and the fleet was once again bound for Louisbourg.[47]

From *Namur*'s high quarterdeck Jeffrey Amherst gazed over the largest combined force England had ever dispatched overseas. Everywhere he looked sails billowed and bluff bows cut the waves as the fleet scudded on before a favorable breeze. Forty men-of-war mounting more than eighteen hundred guns escorting nearly 150 transports filled the horizon. Nearly fourteen thousand soldiers shared space with huge quantities of equipment, stores, and munitions that had been crammed aboard for the short voyage. Aside from four companies of New England rangers, the entire force was made up of regulars. Amherst had little use for provincials.[48]

On June 2, the van of the British fleet drew near Louisbourg. While Boscawen's frigates scouted seaward, lest the fleet be surprised by a French attack, the main body entered Gabarus Bay, three miles south of the fortress. As is usual along this rugged coast, rain, fog, and running surf made it impossible to immediately approach land. The plan agreed to in Halifax called for the landing force to be divided into three divisions: Red led by General Wolfe, Blue under General Lawrence, and White commanded by General Whitmore. Kennington Cove, with its rocky, sloping beach, was the preferred landing site. All was in readiness, except the weather.[49]

For five days Boscawen's ships tugged on their anchor cables in the bay. The admiral sent shallow draft vessels closer in to reconnoiter by fire, trying to tease out and fix the French positions. Franquet had prepared trenches and erected batteries overlooking the beaches. Nearly two thousand troops hunkered down in these positions, ready for the British assault. While the British jogged off shore waiting for better weather, Drucour welcomed some unexpected reinforcements. On May 2 four ships had managed to escape from Rochefort under the command of Commodore Du Chaffault de Besne, carrying the second battalion of the Cambis regiment. Du Chaffault had orders for Louisbourg, but as he neared the coast he learned that the British were present in force, and so he sailed west about fifty miles and landed at the tiny village of Port Dauphin. When Drucour heard of their arrival, he ordered the troops to march overland and the ships to sail for Quebec. The troops arrived at noon on June 6.[50]

The next day began with the usual thick fog and heavy surf, but by afternoon the fog had lifted, the seas calmed, and the sun shone. Amherst decided to gamble that the weather would hold for at least another day. During the afternoon and night barges were brought alongside the transports. In the morning, at the first glint of daylight, soldiers climbed over the sides and crammed into the landing craft. The French held their fire until the boats were within range and then opened on them with artillery. Despite attempts to provide covering fire by the fleet, the French cannon drove the boats back while a fresh breeze churned the waters of Gabarus Bay into a heavy chop. In the midst of this looming disaster, Wolfe ordered his coxswains to steer left. By chance they found a gap in the French defenses. A

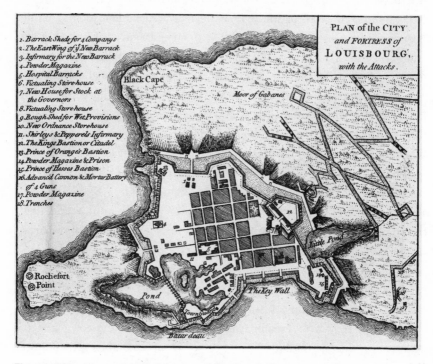

The siege of Louisbourg, June 8–July 26, 1758. (On this map, north is at the bottom.)

boatload of light infantry scrambled ashore and secured a small beachhead. Within moments other boats followed, expanding the landing site.

French grenadiers rushed to plug the growing hole, but it was too late. British soldiers poured ashore, and the French defenders, fearing that their retreat might be cut off, withdrew toward Louisbourg. The British followed but halted when they came within range of the fortress's cannon. By noon four to five thousand British troops were ashore. The siege had begun.[51]

As Amherst gazed over Louisbourg, he had little doubt that he could take it, and the best hope for a quick victory was to have Boscawen force the harbor. This, however, the admiral was unwilling to do—the risk, in his judgment, being too great. Boscawen's reluctance is understandable, for once inside the harbor the British ships would have to endure close and heavy fire from the guns of the fortress. The army took several days to land all its equipment and fortify the camp, but by the twelfth Amherst was ready to begin the siege in earnest. He sent Wolfe with fourteen hundred men to seize Light House Point on the north side of the harbor, while his engineers went to work building three redoubts on the western (landward) side of the fortress. Frequent firefights broke out between probing infantrymen while French cannon did what they could to disrupt British siege operations. At the mouth of the harbor French guns from the island battery poured fire on Wolfe's men at Light House Point.

As the British noose tightened, French morale eroded. To encourage the men, each day Madame Drucour climbed the parapets to fire three cannon at the British. Amherst, the "officer and gentleman," recognized the lady's bravery, and he sent a pair of pineapples to her as a gesture of admiration. She returned the general's beau geste by sending over several bottles of fine champagne.[52]

The conflict turned more serious on June 19 when all the British batteries, more than seventy guns, opened fire. For weeks thereafter the British crashed tons of iron onto the French. Walls crumbled, buildings were demolished and burned. Out in the harbor Gouttes's warships took heavy fire. Early in the afternoon of July 21 a lucky British mortar shot arched up from Light House Point and plunged through the deck of the seventy-four-gun *L'Entreprenant*, one of the largest vessels in the squadron, and set it afire. Fanned by a stiff breeze, flames licked up the rigging and spread to two

Jeffrey Amherst

nearby ships. *L'Entreprenant* blew apart, scattering its splintered remains all the way to the fortress.

On the landward side Amherst's engineers dug their approaches closer and closer to Louisbourg's walls. Drucour's garrison was exhausted. On July 23 at ten in the evening British hot shot plunged through the roof of the King's Bastion and set it ablaze. The Bastion was the largest building in North America, and its loss eroded what little hope lingered among the French defenders. Two days later Boscawen took advantage of a cloaking fog and sent in a cutting-out party that destroyed the last two enemy warships. Now that there was nothing to stand in his way, the admiral prepared to force the harbor. It was not necessary. On the morning of the twenty-sixth the guns fell silent as French and British officers met to parlay.

Contrary to the spirit of pineapples and wine, Amherst turned stern over the discussion of surrender. Given his brave defense, Drucour had every reason to expect the "honors of war." Perhaps because of the memory of William Henry, Amherst flatly rejected the French request, telling Drucour his men would be prisoners of war and that as such he expected them to surrender all their arms, equipment, and battle ensigns. He gave him one hour to reply.

Amherst's demands sent Drucour and his officers into a rage. They vowed to fight to the end, but sounder heads prevailed to protect the hundreds of civilians, many of them women and children, and the wounded. Drucour accepted the humiliating terms, whereas the men of the Cambis regiment broke their muskets and burned their colors rather than hand them over to the British.[53]

As the rest of the garrison laid down their arms, Amherst made preparations to send them back to France. On the first of August he received the disturbing news from Ticonderoga. Fearing that Montcalm might advance south, he dispatched several regiments to New York and made plans to return to Boston. This unexpected development, plus the lateness of the season, made any move on Quebec impossible.[54] But there was still enough time to deliver a few more blows. The general sent Colonel Andrew Rollo to take Prince Edward Island and round up more Acadians for deportation. Some were refugees from the previous cleansing around Fundy. Once again they were torn from their homes and tossed aboard ships.

Amherst gave Wolfe an assignment as well. He ordered the young brigadier to ravage the Gaspé Peninsula. Flushed with victory and eager to move on to greater things, Wolfe thought this despoiling mission was beneath his dignity. He also dreaded being back at sea. He wrote to his mother that he would rather "besiege a Place than pass 4 weeks at sea." He was in an even fouler mood when he wrote to his father that he was on his way "to rob the fishermen of their nets and to burn their hutts."[55]

On August 28 Wolfe sailed to the Gaspé Peninsula with three regiments, escorted by a small squadron commanded by Sir Charles Hardy. As the first troops disembarked at the fishing settlement of Perce, Wolfe told them that if they found so much as a musket they were to put the town to the sword. Homes, fishing vessels, barns, and hundreds of quintals of dried cod went up in smoke. Terrified fishermen and farmers took to the woods. Captain Thomas Bell, one of his officers, noted that they had "left the miserable inhabitants in the woods destitute and deprived of everything." "For our honor," he lamented, "we ought to have proceeded differently."[56]

By the end of September Wolfe and Hardy were back at Louisbourg.

Thoroughly tired of his stay in North America and yearning to be home, Wolfe took advantage of Boscawen's offer to carry him across in *Namur*. Before he left he wrote to Amherst, who had moved his winter headquarters to New York: "If any understanding is determined upon in the River St. Lawrence I should be very glad to return in the Spring. If not I should endeavour to join the Army in Germany."[57] After a fast but miserable passage of a month, Wolfe, seasick as usual, arrived at Portsmouth on November 1.

(9)

Quebec Besieged

If you presume to send down any more fire-rafts, they shall be made
fast to the two transports in which the Canadian prisoners are confined
in order that they may perish by your own base invention.

—Wolfe to Montcalm, July 28, 1759

Despite Wolfe's parting remarks to Amherst about returning to serve in America, the young colonel (his rank as brigadier was confined to America) truly longed for a command in Germany. He was certain that service on the Continent promised more glory than he could ever achieve in the wilderness of North America. Cavalry was his first choice, "because nature ha[d] given [him] good eyes, and a warmth of temper to follow the first impressions."[1]

Wolfe's desire to be in Germany reflected a dramatic change in the military situation on the Continent. Humiliated by his son's concessions at Klosterseven, George II sought and found a way to dissociate himself from Cumberland's agreement, claiming that the French had failed to live up to their part of the bargain by not withdrawing from conquered lands. Whatever the validity of the claim, it was sufficient to justify renewed British participation, which was particularly pleasing to Frederick. In November 1757 England agreed to send troops and money as part of a reconstituted army to be commanded by Prince Ferdinand.

Ferdinand labored during the waning months of 1757 to reorganize his army and make it ready for the spring campaigning season. The plan was for Ferdinand to hold the west against the French while Frederick concentrated on the Austrians and Russians in the east. Although they both paid a high price on the battlefield, each managed to hold their foes at bay and even return some victories. Their success put additional pressure on Pitt to send help. The minister loathed the notion of sending almost anything to Germany, but he recognized that Ferdinand and Frederick were performing a notable service by tying down thousands of French soldiers who might otherwise be sent to Canada. For a modest investment in men and money, Pitt cashed a sizable dividend. In July 1758 he agreed to the posting of six cavalry and six infantry regiments to Ferdinand's army. Wolfe yearned to be part of this "glorious reenforcement."

But Pitt had his own plans for Wolfe. With Amherst he had a logistical genius—a methodical general who had proven that he knew how to feed, supply, and move an army. In Wolfe he found a tactician and daring combat commander who could move fast and strike hard.

Amherst's mission for 1759 was to march north from his Albany headquarters, seize Ticonderoga and Crown Point, take control of Lake Champlain, and then move down the Richelieu to the St. Lawrence. Simultaneous with this attack another smaller expedition under Brigadier General John Prideaux was ordered to move against Fort Niagara. By late summer Pitt expected Amherst to have captured Montreal and be on his way to Quebec, where, if all went well, he would link with a second force, which had advanced on the city from the north via Louisbourg and the St. Lawrence River. Pitt selected Wolfe to command this force.

To attack Quebec from the north required transporting a combined land and naval force on a voyage of nearly nine hundred miles, one-third of it running up the St. Lawrence River.[2] Logistical support was limited, and so was time. Ice often formed on the river in October and stayed until April. Wolfe could not count on Canada's harsh environment granting him more than twelve weeks to complete the campaign.[3] But weather was only part of the problem. Even in the navigable season the river was treacherous. Fogs, currents, dramatic tides, and uncharted shoals made the St. Lawrence a graveyard for the unwary. In 1711 a British expedition led by Sir Hovenden Walker and bound against Quebec had rounded the Gaspé and entered the river only to be wrapped tightly in fog. Within hours several vessels grounded and wrecked, and more than nine hundred men drowned. Walker abandoned the venture, came about, and headed for home.[4] Since the days of Walker's debacle the river had not grown kinder; nor had the British learned more about its navigation.

Picking Wolfe was a daring stroke, but it was only part of Pitt's even bolder strategy. For the second year in a row England would launch massive assaults on Canada. Newcastle and others were deeply troubled, muttering to one another that Canada was as much an obsession of Pitt's as Hanover was to the king.

In France the political wheels at Versailles had taken a new turn. On November 1, 1758, the duc de Choiseuil became minister of foreign affairs. A favorite of the king's mistress, Madame de Pompadour, Choiseuil had recently returned to Paris from Vienna, where he had been serving as ambassador and had successfully scripted the diplomatic coup that joined Austria and France against Prussia. Choiseuil understood that England's true strength lay in its deep financial resources. Despite Newcastle's shortcomings as a manager of foreign affairs, in finance he had few equals.[5] Financial stability, however, rested on the ability of the government to borrow money at decent rates. Rates, in turn, depended upon the government's ability to repay its debt in a timely and orderly fashion. Shake the national faith, and interest rates would rise, while bankers would grow timid. If England ran short of money, Frederick would lose his milch cow, and Pitt would be unable to support costly overseas expeditions. Choiseuil's strategy was to alarm the bankers, and to achieve his goal he revived a plan to invade England.

Regiments of French soldiers marched to the ports and prepared to embark. Thousands of carpenters went to work assembling flat-bottomed invasion barges, while skeptical French admirals tried to figure out how they could protect a channel crossing under the very noses of the Royal Navy. Since Choiseuil's strategy was to divert and panic the English, the French made little secret about their invasion plans. French agents passed on exaggerated reports to credulous English officials, who spread them throughout the kingdom. London newspapers were filled with near hysterical accounts of French preparations. Coffeehouses echoed with rumors. Hapless militia were summoned to duty, while coast watchers scanned the Channel looking for signs of the enemy armada. In London invasion jitters infected the cabinet.

In the midst of this alarm Pitt did not waver. Despite enormous pressure to reduce overseas commitments and strengthen the home island, he
would not back away from his all-out goal of taking Canada. He had, he
said, faith in Lord Anson and the Royal Navy to stop the French from ever
crossing the Channel.

Pitt was disappointed that Wolfe had returned to England. Although he had
yet to inform the colonel of his plans for him, Pitt had intended that Wolfe
remain in America over the winter so that the Quebec campaign could get
off to an early start. When he learned that Wolfe was in London, he began
to have doubts about the young colonel. As soon as Wolfe heard of Pitt's
unhappiness, he rushed off a note to assure him that he was totally unaware of the minister's desire for him to stay in Canada, and that he had
"no objection to serving in America, and particularly in the river St.
Lawrence."[6] Wolfe's apologetic note resulted in a summons to Whitehall.
Reassured by the young colonel's vigor and intelligence, Pitt decided to
defy the claims of seniority. He arranged that by the king's order Wolfe
would command the Quebec expedition. Wolfe wasted no time, and within
a few days he was peppering the ministry with requests for men, matériel,
and transport.

The success of his mission hinged on controlling the St. Lawrence to
block French ships from coming to Quebec's assistance and to provide safe
passage for his army. Wolfe told Amherst, "Let the Fleet carry us up and we
will find employment."[7] He was not convinced, however, that the Royal Navy
was up to the task, and when he learned that Rear Admiral Philip Durrell was
to be second in command of the naval force, with special responsibility for
the blockade, he was filled with even more doubt. Wolfe knew Durrell and
disliked him. The admiral had served under Boscawen and Holbourne and
with Wolfe at Louisbourg. When the senior commanders returned home in
late 1758, the Admiralty left Durrell at Halifax with firm instructions to move
in the spring as early as possible to block the St. Lawrence. In Wolfe's words,
Durrell was "vastly unequal to the weight of the business."[8]

If Durrell's appointment disappointed Wolfe, the posting of Admiral
Charles Saunders to overall command of the naval force offered fair recompense. Saunders had been with Anson on his famous voyage around the

James Wolfe

world, and he enjoyed a high reputation as an aggressive, if taciturn, commander. He was, in Walpole's words, "that brave statue. . . . No man said less, or deserved more."[9] Saunders's modesty notwithstanding, the admiral also wielded political clout, since he served as comptroller of the navy and sat as a member of Parliament for Hedon in Yorkshire. The most junior flag officer was Charles Holmes. Like Durrell, Holmes had spent several years on the North American station, having sailed there early in the war with Boscawen and later commanded a blocking squadron that had attempted, and failed, to shut up Louisbourg.

Wolfe had little say over the appointment of sea officers; if he had, it is likely that neither Durrell nor Holmes would have been on station. He was far less reticent over the issue of army appointments. No question was more important to him than the choice of his subordinates. Here, as he exerted his influence, Wolfe encountered politics, first at the hands of His Majesty and then from his patrons, Pitt and Ligonier.

Colonel Guy Carleton and Wolfe were old friends. Barely a year previous he had tried to get Carleton a command on the Louisbourg expedition, but the king "refused Carleton leave to go."[10] The king's objections were petty and personal. A courtier whispered to him that Carleton had uttered some unkind remarks about Hanover, a slight George II never forgot, and for this the colonel was punished. Despite Carleton's unpopularity at court, Wolfe was determined to press his friend's cause. He presented Carleton's name for quartermaster general in the Quebec expedition. The king rejected him. Wolfe enlisted Ligonier's support, telling his superior in a somewhat untoward tone, "[Unless you] would give me the assistance of such officers as I should name . . . he [the king] would do me a great kindness to appoint some other person to the chief direction."[11] Perhaps seeing in the impetuousness of the young Wolfe his own reflection, the old general twice appealed to the king on Carleton's behalf, but was rebuffed. More anxious to appease the young colonel than to curry favor with an obstinate monarch, Pitt himself wrote to George II "that in order to render any General completely responsible for his conduct, he should be made, as far as possible, inexcusable, if he should fail; and that, consequently, whatever an officer entrusted with a service of confidence requests should be complied with."[12] The king grumbled and signed Carleton's commission.

Pitt's admonition to the king was not one he always followed himself. On at least two occasions Pitt disappointed Wolfe over issues important to the commander: his own rank and the appointment of subordinates. Wolfe was a colonel promoted to the rank of major general, but the higher rank existed only in America. As soon as he finished the business in America and returned home, he would revert to the lower rank. This arrangement was not unusual. Regular officers were often brevetted when commanding in the field, but it was annoying to the proud Wolfe that his promotion was not permanent. He wanted both rank and the money it would bring. He might, however, have let the issue pass with less notice if Pitt hadn't nipped at his authority in a second way.

Wolfe divided his army into three brigades, each to be led by a brigadier.

Like their commander, each brigadier held that rank only in America. Wolfe expected that he would have the right to name these men, and he favored Robert Monckton, James Murray, and Ralph Burton.

As senior brigadier, Monckton took the first brigade. During the War of the Austrian Succession he had served in Germany with Wolfe, and he had also marched with Cumberland to suppress the Jacobite Rebellion led by Bonnie Prince Charlie in 1745–46. In the earliest days of the war Monckton captured Forts Beausejour and Gaspereau. An old hand in Canada, since 1755 he had been serving as lieutenant governor of Nova Scotia. When Wolfe chose him, Monckton was in New York conferring with Amherst in anticipation of taking command in the Carolinas. The posting north was much to his liking.

To Wolfe's great annoyance, command of the second brigade did not go to his choice. Wolfe wanted Ralph Burton, like Monckton, a veteran of the American war. He had been with Braddock at the Monongahela, with Loudoun in New York, and served under Amherst at Louisbourg, where Wolfe had met him. Burton, however, was not Pitt's choice. For political reasons the minister's favor fell on Newcastle's nephew George Townshend, then an unemployed army officer looking for work. A skillful political manipulator, and according to Wolfe's aide Captain Thomas Bell "an excellent Tavern acquaintance," Townshend was infamous for his dripping sarcasm, which he often combined with his talents as a caricaturist to pillory his opponents. Pitt felt obligated to him since Townshend had supported him in Parliament. He was, nonetheless, a troublesome man, and Pitt looked forward to having him out of the country.[13] Since he had gotten most of what he wanted, Wolfe accepted this petty defeat gracefully, and in a restrained letter he welcomed Townshend to his army. Burton joined the expedition with the Forty-eighth Regiment.

While he lost the day with Townshend, Wolfe was pleased that the third brigade went to James Murray. Like Burton, Murray was a comrade in arms from the Louisbourg campaign. He had also served with Wolfe in Scotland and through the ill-fated Rochefort attack. Although the most junior of the three brigadiers, Wolfe viewed Murray as a soldier of "infinite spirit." Others characterized that same "spirit" as "hot headed and impetuous."[14]

Anticipating a siege, Wolfe needed an able artillery commander, and he found one in George Williamson. At age fifty-five, Williamson became the oldest member of Wolfe's staff.[15] Adjutant General Major Isaac Barré served as Wolfe's chief of staff. As large and robust as Wolfe was thin and frail, Barré and his commander had been together at Rochefort. He and Carleton were Wolfe's closest and most loyal friends. In later years, when Barré became the enfant terrible of British politics (and a notable defender of the rights of the American colonies), he remembered Wolfe as that "noble-hearted soldier."[16]

Wolfe valued none of his officers more than Patrick Mackellar, his chief engineer. Mackellar arrived in America with Braddock and survived the Monongahela. He was not so lucky at Oswego, where he was among the prisoners Montcalm trundled off to Quebec. He remained in the city several months under loose confinement, which allowed him considerable leeway to walk about Quebec studying its defenses. Shortly after being exchanged, he returned to England. Blessed with an engineer's eye, a packet of notes, and a good memory, Mackellar drew a detailed map of the city and its defenses for the Board of Ordnance. In 1758 Mackellar joined the Louisbourg expedition as Chief Engineer John Henry Bastide's deputy. When Bastide was wounded, Mackellar took over his duties. Wolfe had been impressed by the engineer's skill, and since Mackellar was the only senior officer to have seen Quebec, his personal and professional knowledge were key to the operation.[17]

By "Secret Instructions," the king ordered Wolfe to get under way from England in time to arrive at Louisbourg no later than April 20, 1759, "if the season will permit."[18] The Admiralty told Saunders to rendezvous with Wolfe at Cape Breton. The combined force was to be on its way up the St. Lawrence by May 7. Pitt promised Wolfe an army of twelve thousand soldiers and a naval armada sufficient to his needs. To ensure that the land force would be ready in a timely way, rather than wait to muster all the troops in England Pitt stripped the garrisons at Halifax, Annapolis, and Louisbourg to provide regular battalions, which he promised would be replaced by provincial levies. In addition, he put Amherst on notice to prepare transport and provisions in New York and Boston.

Wolfe, however, was not satisfied. Beset by his chronic seasickness, he wrote to Amherst while aboard *Neptune* in mid-Atlantic. He complained bitterly about the ministry's lack of support for his expedition. "The Government have fail'd in the most material article which is the Number of Troops." In his estimation too many battalions had been posted to the Champlain route and not enough to the St. Lawrence. He had no faith "that the Militias will get to their posts." Should he fail to take Quebec, he assured Amherst that before he retreated he would "set the Town on fire, . . . and leave famine and desolation behind."[19]

On February 14 the vanguard of a fleet that eventually numbered nearly a quarter of the entire Royal Navy cleared Spithead under the command of Admiral Holmes. Six ships of the line, nine frigates, and sixty transports headed for New York to rendezvous with additional forces gathered there by Amherst. Three days later the main body under Saunders, with Wolfe, left the same port bound for Louisbourg. The plan was for both fleets, plus the expected colonial contingents, to meet at Cape Breton by Pitt's deadline of April 20.

According to Murray, the winter of 1758–59 was "uncommonly severe" in Nova Scotia.[20] Durrell did what he could at Halifax to prepare his vessels to sortie early in the season to blockade the St. Lawrence, but unusually persistent ice made navigation dangerous. The admiral opted to stay snug in port.[21] During the long winter Durrell and his officers spent much of their time debating the naval aspects of the upcoming Quebec campaign. From the perspective of sea officers, they worried chiefly about getting up the St. Lawrence. No officer in the fleet had ever sailed the river, and the only available English chart, which was based on French surveys, was a poor one drawn and published in 1757. They had found several French charts at Louisbourg, but these plotted virtually no information on the river, particularly the 125-mile stretch of water between the Saguenay River and Quebec.

Discussions often took place in the captain's cabin aboard *Pembroke*. Among those at the table was the ship's master, James Cook. Born near Whitby in 1728, Cook spent many years sailing aboard colliers in the Newcastle coal trade. When war broke out in 1755, Cook, moving a few steps ahead of the press gang, decided to volunteer for naval service. He signed on as a seaman, but his skills as a pilot and ship handler advanced him and in May 1759 he was warranted a master and posted to *Pembroke*. As a skilled pilot, Cook was expert at handling ships in treacherous waters.[22]

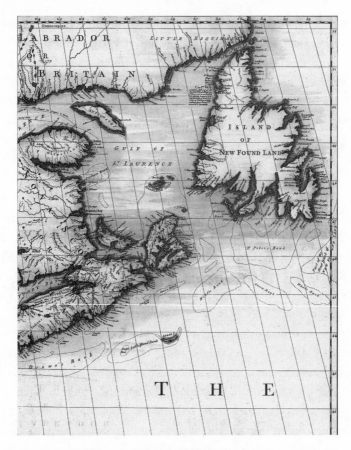

Nova Scotia, Newfoundland, and the Gulf of St. Lawrence

On April 21 Saunders drew within sight of Cape Breton's rocky head-
lands. Despite the season, the ice had yet to leave Louisbourg Harbor. Unable to enter the harbor or anchor in Gabarus Bay, Saunders took his fleet
down the coast to Halifax. Upon entering the harbor, Wolfe was astonished
to see Durrell riding at anchor. "Military affairs that depend upon naval
ones are uncertain" was his terse comment.[23] The memory of Rochefort
must have echoed in his head. Durrell got the message, and three days
after Wolfe's arrival he sailed for the St. Lawrence with ten ships—too late,
however, to prevent French reinforcements from getting through. While
Durrell's ships had been swinging on their winter moorings in Halifax

Harbor, twenty-three French store ships and three frigates cleared Bordeaux and battled their way past dangerous ice floes up the St. Lawrence and arrived at Quebec in early May.[24]

Saunders and Wolfe wasted no time. Less than a week after Durrell's departure Halifax Harbor emptied as warships and transports got under way for the rendezvous at Louisbourg. The weather was raw and cold, and as the ships approached the rugged coast lookouts warned of bobbing ice floes amid the "gloomy air" and pounding surf. At least one transport failed to heed the warning and ran on the rocks.[25] For more than two weeks Wolfe and Saunders waited at Louisbourg while the remainder of the transports and warships from Halifax, Annapolis, Boston, and New York straggled into the anchorage. The admiral and general spent hours conferring. Staffs met and sorted out matters of logistics and transportation. To help in navigation, Saunders "acquired" some Canadian pilots, who, being threatened with hanging, agreed to guide the fleet up the St. Lawrence. Even without the pilots, however, Saunders was confident that his own sailing masters and captains could do the job.

While Saunders and his officers plotted the course to Quebec, Wolfe drilled his soldiers. Instead of the twelve thousand promised by Pitt, the general counted fewer than nine thousand. Contingents promised from America did not materialize, and those that did report, particularly the rangers, were men in whom Wolfe placed little faith.[26] Each day Wolfe's men practiced the demanding task of climbing down the sides of rolling transports into flat-bottomed boats tossing about on the waves. Shore landings were repeated again and again until both the sailors and soldiers mastered the drill. Signal officers and semaphore men memorized and rehearsed dozens of flag combinations used to send orders. On board ship division officers and gun captains put their batteries through endless rounds of practice, while down below, other crewmen checked to make sure that supplies were properly stowed and easily accessible.[27]

Nearly six weeks after Pitt's departure deadline Wolfe and Saunders were ready to sail. On the first of June Wolfe ordered, "The troops to land no more for exercise; the flat-bottomed boats to be hoisted up, that the ships may be ready to sail on the first signal."[28] On the morning of the fourth, three guns were fired from the fortress as a signal to get under way, and the first contingent of the fleet headed for sea. "Weather wet and foggy" read the logs. After giving a wide berth to the tip of Cape Breton, the fleet rounded the Gaspé and by the sixteenth was well within the St. Lawrence at the island of Bic, where it anchored for the night to await news from Durrell. In the morning the frigate *Richmond* hove into sight from upriver delivering news that Durrell had taken the island of Coudres only fifty miles downriver from Quebec, and that he was moving closer to the Île d'Orléans, directly opposite the city. Pushed on by a fair wind, and with his survey vessels in the van sounding the river and buoying the channel, Saunders made his way toward Quebec. For more than a week the fleet crept up the river. On deck the watch kept a keen eye for swirling eddies that might mark hidden rocks and shoals while swatting away hordes of "musketas." Summer thunderstorms swept across the river valley, and on occasion, defiant habitants took shots at survey vessels that prowled too close to shore.

On June 26 the fleet hove to within view of the Île d'Orléans. Captain John Knox of the Forty-third Regiment described the bucolic scene: "Here we entertained with a most agreeable prospect of a delightful country on every side; windmills, water-mills, churches, chapels, and compact farm-houses, all built with stone, and covered, some with wood, others with straw. The lands appear to be every-where well cultivated, and, with the help of my glass, I can discern that they are sowed with flax, wheat, barley, pease, etc and the grounds are enclosed with wooden pales."[29] Ahead of them lay the imposing heights of Quebec City. That night Wolfe issued orders to land on the island, and just before dawn small boats carrying rangers and light infantry assembled in the lee of the frigate *Lowesdorf.* Shallow-draft sloops, with crew standing forward heaving lead lines to sound the water's depth, approached the beach to lay down covering fire. About midnight forty rangers landed to secure the beachhead. As they moved beyond the river edge, they encountered a small force of local militia. After a brief firefight the Canadians disappeared into the woods. There was no other opposition.

At first light Montcalm and his officers looked out over a vast British armada. They watched from the heights of the city as dozens of small boats, their dripping oars flashing in the morning sun, dashed quickly from ships to shore ferrying thousands of men and tons of equipment. The British had arrived, and they were prepared for a siege.[30]

The relief ships that had dared the St. Lawrence in May not only had brought much needed supplies but had also delivered new orders from the king. "His Majesty having been informed of all that occurred last year in Canada" was pleased to promote "the Marquis de Montcalm . . . Lieutenant General of his armies." With his new rank Montcalm stood over Vaudreuil. Perhaps as a consolation to the governor, the king awarded him the Honorary Grand Cross of the Order of St. Louis, commenting, with a bit of unwitting irony, that by this honor "the troops of the Colony [Troupes de la Marine], the farmers, [and] the Indians" will be impressed.[31]

At Quebec Montcalm had soldiers from seven regular battalions totaling nearly four thousand men. Also present were one thousand men of the Troupes de la Marine, and nearly ten thousand militia drawn from the districts of Quebec, Trois-Rivière, and Montreal. Rounding out the force were as many as two thousand sailors and marines drawn from the idle

Brigadier General François de Lévis

ships anchored in the St. Charles River. Mingling about were several hundred Indians whose role was uncertain.[32]

Lévis was Montcalm's second in command. In diplomacy and politics
Lévis was everything that Montcalm was not. While he may have shared his
commander's snobbish disdain for Canadians, he held his temper and his
tongue. When Vaudreuil and Montcalm fell out, it was Lévis to whom they
turned as a go-between. Bougainville was also at Quebec. The year before,
Montcalm had sent him to Paris to make a case for the king to send more
troops. Bougainville was unable to pry any loose. Indeed, in the face of
France's commitments on the Continent, Bougainville's request to Nicolas-
René Berryer, the minister of war, provoked the sarcastic reply "that one
did not try to save the stables when the house was on fire."[33] Etienne-
Guillaume de Senezergues was third in command. Personally brave (allegedly to the point of foolhardiness), he had served with Lévis and was
with him and Montcalm at Ticonderoga, where the general declared him to
be the only senior officer fit to remain in Canada after the hostilities.

Montcalm's chief of engineers, Nicholas Sarrebource de Pontleroy, had
designed the defenses at Ticonderoga. Pontleroy reminded Montcalm that
although Quebec's high bluffs offered protection against assault from the
river side, the city stood open to attack from other points of the compass.
Upriver was particularly troublesome since the ground in that direction,
running along a small east-west ridge called Buttes à Neveau, was actually
high enough to overlook the city's walls. On the other side of the ridge was
an open rolling field known as the Plains of Abraham, after the farmer who
once owned the land. Should an enemy come across the Plains and take the
ridge, it might easily rain shot on the town and breech the walls. Pontleroy
advised that ditches and other hasty outer defenses be erected immediately to keep the enemy at bay in that sector. Montcalm agreed, but with the
British at his gates he had neither sufficient time nor enough men to mend
the flaw. His best hope was that Wolfe would never be able to pass below the
heights, get upriver, then land and advance on him from the south.

Quebec was a two-tiered triangular cake.[34] On the top layer stood the
upper city protected on the land side by a stone wall nearly twenty feet high
and several feet thick. The wall stretched from the edge of the bluff northwest to the steep slope down to the St. Charles River. Mackellar's report

that the wall was unfinished on the side close to the St. Charles was erroneous. Two roads entered the city through the wall at the gates of St. Louis and St. John.

Tucked under the high bluff overlooking the St. Lawrence was the cake's bottom tier: the lower city, la Basse-Ville. Only a few hundred feet wide, this portion of the city lay on an incline between the river and the foot of the high bluff. It was crowded with wharves, warehouses, shops, and the homes of workers. The small church of Notre Dame des Victoires, named in honor of the times when Quebec had been saved from English conquest, was near the center. The lower city was Montcalm's most exposed position, since it was within easy range of cannon from passing ships as well as any

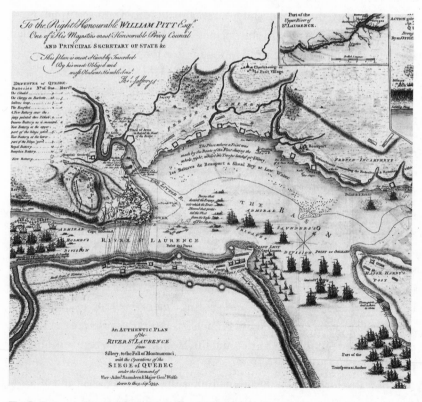

The St. Lawrence River, with Quebec (upper left), the Beauport shore northeast of the city, and the Île d'Orléans (lower right).

land batteries that the enemy might erect across the river. A steep and winding road coiled its way up the face of the escarpment connecting the lower and upper towns.

Montcalm assumed that the British would not risk a direct attack on the city. They might, he thought, attempt to advance upriver and attack from the south, as Pontleroy feared, but that would pose heavy risks. Vessels moving upstream would have to pass directly under Quebec's guns while coping with the St. Lawrence's strong currents. Such a maneuver would have to be timed to the tides, thus eliminating any chance of surprise, and since favorable tides and currents would only be available for a few hours each day, the attacker would most likely have to divide his force for passage, thus risking defeat. Even if an upriver landing could be effected, once in position at the top of the bluff the assaulting force ran the risk of being trapped between the walls of Quebec and a relief force from Montreal. Reviewing these options, Montcalm decided that the British would most likely attack him from the opposite direction, across the St. Charles River along the Beauport shore. To that location he sent the bulk of his troops.[35]

The St. Charles River flows from a northwesterly direction, emptying into the St. Lawrence at the foot of Quebec's northwest face. Across the river and stretching along the edge of the north channel of the St. Lawrence (a relatively shallow body of water extending for twenty miles between Île d'Orléans and the mainland) are the Beauport flats. With a tidal range of more than twelve feet at low water, the flats are a broad muddy apron. Approximately five miles north of the St. Charles the Montmorency River cuts the shoreline.

From its source at Lac des Neiges the Montmorency flows 120 miles southeast to cascade over a 272-foot-high cliff only a few hundred yards inland from its confluence with the St. Lawrence. Once over the falls, the river slices across the flat shore, presenting a natural barrier to an advancing army. The river protected the French left. Montcalm viewed the Beauport flats between the St. Charles and the Montmorency as the most likely place for an amphibious attack.[36]

Montcalm fortified the Beauport line using the St. Charles and Montmorency to anchor his flanks. On the right he built a temporary bridge across the St. Charles to link him with the city. He protected the exposed bridge with a series of floating batteries. Lévis commanded the left near the Montmorency and fortified his position by digging a series of entrenchments on the high land overlooking the tidal flats. Vaudreuil remained on the right near the St. Charles. Montcalm made his headquarters in the center.

Before marshaling his assault, Wolfe organized his camp. A strict disciplinarian, the general entertained no romantic illusions about the character of his men. "The Infantry," he wrote his father "are easily put into disorder." "Their discipline [is] bad, and their valour precarious. . . . They frequently kill their officers through fear, and murder one another in their confusion."[37] To keep control, Wolfe demanded that his officers know their men by name, and he held them strictly accountable for the behavior of their troops. As usual, American rangers were a special problem, particularly when they insisted on firing off their muskets in camp. Wolfe ordered that no soldier was to fire his weapon in camp, and he insisted that musket flints be covered with cloth to prevent any accidental discharge. No soldier was to harm any habitant or seize and destroy private property without express orders. Exceptions could be made—"The General strictly forbids the Inhuman practice of Scalping except when the Enemy are Indians or Canadians dressed as Indians." Yet he warned his men, "If any violence is offered to women the Offender shall be punished with death." He told them, "The object of the campaign is to Compleat the conquest of Canada, and to finish the war in America."[38]

Reams of orders gushed from Wolfe's headquarters. In the presence of his troops the general was energetic, firm, and determined, yet his precarious health began to deteriorate. Almost as soon as he stepped ashore he "was seized with a fit of the stone and made bloody water." For the moment, he endured the pain stoically and disciplined his mind to plan the attack.

Wolfe's legendary prickliness is often attributed to his poor health. He suffered, he said, from rheumatism and gravel. His fits of illness often coincided with moments of great emotional stress. He fell ill, for example, in 1743 after the fighting at Dettingen, and later in Scotland, a place he loathed for both its people and its climate. Whether the causes were physical or psychosomatic at Quebec, Wolfe suffered pain and chronic illness.

*　*　*

Control of the St. Lawrence above and below the city was essential to British strategy. Vastly outnumbered by Saunders's fleet, Montcalm's pitiful naval force was powerless to challenge the English on the river. On the other hand, the dense mass of British ships tugging on their anchors in the stream presented an inviting target for a tactic of last resort: fireships. After dark on June 28 parties of French sailors went to work cramming seven vessels with combustible material. They stuffed cannon with powder and shot, then plugged the muzzles with wadding. Bundles of hay and dry timber were stowed below decks. Powder kegs and barrels of tar and pitch were placed in key locations. As the tide ebbed, these "infernal machines" were towed into the current. At the last possible moment French volunteers lashed the ships' wheels to keep the vessels on a steady course downstream toward the anchored British warships and transports. Below decks other crew scrambled to set fuses and kindle fires. As the flames licked out of the holds, the men hurried over the side to boats waiting to take them to safety.

Saunders expected that the French might try such a gambit. As a precaution, from the first night at anchorage he had assigned small craft to patrol around the men-of-war. He ordered his captains to send extra lookouts aloft and to reinforce the anchor watch. About midnight on the twenty-eighth, as the tide was running out, the alarm went up. From mastheads keen-eyed British seamen saw moving shadows and the faint glow of flames drifting out of the St. Charles. The French crews had set the fires too soon, allowing Saunders's men ample time to prepare for the attack. As the vessels drew nearer, flames shot up the rigging as cannon blew apart, hurling iron fragments in all directions. The blazing ships bore down on the British fleet, but Saunders's men did their work well. Officers bellowed to the small boats to grapple and tow the menacing "infernals" away from the fleet. On the decks of the British ships marine drummers called all hands to stations. Gangs of sailors heaved around the capstans hauling on anchor cables to move the ships away, while others climbed over the bulwarks and stood in the chains with long pikes preparing to fend off the fiery craft. Some crews had no time to haul the anchor, and seamen went forward with axes to cut the cables and let their vessel drift out of harm's way. Not a single British ship was damaged. At daybreak men crowded the rails to look over the St. Lawrence at the charred French hulks. Some had stranded on shore, while others drifted harmlessly downstream.

As the fireships smoldered, Wolfe made his first move off Île d'Orléans. The heights at Point Lévis, directly across from the city, were well within cannon range of Quebec. Wisely preferring not to divide his regular forces, Montcalm had assigned local militia and Indians to the defense of the point. Late in the afternoon light infantry, rangers, and a single regiment under Monckton's command crossed over from Île d'Orléans and landed at Beaumont a few miles to the east of Point Lévis. Despite stiff resistance, Monckton's force took the point with a loss of only thirty men. As the French defenders withdrew, rangers scurried after them and returned with six scalps. By the morning of the thirtieth Wolfe's engineers and artillerymen were sighting their batteries on targets across the river. In the meantime Saunders steered his fleet within range of the lower town. Wolfe ordered Carleton to finish fortifying the sprawling encampment on Île d'Orléans while he crossed over to Lévis. From the heights the general got a good view of Quebec. As he scanned across the river, he saw Montcalm's troops working to improve what was already a formidable set of defenses. He urged Monckton to bring the guns ahead while he gave thought to an assault at Beauport.

With his bases on the Île d'Orléans and Point Lévis secured, Wolfe was ready to swing to his right and take a lodgment on the Beauport shore. His plan was to land on the north side of the Montmorency River and take a position on the French left. Between six and seven o'clock on the rainy morning of July 9, Saunders sent in a squadron of frigates and bomb ketches to lay down fire along the shore. The bombardment forced the French to pull back from their positions near the river and redeploy inland on higher ground. Their withdrawal gave Wolfe his opening. The grenadiers went in first, followed by Townshend's brigade. While the main body, including artillery, dug in, rangers and light infantry drove farther inland to secure the perimeter. As they probed through the woods near the river, they encountered Indians attached to Lévis's command. Both sides took heavy casualties and withdrew.

Three days after the landing on the Beauport shore, Monckton's guns on Point Lévis were ready to open fire on the lower town. Mortars arched their rounds high over the river, dropping them with devastating effect. Houses, shops, and even Our Lady of Victories church were crushed under the weight of falling metal. Because of distance and height, British guns could not so easily target the upper town, though it too suffered greatly.

Wolfe had secured three positions: Île d'Orléans, Point Lévis, and Montmorency. Although he held the initiative, he had put his army at risk. In the face of a larger enemy force, Wolfe had divided his troops into three weaker divisions, separated from each other by the river. His plan was to hold the enemy on his left (Point Lévis) and center (Île d'Orléans) and strike on his right (Beauport). His entire tactical plan depended upon Saunders controlling the river. Had Montcalm been a bolder commander, he might have ordered a quick strike across the Montmorency to hit the British before they had a chance to secure their positions. As it was, Montcalm preferred to remain where he was "intrenched up to the chin" to wait out the British, hoping that the harsh Canadian winter eventually would drive the enemy away.[39]

The siege wore on. Cannon and mortars traded fire across the river, but the British got the better of the exchanges, and each day the piles of rubble in Quebec grew larger. On the night of July 18 the *Sutherland* and *Squirrel* passed under the city and moved upstream. Three days later Wolfe went aboard *Sutherland* to inquire about the difficulty of the passage. It had, reported *Sutherland*'s captain, not been hard.[40] On the twenty-seventh the French made another try at the fleet with fireships. After fending them off, Wolfe wrote to Montcalm, "If you presume to send down any more fire-rafts, they shall be made fast to the two transports in which the Canadian prisoners are confined in order that they may perish by your own base invention."[41]

As the siege wore on, Wolfe showed increasing signs of strain. He was often confined by his painful maladies to his headquarters. Communications with his senior officers became difficult, and they grew uncertain about their commander's intentions.[42]

Finally, Wolfe decided to launch a frontal assault at the place where the French were strongest: the Beauport shore. In late July he presented his plan to Monckton, Townshend, and Murray. None of them favored the scheme, but Wolfe was fixed on his idea.

About a mile upstream toward Quebec from the Montmorency, Montcalm had constructed a strong point named for Chevalier James Johnstone, a Scot Jacobite serving the French. The Johnstone Redoubt stood between the river and the main French position, which ran along the crest of a rise two hundred yards to its rear. Wolfe later explained his plan to Pitt: "I proposed to make myself Master of a detach'd Redoubt near to the Water's Edge, and whose situation appear'd to be out of Musquet Shot of the Intrenchment upon the Hill: If the Enemy supported this detach'd piece, it would necessarily bring on an Engagement, what we most wish'd for; And if not, I should have it in my Power to examine their Situation, so as to be able to determine where we could best attack them."[43] Once he had enticed the French off the high ground and toward the flats, Brigadiers Townshend and Murray would ford the Montmorency and hammer them on their left. Wolfe chose his grenadiers—thirteen companies numbering nearly one thousand men, the cream of his command—to lead the amphibious assault. At high water Saunders deliberately ran two of his armed transports onto the shore in order to get their guns within range of the redoubt. At the same time detachments of light infantry and rangers from Townshend's and Murray's camp marched inland along the Montmorency to feign a crossing and draw French defenders in that direction. Before dawn on the thirty-first, sailors from Saunders's ships beached dozens of flat-bottomed boats along the shore of the Île d'Orléans and Point Lévis. By midmorning the boats were pulling for the Beauport shore. Captain John Knox described the scene.

Eleven o'clock.—Two armed transport-cats, drawing little water, worked over, and grounded a-breast of the Point de Lest, westward of the fall of Montmorency. A smart cannonading ensued.

Twelve o'clock—Weather extremely hot. The enemy throw shells at the troops who are in their boats half channel over.

Four o'clock—The Centurion, and the two armed cats, renewed a very brisk fire on the enemy's detached works.

Five o'clock—Very gloomy weather; some of the boats, in attempting to land, struck upon some ledges.

Half past five o'clock—The first division of the troops, consisting of all the grenadiers of the army . . . landed at Point de Lest.[44]

For nearly the entire day Lévis had watched calmly. He ordered reinforcements to march parallel to the Montmorency to repel any attempt by
the British to ford the stream and come at him from that direction. Additional militia took positions on the rise, looking down on the British drifting off shore.

Once ashore, the grenadiers formed up and advanced on the redoubt. It
was empty: the French had flown up the hill and joined their comrades behind the entrenchments. In the meantime the diversionary feint by rangers
and light infantry up the Montmorency had been abandoned, and the men
were back in camp. Having seen no action for more than a month, and after
spending an afternoon steaming in the sun, the grenadiers were tired,
angry, and agitated. They were determined to attack the enemy on the
rise.When the drummers began to beat "The Grenadiers March," emotion
overcame sense, and without forming up properly or waiting for orders one
thousand men advanced in a "disorderly" and "strange" manner."[45]

Many of the French soldiers staring down at the red mass coming at them
were veterans of Ticonderoga, where they had seen a similar brave but fool-
hardy British assault. From their entrenchments the Frenchmen poured
withering fire down on the grenadiers, who despite heavy losses continued
to charge. They might even have taken the heights had the late afternoon
sky not opened up with a thunderstorm. The downpour silenced the muskets and turned the grassy slope into a slippery, treacherous trap. Unable to
see the enemy through the driving rain or fire their drenched weapons, the
grenadiers slid back down the slope and retreated across the mud flats
toward the Montmorency and the covering fire of Townshend's and Murray's brigades. In great disorder and confusion the dispirited men waded
across the river and fell exhausted. It was a shocking debacle brought about
by a lack of intelligence compounded by poor command and control. Nearly
half of the grenadier force was killed or wounded. Vaudreuil proclaimed, "I
have no more anxiety about Quebec."[46]

Wolfe was growing increasingly worried. The dread of defeat consumed
him. On August 31, 1759 he wrote to his mother that he feared coming home
in failure to be exposed to an ignorant populace. He would, he claimed, resign at the first opportunity.[47] In rapid fire he issued orders and then as
quickly canceled them. Montcalm, it seemed, had beaten him.

The French would not come out from their walls and entrenchments. If he could not tease them out, Wolfe thought he might starve them into submission. He ordered Saunders to send additional ships upriver to cut Quebec's water communications. On August 4, Wolfe ordered "Brigadier Murray, with a strong detachment . . . to proceed on board of Admiral Holmes's division to make a diversion above the town, with a view to divide the enemy's attention."[48] Murray sailed past the Chaudière River and swept up the shoreline, burning the villages of St. Nicholas, St. Antoine, and St. Croix on the south side. On the eighth he attacked Pointe aux Trembles on the north side but was repulsed. Twelve miles farther upstream he landed at Deschambault, where he destroyed a large stock of supplies. Murray's raid forced Montcalm to detach Bougainville with a flying column upriver to prevent the British from enveloping his position. Having never planned a permanent lodgment, Murray withdrew his forces and returned to the main camp, his mission a success.

In addition to spoils, Murray returned with welcome news. He had intercepted French dispatches, intended for Montcalm, announcing the fall of Niagara to a force under John Prideaux and William Johnson.

In June, coincident with Wolfe's advance up the St. Lawrence, Prideaux and Johnson left Albany with an army of 3,300 men. They followed the usual route west: up the Mohawk and via portages to Oswego. Along the way they dropped off about 1,300 men at various forts and land carries to protect the supply line. From Oswego, the remaining men traveled by small boats along the south coast of Lake Ontario to the Niagara peninsula. They encountered no opposition, and by July 7 they were within sight of the fort.

On the ninth an English drummer approached the walls of the fort and beat the call to parley. Captain François Pouchot, the fort's commander, ordered the main gate opened and the English emissary, Lieutenant Walter Rutherford, entered to present General Prideaux's compliments and a summons to surrender. All the pleasantries were observed. Pouchot replied to the lieutenant that "before he became acquainted with them [the English], he should at least assuredly gain their esteem."[49]

Montcalm had in fact anticipated the loss of Niagara. In April, when he had sent Pouchot to command the fort, he told him that if the British arrived he should do no more than put up a good defense. "If Niagara is besieged it will be taken. We must look forward to the siege, but it is not necessary to sacrifice too large a garrison."[50]

True to his word, Pouchot held out for nearly a month. The siege could have been scripted by Vauban himself. Trenches were dug, approaches were made, while cannon and mortars pummeled the walls. On the twenty-first the British suffered a serious loss when a mortar exploded in one of the trenches, killing Prideaux. An even more serious blow fell on the French three days later when an Indian-British force commanded by Johnson ambushed a relief force coming up from the Ohio. With his men exhausted, his fort in shambles, and no relief in sight, Pouchot surrendered on the twenty-sixth. His fierce resistance did indeed gain the "esteem" of his opponents.

Niagara's surrender coincided with Amherst's slow march northward. In his usual cautious manner the general edged toward Ticonderoga. The French made a show of defense, but their real plan was to abandon the fort. Amherst's slow approach left Bourlamaque, Ticonderoga's commander, with ample time to evacuate his troops. While the main force left without notice, a detachment of engineers stayed behind to set demolition charges. Before Amherst's advance party reached the gates, the fort went up in a thunderous roar. Amherst made camp near the rubble.

A few days later Bourlamaque repeated his tactic at Crown Point, reducing it too to a heap of ashes and broken stone. Although there were still several weeks of good campaigning weather left, Amherst decided to consolidate his positions at Ticonderoga and Crown Point and await the spring for a move north. Although the fall of Niagara, Ticonderoga, and Crown Point were important, these victories did little to assist Wolfe. Neither Amherst nor Johnson would march to his aid in 1759.

Montcalm knew that the fall of Niagara and Ticonderoga left Montreal exposed from two directions. On Champlain all that stood between Amherst and the St. Lawrence was a force of less than three thousand men commanded by Bourlamaque at Île aux-Noix. To the west the French position was even more exposed: Only Luc La Corne with a handful of militia and

Troupes de la Marine at the mission of La Presentation (Fort Lévis) remained on the St. Lawrence between the British and Montreal. On both fronts the British tide was rising. On August 9 Montcalm sent Lévis to organize Montreal's defense. British pressure had taken his two best generals from him.

10

The Fall of Quebec

Wolfe had dug a grave for his army, but Montcalm
marched his own army into it.

The Marquis de Montcalm is at the head of a great number of bad
soldiers and I am at the head of a small number of good ones.

—Wolfe to Henrietta Wolfe, August 31, 1759

Thus far Montcalm's defense of Quebec had been prudent. The Beauport line held as planned, and Bougainville's flying column had prevented the British from making a secure lodgment upriver. Wisely, the marquis had steadfastly refused to abandon his entrenchments and expose his army to Wolfe. Although he had the advantage of greater numbers, Montcalm feared that his Canadians, Indians, and even the Troupes de la Marine, the majority of his force, would crumble if he sent them to face Wolfe's disciplined regulars.[1] Better, thought Montcalm, to hunker down behind the walls and entrenchments, and let the enemy impale themselves on his defenses. The carnage on the muddy slopes near the Montmorency confirmed the soundness of his plan. What Montcalm could not defend against was Saunders. Montcalm's batteries had proven noticeably ineffective in preventing the admiral's ships from enjoying virtually free rein on the river. Aside from the armed transports he deliberately ran aground at Beauport, Saunders had not lost a single ship; nor had he suffered any significant damage from enemy shot. Montcalm's fireships had turned out to be little more than a feckless display of pyrotechnics.[2]

Despite the impressive performance of Saunders, Wolfe was plagued by frustration, stress, and anxiety. The young general knew that Amherst's advance had ground to a halt at the southern end of Lake Champlain, and that by early October the cold Canadian weather would begin to sweep in and endanger his presence in the St. Lawrence. Adding to his frustration was the fact that his best troops—the grenadiers—had failed him miserably. Their reckless charge at the Montmorency was a worrisome sign of collapsing discipline. The day after the bloody repulse Wolfe issued a stinging rebuke, calling the grenadiers' behavior "impetuous, irregular, and unsoldierlike."[3] Furthermore, his brigadiers, particularly Townshend, were at officer's mess and in private conversation taking every opportunity to snipe at Wolfe. Townshend's verbal jabs, however, were nothing compared to the caricatures he drew of the general and circulated for amusement in the camp.

Sieges are tiresome and boring, and Quebec was no exception. The army was restless, and the sick list was growing as the usual "fluxes and fevers" meandered through the camp. All the time, Wolfe's artillery and Saunders's broadsides belched iron "warmly on the town." On August 9 a hot shot dropped into the lower town, turning the neighborhood into an inferno. Still, the French endured, and they showed little sign of weakening. Outside the city Indians and Canadians continued to harass Wolfe's pickets, scalping men foolish enough to wander too far from camp. Wolfe and Saunders continued to probe at the French. While the guns of the Royal Navy played on the shore and the city, Wolfe attempted to confuse his foe by marching men along the opposite bank to feign crossings. In another ploy he dispatched landing craft toward the Beauport shore to draw the enemy in that direction.

In August Wolfe turned his attention away from the environs of Quebec and looked downriver, where he reverted to a cruel form of war reminiscent of his campaigns in the Scottish Highlands and along the Gaspé shore. Putting Brigadier Monckton, who four years before had cleared the Acadians out of Nova Scotia, in command of the operation, he hit at the habitants. On August 4 Monckton burned the village of Baie St. Paul. Over the next several days nearly twenty other small parishes were torched and plundered. Household goods, food, cattle, and "a library said to be the property of a priest" were hauled away. At the village of St. Anne a priest and his parishioners "fortified themselves in a house." Light infantry and artillery were sent "to reduce them." The detachment arrived and "laid an ambuscade in the skirts of the wood near to [the] fortified house, and as soon as the field-piece was brought up, and began to play, [the priest], with his men, sallied out, when falling in to the ambush, thirty of them, with their leader, were surrounded, killed, and scalped."[4]

The earlier attacks upriver had had a strategic purpose, threatening Montcalm's supply line from Montreal and forcing him to divert forces from the defense of Quebec. The pillaging of settlements downriver had no purpose other than punishment and terror. Although he lamented the sad fate of the locals, Montcalm had no intention of marching to their defense. Indeed, he took encouragement from Wolfe's savagery, viewing it as the work of a desperate commander, who having been bloodied at Montmorency shied away "from any sort of landing unless [he found] absolutely no resistance." As Montcalm watched the summer days grow shorter and the evenings turn cooler, he noted in his journal that his enemy's only remaining hope was "a bold stroke, a thunderbolt."[5]

On the morning of August 19 Captain Hervey Smith, the general's aide-de-camp, emerged from headquarters to announce that the general "could not rise."[6] Wolfe's health had grown worse. From his bed at headquarters he wrote to Saunders that he was "ruined." Morale plummeted, and rumors swept the camp that the general was preparing to retreat.[7]

Having recovered somewhat, Wolfe wrote to his brigadiers on August 28, outlining three tactical options—all centering on Beauport. His first plan argued for a night march inland along the Montmorency to a ford eight or nine miles inland. The army would then cross the ford and sweep down behind the French. To succeed, this plan required complete surprise—an impossibility. Troops were massed on both sides of the Montmorency, and Canadian and Indian scouts were posted everywhere. The stirring of even a single British soldier would sound the alarm. A second plan, only slightly less imaginative, called for a night assault up the same hill from which the grenadiers had been driven with devastating losses nearly a month before. Wolfe's third option was simple: "All the chosen troops . . . attack at Beauport at low water." Inserted in all three plans was the injunction that "the General thinks the country should be ruined and destroyed."[8]

Monckton, Townshend, and Murray read Wolfe's plans and replied the next day. Beauport, in their view, was a British graveyard. A month before, the French had repelled a major attack there, and in the interim they had strengthened their entrenchments. Attacking the French at their strongest point made little sense. Instead, the brigadiers recommended abandoning Beauport and bringing "the troops to the south shore [opposite Quebec] and to carry operations above the town." The brigadiers urged Wolfe to cross the St. Lawrence at a place upriver where he could drive a powerful wedge between Montcalm and his supply depots. If, Townshend, Monckton, and Murray declared unanimously, "we establish ourselves on the north shore [between Quebec and Montreal] Montcalm must fight us on our own terms. . . . If he gives battle and we defeat him, Quebec, and probably all of Canada, will be our own, which is beyond any advantage we can expect by the Beauport side."[9]

Wolfe had little choice but to abandon his Beauport plans, explaining to Saunders, "The generals seem to think alike as to operations; I therefore join with them, and perhaps we may find some opportunity to strike a blow."[10] He ordered the troops remaining at Beauport to withdraw. As the men boarded the boats ferrying them back to camps on the Île d'Orléans and Point Lévis, a despondent Wolfe poured out his frustration to his mother.

No personal evils, worse than defeats and disappointments, have fallen upon me. The enemy puts nothing to risk, and I can't in conscience, put the whole army to risk. My antagonist has wisely shut himself up in inaccessible intrenchments, so that I can't get at him without spilling a torrent of blood, and that perhaps to little purpose. The Marquis de Montcalm is at the head of a great number of bad soldiers and I am at the head of a small number of good ones, that wish for nothing so much as to fight him; but the wary old fellow avoids an action doubtful of the behaviour of his army.[11]

Even at the last minute Wolfe hoped that the sight of his troops marching to the boats might draw Montcalm into the open for a fight, but the "wary old fellow" refused to budge. By September 3 all the troops had been withdrawn. Three months of effort had cost Wolfe nearly nine hundred men killed, wounded, or missing. His remaining force, including marines, numbered approximately 8,500 men. Provisions were running short, sick lists were growing, and the troops, officers included, mumbled about going home.

* * *

Life was also stressed within the French lines. Montcalm had suffered only a fraction of the British casualties and his regulars and the Troupes de la Marine stood firm, but they represented less than half of his force. The Canadian militia were edgy and weary from the siege and were anxious to get home for the harvest. The few Native American allies present were also eager to leave.

Wolfe's greatest advantage remained his naval superiority. Saunders's ships held complete control of the river and passed easily under the guns of Quebec. At the same time Murray's assaults upstream demonstrated that amphibious attacks were possible.[12] By the time his last boats pulled away from the mudflats of the Beauport shore, Wolfe had made up his mind. In line with the recommendations of his brigadiers, he laid plans to launch a major attack behind the enemy to cut his supply lines and force him to battle. Since Saunders had taken control of the river, an upstream landing had been possible, but Wolfe had shied away from it. The most accessible landing sites were several miles upriver. Landing so far from Quebec posed serious risks: His troops would be exposed to counterattack from Bougainville, and at the same time they would be at least a full day's march from Quebec, thus allowing Montcalm sufficient time to consolidate his positions. But since Wolfe had failed on every other avenue of attack, he decided that an upriver approach would have to be made. However, to succeed, the landing would have to be close to the city and done in secret.

Given the lateness of the season, Montcalm assumed that Wolfe would let loose his men to sack the countryside, and then withdraw downriver to winter quarters in Halifax. Under those circumstances he ought to have considered tightening his lines by withdrawing even closer to the city, but he opted instead to maintain his long left flank along the Beauport shore. At the same time he stretched his lines thinner by sending reinforcements to Bougainville.[13] As a result, Bougainville's three thousand troops, mostly regulars, were drawn beyond quick supporting distance from Quebec. Wolfe's mobility by water forced Montcalm to cover a twenty-mile front. Wolfe knew that somewhere along this line there had to be a place to land.

Wolfe's personal knowledge of the terrain surrounding Quebec was fragmentary. He had listened carefully to Mackellar, read the intelligence reports, and scrutinized maps. None of this satisfied him. He decided on a personal reconnaissance. Throwing off his elaborate uniform so that the French would not recognize him, the general rode for several days with his officers along the river, looking for potential landing places on the opposite shore. He also went aboard the sloop of war *Hunter* and sailed the river to examine the possibilities more closely.[14] After Rochefort and Louisbourg, this was Wolfe's third amphibious challenge. He had no illusions about the huge difficulties awaiting him.

Wolfe moved his headquarters on board *Sutherland*, anchored upriver from Quebec. From the ship he issued orders directing regiments to assemble at Gorham's Post near where *Sutherland* lay. At the general's direction, other troops left camp and went aboard transports, which Wolfe ordered to move along the river to feign landings and confuse the enemy. For the embarked soldiers, it was a miserable business. Crammed below decks in the steamy weather of early September, the men sickened quickly and had to be rotated ashore to recover. Wolfe himself fell ill again, and his officers, kept in the dark, gossiped that he was too sick to command the grand enterprise.

On September 9 Wolfe made another reconnaissance. Based upon what he saw on this excursion, he decided to land at L'Anse le Foulon, a small cove tucked away under high bluffs about a mile and a half upriver from the city.[15] The cove was one of the few places where the tidal shore was firm and wide enough for troops to land safely. Most important, a decent path led up from the river's edge to the Plains of Abraham, and although Montcalm had posted a guard at the top, Wolfe was confident that his men could move quickly enough to surprise and overwhelm the French sentries. The Plains were the perfect stage for the set-piece battle Wolfe yearned to have with Montcalm. If he could marshal his ranks on the Plains, he believed, Montcalm would come out and fight. Surprise and speed would be his keys to victory.

On the tenth Wolfe took Monckton, to whom he had given command of the first wave ashore, Holmes, who was commanding the supporting naval squadron, and Captain James Chads, the naval officer in charge of the landing craft, down to Gorham's Post to view the landing place. After pointing out the cove, he told them that he planned to land on the thirteenth at daybreak. Chads objected that the tide would not be favorable at that hour, and he asked if they could move earlier. Wolfe replied that the risks of a night attack outweighed the problems of an unfavorable tide.

The following day Wolfe issued general orders detailing the embarkation. The men were to go to their boats at nine o'clock the next evening. They were to carry "Arms, Ammunition and two days provisions."[16] Townshend and Murray, neither of whom Wolfe had thus far taken into his confidence, were angry. They managed to draw Monckton, who did know the plan, into collectively writing a peremptory note to their commander. They complained that they were not "sufficiently informed" of the plans for the "execution of the descent." The "public orders" were vague, and they did not view it as appropriate that they should have to depend upon a naval officer (Chads) to instruct them. To avoid "any mistakes," they requested "distinct orders."[17] Wolfe shot back to Monckton, reminding him of what he already knew. So that there could be no mistake, Wolfe told Monckton: "It is my duty to attack the French Army. To the best of my knowledge and abilities I have fixed upon that spot where we can act with the most force and are most likely to succeed. If I am mistaken I am sorry for it and must be answerable to his Majesty and then the public for the consequences."[18] Wolfe was less courteous to Townshend. He informed him curtly that he should follow Monckton ashore, where he was to give his "best assistance" "to beat the French Army."[19]

About midnight a signalman hoisted a single lantern into *Sutherland*'s maintop. Across the water lookouts watching from the waiting barges quietly passed the word. Silently, oarsmen dipped their sweeps into the river, and soon a flotilla of boats bearing sixteen hundred troops emerged from the lee of the transports and slipped into the stream. The barges took position between *Sutherland* and the south shore, about eight and a half miles above the proposed landing site. There they held while Wolfe joined them. By 2 a.m. the tide was ebbing sufficiently to carry them quickly downriver.[20] *Sutherland* hoisted two lights, and the barges cast off, heading downstream. The weather was fine and the moon in its last quarter. In the lead were eight barges carrying the light infantry under the command of Lieutenant Colonel William Howe, brother of George Howe, the fallen hero of Ticonderoga.[21] In the first boat were twenty-four men commanded by Captain William DeLaune, an officer with whom Wolfe had served at

Louisbourg. DeLaune's orders were to hit the beach quickly, find the path up the bluff, and strike for the top.

As Wolfe's flotilla floated down toward L'Anse le Foulon, Montcalm was on the other side of the city inspecting defenses along the St. Charles River. The marquis understood the threat from upriver, but he still held that Beauport was the most likely point of attack. He felt confirmed in his opinion during the night when he heard Saunders's guns playing along the shore, and saw small boats milling about the fleet as if preparing to land soldiers. Saunders's movements were a deliberate deception.

In midstream Wolfe's boats passed close by the sloop *Hunter.* Its commander informed the general that a French deserter had told them that provision boats from Montreal were expected at any moment. As the barges edged closer to shore, a sentry heard noise and called, "Qui vive?" A French-speaking officer in the lead boat called back, "La France." "A quel régiment?" The Englishman called back, "De La Reine." As they approached the landing site, another sentry challenged. Captain Donald MacDonald of the Seventy-eighth Regiment called back in French, "Provision boats. Don't make such bloody noise. The English will hear us."[22]

The faint glow of daybreak came over the river at 4 a.m. as the first boats grounded. Howe ordered three companies of light infantry up the slope in front of him. The French-speaking Captain MacDonald led the first company up. For a second time that morning he saved the attack: "As soon as he [MacDonald] and his men gained the height, he was challenged by a centry, and with great presence of mind, from his knowledge of the French service, answered him according to their manner."[23]

MacDonald's quick thinking bought the British enough time to bring more troops up the slope. The officer in command of the French guard, upon whom rested the fate of Quebec, was Louis Du Pont Duchambon de Vergor, who had surrendered Fort Beausejour to Monckton in 1755. He was, according to one historian, "unfit for military command," and in the view of a contemporary "the most dull witted fellow I have ever met."[24] When Vergor's men realized that they had been deceived, they belatedly sought to defend their post. In a sharp exchange of musketry Vergor was hit in the right leg and hand. As he fell, most of his men fled for Quebec. Light infantry quickly mopped up the rest of the scattered French and secured a defensive perimeter. Soon hundreds more red-

The Plains of Abraham

coats swarmed over the top and formed up in ranks. By 6 a.m. the tide had slacked sufficiently that Wolfe could ferry additional troops across the river.

Downriver Montcalm was in his Beauport headquarters monitoring Saunders's movements on the river. Shortly after dawn a breathless Canadian messenger arrived at headquarters with the news. Within the hour French battalions were double-timing toward the Plains of Abraham, led by a brigade of militia and Troupes de la Marine.

By 8 a.m. Wolfe had brought his entire force to the top of the bluff. He had also managed to haul up two brass fieldpieces. It was an extraordinary accomplishment. The regiments wheeled onto the Plains of Abraham and formed up on an axis facing the city. The British line stretched for about a half mile. Wolfe's officers and NCOs stood to the front and barked orders at the men to dress ranks and fix bayonets. On the left near the road Canadian militia and Indians managed to come close enough to fire into the British ranks. Townshend, to whom Wolfe had given command of the left, sent skirmishes to clear away the enemy.

By 9 a.m. the Beauport regiments arrived. Montcalm took personal command and faced an immediate dilemma. The British were entrenching in front of him. If he waited too long, the enemy would have time enough to prepare positions that would make an assault against them a costly and probably futile venture. He had to attack immediately or else withdraw. The latter was impossible as his troops were still moving into position and any rearward movement would confuse them and panic the militia. While he wrestled with his options, Montcalm must have considered the Bougainville factor—a "flying camp" of three thousand men were only a few miles away and were undoubtedly on the march, though how soon they would arrive was unclear. For weeks Montcalm's favorite dinner companion had been marching up and down the river following the tide and the British. Not until 9 a.m., however, more than four hours after the British had come safely ashore, did Bougainville hear the news of their landing. He rallied his troops and set out on the road toward Quebec.

Wolfe had his dilemmas as well. He needed to bring the French to action soon, for Saunders and Holmes had made it clear that to avoid the perils of winter, they would depart by the end of the month. Now that Wolfe had gambled and reached the Plains, he was caught between two enemy forces: Bougainville and Montcalm. He could only win if he took them on one at a time.

In the end Montcalm acted first: He ordered an attack.

After more than two centuries of debate, the marquis's fateful decision to advance remains controversial. We can never know for certain what the general thought as he rode out through the St. Louis gate. Perhaps the old cavalryman was overwhelmed with romantic thoughts of glory and victory, or he may have been reconciled to the inevitability of battle and defeat. Since Montcalm had no faith in the ability of his Canadian or Indian allies to stand and volley against British regulars, he placed all his reliance on his own regular troops.

By 10 a.m. Montcalm had organized his formation. On the right he positioned the Quebec and Montreal militias standing close to the St. Foy road. To their left stood the Troupes de la Terre in order: La Sarre, Languedoc, Bearn, Guyenne, and Royal Roussillon. On the far left the Montreal and Trois-Rivières militia held ground. Out on the distant flanks an undetermined number of Indians hovered. Montcalm did enjoy the advantage of superior artillery and a slightly larger number of troops. To Wolfe's two field guns, he answered with four.

Wolfe, concerned that the enemy might try to flank him, drew his force

Louis-Antoine de Bougainville

into a three-sided formation. Six regiments stood to the front, facing the enemy, while strong detachments deployed to either side, facing out. The Louisbourg grenadiers held the right, and two battalions from the Royal Americans held the left rear flank. Slightly more than five battalions held the center. A third battalion of Royal Americans stayed to guard the path up from the river, and the rough equivalent of two battalions were held in reserve. Wolfe took his post on the right with the grenadiers. Monckton and Murray were to his left, and Townshend commanded the left flank and reserve. Wolfe's two brass guns faced the French on either end of his line, as he waited for Montcalm to make the first move.

While Bougainville was hurrying to his commander's side, Montcalm rode to the front of the French line. Years later Joseph Trahan, a Canadian militiaman, remembered the scene. The marquis "was riding . . . a black horse in front of our lines, bearing his sword high in the air." The troops cheered and moved forward, but they were not in good order. Instead of a straight and steady line, some men advanced headlong too quickly, while others faltered and fell behind. When the French artillery began to belch canister, Wolfe ordered his men to fall on the ground. All the time the British held their fire. As the enemy advanced, Wolfe might well have remembered that day fourteen years before when he watched the rebellious Highlanders surge forward at Culloden. What he said about the Scots then applied to the French now: They came "with more fury than prudence."[25]

Canadian militia and Indians laid down fire on the flanks. According to some reports, instead of advancing in a solid line formation, the regular troops in the French center moved forward in a mix of line and column. At 140 yards they let loose a volley of musketry, which at such a long distance had virtually no effect on the British. Once they had fired, the militia and Indians, true to form, fell to the ground to reload. The regulars standing in the center were confused by this maneuver. Their advance became even more jagged.[26]

Wolfe stood with his men. He ordered them to load two musket balls at a time and hold their fire. When the French were only forty yards away, officers and NCOs behind the British line ordered "present" and then "fire." Thousands of lead balls tore through the French center. Men fell in windrows. Covered and protected for the moment by a shroud of smoke, the French fell back. The redcoats reloaded and advanced steadily.

On the right Wolfe stood with the grenadiers. Canadians and Indians hidden in nearby brush fired into their ranks. As he advanced with the grenadiers, a musket ball slammed into his right wrist. Wolfe wrapped the wound and pushed on. The enemy sighted on him again, and this time

The death of James Wolfe

he took a ball in the stomach and another in the breast. He crumbled to the ground. Lieutenant Browne of the grenadiers, Mr. Henderson, "a volunteer," and an unknown officer of artillery lifted him carefully and carried him to the rear. When asked if he would have a surgeon, Wolfe replied, "It is needless; it is all over with me." One of the officers cried out, "They run, see how they run." "Who runs?" asked Wolfe. "The enemy, Sir; Egad they give way everywhere." Wolfe gave his final order. "Go one of you, my lads, to Colonel Burton; tell him to march Webb's regiment with all speed down to the Charles river, to cut off the retreat of the fugitives from the bridge." Wolfe then turned on his side and said, "Now God be praised, I will die in peace."[27] News of the general's fall and then death swept through the British lines. Command passed to Monckton, but he too had been hit and taken to the rear, leaving Townshend to hold the field.

While Wolfe lay dying, the battle continued to rage. On the other side Montcalm rode to the front presenting a perfect target astride his black charger. According to Wolfe's artillery commander, George Williamson, Montcalm was brought down by Williamson's "grape shot from a light six pounder."[28] Whatever the case, the marquis was hit several times. Two officers came to his side and held him in his saddle as they turned about and

The Marquis de Montcalm astride his black horse on the Plains of Abraham

rode through the St. Louis gate to the home of a surgeon named Arnoux. According to an apocryphal story, a crowd of women who saw him struggling in his saddle called out, "My God, my God, the marquis is wounded!" To which he replied, "It is nothing, it is nothing. Do not worry about me. Take care of my good troops." At the surgeon's home he asked Arnoux to "tell the truth like a sincere friend." The doctor told him he would be dead by morning, to which the marquis responded, "Good, I will not see the English in Quebec." His men buried him in the chapel of the Ursuline convent.

Townshend took command of the British forces. On the left the Highlanders pursued the fleeing French with bayonets and claymores. At a wooded escarpment overlooking the St. Charles River a strong detachment of Canadian militia and Indians turned to meet the charging Scots. With a quick volley they tore up their formation. Only after reinforcements arrived did the British manage to drive the enemy from the woods. On the right the grenadiers and the Twenty-eighth Regiment tried to approach the city walls, but they were driven back by heavy cannon fire.

Finally, as the smoke cleared and the battlefield fell quiet, Bougainville appeared suddenly on the west side. Townshend sent Burton's Forty-eighth, along with additional light infantry and artillery, to drive them away. Bougainville, not fully aware of the shape of the battle, decided to withdraw toward Loriette, preferring to maintain his force rather than

The death of the Marquis de Montcalm

risk it in an unknown environment. By noon the Plains of Abraham were quiet, disturbed only by the cries of the wounded and the voices of those coming to help them. The day had cost the French nearly 650 men killed, wounded, and taken prisoner. British losses were estimated to be about the same.

That night the remainder of the troops at Beauport left their lines and joined Bougainville and Montcalm's survivors at Loriette, where they tended their wounded and tried to reorganize. The city's commander, Jean-Baptiste de Ramezay, surveyed his unhappy position. Although a French army still existed, it was defeated and demoralized. Quebec was a carcass. After a three-month siege the city was in ruins, men were deserting, and supplies were low. If the British assaulted and took Quebec, it was likely to be a scene of bloody carnage. Some of the British had been at Monongahela and William Henry; those veterans ached for revenge. The whole army remembered what had happened at Montmorency. Rather than risk an assault and the carnage likely to follow, on the fifteenth Ramezay sent a messenger to Townshend to ask for terms.

Despite the victory on the Plains, Townshend's army was still outside the city. Bougainville was to his rear with a large intact force. Worst of all, winter was on its way. When Saunders came up the hill to pay his respects and congratulate Townshend on the victory, he informed the general that the fleet was anxious to depart. Under the circumstances all that had been gained might well be lost. Townshend's army had to be in the city or else leave with Saunders. They could not spend the winter in an exposed winter encampment. Realizing his predicament, Townshend offered Ramezay generous terms, including the "honors of war." He told the French that "the garrison of the town" would be permitted to "march out with their arms and baggage, drums beating, matches lighted, with two pieces of cannon, and twelve rounds for each piece." He further promised that the prisoners would "be embarked as conveniently as possible . . . to the first port in France."

Townshend's generous terms were persuasive. Ramezay called a council of war, and his officers voted 13–1 in favor of surrender. At 3 p.m. on September 17 Ramezay ordered a white flag hoisted on the wall. On the eighteenth the final surrender was signed, and the following day, in accordance with the "honors of war," the French marched out of Quebec City as "the Louisbourg grenadiers marched in, preceded by a detachment of the artillery, and one gun, with the British colours hoisted on its carriage." That evening across the river the crew of the *Royal William* stood to attention as the admiral's barge, bearing the body of James Wolfe, came alongside.[29]

11

The Year of Great Victories

The English hold no more than the ruins of Quebec;
only four houses remain standing in the town.

—Gazette de France

I have an army that can take Canada, and I will do it.

—Jeffrey Amherst to William Pitt, July 13, 1759

Inside the walls of Quebec the victorious British walked amid rubble. Their relentless bombardment had demolished at least five hundred buildings and damaged many more. The granaries and storehouses were empty, fires smoldered, and food was scarce. Beyond the walls the French army still existed. The British held "no more than the ruins of Quebec."[1]

While the British secured the city, Bougainville moved his defeated force from Loriette to Pointe-aux-Trembles, about twenty-five miles upriver from Quebec, hoping that by taking a position between the British and Montreal he would be able to rendezvous with the relief force that he anticipated was on its way. Vaudreuil was with him, and as usual the impetuous Canadian urged action. He wanted to counterattack and retake the city, but wiser heads urged caution. Lévis soon arrived from Montreal and took command. He had, however, not brought reinforcements. With little hope of retaking Quebec, he posted small garrisons at Pointe-aux-Trembles and at the Jacques Cartier River to maintain a watch over the British, while withdrawing the rest of the army to Montreal to prepare for the spring.[2]

It was too late in the season, and the British were too spent, to pursue the French. Although the cost had been extraordinary, Montcalm had held the British long enough at Quebec to buy Canada another year. Anxious to avoid winter in Canada, most of Wolfe's staff booked passage for more hospitable climes. Townshend, embarrassed by allegations that he had conspired against Wolfe, hurried home to protect his reputation.[3] Monckton, still recovering from his wounds, took dispatches to Amherst in New York. Saunders and Holmes bid their farewells. Murray, the only general left, was in command.

Nations adore military heroes, and none more so than the English, particularly when the idol falls in battle. As the Quebec veterans arrived home, the stories of their triumph grew more grand and romantic with each retelling. Most compelling and popular were the elegiac tales surrounding the death of Wolfe. He fell with his men, dying in the arms of his comrades at the moment of victory. It was drama worthy of Shakespeare, and the public loved it. Tirelessly, writers, poets, sculptors, and painters went to work fashioning monuments to Wolfe in words, stone, and on canvas.[4]

Pitt had the best combination a politician could hope for: a glorious victory and a fallen hero. In Parliament he rose to deliver a eulogy to Wolfe and a paean to his victory. The speech was a dense discourse filled with so many classical allusions that Walpole thought it was "the worst harangue he ever uttered."[5] As usual, however, Pitt knew better than his critics. The public loved him for his sentimental eloquence as they mourned the fallen Wolfe.

Nor did Montcalm escape hagiography. Although a tragic figure, the marquis had stood bravely against overwhelming odds. Indeed, Quebec was the only battle Montcalm lost in America, and there were many who claimed that had it not been for the perfidy and corruption of a rotten Canadian bureaucracy, he might have triumphed.

Indisputably, Montcalm and Wolfe were brave soldiers. Neither, however, were brilliant commanders. Wolfe, for example, stubborn and unwilling to listen to advice, wasted a summer. Only after his generals forced him to abandon another fruitless attack at Beauport did he embrace their option—an attack upriver. Montcalm's fatal error was his decision to abandon the protection of Quebec's walls and commit himself to a set-piece battle where he knew he was at a disadvantage. Whatever their tactical errors, they did act boldly. Jeffrey Amherst did not.

* * *

On the day when Wolfe lay dying on the Plains of Abraham, Amherst sat comfortably in his headquarters at Crown Point. As far as the general was concerned, the next year would be soon enough to move north. Although unwilling to risk a major move north, Amherst did at least order a raid in that direction. To gain intelligence about Wolfe's situation, Amherst sent Ensign Thomas Hutchins to Quebec via the Kennebec and Chaudiere on August 7. The next day he sent a second party, led by two regular officers, Captain Kinton Kennedy and Ensign Archibald Hamilton, accompanied by seven Stockbridge Indians, to travel via Missiquoi Bay and the Yamaska River to the Abenaki village of St. Francis. Although they traveled under a flag of truce, claiming to be emissaries to negotiate prisoner exchange, Abenaki guarding the northern end of Lake Champlain intercepted the party, seized the men, and sent them off to Trois-Rivières. Amherst, furious at this apparent breech of international etiquette, vowed revenge against "the enemy's indian scoundrels."[6] On September 12 he summoned Major Robert Rogers and ordered him to attack the Abenaki mission on the St. Francis River, located a few miles upstream from the St. Lawrence. Amherst told Rogers, "Take . . . revenge."[7]

Although often referred to as an Abenaki village, St. Francis was a cosmopolitan gathering place where members of several tribes dwelled. Originally founded by the Jesuits on the nearby Chaudiere River, the mission moved to the St. Francis about 1700. A well-established settlement with European-style homes, it was infamous among New Englanders as a staging point from which French and Indian war parties had for generations sortied against their settlements.

Moving at night, Rogers rowed north with 200 rangers and Indians from Crown Point, hugging the east shore of Lake Champlain. They landed at Missiquoi Bay. For nine days they trudged northeasterly through swamp and brush until they reached the St. Francis River about fifteen miles upstream from their target. Rogers and his men, reduced to 150 because of sickness and accidents, forded the river and made their way quietly along the riverbank toward the village. Late in the afternoon on October 3, Rogers's scouts spotted smoke rising from the village. The men paused, and after dark, Rogers and two other rangers moved closer for a better view. According to the major's account, the Abenaki were "in a high frolic or dance." Rogers returned to his men and issued orders for the attack.[8] They would wait for the early morning hour, hoping that the "frolic" would put the Abenaki in a deep slumber. Before dawn the rangers took up positions on the right, left, and center along a line that left the Indians no retreat except into the river. Rogers described the attack to Amherst.

> *At half an hour before sun-rise I surprised the town when they were all asleep . . . which was done with so much alacrity by both the officers and men, that the enemy had not time to recover themselves, or take arms for their own defence, till they were chiefly destroyed, except some few of them who took to the water. About forty of my people pursued them, who destroyed such as attempted to make their escape that way, and sunk both them and their boats. A little after sunrise I set fire to all their houses, except three, that I reserved for use of the party. The fire consumed many of the Indians who had concealed themselves in the cellars and lofts of their houses. About seven o'clock in the morning the affair was completely over, in which time we had killed at least two hundred Indians, taken twenty of their women and children prisoners.[9]*

Rogers, never one to underestimate his own role, exaggerated the number of enemy casualties. Most estimates place the number of Indian dead at twenty to thirty. Having accomplished his mission, Rogers and his men faced the much tougher challenge of returning home.

Aroused by the attack, French and Abenaki moved quickly to hunt down and kill the retreating rangers. Rogers, who realized the folly of returning by the same route, ordered his men to march east and then south. Their goal was Fort Number 4 on the Connecticut River, more than one hundred miles distant. Rogers's retreat turned into a nightmare. Slowed down by the sick and wounded, his men needed eight days to cover the fifty miles to Lake Ampara Magog, where Rogers divided his command into "small companies of twenties" so that they could move faster and forage more easily.[10] As provisions ran out and the men weakened, the wounded and sick fell behind, to be killed and scalped by the fast-approaching enemy. "Being not a season for distinctions,"[11] men turned to eating ground nuts and roots. Some roasted their shoes and powder horns. As a last measure, one group of rangers resorted to cannibalism, devouring the bodies of those who had died.[12] On the fifth of November, one month after the attack, Rogers reached Fort Number 4. He quickly dispatched supplies upriver, hoping that they might find his starving men. Rogers had lost only one man and had six wounded at St. Francis. However, eighteen rangers were killed on the retreat, and thirty more died of starvation. As one New England balladeer wrote after the attack:

> *The rest there fled into the wood*
> *where they did dy for want of food*
> *these men did grieve and mourn and cry*
> *were in these howling woods must dy.*
>
> *few of these men rogers there fore*
> *conducted safe to numbr four*
> *the rest behind did their remain*
> *wheir they with Hunger firce were slain.* [13]

Amherst's desire for revenge had come at a very high price and accomplished virtually nothing.

Through the winter in Montreal Vaudreuil and Lévis pondered their plight. The British were closing in on them from three sides (Quebec, Champlain, and Ontario). In the aftermath of the fall of Quebec, colony officials, including Lévis, Vaudreuil, Bigot, and others, spent hours writing self-serving reports that exculpated themselves from all responsibility for the defeat while laying the blame on the dead. [14]

Like his fallen commander, Lévis knew his duty: to hold out as long as possible. He asked Versailles for reinforcements, knowing that there was little chance of any arriving. Lévis hoped for a long winter, uncertain what spring might bring.

Lest the British army overshadow it, the navy too delivered grand news. Under Anson's direction the fleet had maintained a close blockade of the French coast. The navy's vigorous activity, as well as the overzealous behavior of English privateers, thoroughly annoyed the Continent's neutral powers: Spain, Sweden, Holland, and Denmark. English captains had scooped up their ships, offering little regard for the niceties of international law. Pitt and Anson saw neutral complaints and threats of retaliation as a small price to pay for keeping the French in check. Underscoring British naval supremacy were the victories of Boscawen off Lagos and Hawke in Quiberon Bay.[15]

Since the middle of May 1759, Boscawen had been patrolling the Mediterranean coast between Marseilles and Toulon. For six weeks he kept his ships in perpetual motion prowling near the shore. The strain on his men and ships was beginning to show. Provisions were running low and the fresh water was turning foul, so the admiral ordered the fleet to Gibraltar for victualing and repair. Wasting no time, the French commander, Admiral Sabran La Clue, sailed from Toulon with ten ships of the line screened by two 50-gun ships and a trio of fast frigates and dashed for the Straits of Gibraltar. Once through the straits, La Clue intended a course for Brest to combine with the fleet awaiting him there. La Clue came south and hugged the Barbary Coast bearing west. As he neared the straits, Boscawen's scouting frigates spotted him and gave chase. In rapid order the main force got under way from Gibraltar and pursued the French toward Cape St. Vincent. On the afternoon of August 18 Boscawen's van led by *Culloden* came within range of La Clue's rearmost ship, *Centaure*, and the battle was on. Through the remainder of the day and into the night the English got the better of the exchange. By morning La Clue was running northeast toward neutral Portugal, making for the port of Lagos.

Boscawen was relentless. Two of the French fleet made good their escape, but La Clue, unwilling to suffer the humiliation of surrender, ran his flagship, *Ocean*, aground on the Portuguese shore. *Redoubtable* followed his example. Two other ships, *Temereire* and *Modeste*, sought shelter close to shore under Portuguese batteries. With their traditional disregard for neutrality, Boscawen's captains followed in hot pursuit, brazenly sailing into Portuguese waters, where they burned *Ocean* and *Redoubtable*, and took *Temeraire* and *Modeste* as prizes.

Boscawen's rout of La Clue crippled the French navy. Two months later it suffered an even greater defeat.

On November 16 Admiral Sir Edward Hawke received intelligence that a French fleet under Admiral the Marquis de Conflans had slipped the Brest blockade and was at sea with twenty-one ships of the line. According to the report, it was bound south toward Quiberon Bay, where Conflans intended to rendezvous with a fleet of troop transports and supply vessels. Their intention was clear: a cross-Channel invasion. The next morning Hawke signaled his fleet of twenty-three ships of the line to make sail for Quiberon. At the same time he dispatched a message to the Admiralty, announcing "[I am] in pursuit of the enemy, and make no doubt of coming up with them at sea or in Quiberon Bay."[16]

By the nineteenth Conflans was seventy miles northwest of Belle Isle in Quiberon Bay. As is so often the case in those waters, winds sweeping down off the land collided with weather coming in from the ocean, stirring up a boisterous sea. Undaunted, Hawke held his course and pressed ahead to "court the prosperous gale."[17] Sailing in the van was *Magnanime*, commanded by Captain Richard Howe. *Magnanime* was listing so severely that the lower tier of her lee gun ports were under water. At nine in the morning of the twentieth a lookout called out that there was a fleet ahead. Despite the continuing strong winds and heavy seas, Hawke set his topsails and signaled a full chase. "All the day," reported Hawke, "we had very fresh gales at northwest and west-north-west, with heavy squalls. M. Conflans kept going off under such sail as his squadron could carry and at the same time keep together; while we crowded after him with every sail our ships could bear."[18]

Hawke bore down on the retreating French as they scurried through the narrow entry north of Belle Isle into the treacherous waters of Quiberon Bay. A cautious commander would have paused seaward of the bay to avoid the confined waters and the danger of being thrown up onto a lee shore, but Hawke charged into the bay. Conflan's fleet fell into complete confusion and disorder. "Had we but two hours more daylight" reported Hawke, "the whole" would have been "totally destroyed or taken."[19] Even so, French losses were heavy, and once again the Royal Navy took the laurels.

The battles at Lagos and Quiberon Bay broke the back of the French navy. "The glory of the . . . enemy is vanished into empty air," reported the *Gentlemen's Magazine*.[20] So great was the rejoicing that in London, reported Horace Walpole, "our bells are worn threadbare with ringing of victories."[21]

The good news from Lagos, Quebec, and Quiberon helped offset grim news in the dispatches from the Continent. For three years Frederick had been fighting on multiple fronts. Vastly outnumbered by his enemy, he had managed to survive by dint of his own military genius and the inability of his foes to coordinate their efforts. His success, however, had come at a high cost. In three years of tough campaigning Prussia had lost nearly seventy-five thousand men. These numbers were staggering to a nation whose entire population totaled less than three million, but even worse was the fact that these casualties took from the emperor a cadre of trained soldiers. Not only was his army growing smaller, but its ranks were increasingly filled with green recruits.

Prince Ferdinand continued to command the allied army of British and German soldiers facing the French in the west, while Frederick held command over the Prussian army in the east against the superior forces of Russia and Austria. On Good Friday, April 13, 1759, Ferdinand had advanced against the French near the city of Frankfurt. The engagements around the city were indecisive, but in the following weeks the French recovered quickly and were able to take the offensive and threaten Hanover. The prince planned to fall back slowly toward his main supply base at Minden on the Weser River. The French, however, outmaneuvered Ferdinand and marched into the city before the allies could arrive to defend their base. Ferdinand had no choice but to attack, and on August 1 the two armies met on the outskirts of the city. Marshal Louis Georges Erasme de Contades, the French commander, had an army of fifty-four thousand supported by 160 cannon. Ferdinand marched out with forty-two thousand men and 170 guns.

Contades arranged his men on the field in an unconventional manner. Instead of placing his cavalry on the flanks, where they might be used to harass and pursue, he put them in the center. As the battle got under way, Ferdinand ordered his infantry battalions forward to a position opposite the French cavalry. With bayonets fixed, the battalions formed ranks and held their fire as the French horse charged their line. Although the charging French made a fiercesome sight, it was more bluster than power. Their drawn sabers were a poor match for the wall of lead let loose by Ferdinand's infantry when they were less than one hundred feet away. Troops and horses fell in a tangled, bloody mess. A second charge met with the same result. With their center crumbling, the French had no choice but to retreat.

Watching the French withdraw, Ferdinand ordered his cavalry, under their English commander, Lord George Germain, to pursue. For uncertain reasons Germain failed to follow orders, and the French managed to fall back in good order. Contades lost seven thousand men. The allies lost barely half that number, but nearly all their casualties were in the British regiments. Lieutenant Hugh Montgomery of the Twelfth Regiment of foot reported to his mother that this "astonishing victory" had cost his regiment dearly. "We fought that day not more than 480 private and 27 officers, of the first 302 were killed or wounded, and of the later 18."[22]

Ferdinand's victory at Minden was one of the few bright spots in the German campaign. With their superior numbers the Austrians and Russians were hammering the Prussians in the east. In June, while Wolfe was preparing to lay siege to Quebec, an army of seventy thousand advanced, hoping to trap the emperor in one final climactic campaign. To divert them, Frederick ordered General Johann Von Wedel to attack the Russians at Paltzig. They mauled him, forcing Frederick to rush to save his army. But instead of advancing, the Russian commander, General Peter Semenovich Soltykov, opted to retire to a fortified position at Kunersdorf on the eastern side of the Oder River. Frederick, the master of march and maneuver, was out of his element. He probed for a hole in the Russian line, but finding none he ordered a full attack. It was hopeless. On August 12 Russian artillery tore through the Prussian ranks, and by the end of the day Frederick's army was battered and beaten. He lost nineteen thousand men killed and wounded. Soltykov crossed the river and began to drive toward Berlin. He might well have taken the city and forced Frederick to sue for peace had he not been unexpectedly forced to march south to relieve his beleaguered Austrian allies, whose supply lines were being threatened by a small Prussian force.

While Frederick struggled to rally his army, a few weeks after the disaster at Kunersdorf the French took Dresden, and in November he was beaten again at Maxen. That Frederick survived the horrible year of 1759 was due less to his tactical genius than to the ineptness of his Austrian and Russian foes, who preferred to squabble among themselves rather than coordinate against the Prussians.

Elsewhere around the world, in India, Africa, and the West Indies the British undertook smaller "eccentric" attacks. More commercial than strategic in their goals, these operations, particularly those in India and Africa, were designed to divert enemy forces while seizing important trading opportunities.

In distant India the war was carried on by a combination of forces both public and private, the latter in the guise of trading companies, namely the British East India Company and the French Compagnie des Indies. British affairs there were largely in the hands of one of the most enigmatic figures in imperial history: Robert Clive. Born into a middling Shropshire family in 1725, Clive was a bright and combative child who developed a lifelong love for fighting. Although he never attended university, his family provided a solid education, and in 1743 he joined the British East India Company as a clerk. The following year the company posted him as chief clerk in Madras. Two years later, during the War of the Austrian Succession, the French took him prisoner when they swept into the city from nearby Pondicherry. Clive managed to escape, and eager to exchange the pen for the sword, he applied for an ensign's commission and served with distinction during the British siege of Pondicherry. In 1748, the Treaty of Aix la Chapelle returned Madras to England and Clive to his clerkship.

But Clive was too ambitious and restless to spend his days keeping accounts. In the turbulent world of Indian politics, where the British and French trading companies were constantly inciting local princes against one another, Clive found ample opportunity to advance his military career as a company mercenary. A Kipling-like character who earned a reputation for swashbuckling derring-do and rashness, in 1753 he returned briefly to England, where news of his exploits made him a popular figure. Much impressed by his military service, the company appointed him lieutenant governor of St. David and also secured him a king's commission as a lieutenant colonel. By the time Clive returned to his post in June 1756, war had already been declared, but the official news did not reach him until months later. In the meantime, however, he had a more immediate crisis on his hands.

Suraj ud Dowlah was the nabob of Bengal. An ambitious and impetuous young man, he had recently inherited the throne from his grandfather. In the kaleidoscopic mix of Indian and European politics Suraj used bribery and assassination to consolidate his authority. One of his kinsman challenged the new nabob but then, having second thoughts, fled for his life

Robert Clive

and found sanctuary in the British-held city of Calcutta. Furious at the British for harboring the "traitor," Suraj stormed the city on June 20. Most of the Europeans fled, but at least 150 were taken prisoner. What happened next remains a matter of controversy. The only documentary source is a memoir written by John Zephaniah Holwell, an Englishman who claimed that the nabob's guards threw everyone into a small room, barely eighteen by fourteen feet, with only two tiny windows for ventilation. Holwell wrote that the intense summer heat turned the room into a death chamber, and that by morning only twenty-three people were left alive. Whether true or not, the story of the "Black Hole of Calcutta" gained wide currency.[23]

When news of the disaster reached Madras, the company ordered Clive to advance north and retake the city. His force approached by sea, escorted by a naval squadron under Admiral Charles Watson. Clive and Watson retook the city in December with little difficulty and then repulsed a counterattack by the nabob. A few weeks after the retaking of Calcutta, official word reached India that Britain and France were at war. Clive thus had a free hand to attack the French. In order to concentrate his forces, Clive, against the advice of his officers, negotiated a peace with the nabob. Then he urged a reluctant Watson to help him seize the French post at Chandernagor, fifty miles up the Hooghly River. By the end of March 1757, Chandernagor was in British hands. In the meantime the wily Suraj ud Dowlah was secretly talking with the French. Clive decided to rid himself of the

unreliable nabob. By promising the nabob's uncle, Mir Jaffer, that he could
have the throne once his nephew was disposed of, he was able to secure
local support.

On June 13, 1757, while Loudoun was marshaling his forces for the attack
on Louisbourg, Clive marched north from Chandernagor with a small
army of one thousand Europeans, two thousand native troops (Sepoys), and
ten cannon. They reached Cutwa Fort on the eighteenth, and by the twenty-
second they had crossed the river and made camp at Plassey Grove. The
next morning the nabob's army—estimated by Clive to be fifteen thousand
cavalry and thirty-five thousand infantry supported by fifty cannon, many
of them manned by French artillerymen—made their approach. The heavy
guns played on the British. Clive had chosen his position wisely, and indeed, his preparations went beyond the military. Over the previous weeks
his agents, aided by Mir Jaffer, had distributed hefty bribes among the
nabob's army, greatly reducing their enthusiasm for the upcoming battle.

High mud banks provided cover for Clive and his men. When the enemy
cavalry advanced, Clive's cannon delivered withering close-in fire that
made mincemeat of their formation. After several hours of bombarding
the English with little effect, the nabob's army withdrew. Clive ordered his
men forward, and within minutes they had the enemy in flight. Clive estimated five hundred enemy dead; his own losses were twenty-two killed
and fifty wounded.

Clive's astounding successes gave the British control of Bengal, albeit
through his puppet, Mir Jaffer. Shortly after the victory at Plassey Grove,
Watson died of fever and was replaced by his second in command, Admiral
George Pocock. Both Clive and Pocock realized that, while they held the
upper hand, their theater of operations was so distant and isolated that
they were on their own. Little help was likely to come from England, and
the French remained in control at Pondicherry. The slightest alteration in
strength on either side might quickly upset the balance of power. This was
particularly the case at sea, where the presence or absence of a single ship
could make the difference between victory and defeat.

Pocock's main objective was to secure communication between Madras in
the south and Calcutta in the north. In the spring of 1758, following Clive's
triumphs on land, communications between the cities was threatened by the
arrival of a French naval squadron and troop reinforcements under the

command of Admiral the Comte d'Ache and Comte Lally de Tollendal. Their orders were to reinforce the French garrison at Pondicherry and take the English fort at St. David. As soon as he heard of their arrival, Pocock beat southward from Madras, hoping to intercept them before they reached Pondicherry, but he missed them. The French moved overland against St. David with one thousand regulars and as many native troops while d'Ache tacked along the shore. On April 29 Pocock and d'Ache fought an indecisive battle. At the same time French land forces captured Cuddalore near St. David. Unable to reinforce the garrison, the British surrendered St. David on June 2. For several months the French did all they could to take Madras, but they failed. By the end of the year the French held firmly to Pondicherry, while the British remained steadfast at Madras and Calcutta. The stalemate held, neither side having sufficient force to overwhelm the other. Clive received orders in late 1759 to return home. In his place Sir Eyre Coote, a veteran of the battle at Plassey Grove, took charge.

India was not the only exotic place where commercial competition fueled Anglo-French rivalry. In West Africa, for example, on the island of Goree (Dakar) and the nearby coast of Senegal, British and French slave traders battled for profits.

For nearly two centuries Goree Island had been an important center for the slave trade. Barely three miles off shore, the island was a low, uninviting piece of rock less than one hundred acres in area. Refreshed by constant sea breezes, however, its climate was far more salubrious than the pestilential mainland, where "the hottest summers in Europe would be winters in Senegal."[24] Traders shipped slaves to the island from the mainland, where dealers shackled them in stone dungeons to await sale and shipment. The Portuguese were the first Europeans to set up shop on the island. The Dutch took it from them in 1621 and then lost it to the French in 1677.

Slave trading was brutish, violent, and despicable, and Thomas Cumming was one of its chief practitioners. Despite his horrid credentials, Cumming was a Quaker, known in London circles by the oxymoronic nickname the "Fighting Quaker." Greedy to control the lucrative West African trade, Cumming pestered Pitt and Anson to launch an expedition against

Goree and Fort St. Louis. The fort, 120 miles north of the island, controlled the entrance to the Senegal River, a major sluiceway for slave traffic, which reached hundreds of miles into the interior.[25]

Cumming's hectoring paid off. On March 9, 1758, Pitt sent six ships and two hundred marines, along with a detachment of artillery, to seize the island and the river fort. Commodore Henry Marsh commanded the whole, while Cumming went along as a political adviser; in reality Cumming managed the affair.[26] They arrived off the Senegal River on April 24. After bumping over the bar at the mouth, the commodore made his way twelve miles upstream to Fort St. Louis. Built on a low sandy spit, the post was decidedly unimpressive. As soon as the French defenders saw Marsh's ships, they sued for peace. Within a few days Marsh fell down the river and sailed south toward Goree. Resistance was much stronger on the island than at Fort St. Louis, and he was forced to withdraw.[27] Despite the repulse at Goree, for a small military and naval investment the English, Cumming in particular, reaped a huge profit.

Although the West Indies might be lumped in with India and Africa, the islands were in fact far more central to the conduct of the war. Sugar, and its waste product molasses (the raw material for rum), were the most valuable commodities in the Atlantic trade. The Caribbean islands that produced these products were prime targets for competing empires.[28] In addition, their geographic proximity to North America made them key strategic and diplomatic assets.

Almost from the day of Columbus's "discovery," Spain, England, and France had competed for trade and territory in the West Indies. By the eighteenth century Spain's principal base was Havana on the island of Cuba. England's key positions were its naval bases at Antigua and Jamaica and the rich sugar islands of the Barbados. France's most valuable possessions were the large islands of Guadeloupe and Martinique. In November 1758 Pitt dispatched an expedition to seize Martinique.

Pitt was haunted by the unhappy memory of the peace made in the last French war at Aix la Chapelle in 1748. By returning Louisbourg to France and leaving the borders of North America in a confused state, and by permitting the French to keep a strong presence in the Caribbean, Pitt's predecessors, he believed, had made the current war inevitable. Bellicose and bold, Pitt was determined to reduce France's New World empire. But he was also a realist who understood the political and diplomatic dynamics surrounding him. He knew that at any moment pressure from the king, Commons, or his own cabinet colleagues might drag him to the peace table. If that were the case, Martinique would provide a valuable bargaining chip in the traditional (and inevitable) swap of territory that would come with peace. Elements of the Martinique expedition sailed from Portsmouth and Plymouth on November 10, 1758, with Major General Peregrine Thomas Hopson in overall command.[29] At least seventy years old and infirm, Hopson had not been Pitt's choice. He preferred John Barrington, but the king insisted on Hopson. The king did agree, however, that Barrington might go as second in command. The year before, when he was stationed in Nova Scotia, Loudoun had asked Hopson to command the Louisbourg expedition, but Pitt reversed the decision and summoned him home out of fear for his health.

After a passage of seven weeks "without any material occurrence," the fleet rendezvoused at Carlisle Bay in the Barbados, where Commodore John Moore, a protégé of Anson's, took command of the sea forces.[30] After two weeks of additional preparation Moore and Hopson departed for Martinique. They arrived off Fort Royal on January 15. Fortified by nature and art, Martinique presented a serious challenge to an attacker. Numerous obstacles along the coastline made any close approach by warships extremely dangerous. Ashore, the French had prepared strong defenses.

With covering fire from the fleet, on January 16 Hopson landed 5,500 men at Negro Point, five miles west of Fort Royal. He took the post easily and the next day began his march toward the town. Wisely, the French defenders withdrew behind the walls of the local fort. Nearly four thousand troops, mostly Swiss and Irish, stood ready on the ramparts. As Hopson's soldiers approached the town, the fleet's guns were having a tough time. The French engineers who laid out the fort sited it high enough on the hillside that ships in the harbor could not elevate their cannon to a steep enough angle to train on it. While Moore's gunners futilely tried to lay fire on the fort, the infantry trudged ahead. As the afternoon temperature and humidity climbed to their normal oppressive range, the men stumbled through the heavy vegetation, swatting away squadrons of pestering insects. The soldiers had barely ad-

vanced two miles when their progress ground to a halt on the edge of a steep
ravine. To go around it would require a five-day detour, to bridge it "would
take ten days work by a thousand men . . . and another thousand . . . to carry
water to the workers."[31] Hopson elected to abandon the attack, and by midnight the troops were back aboard the transports.

Having failed to take Fort Royal, Hopson and Moore sailed along the
west side of the island to try their luck against the town of St. Pierre, the
commercial center of the island. The squadron arrived early on the morning of January 19, 1759. Although the town had plenty of notice that the
British were coming, the harbor was crowded with at least forty merchantmen laden with sugar. Sugarplums danced in the heads of the English as
they calculated the potential prize money anchored before them. Moore
ordered *Panther* and two bomb vessels to sail close to the town in order to
sound the harbor and draw fire so that he might assess the enemy's
strength. The island batteries showed remarkable strength, however, so
after several hours of engagement Moore decided that the French position
was simply too strong to risk an assault, and St. Pierre, with all its promise
of booty, was abandoned as well. Having "wasted balls, brawn and blood"
against Fort Royal and St. Pierre, Moore and Hopson decided to abandon
Martinique altogether and try their luck against another nearby French island, Guadeloupe.[32]

After a blustery three-day passage north past the island of Dominica, the
fleet arrived off Basse Terre on Guadeloupe's southwest coast. At seven in the
morning on January 23, 1759, the fleet opened fire on the town. They kept up
the barrage all day. British "hot shot" sent several waterfront warehouses
bulging with rum and sugar bursting into flames. The next morning Hopson's troops landed. "The governor, principal inhabitants, and armed ne-
groes having retired into the mountains," Hopson's soldiers easily took
control of the town.[33]

Hopson sent messages into the island's interior, summoning the French
commander, Nadau D'Utriel, to surrender. D'Utriel replied: "The terms . . .
offer[ed] me, are such as can only be dictated by the easy acquisition you have
made of the town and citadel of Basse-Terre; for, otherwise, you must do me
the justice to believe, that I would not have received them. The force you have
with you is indeed sufficient to give you possession of the extremities of the
island, but as to the inland part we have there an equal chance with you."[34]

D'Utriel's prediction proved correct. Whenever Hopson's men ventured beyond the safety of their own camps, they encountered a fiercely hostile populace, who fired at them "from every sugar plantation." "With the valour of an Amazon" one planter, Madame Ducharmey, armed her slaves and led them in person against the invaders.[35] Hoping to crush resistance, the British put to the torch every house, barn, and sugar mill they found. According to one report, their campaign of terror reached a vicious low when soldiers trapped slaves in a cane field and set it on fire, incinerating them. For nearly two months the British futilely attempted to corner D'Utreil. Hopson died in the midst of the campaign, a victim of heat and disease. Major General John Barrington took over.

Barrington quickly abandoned Hopson's slogging tactics. On March 7, leaving behind a small garrison at Basse Terre, Barrington embarked most of his force aboard twenty-five transports. With Moore's squadron escorting them, they made their way toward Grand Terre Island. The fleet had to tack around Old Fort Point and then beat into the prevailing easterlies, taking four days to make thirty miles.

Barrington landed without the loss of a man. The next day Moore informed him that a French squadron had been sighted north of Barbados. Moore was in a pickle. Although he was in support of Barrington, his orders from the Admiralty were also to protect British trade in the West Indies against French depredations. The squadron posed a serious threat, and Grand Terre was too far removed from the principal sea-lanes to be a proper base. Moore decided to move his ships to Prince Rupert's Bay on the north shore of Dominica. From there he could keep an eye out for the French and still be within a few days' sail of Barrington. On March 13 Moore sailed, leaving behind most of the transports and the frigate *Roebuck*.

Heavy rains and mud made life miserable, but Barrington persevered. With his transports and small boats he darted about the islands for two agonizing months, pursuing the enemy through the settlements of Arnoville, Petit Bourg, and Goyave. Finally, by late April, the British managed to chase D'Utreil to ground on the east side of Basse Terre near Petit Bourg. On April 22, D'Utreil entered the town and presented himself to the British.

Both the English and French had suffered much, and with the dreaded tropical summer approaching, neither side was anxious to prolong the struggle. Barrington offered generous conditions, which D'Utreil quickly accepted. On May 1, 1759, the French surrendered Guadeloupe along with the small neighboring islands of Deseada and the Saintes. The victory on Guadeloupe was part of a triumphal pattern. Aside from the Continent, where Frederick continued to struggle, British forces were victorious everywhere. The combination of strength at sea and disciplined troops ashore seemed unbeatable.

Fall arrived in Canada in 1759 bringing "frost and sleet."[36] Behind the walls of Quebec, Murray prepared his troops for the harsh winter. His ranks totaled 7,313 soldiers. Although Murray held most of his men within the city, he did post detachments across the river at Point Lévis and along a line from the Sillery Woods to Lorette to keep marauding French and Indians at a distance. Fresh food was scarce. Dysentery and scurvy, brought on by a relentless diet of salt meat without fresh vegetables, ravaged the ranks. Sentries who normally stood their posts for two hours could barely survive a single hour standing in the wretched cold. Regimental surgeons did what they could, which often meant amputating fingers and toes. Nuns at the General Hospital comforted the sick and dying. Bodies were "laid in the snow until the spring, the ground being, at this time, impenetrably bound up with frost."[37]

In their more comfortable quarters at Montreal, Lévis and Vaudreuil laid plans for a spring offensive to retake Quebec. The odds were heavily against them, and neither the governor nor the general had any illusions about their chances of success. Their only hope was to move early in the spring and strike quickly before the English could bring reinforcements up the river. Once Murray was defeated, they reasoned, they could turn against the British armies coming at them via Champlain and Ontario.

They expected little help from France. Versailles was teetering toward bankruptcy. Reeling from the incredible expenses of its huge European armies, in October 1759 the government issued a decree halting payment on all Canadian bills of exchange.[38] Having clearly signaled their intention not to honor their financial obligations in Canada, the ministers then spent weeks debating whether to commit troops and supplies to the colony. Although Vaudreuil and Lévis were unaware of how completely the ministry had abandoned them, they knew that they were far down on the list of national priorities. Hoping for the best, the governor and the general prepared to attack Quebec.[39]

Murray watched Lévis's movements carefully. Despite his official muster roll, fewer than five thousand soldiers were fit for service. A third of his army had been lost to "fevers, dysenteries, and most obstinate scorbutic disorders."[40] Faced with an imminent attack, he decided to call in his outposts and consolidate his forces nearer Quebec. At the same time, fearing that French civilians within the city might act as a fifth column, he ordered them expelled. The French citizens of Quebec, who had done nothing to warrant this treatment, marched sadly through the St. Louis gate, muttering curses about the lying and faithless English.

As usual, spring arrived late in the St. Lawrence Valley in 1760, and Lévis did not leave Montreal with his army until April 20. Five days later he landed at St. Augustin, about thirteen miles upstream from Quebec. By the evening of April 26 Lévis was crossing the Cap Rouge River on his march toward Quebec. That night, according to Captain John Knox, who was with Murray, there was "violent thunder and lightning . . . , surpassing any thing of the kind that has been known in this country for many years; and was succeeded by a most tremendous storm of wind and rain, threatening desolation to trees, houses, etc. the river was so agitated by this uncommon storm, which came from the south-east quarter, as effectually to tear up and disperse all the remaining ice."[41] Shortly after the storm passed, about two in the morning of the twenty-seventh, "the watch on board the *Racehorse* . . . , hearing a distressful noise on the river," found "a man almost famished on a float of ice."[42] He turned out to be a sergeant of the French artillery, the sole survivor of a bateau that had overturned in the storm. After some hot rum the sergeant told his captors that Lévis was on his way toward Sillery with twelve thousand men. In fact Lévis had only seven thousand.

Murray prepared to march out from the city toward the Sillery Woods. For several hours British guns fired toward the woods, harassing the French. As Murray watched, however, the French force grew in strength. Not wishing to risk an engagement, toward evening Murray gave the order for withdrawal, and his troops returned to the city. That night Murray held a council of war and decided that he would march out again the next morning. He explained to Pitt: "The enemy was greatly superior in numbers, it is true; but when I

Brigadier General James Murray

considered that our little army was in the habit of beating that enemy, and had a very fine train of field artillery; that shutting ourselves at once within the walls was putting all upon the single chance of holding out for a considerable time a wretched fortification, I resolved to give them battle."[43]

Early on the morning of April 28, Murray's infantry marched through the city gate. Some men carried entrenching tools; others were harnessed to pull artillery. Most of the horses had starved or been eaten. The general halted his men a half mile from the city on the Plains of Abraham, the same ground made sacred by Montcalm and Wolfe. Murray intended to dig in, though how far down his men might have been able to dig remains unknown since in several places the earth was still rock-hard from the lingering winter freeze. From a rise on the Plains Murray looked south and saw Lévis's van approaching through the woods of Sillery. The mass of the army was on the French left, marching close to the St. Foy road. It was, in Murray's words, a "lucky Moment."[44] He ordered his men to halt digging, throw down their tools, fix bayonets, and advance on the French before they had a chance to deploy. By advancing so quickly, Murray gave up his chief advantage: position. Although he had fewer men in the field than the French, he did have considerably more artillery. But by moving down from the rise and onto soft muddy ground, he lost the advantage of his cannon. His advancing infantry masked their fire, and the mud churned up by the marching men made it nearly impossible to move the guns and ammunition forward. All along the line the action was fierce. In a mill along the St. Foy road French grenadiers and Highlanders struggled hand to hand—Highland claymores versus French bayonets. The French pressed hard, and Murray realized that if Lévis could turn his flank, he would be able to drive behind the British line and stand between them and the city. Murray ordered a full withdrawal. It was a disorderly retreat, and without horses the artillery could not be moved out of harm's way. Murray's entire artillery train, more than twenty guns, was left to the French. Hoping to cut off the British retreat, Lévis ordered one of his regiments to sweep around the British. In the confusion of battle the order went awry, and the battalion failed to carry out the movement, allowing the British to reach the safety of the city's walls. By midday Lévis's army had the city under siege.

Both sides suffered heavy casualties. Murray's losses (killed and wounded) numbered 1,088, while Lévis reported 833. Two days after the battle Murray dispatched *Racehorse* to carry the ill news to Halifax. Governor Lawrence was stunned. Wolfe's work, he feared, was unraveling. Lawrence dashed off a long message to Pitt. In a tone meant to convey alarm, he told the minister that he had good reason to believe that by then, May 11, Quebec was in the hands of the French.[45] In fact, Murray had provisions enough to hold out against Lévis for about two weeks. If relief did not reach him before then, he would be forced to capitulate.

Lévis's position was little better. He hoped that a relief fleet was en route to him. In November Vaudreuil and Lévis had sent their chief of artillery, François-Marc-Antoine Le Mercier, off to Paris to plead for help at court. Had they known the miserable results of Mercier's mission, they would have despaired. Not only did the ministry ignore his plea; the ministers imprisoned him and charged him with fraud and embezzlement. And then, in a gesture that came too late, they sent a pitiful convoy of five merchantmen, accompanied by a single warship, to Quebec. They made it as far as the mouth of the St. Lawrence before British patrols out of Halifax took them as prizes.

On May 9, a British sentry called out from his post that a vessel was coming around Île d'Orléans. As the vessel drew nearer and glasses focused, there was no mistaking the fluttering Union Jack. While HMS *Lowestoft* was still coming to anchor in the St. Charles, its captain came ashore and hurried up the heights to inform Murray that Admiral Alexander Colville was on his way upriver with a relief squadron, and that he should be at the city within a few days. The officer also delivered a bundle of London newspapers filled with news of British victories. Murray dispatched copies of the papers through the lines to Lévis. With Gallic indifference Lévis dismissed the news as "vague and uninteresting."[46]

Despite his pretended indifference, Lévis knew then that he had no hope of retaking Quebec in this campaign. In a soldiery gesture of defiance, on the eleventh he ordered his batteries to open fire on the city, a desultory barrage that continued for several days. But with more British vessels making their way upriver, there could be little doubt of the outcome, and Lévis ordered his men to abandon their entrenchments and fall back across the Cap Rouge River.[47]

Lévis's rapid withdrawal toward Montreal endangered the French forces remaining on Lake Champlain and the Richelieu River. After blowing up Ticonderoga and Crown Point, Bourlamaque had consolidated his position at the northern end of the lake. He left a small guard force on Île aux-Noix, to guard the entrance to the Richelieu River, while concentrating his main force farther upstream at Fort Chambly. His men had spent a hard winter enduring frostbite, dysentery, and scurvy. In February 1760 Lévis summoned Bourlamaque to Montreal to help him plan the retaking of Quebec and dispatched Bougainville in his place to command the Richelieu area. Bougainville's situation was precarious. Lévis's retreat toward Montreal meant that Murray could easily move upriver and stand between him and Montreal, while on his southern flank Colonel William Haviland was creeping up the lake with a strong military and naval force. Bougainville was being squeezed, and on August 27 he abandoned Île aux-Noix and gave orders to blow up the fort at Chambly. He marched his men to join Lévis at Montreal. Bougainville's withdrawal left Haviland and Murray a clear path to Montreal.[48]

Amherst moved his headquarters west to Oswego in July 1760 to organize an attack against Montreal via the St. Lawrence. Murray's orders were to proceed along the river from the other end and join up with Haviland. Together Murray and Haviland were to close in on Montreal from the north, while Amherst attacked from the south.

Lévis's position was desperate. The enemy outnumbered him and were traveling with mountains of supplies. But if he could not deny his attackers victory, he could at least, he hoped, stall it. His best hope was to delay the main force under Amherst, which might allow him time to fend off the weaker forces coming at him from the north. To help him, he looked to the old soldier François Pouchot, the officer who had so admirably sustained the long siege at Niagara.

Lévis dispatched Pouchot up the St. Lawrence to complete the fortifications at the river's first set of rapids near the mission of La Presentation.* With his usual zeal Pouchot went to work, and within a few weeks he managed to erect a strong post, Fort Lévis, that covered nearly two-thirds of the low-lying island.[49]

As was his wont, Amherst massed his army slowly. From Oswego he wrote Pitt, "I have an army that can take Canada, and I will do it."[50] On August 10 "at the Peep of day the whole embarked," consisting of ten thousand men, mostly regulars, but including provincials from New York, New Jersey, and Connecticut as well. Also along were more than seven hundred Indians under William Johnson.[51]

The main body moved in bateaux crammed with tons of supplies. After three days on the lake the army entered the St. Lawrence. It passed Frontenac, moved into the current, and floated downstream through the treacherous Thousand Islands. Light infantry, provincials, and Indian scouts ranged along both banks of the river, providing security. By August 16, Amherst's advance guard was within a few miles of Pouchot. The next morning the brig *L'Outaoais*, the last remaining vessel in the French fleet on the lakes, sortied against the British. A swarm of British row galleys descended on it. After a three-hour battle the brig surrendered and was taken into Amherst's service.[52]

Amherst planned his approach to Fort Lévis very carefully, even though Pouchot's weak garrison could not do much more than puff smoke at the passing British. Had he wished, Amherst could have easily leapfrogged past Fort Lévis and been on his way to Montreal, but he was determined to pause and humble Pouchot. Pouchot, the great delayer, had put out the bait, and Amherst took it.

The British took two days to complete their encirclement of the island, and then five more to position cannon. Finally, on the twenty-third

---

*Ogdensburg, New York.

Amherst's batteries opened up. Remarkably, Pouchot held out for two days before surrendering. Amherst then spent four days rebuilding the fort he had just destroyed, renaming it William Augustus. At the price of twelve men dead and forty wounded, Pouchot and his brave garrison had delayed Amherst for nearly two weeks.[53]

Amherst's Indian allies voiced their displeasure. Having come across the lake with the British and fought against the French, they expected to be rewarded by being permitted to sack the fort, strip the French, and take prisoners for ransom and revenge. Johnson made the case for his allies and asked Amherst to grant them their customary reward. If they were not satisfied, he warned, they would abandon the campaign and return home. Amherst could not have cared less. His disdain for Indians was even greater than his disgust with provincials. He summarily rejected Johnson's request, telling him that "he believed his army fully sufficient for the service he was going upon, without their [Indian] assistance. . . . he could not prevail on himself to purchase [their friendship] at the expense of countenancing the horrid barbarities they wanted to perpetrate."[54] Johnson did his best to disguise the unpleasant news, but his friends were not fooled. Disgusted at the faithlessness of their allies, by morning more than six hundred warriors had left.

Aside from the departure of his Indian allies, Amherst's losses thus far had been minimal, and the only remaining obstacle between his army and Montreal was the wild rapids of the St. Lawrence. On the thirty-first Amherst renewed his sluggish advance downriver. Rumors of rocks and rapids raised anxiety among the men. For more than a century, French soldiers, trappers, and missionaries had paddled this route. To Amherst and his men, however, the ferocious white water of the St. Lawrence was new.

Amherst's first division managed to make eighteen miles downriver through rapids "more frightful than dangerous" until they reached Isle aux Chat (Cat Island), where they encamped for the night. The next day Brigadier Thomas Gage brought the second division. Together the divisions shot the Long Sault Rapids, where Amherst reported that "broken waves" filled the bateaux and a corporal and three soldiers of the Royal Highlanders were lost. That night they encamped at Johnson Point near the entrance to Lake St. Francis. The following morning the whole force proceeded two-thirds of the distance across the calm waters of the lake to

Pointe aux Boudets (Point Bodet). "Very violent Rain and Wind" held the army at the point for an extra day, but finally on September 4 they rowed across the remainder of the lake and reentered the current to face the most dangerous rapids between them and Montreal. It was "the worst part of the river."[55]

Eighty-four men drowned in this eighteen-mile stretch of white water, more men than Amherst had lost to enemy action in the entire campaign. Tired, wet, and weary, Amherst's army encamped on the Isle Perrot near the head of the La Chine Rapids, where the Ottawa and St. Lawrence rivers join. After a day of rest the army broke camp on the sixth and prepared for the final push to Montreal. A few hours later they landed without opposition within a few miles of the city. That afternoon Murray, coming upriver from Quebec, landed on the east side opposite the city. The following morning Colonel Haviland's men emerged from the woods near Murray's camp. Montreal was besieged.[56]

Neither the walls of Montreal nor the garrison within were sufficient to offer more than token resistance to the British. Most of the militia and Indians had already left, and even some of the regulars had deserted. As Amherst's engineers prepared the siege, Vaudreuil, Lévis, and Bigot discussed surrender. They had barely three thousand men. Although the situation was hopeless, Vaudreuil opted to play for time, sending the elegant Anglophile Bougainville to offer Amherst conditions: a one-month cease-fire. That drew a quick rejection from Amherst, who responded that the French had until noon to surrender or suffer the consequences. More talk followed until finally Vaudreuil agreed to a full and complete surrender. The terms were generous and allowed the French troops, both the Troupes de la Marine and la Terre, the right to parole, that is, the freedom to return home, offering in exchange a pledge not to fight again in this war against the British. In one particular, however, Amherst stepped outside the canon. He refused to offer his foe the "honors of war." Lévis protested vigorously, but Amherst was firm. The French, according to him, had excited "the savages to perpetrate the most horrid and unheard of barbarities."[57] Yes or no were the only answers that Amherst would accept.

Lévis and his fellow officers were stung. They were not, they felt, responsible for the "barbarities" of their allies and believed that as many "barbarities" had been committed on the British side as on the French. To save the city and preserve the honor of his soldiers, Lévis asked Vaudreuil's permission to withdraw and make a last stand. Vaudreuil dismissed the chevalier's bravado and signed the capitulation. In a final act of defiance Lévis ordered the regimental colors burned. In retaliation Amherst threatened to search the personal luggage of the French officers, an insult of the first order. Lévis stood firm in his defiance, and Amherst backed down. The French officers were secure in their personal baggage, and Amherst was denied the honor of presenting the colors of a vanquished enemy to his king.[58]

At six o'clock on the morning of September 8, almost a year after the battle on the Plains of Abraham, Amherst announced the surrender of the French and ordered his troops to cease operations. That night the general entered in his journal, "I believe never three Armys, setting out from different and very distant Parts from each other joyned in the center, as was intended, better than we did, and it could not fail of having the effect of which I have just now seen the consequence."[59] The next morning grenadiers and light infantry under the command of Brigadier Frederick Haldimand entered Montreal and marched to the Place d'Arms.

Vaudreuil's capitulation included all the troops in Canada. Over several weeks the news reached across the lakes and down the Ohio Valley. The war in North America was over. The fate of North America, however, was yet to be decided.

(12)

Pitt Departs, the War Expands

I will be responsible for nothing that I do not direct.

—William Pitt, minutes of cabinet meeting, October 12, 1761

No one had a greater stake in the fate of North America than its native in-habitants. On September 16, 1760, eight days after Vaudreuil surrendered to Amherst, a delegation of Canadian Iroquois arrived at Montreal to meet with William Johnson. Johnson opened the council by thanking "the Great Spirit above who allows us to meet together this Day in so Friendly a Man-ner." The chiefs responded by celebrating the renewal "and strengthening [of] the old Covenant Chain which before this War subsisted between us." They were pleased, they told Johnson, that the road from their villages to Al-bany was once again open for trade. They promised to return all captives and to "burry the french hatchet we have made use of, in the bottomless Pit."[1]

In return for burying the hatchet, the Iroquois asked for three con-cessions.

There is one thing we understand [British] have great Plenty of, which is Liquor, as that is the only thing [which] can turn our heads and prove fatal to us, we . . . entreat you in the most earnest Manner not to suffer any of your People to sell or give any to us.

It is proper for you to know the Way our Affairs were managed while under the Care of the french [which] is that Smiths &etc were allowed to work for Us upon the Government expense.

We are heartily thankful to the Genl for his Goodness in allowing our Priests to remain & instruct us as usual, and we shall endeavour to

make a good Use of it, as He is now the head of all here, & had subdued
our former Superiors, who maintained our Priests, they must now suffer
& cannot subsist without your Assistance; Therefore we beg you will not
be worse than our former Friends the french. And also beg that you will
regulate Trade so that we may not be imposed upon by [the] People our
new [Allies]. [2]

These requests reflected the growing plight of all the Indians who had
watched, and sometimes fought, during the war. Whether they were French
or English allies, the war had exacerbated their growing reliance upon European goods and technology, but their own declining economic condition
made it difficult for them to afford them. The British victory in North America accelerated this downward spiral of Indian impoverishment. Whatever
might be said of French attitudes toward the Indians, an economic relationship based on the fur trade was far more tolerant of native culture than the
expansionist agrarianism characteristic of English settlement.

Despite promises of renewed friendship, Johnson's meeting at Montreal spelled somber times ahead for the northern tribes. Tidings from
Pennsylvania carried equal concern for the natives of the colonies to the
south. By a royal charter of 1662 Charles II granted to Connecticut not only
the land within the generally acknowledged boundaries of the colony but
also a narrow swath of territory that stretched from Narragansett Bay to
the South Sea. Neither the king nor his ministers had any notion of what
they had given away, so it was not surprising that two decades later they
presented William Penn a charter granting to him portions of the land
previously given to Connecticut. In neither case did the king consult with
either the Delaware or the Iroquois, who both claimed a portion of this
territory in northern Pennsylvania and southern New York known as the
Wyoming Valley.

While legal title to this rich agricultural region stood contested for nearly
one hundred years, in a practical sense the issue of who owned the valley
was moot. The tide of white settlement had yet to reach that far inland, and
in any case, the presence of powerful Indian forces allied with the French
made the Wyoming Valley too dangerous for farmers to settle. Beginning in
1753, however, the region began to open up as European immigration grew
and Indian influence lessened. Land-hungry settlers and speculators eyed

the valley with keen interest. Attention peaked in Connecticut—which had a claim to the valley—where farmers laid plans to develop the Wyoming. In 1753 they gathered at the town of Windham, Connecticut, and formed the Susquehanna Company. The company's purpose was to buy land in the Wyoming Valley. The next year the company stockholders took advantage of the gathering at Albany and hired the infamous John Lydius to treat with the Indians at the conference in order to acquire title to the valley. Lydius did as he was told, and by any method he could employ. Unfortunately, the Iroquois who sold the land to Lydius also sold the same parcels to Pennsylvania interests. These convoluted machinations might have led to immediate conflict had anyone actually tried to settle on the disputed lands, but the explosion of warfare in the area intervened.[3]

With the surrender of Duquesne to Forbes, and the collapse of French power in the west, the Wyoming Valley took on new luster. Denying that they had ever abandoned or sold their ancestral claim, both Delaware and Iroquois, with the support of William Johnson, asserted that they still owned the valley. The colony of Pennsylvania, led by William Denny, put forth its own claim, and so too did the Susquehanna Company investors, who produced documentary evidence to support their position. It is difficult to know where the smell of fraud was the strongest.

As the parties contended, sharp divisions formed. On one side were the Connecticut men, and on the other were Denny and William Johnson. In a remarkable turnabout these two men who had spent most of the war tossing barbs at each other, combined to keep Connecticut at bay. To succeed, they needed Indian support—especially from the omnipresent Delaware Teedyuscung. On June 18, 1762, the disputing parties gathered at Easton, Pennsylvania. With Johnson presiding, they met almost every day for ten days. Teedyuscung laid out the Indian grievances. It was a matter of Indian oral tradition versus European documents. The Indians recounted what had been said at previous councils. The Pennsylvanians laid documents on the table that disputed their oral testimony. When Teedyuscung asked that the Indians have their own clerk to record the proceedings, Johnson replied that he was "surprised" at the request and assured Teedyuscung that the king's clerk—that is, the person appointed and paid for by Johnson—would make a good record. Suspicious of having his fate resting in documents he did not understand, four days into the conference Teedyuscung spoke in council to Johnson, "I desire you'll let me have the Writings which were read yesterday, that I may have time to Consider of them, as We did not understand what was said." He then added: "You promised to see Justice done, but when you refused to let me have a Clerk, I began to Fear you intended to do as George Croghan did, when We were here five years since,—King George has ordered you to hear me, and all the Indians fully. But how do you think I can make Answer at once to as many Papers as your Clerk was four Hours reading, in a Language I do not understand, and which have not been interpreted to me?"[4]

As soon as Teedyuscung finished, the Quaker leader Israel Pemberton stood and spoke in his support. Other Quakers chimed in, and Johnson found himself in an embarrassing position. The next day Johnson responded vigorously, charging that Teedyuscung and the Quakers were "Abusing" him and showing "Contempt." Something unrecorded occurred that evening that caused a sea change in the tone of the meeting. In the morning Teedyuscung announced that he and the other Indian leaders present "were ready . . . to Sign a release for all the Lands in Dispute."[5] No one has ever been able to explain the overnight change of heart. Bribery is a distinct possibility.

If Teedyuscung did receive payment, he did not live long enough to enjoy it. He spent lavishly, at least by his poor standards, trying to ape his white neighbors. He wore their clothes, lived in a settler's style cabin, and drank cheap English rum. His ill behavior undermined his standing in both the European and Indian camps. Although he railed against the inevitable white invasion of the Wyoming Valley, there was little he could do to prevent the takeover. On April 19, 1763, he and his wife burned to death when their cabin was engulfed in a fire of suspicious origin.[6]

By any measure the Indians were the biggest losers in the war, but the French in Canada suffered as well. While officers and men of the Troupes de la Terre, along with the Creole elite, including Vaudreuil and Bigot, boarded ships at Quebec to return to France, most of the sixty thousand French-speaking Canadians remained in their native land. Since there were so many of them, an Acadian-style cleansing was not possible, nor was it necessary. Incorporating these Francophone Roman Catholics into

an Anglo empire, however, posed problems. The example of the conquered Scots and the Irish weighed on British minds. In Ireland, and to a
lesser degree in Scotland, military defeat had been followed by land con-
fiscation, religious discrimination, and political disenfranchisement. Re-
pression is costly. Military occupation and constabularies are expensive to
maintain, and their presence often provokes violence. If the Acadian and
Celtic examples were followed in Canada, it would likely result in a heavy
bill of costs.

Equally unacceptable, however, was the notion of extending to Canada
the laissez-faire policy of previous administrations that had encouraged
the American colonies to assert their own prerogatives and challenge the
authority of king and Parliament. Both the king and his ministers were determined not to repeat in Canada the mistakes they had made in America.
In their goal of imposing firm rule over Canada, the English enjoyed two
great advantages. First, unlike the British colonies, Canada had no experience in self-government. The colony lived in the Bourbon world of "enlightened" despotism. Representative government had no meaning other
than the occasional meetings of the elite summoned to rubber-stamp the
decisions of the king's servants. No French Canadian could claim that the
new English rulers were taking his/her rights since they had so few to
begin with. Second, whatever attachment the French Canadians felt for
France was severely compromised by the arrogant behavior of the men the
king sent to defend them. Not only did they fail to beat the British but their
haughty and dismissive attitude toward all things Canadian was alienating.
In short, French Canadians cared little for Louis XV and his government.
What did matter to them was the preservation of their culture and religion.

While Amherst celebrated his victory at Montreal and negotiated with the
French Canadians and Indians, disturbing news arrived from the south:
The Cherokee were in full rebellion in the Carolinas. The uprising had little to do with the English struggle against the French. The Cherokee had
their own list of grievances against the settlers of the Carolinas and Virginia. Henry Timberlake, a young Virginia militia officer who had lived
with them, described what he saw as the English invaded Cherokee lands:
"The English are now so nigh, and encroached daily so far upon them, that

they not only felt the bad effects of it in their hunting grounds, which were spoiled, but had all the reason in the world to apprehend being swallowed up, by so potent neighbors, or driven from the country inhabited by their fathers, in which they were born, and brought up, in fine, for their native soil, for which all men have a particular tenderness and affection."[7]

The Cherokee understood the threat from the English traders as well as the danger of their dependence upon them. When a band of young men at Keowee, the principal village of the lower Cherokee, argued for an attack on the English, Round O, one of the headmen of the Stecoe Cherokee, rushed to the village. In an open council he asked his young kinsmen pointedly how they planned to get along without the British traders. "Had they found a mountain of powder? Had their women learned to make clothes and their men to make knives? Hatchets? . . . where was their store?"[8] Round O's sarcasm hit the mark. While the French governor at New Orleans, Louis Billouart, Sieur de Kerlerc, was adept at stirring the pot among the Indians of Georgia and the Carolinas, he could not provide the Cherokee with what they and their brothers needed most: trade goods. For that they turned to the English.

Other tribes in the region faced a similar dilemma as they struggled to maintain their lands against English and French encroachment. Traditionally, the Chickasaw and Choctaw allied with the French, whereas their neighbors the Creek exhibited caution. Fort Toulouse was in their homeland, which made them vulnerable to French retaliation should they sidle too close to the English. A fourth tribe, the Catawba, who lived in the northeastern part of South Carolina, had once been a powerful force, but the ravages of smallpox and Iroquois raids had weakened them considerably.[9]

In an attempt to further secure his colony's position among the Cherokee and forestall any French incursions, in the fall of 1753 South Carolina's governor, James Glen, marched two hundred miles west along the Charleston Path with a small force of colony militia. He stopped at the Keowee River, and with the help of Indian labor built Fort Prince George across from the village of Keowee on the opposite bank.[10] Following this policy of armed intrusion into the Cherokee country to a risky extreme, Glen's successor, Governor William Henry Lyttleton, advanced 150 miles west beyond Fort Prince

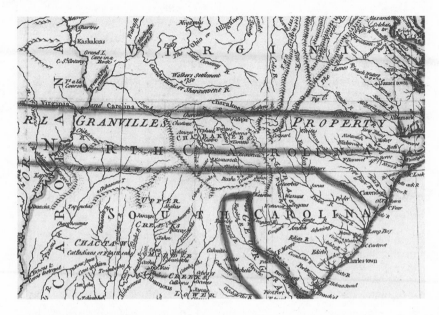

Virginia and South Carolina in 1762

George into the remote "Overhill" country, where on the banks of the Little Tennessee River he erected Fort Loudoun in 1756. The new fort was at the end of a very thin logistical line that snaked nearly four hundred miles from Charleston.

These repeated incursions into Cherokee lands raised tensions to the breaking point. Sensational reports of "murders" of both whites and Indians circulated in the colony. Finally, in the fall of 1759 the frontier erupted when a band of Virginia militia stumbled upon a group of Cherokee making their way home from Pennsylvania, where they had traveled to assist General Forbes. Like most colonies, Virginia offered a bounty for Indian scalps, and these militiamen were anxious to turn a profit. "Mistaking" the Cherokee for horse thieves, the Virginians attacked the unsuspecting warriors, killed several, and took their scalps in order to collect the bounty. One of the victims managed to escape, and soon news of the murders swept through the country.[11]

Years of pent-up resentment at their treatment by greedy traders burst out, particularly among the younger Cherokee warriors, and soon war parties were raiding border settlements. In an attempt to quiet the uprising Governor Lyttleton invited a group of headmen to Charleston. As soon as the chiefs arrived, officials seized them. With the hostages in tow, Lyttleton marched west with a force of sixteen hundred men. He camped at Fort Prince George and from there sent messengers to the Cherokee villages, demanding that they turn over the warriors responsible for the deaths of settlers.[12]

Thanks to the efforts of Attakullakulla (the Little Carpenter), the Cherokee's most able orator and diplomat, some of the hostages were freed, including a leading headman, Oconostota (Great Warrior of the Chote).[13] Releasing only some of the hostages, however, did not end the crisis. By the end of December the situation had deteriorated badly.[14] Lyttleton returned to Charleston, leaving Lieutenant Richard Coytmore in command of the fort and the remaining hostages. On the morning of February 16, 1760, Oconostota appeared at the gates to the fort and invited Coytmore to parley. The lieutenant agreed. Cotymore exited the fort under a flag of truce. He had only gone a few paces beyond the gate when a "Warrior gave a Signal [and] off went about 25 or 30 Guns from the Indians that had concealed themselves under the Banks of the River." Cotymore stumbled back with a ball "through the left breast." While the rest of the garrison laid down covering fire, Cotymore's men rushed outside the stockade and carried the lieutenant back to the fort, where he died a few hours later. Enraged at the betrayal, Cotymore's "men swore bitterly that they would kill every Indian in the fort." When one of the hostages, in fear of his life, stabbed a militiaman, the Carolinians took this as their excuse and they let loose "and fell to work [and] laid them lifeless."[15] The affair at Fort Prince George gave both sides ample reason to hate each other.

Lyttleton sent to Amherst for help. Although he was in the midst of preparing his push against Montreal, the general, accusing the Cherokee of "an infamous breach of the peace," dispatched eleven hundred men, under the command of Colonel Archibald Montgomery, to "chastise" the Cherokee.[16] After landing at Charleston in early April, Montgomery marched his men inland. Through the spring Montgomery's tough Highlanders burned numerous Cherokee towns, killed more than one hundred warriors, and tracked hundreds of miles chasing down the enemy.[17]

Montgomery, however, had too few men to leave any detachments to garrison the countryside, and as soon as he left, the Cherokee returned. By late June Montgomery's ranks were thinning. Disease, heat, and the Cherokee had taken a considerable toll. Deep in Cherokee territory, far from his base, Montgomery was learning that the interior of South Carolina was a place where "a handful of men may ruin an army."[18] Believing that he had punished the Cherokee as much as he was able, Montgomery withdrew his exhausted men to Fort Prince George. He allowed only a short rest before he and his Highlanders made a quick march to Charleston, where they boarded transports for the voyage back to New York. The Cherokee nation had been damaged but not defeated.

Montgomery's "success" had accomplished very little. On August 7, barely one month after Montgomery departed, Oconostota captured Fort Loudoun. As a condition for an honorable surrender, the headman demanded that the South Carolinians leave the fort's magazine and cannon intact. They did not. Angered at the deception, Oconostota's men waited until the militia marched from the fort and then ambushed the retreating column, killing at least twenty-nine and taking the rest captive. By late summer 1760, as Amherst advanced on Montreal, the Cherokee had come close to their goal of driving the English from their homeland.

Despite this remarkable success, shortages of food made the winter of 1760–61 a difficult time for the Cherokee. In January 1761 Colonel James Grant, who had formerly served with Forbes on the Duquesne expedition, arrived at Charleston with eleven hundred regulars. Given the alarming reports from Fort Prince George and Fort Loudoun, William Bull, Governor Lyttleton's successor, had no difficulty rousing South Carolina to launch a counterattack against the Cherokee. By spring Grant was ready to "reduce them to the absolute necessity of suing for pardon."[19] Grant marched into the interior, burning every home, tearing up cornfields, chopping down orchards, destroying livestock, and laying waste to everything his soldiers could find. For thirty-three days his force ravaged Cherokee country in a campaign with little mercy. In one instance Captain Christopher French was ordered to put the Indian town of Tasse to the torch and "put every soul to Death."[20]

Pressed by the British, the Cherokee fled deeper into the mountains. Resistance crumbled as their supplies of food and ammunition ran out. In the midst of the disarray Attakullakulla, who had earlier been thrust aside by the hard-line headmen, reemerged as the voice of moderation. After meeting with the other headmen, he journeyed to Charleston to seek an end to the war. Some embittered South Carolinians urged harsh punishment, but others argued that peace was cheaper than war. Both sides were exhausted, and for weeks they discussed terms for ending the killing. In the ultimate agreement, reached on September 23, 1761, all prisoners were returned, but the Cherokee were also required to surrender considerable territory and forced to permit the English to build forts in their country. Although the Cherokee nation survived, like the other tribes of the region, as of 1761 it became a vassal of the English.

Almost at the same moment that Grant landed at Charleston, January 1761, Amherst received orders from Pitt to open a campaign against Martinique. Timing was critical. Nothing could be done "till after the Hurricane Months, that is to say, about the end of September, or the first days of October." Amherst, a masterful logistician, was to prepare the campaign, but he would not command it. The king, according to Pitt, wanted Amherst, whose "Abilities, Prudence and Application" were so valuable, to remain in North America.[21] In an unusual demonstration of faith in a commander, the king vested in Amherst the authority to choose his own field commander. Amherst picked Robert Monckton.[22]

Even as he recognized the need to properly plan for Martinique, to maintain support in his cabinet, Pitt needed a triumph sooner than the one Martinique could provide. To secure his "Influence . . . both at Home and Abroad," a "Success" before late fall was essential, and so in the same January dispatch he ordered Amherst to make an immediate descent upon the small French Caribbean islands of St. Lucia and Dominica.[23] Amherst had barely three months to prepare, with the added complexity of Pitt's insistence that aside from naval support he would have to draw all the men and matériel necessary for the Caribbean expeditions out of his own resources.

To lead the Dominica–St. Lucia attack, Amherst selected Colonel Andrew Rollo, an officer who had served with him at Louisbourg, and who after the capture of the fortress had been charged with pacifying Prince

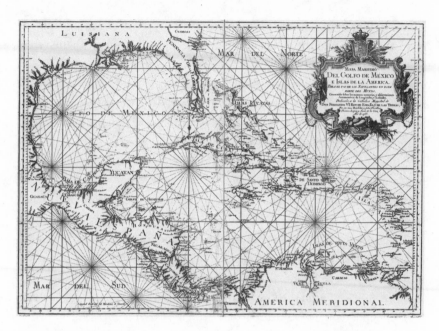

The Caribbean in 1757

Edward Island.[24] Amherst assigned him a modest force of less than two thousand men. Rollo sailed from New York in early May and rendezvoused at Guadeloupe with additional forces, including a small naval squadron under Commodore Sir James Douglas. They were off Roseau, Dominica's chief town, on June 6. Immediately, he demanded surrender. After the French refused, Rollo landed without firing a shot, and by evening had swept the small French forces aside "with very little loss." In the morning the island surrendered.[25]

Although Dominica had been an easy victory, Rollo's "little army" was suffering the usual medley of tropical diseases. Those men who remained well enough for duty were policing the interior, where a few French diehards were still holding out. Rather than strip his garrison and risk losing the island, the colonel decided to pass on St. Lucia and keep his men in place while he awaited the arrival of reinforcements for the expected assault against Martinique in the fall.

* * *

Following the capitulation of Canada, Amherst moved his headquarters to New York City. From there he supervised the consolidation of British authority in North America, dispatching emissaries to accept the surrender of distant French frontier posts and to bring news of the English victory to Indians beyond the lakes. These day-to-day activities were interrupted on October 25 when in the presence of his officers by order of the king, Amherst was invested with the gold collar and red ribbon of the Order of the Bath. The ceremony offered a brief break from the business of preparing Monckton's force for Martinique.

At the very moment that his friend General Monckton presented Amherst with the symbols of his honor, the king who ordered them was dead. George II was a man of routine. On the morning of October 25, 1760, he rose as usual at six and drank his chocolate. A quarter after seven he went into his "closet." Shortly afterward his German valet heard a thump, "and running in, found the king dead on the floor."[26]

Few people mourned the death of the old monarch. He was vulgar, cantankerous, and German. His disdain for popular opinion and clumsy political maneuvering had seriously diminished the influence of the monarchy in English politics. In contrast, the new king, George III, was English born, politically savvy, and a monarch determined to use all the tools he had at hand (mainly patronage) to reverse the political decline of the throne. In that regard George III viewed Pitt as a political rival and did not necessarily share his war aims.

The arrival of George III did not affect the plans for Martinique, however. Admiral George Rodney was already under way from Spithead with a squadron bound for Barbados, where he rendezvoused with transports carrying two thousand men under Colonal William Rufane. On Christmas Eve the largest piece of this elaborate force fell into place when Monckton's transports arrived from New York with the main army of seven thousand men, followed shortly by Colonel Rollo from Dominica, with the few hundred soldiers he could spare.

On January 5, 1762, sixteen ships of the line, thirteen frigates, and several other smaller vessels of the Royal Navy hoisted sail, came onto a port

King George II of England

tack, and formed a protective circle around a flotilla of troop transports, store ships, hospital ships, and baggage ships bound for Martinique. Monckton's force numbered nearly fifteen thousand men, including fifteen hundred blacks impressed for service from the islands of Antigua, Barbados, St. Christopher's, and Montserrat. By the morning of the eighth the armada lay to off the island and "fell down gently by the current" toward Fort Royal.[27]

From the quarterdeck of HMS *Marlborough* Monckton and Rodney cast a careful eye toward Martinique's forbidding coast. The sharp shoreline taught them a quick lesson. In a calm sea *Raisonable*, with sixty-four guns, ran aground on a hidden reef. Its keel struck so hard that its masts shuddered violently and within minutes they toppled over the side. A massive tangle of rigging, spars, and sails collapsed onto its deck, while down below, its hold filled fast with water. In surreal silence *Raisonable* settled slowly to the bottom. Rodney turned cautious. He signaled his deep-draft warships to lay offshore and keep to deep water. Lighter-draft vessels crept closer to the breakers but kept a careful watch.

Notwithstanding the perils of navigation, mobility on the water was Monckton's greatest tactical asset. To confound the enemy, Rodney dispatched fast frigates to bombard various villages around the island shore, hoping to draw defenders off on wild chases. In the meantime the commanders planned their attack. Neither Monckton nor Rodney needed lessons on the intricacies of combined operations. Monckton had been an understudy to Wolfe and Saunders. Rodney had commanded the amphibious assault against the French at the port of Le Havre in 1759. "Both fleet and army [were] at home with the work, and schooled for it, hand in hand, by constant and well-ordered practice."[28]

On the morning of the sixteenth the main attack got under way. Several ships of the line and frigates moved carefully to within range of Fort Royal and laid down a barrage of fire that lasted for nearly the entire day. While naval gunfire pinned the enemy down in the town, seven thousand men landed safely at a small bay, Cas de Naviere, six miles to the west. After securing the landing site, Monckton scattered patrols to reconnoiter the ground between him and the town. It was rough, hard terrain sliced by deep gullies, tangled with heavy undergrowth, and covered by "militia and mulattoes [who] were numerous, well armed and well skilled in the only kinds of war which could be carried out in a country like this."[29] On the twenty-fourth Monckton ordered the main force to advance. Two columns of troops moved toward Fort Royal. One hugged the beach line, while the other held the inland flank. As the troops inched forward, stumbling over the dark volcanic rock and cutting through dense brush, one thousand seamen paralleled them, rowing small boats a few hundred feet off shore that carried supplies and cannon. By evening the British had seized Mount Tortonson, a small hill overlooking the town. The march, however, had been extremely difficult. Although they had managed to get past the ravine that had thwarted Hopson, the vicious terrain and heat took a heavy toll on the weary soldiers, and the French still held the town and Mount Garnier, another nearby hill.

On the twenty-seventh the French defenders turned the tables on Monckton and launched a furious counterattack. They were beaten back; by evening the British had taken Mount Garnier.

On February 3 Fort Royal surrendered. The town's capitulation did not immediately end resistance. Forces under the French governor-general Le Vassor de la Touché still controlled most of Martinique, including the towns of St. Pierre on the west side and La Trinite on the north. The British took La Trinite by amphibious assault on February 9. Recognizing the hopelessness of his situation, de la Touché surrendered the entire island on February 13.

Over the next few weeks Rodney swept up the other French islands in the region, including Grenada, St. Lucia, and St. Vincent. The admiral was in his full glory. In his dispatches home he proclaimed triumph after triumph, and in his private account books he quietly tallied the booty that was to make him a rich man.[30]

In late January 1762, in the midst of his conquest of Martinique, Rodney received important news: England and Spain were at war. Like England, Spain had a relatively new king, Charles III, who, like George III, brought a new perspective to diplomacy and politics. Although both the French and Spanish thrones were held by members of the Bourbon family, the late king Ferdinand VI had tried his best to keep Spain out of the war. His younger brother and successor, however, was less able, and on August 15, 1761, he secretly signed the Family Compact, pledging to act in concert with France against England. Most important, Charles III agreed that if peace was not secured between the two warring powers by May 1, 1762, Spain would declare war against England.[31]

Thanks to his ring of spies, Pitt was well aware of the discussions between France and Spain. Firm in his determination to see the war concluded in a manner entirely favorable to England, he had for some time been fending off peace overtures from France. Why make peace when there were more victories in the offing and more territory to be gained? Rumors of Spain's secret negotiations with France stiffened him in his determination to push on to victory. His goals remained steadfast: take the French colonies in North America and the West Indies; hold to the treaty with Prussia; guarantee a settlement in India suitable to the interests of the East India Company; control the Atlantic fisheries; and dominate trade to Africa. Newcastle shared Pitt's war aims, but he was unwilling to pay the price for their purchase. The old minister was ready to make peace. He, and the majority of the cabinet, were weary of the war and tired of its expense.

Despite peace overtures wafting over from France, Pitt was convinced that the French were only playing for time while they consolidated their position in Germany. He was equally certain that Spain's diplomatic dance was a charade behind which it was arming for war. Through the summer and into the early fall of 1761, Pitt urged Newcastle and others to support a preemptive strike against the Spanish. Ships of the Royal Navy, he told them, stood ready off Cape Finisterre to intercept the returning treasure fleet from the Americas. Panama and Havana, he argued, could be taken with the forces already present in the West Indies, and Manila, far away and weakly defended, was ripe for the picking. Pitt's penny-wise colleagues shuddered at the expense of widening the war, and they resented the minister's haughty demands.

As Newcastle wavered, the king organized opposition against Pitt. In this he had the help of Lord Bute, a Scottish peer and a close friend of his mother and late father. Thanks to the king, Bute, over the vehement objections of Pitt, had entered the cabinet in March 1761. At an October 2, 1761, cabinet meeting, called to discuss the Spanish crisis, Anson and Ligonier gave expert testimony.[32] Both spoke against war with Spain. The fleet, according to the first lord, was not ready, while the general argued that the addition of Spanish troops in Germany would tilt the scales against England's allies. Pitt knew he was beaten. He told the cabinet, "I will be responsible for nothing that I do not direct." Three days later he surrendered the seals of his office.[33]

Pitt's departure left Newcastle as the nominal head of government, but the real power rested with Bute and the young king. Ironically, once confronted with the reality of the Franco-Spanish alliance, the new government found itself on the path to war. Only a few weeks after Pitt stepped aside, the British ambassador in Madrid, Lord Bristol, asked Richard Wall, the Spanish foreign minister, point-blank if he might see the treaty reported to have been signed between Spain and France. Wall lambasted the ambassador for his impertinence. Four days later Charles III sent orders to seize all British ships in Spanish ports. Within a month both sides declared war. Spain entered the fray too late and with too little. But war with that nation offered lucrative opportunities for Britain. Having scooped up nearly all the French colonies and merchant marine, the Royal Navy was running short on prey. Spain's ill-timed entry provided fresh and inviting targets.

* * *

As soon as he learned that war with Spain was official, Rodney wasted no time taking advantage of his opportunities. He ordered the island garrisons and nearby squadrons to stand ready while he sent fast frigates to warn ships on station to keep a watch for the Spanish. Rodney's actions were aggressive and prudent. He anticipated that the Admiralty would send him new orders to seize Spanish possessions in the Caribbean.

On March 5 Rodney received worrisome news. According to dispatches dated December 23, the entire Brest squadron under the comte de Blenac had given the slip to the British blockading force. The Admiralty assumed that they were bound for Martinique. Rodney called in his scattered squadrons and ordered cruisers to find the enemy. Blenac had his own plan. When he arrived near the islands and discovered that Martinique had fallen to the English, rather than undertake a risky counterattack he slipped away and headed north for Cap François, located on the northwest coast of the island of Santo Domingo only a few days' sail from Havana. Blenac's move caused Rodney to fear for the safety of his main base at Jamaica. If the French fleet combined with the Spanish at Havana, they would pose a serious threat to England's position in the Caribbean. Without faltering, Rodney gathered his ships and sailed toward Jamaica, leaving behind a small force to cover his rear. He ordered the commander at Jamaica, Captain Arthur Forrest, to join him with all available force in the Windward Passage (between Cuba and Santo Domingo), where they could stand and block any enemy descent on the island.

En route to his rendezvous with Forrest, Rodney put into St. Christopher's. Captain John Elphinstone of the frigate *Richmond* was there to meet him with new orders from the Admiralty. Their lordships instructed him "to desist from any enterprise he might have in view."[34]

Rodney was, after all, a relatively junior flag officer, and it was never likely that the Admiralty would entrust a major campaign in the West Indies to him when a small squadron of senior officers would have lined up for the post, anxious for the glory and spoils that might come by plucking Spain's Caribbean treasures.

Havana, "the Pearl of the Antilles," was the juiciest prize. Located on the northwest side of Cuba, it was one of the largest European cities in the New World. Its deep and spacious harbor was the finest and best defended in the Caribbean. At the harbor's narrow entrance the Spanish had built two imposing forts: Morro Castle on the east side and Punta on the west. Their walls stood watch over a narrow passage leading from the sea to the inner harbor. Havana was the key to the Greater Antilles. Pitt had advocated its seizure when in office, and now that the nation was at war with Spain, not even those who had dumped him from power could argue against his logic. With the advice of Bute, Anson, and Ligonier, the king appointed Admiral George Pocock, Clive's naval partner in India, to overall command. Pocock's second was Commodore Augustus Keppel. The land forces were under Keppel's older brother George, earl of Albemarle. The earl had once been colonel of Wolfe's regiment when the hero of Quebec was serving in Scotland. Wolfe had detested him, describing him to his mother as a "showy" officer who "professes fairly, and means nothing."[35]

Anson and Ligonier moved quickly. Their "secret plan" was to rely mainly on forces already in the field. The Admiralty could spare only six ships of the line fom home waters.

On March 5, Pocock and Albemarle came aboard the flagship *Namur* at Portsmouth. That same day *Namur* departed, in company with several men-of-war, sixty-four transports, and three East India ships.[36] *Namur* made its landfall at Barbados on April 20. Pocock sent a fast boat ahead to get the latest intelligence. When he learned that the main British force was waiting at Martinique, he hurried to the island. Rodney did not welcome Pocock in person. "It gives me real pain," he wrote to his successor, "that my ill state of health prevents my paying my respects to you in person."[37] Monckton transferred his regiments to Albemarle's control. All told, Pocock had a fleet of thirteen ships of the line, while Albemarle's land force totaled nearly sixteen thousand men. Five thousand of Albemarle's men, however, had to be left in the islands for security. To compensate for the loss of manpower, the admiral purchased one thousand slaves for a labor force. On May 6 the expedition sailed for Cape St. Nicholas on the Windward Passage, where on the twenty-third they were joined by nine more ships of the line that had been dogging the enemy off Cap François. Once again the Admiralty had demonstrated a remarkable ability to assemble land and sea forces.

Pocock faced a difficult decision. Looking at the charts, he realized that he had two ways to approach Havana. He could sail his fleet through the relatively safe waters off Cuba's southern coast and then pass northwesterly through the Yucatan Channel, coming onto a northeasterly course toward Havana. Although this offered safe water, it was a lengthy passage, and for his lubberly transports it posed a special problem, since once they exited the channel and came onto an easterly heading they would have to beat against both wind and current. It could take them weeks to cover the distance to Havana. Pocock's other choice was to bear north through the Windward Passage and then set a westerly course along Cuba's north shore. This route was shorter and blessed with a fair current and a favoring breeze. The curse was that the fleet would have to negotiate the Old Bahama Channel, which included some of the most treacherous waters in the Caribbean. Shallow banks, shoals, and serpentine reefs dotted the wreck-strewn waters between the Bahama Islands and Cuba's northern coast. Despite the horrendous obstacles, the admiral chose tactical advantage over navigational risk. He ordered his captains to lay a course along the northern shore.[38]

Before carrying out his mission against Havana, Pocock still had to deal with Blenac. The French fleet had dashed into Cap François and was riding at anchor waiting for the Spanish to join them. Luckily for Pocock, the Spanish admiral at Havana, Don Gutierre de Hevia, was under strict orders to keep his fleet intact at Havana, and not to undertake anything that might leave the city unprotected. To ensure that Blenac would not hit him from the rear, Pocock dispatched eight ships of the line to guard the port. But Blenac was not about to aid an ally that he believed had abandoned him.[39]

Pocock's advance on Havana was similar to Saunders's earlier movements up the St. Lawrence. Both admirals faced the challenge of bringing a large naval force through dangerous waters. To simplify control, Pocock divided his fleet into seven smaller divisions. At four in the afternoon of May 27 *Namur* signaled the divisions to get under way. Decks were cleared, sailors sprang aloft to let go topsails, and dozens of small boats were put over the sides and trolled along on painters, ready to be sent ahead to sound and buoy the uncertain channels. Although the wind was fair, Pocock moved slowly. For safety the fleet anchored at night. A few days out, Pocock grew anxious that his snail-like advance might cost him the element of surprise. To close faster, he decided to risk night sailing. He ordered the small boats to go ahead, where they anchored on either side of the channel and displayed lanterns to guide the men-of-war and transports. By then Cuba was clearly visible on the larboard side.

After ten anxious days of sailing, his fleet hove to about fifteen miles east of their objective. They had achieved near complete surprise over the enemy. As ships let go their anchors and swung into the wind, sailors on the troop transports struggled to release the lines that held the landing barges on deck. Pocock dispatched a fast frigate with Colonels William Howe and Guy Carleton aboard to reconnoiter possible landing sites. The admiral wanted to secure the beach as soon as possible, but squalls flying in from the north churned the sea and made it too dangerous to launch small boats.

On the morning of June 7 Pocock sent several warships to Chorera, just west of the harbor entrance, hoping to draw defenders in that direction. While his ships feigned an attack, the main body went ashore four miles east of the city at Coxima, where Howe and Carleton had chosen the landing site. Spearheaded by the grenadiers, an advance corps secured the beach, and within a few hours several thousand British troops were safely ashore, ready to advance inland.[40]

Although the British had caught the Spanish unprepared, they still had to face the formidable defenses of the city. Most impressive was Morro Castle. Rocky ground at the base of its walls made it impossible to dig trenches for a siege, and the thin soil provided almost no earth to mound up for hasty defenses. In the harbor itself Hevia had a dozen ships of the line. Not one of them raised anchor to sortie. True to his instructions, the admiral remained snug in the harbor. With fewer than five thousand regular troops available to defend the city, the Spanish commanders thought it a better course to keep the nine thousand sailors and marines on the ships close by for land defense.

Once Albemarle's troops were ashore, the speed and daring that had thus far characterized the operation evaporated under the hot Cuban sun. Boldness gave way to convention. Instead of using his mobility to strike quickly and hard at the key to Havana—Morro Castle—Albemarle opted for a conventional siege.

Grenadiers and light infantry moved in a wide southwesterly arc around the city, easily sweeping aside the few Spanish defenders they encountered. Having secured the countryside, Albemarle gradually tightened the noose. On June 11 Carleton's light infantry secured the heights of Cabana, giving British artillery range on the enemy fortifications. By the end of June siege guns and mortars were in place, ready to begin the bombardment. To Pocock's dismay, the fleet was of little use in the assault on the fortress.[41] The walls loomed so high over the water that the ship's gunners could not elevate their cannon to a sufficient angle to strike them. Albemarle's tactical success came at a high cost. The general had yet to fight a single major battle, but he was already suffering heavy losses from tropical heat and disease.

Engineers and slaves labored and died as they struggled to cut roads through heavy undergrowth and across sharp volcanic rock. The average daily temperature spiked above eighty degrees Fahrenheit, rising to near one hundred degrees at midday, with little rain.[42] Night brought no relief. Fresh water was the fuel upon which the besiegers depended, but there was none to be had except from the Chorera River several miles to the west. On June 15 Pocock ordered Colonel Howe to land at the river mouth and secure the supply. Soon a constant convoy of vessels plied back and forth, carrying thousands of barrels of water to parched sailors and troops.[43] Nonetheless, the situation remained difficult. James Miller, a soldier at the siege, remembered that "The fatigues on shore were excessive, the bad water brought on disorders, which were mortal, you would see the men's tongues, hanging out like a mad dog's, a dollar was frequently given for a quart of water."[44]

On July 1 British gunners opened their barrage against the Spanish. It was a fierce bombardment. By the artilleryman's manual, a per-gun rate of 80 to 90 rounds a day was considered expert; these guns fired at the pace of 149 shot in sixteen hours—more than twice the standard rate. The weather was oppressive, and the gun barrels were blistering hot. Since there was so little earth available to mound up to protect their positions, the artillerymen fashioned fascines from brush and palm leaves, piling the bundles close to their guns to shield themselves from enemy fire. The fierce sun dried the bundles to kindling. On the second day of bombardment a spark flew from a muzzle, igniting the fascines. In minutes a firestorm swept the batteries, men ran to escape exploding powder, and "the labor of six hundred men for seventeen days" was destroyed.[45]

By mid-July more than eight thousand soldiers and sailors were down, stricken with fever, dysentery, and scurvy. Like the Canadian winter, the Cuban summer threatened to destroy British plans. Albemarle's regiments were on the verge of collapse when they were saved by the arrival of fifteen hundred slaves from Jamaica. The Jamaican legislature had, according to a contemporary, behaved with "infinite honor" by offering to supply the labor of these men at only one-third of the going rate, that is, five pence per day rather than the usual fifteen. Strangely enough, there had even been a proposal to arm some of them, but fear of a slave revolt trumped the desperate need for soldiers; in the end, only one company of slaves was given arms to join in the siege. The rest labored and many died in the Cuban sun.[46]

Encouraged by the arrival of reinforcements Albemarle pressed the siege. For the Spanish the situation was critical. Under the weight of the English attack, the walls of the fortress were crumbling and the men inside were collapsing. On July 27 fresh troops arrived from New York. Three days later, after a party of engineers had blown up part of the wall, the British stormed through the breech, capturing the fort and mortally wounding the commander, Don Luis Vicente de Velasco.

Although they had lost the Morro, the Spanish still held Havana—but not for long. On August 2 more reinforcements arrived from North America. On the ninth Albemarle summoned the dying Velasco to surrender, warning him that if he should force the British to storm the city he and his men might not expect any quarter. In no condition to respond, Velasco turned command over to his subordinate Juan de Prado, who politely refused the British demand. Early in the morning of the eleventh the British batteries opened a tremendous fusillade. By midafternoon Prado was ready to parley. At 3 p.m. "flags of truce were hung all around the town."[47]

Nearly one thousand Spanish soldiers and five thousand sailors laid down their arms, but the real prize was the fleet in the harbor and the town itself. The English had become masters of the greatest trading port in the New World. They had taken or destroyed one-third of the entire Spanish navy and captured a huge store of sugar, tobacco, and other spoils. The cost, how-

The capture of Havana, 1762: the Morro Castle and the boom defense before the attack

ever, was heavy. More than six thousand British seamen and soldiers had died, mostly from disease.[48] Albemarle, Keppel, and Pocock tallied their booty. The admiral took home £122,700, while each lowly seaman pocketed an impressive £3 14s 6p. Havana was the richest prize of the entire war.

Across the globe another British force was closing in on an equally rich Spanish city—Manila in the Philippines. Called Manilad by the natives after the nilads, a beautiful white flower common in the area, Manila was occupied by the Spanish in 1565. It soon became Spain's principal post in the Pacific and the center for the immensely lucrative China trade. Taking the city had been part of Pitt's plan for the war against Spain. Bute carried it forward. Colonel Eyre Coote, Clive's successor in India, had managed to defeat the French at the Battle of Wandiwash (January 22, 1760) and take the city of Pondicherry. Coote's victories put India firmly under English control. He could easily spare men and ships for the descent on Manila.

Coote ordered Colonel William Draper to assemble a small army of two thousand men composed of "Seamen, Soldiers, Seapoys, Cafres, Lascars, Topasees, French and German Deserters."[49] Escorted by a squadron commanded by Admiral Samuel Cornish, the force left Madras in late summer

1762. Cornish sent a screen of frigates ahead of the main convoy to intercept any vessels that might bring the Manila garrison news of Spain's entry into the war. The admiral hoped to keep the enemy garrison ignorant, isolated, and unprepared. The plan worked. On September 23, 1762, the British force entered Manila Bay, catching the Spanish completely by surprise. They landed on the twenty-fifth and set to the siege. All went well, and on the sixth of October Draper stormed the town and broke through the Spanish defenses. Intoxicated by their victory and eager to seize booty, Draper's motley force was not easy to control. Looting, even beyond what was normally expected, broke out. To save themselves and the city, the Spanish pleaded for a truce. An agreement was struck: The governor-general of Manila, who also happened to be the archbishop, would see to it that his government paid a ransom of four million dollars. In return, Draper and Cornish promised to restrain their men. With that, Manila surrendered.

Beguiled by the riches offered by Havana, Manila, and India, England neglected its oldest overseas possession: Newfoundland. For almost five years two companies—one from the Fortieth Regiment and commanded by Captain Walter Ross, and the other a company of Royal Artillery under Captain John Boxer—were all that guarded it. While their brothers shared the booty at Havana and Manila, these men begged for bedding and clothing to protect them against the fierce Newfoundland winter.

Although forgotten by London, Newfoundland did not go unnoticed in Paris. Desperate for some victory, and anxious to grab any chip that might be traded at the peace table, Choiseuil decided to take advantage of Britain's distraction and descend upon the island. To command the expedition, Choiseuil chose a young naval officer, the chevalier de Ternay, assisted by Choiseuil's nephew, the comte de Haussonville. On May 18, 1762, de Ternay eluded the British blockade and headed west from Brest with two ships of the line and two frigates carrying a landing force of twelve hundred men. The French landed at the Bay of Bulls near St. John's on June 20, and within a week they took the town. Not until the end of July did Amherst learn of the attack on his rear. Embarrassed by the French success so close to home, Amherst the plodder reacted with unwonted speed. He dispatched his brother, Lieutenant Colonel William Amherst, to dislodge the enemy. The latter left New York with six troop transports ferrying fifteen hundred men, a supply ship, and artillery. His brother's orders were to proceed to Halifax and rendezvous there with a naval escort to be provided by the commander in chief of the North American station, Lord Colville.

When de Ternay saw the size of the British force, he withdrew, leaving Haussonville to fend for himself. Amherst landed on September 13, and five days later the French surrendered. Forgetting protocol, Colonel Amherst wrote to his commander, "My Dear Brother! I have done the business, I hope to your satisfaction," telling Amherst, "You can't conceive how determined I was. I believe I have learned from you."[50]

Seventeen sixty-two was a profitable year. Thanks to Spanish weakness, in the space of a very few months England had taken millions of pounds in prizes. From their shares of the spoils generals and admirals had grown rich, and even common soldiers and sailors had profited. Havana and Manila helped replenish the coffers of the British exchequer that had been so woefully depleted by the long war with France.

(13)

The End, the Beginning

*Here lies the Earl of Bute, who in concert with
the King's ministers made the Peace.*

—Horace Walpole

Even before the glorious news from Havana and Manila arrived, peace was
in the offing. Both the king and Bute wished to end the costly war, and they
were willing to settle on terms far more generous than anything Pitt might
have been willing to offer. Affairs in Germany, however, were not working
in their favor. Czarina Elizabeth of Russia had died on January 5, 1762,
leaving her son Peter, a fawning admirer of Frederick's, to inherit the
throne. Almost immediately he made peace with Prussia, giving Frederick
renewed opportunity to consolidate his forces and move against France
and Austria. When told by the Russian ambassador that Frederick intended
to continue to prosecute the war, Bute, next to Newcastle the most important person in the cabinet, replied that "it was not the intention of England
to make eternal war to please the King of Prussia."[1]

Bute was playing a double game. For months, via various shadowy inter-
mediaries, he had been secretly exchanging notes with the French. Aside
from the king no one, either in Berlin or London, was aware of the correspondence. But it was only a matter of time before the news leaked. Frederick's intelligence services were not idle. By late winter 1762 he was aware
that the English were in conversation with the French. He feared that England and France would make peace at his expense.

Bute moved to consolidate his position within the cabinet. In May 1762
he engineered Newcastle's resignation, thus ending the duke's four decades

John Stuart, the earl of Bute

of public service. In less than nine months Bute had managed to topple Pitt and Newcastle, two politicians who, although distinctly different and not overly fond of each other, had forged a coalition government that had led England to the greatest military and naval triumphs in its history. Having rid himself of Newcastle, Bute moved to the head of the table. Within weeks he arranged the appointment of the duke of Bedford as minister plenipotentiary to France. Bedford's appointment was gleeful news for the French, who dispatched their own pro-peace envoy, the duc de Nivernois, to London. Weary and nearly bankrupt, the French government ached for an end to the war. Pitt was the agent of their misery. Like Rome's Cato, Pitt would hear of no terms of peace other than those that brought devastation and humiliation to the enemy. No one in Paris could talk to Pitt, particularly the king's chief minister, the duc Choiseuil, who remarked that he "would rather go and row in the galleys than to have to discuss any kind of peace with Mr. Pitt." Bedford and Bute were more reasonable men.[2]

Bute kept Bedford on a short leash, instructing the duke to send home any preliminaries before signing. Although he was annoyed at the restraints fastened upon him, Bedford moved ahead and engaged in discussions with Choiseuil and the Spanish ambassador, the marquis Grimaldi.

Grimaldi behaved as if Spain was winning the war. In private he insisted repeatedly to Choiseuil that the English must be barred from any new entry into the Caribbean. How he proposed to do this was a mystery since there was little left of the French navy and the Spanish were hardly up to the task on their own. The marquis was posturing. Choiseuil detested him, and Bedford thought that "either [Grimaldi] or his Court have lost their senses."[3] Ultimately, to secure Spanish agreement to a peace, Choiseuil signed a secret treaty with Spain by which France ceded all of Louisiana, with the exception of New Orleans, to Spain in recompense for Spain's agreement to surrender Florida to England.

Late in September the glorious news from Havana arrived. Although the victory took place on his watch, Bute had had nothing to do with its planning or execution; indeed he had been noticeably cool toward the enterprise. Havana was Pitt's prize and another dazzling jewel in his crown. Bute feared that this new wave of victories might sweep him from office and return Pitt. Peace had to be made quickly. Bedford, too, understood the need to move quickly, and on February 10, 1763, with Bute's support, he signed the Treaty of Paris.[4]

North America was at the center of the treaty. Neither the French nor the English desired a return to the bitter and incessant border warfare that had characterized their joint occupation of the continent. Surely the violence would continue if both nations continued to support competing colonies set side by side in this vast wilderness. Choiseuil cared little for Canada, and so he agreed to renounce "all the pretensions which [France] has heretofore formed, or might form, to Nova Scotia, or Acadia, in all its parts," and France ceded "to his Britannic Christian majesty, Canada, with all its dependencies, as well as the island of Cape Breton, and all other islands and coasts in the gulph and River St. Laurence." Having solved the boundary mess in the northeast, Bedford and Choiseuil turned their attention to the west. Here their goal was "to remove forever all subject of dispute with regard to the limits of the British and French territories on the continent of America." With the exception of "the town New Orleans, and the island on which it is situated, which shall remain to France," all other territory would be "fixed irrevocably by a line drawn along the middle of the river Mississippi." Everything on the river's left side (east) was henceforth British.

Although the French vacated nearly everything they possessed in North America east of the Mississippi (except New Orleans), they did retain two tiny islands, St. Pierre and Miquelon, located a few miles off the south coast of Newfoundland between Placentia and Fortune bays. Their commercial and strategic importance was out of all proportion to their size. From the outset of the war Pitt had been obsessed with destroying French naval power. Like all eighteenth-century navies, the French fleet depended upon a ready supply of skilled sailors who could be brought quickly into service during wartime. Fishermen were an important manpower reservoir, and a great number of those men fished the banks of Newfoundland. Without a secure location near the banks of the western Atlantic, French fishermen would not be able to carry on the cod fishing. The economic loss would be devastating, and so too would the loss of seamen. This was precisely what Pitt desired. Allowing France to keep these two dots of land in the western Atlantic threatened to undermine his goal of sinking French naval power once and for all. Nonetheless, Bedford acceded, and the islands stayed with France. In the matter of fishing Choiseuil also managed to drag out of Bedford the right of French fishermen to drop their lines in the Gulf of St. Lawrence beyond nine miles from shore and to enjoy a similar privilege in waters off Cape Breton and Nova Scotia at a distance of forty-five miles from the coast. These were significant concessions to France.

Having been enticed to join the war by its Bourbon partner with the promise of spoils, Spain faced instead a staggering bill of costs. It had already secretly agreed with France to surrender east Florida in exchange for Louisiana. But now the bill grew higher. In addition to east Florida, the British demanded west Florida. Spain agreed to the terms, and in return England gave back Havana. England now possessed the entire east coast of North America, from the Arctic to the Mississippi Delta.

The West Indies were particularly troublesome. Pitt and his supporters argued vociferously that both Guadeloupe and Martinique, along with St. Lucia, ought to be held. But Bute, bent on a quick peace, knew that quibbling over those islands would delay the final settlement. On this specific point he had help from some of his Whig opponents. Wealthy West Indian planters, most of whom lived in London, were a powerful lobby in Parliament. Some of these gentlemen were dismayed at the thought of the French Islands being incorporated into the empire. Sugar production on Martinique and Guadeloupe dwarfed the English islands. The volume of imports from those islands into the English market would drive prices down. Whether to keep the islands, however, depended less upon the views of the planters and more upon the need to end the war and establish peace. Although England was triumphant, its victories did not give it sufficient leverage to demand both Canada and the sugar islands. Bute chose Canada, both to end the war and to eliminate the French in North America so as to ensure British domination over the entire continent.[5] England did, however, take several other islands, including Grenada, the Grenadines, St. Vincent, Dominica, and Tobago. It also managed to extort from Spain the right to cut and export valuable logwood from the bay of Honduras.

England held the upper hand on the African coast. Having failed to take Goree Island in 1757, the Royal Navy did so early in 1759. Returning the island to France represented a small concession, since in compensation England kept its position one hundred miles north at the mouth of the Senegal River (Fort St. Louis). Standing astride the river gave British slave merchants control over a vast hinterland that disgorged a seemingly endless procession of slave caravans every season. It was a far more valuable place than the collection point on Goree.

In India, too, commerce was at the heart of English desire. To speed the peace, the ministry offered to return Pondicherry. French factories, that is, trading stations, were permitted in a limited number of locations, but fortifications were banned. Both sides retained the fiction of rule by local princes, and they agreed to recognize them as the legitimate authority. In point of fact, however, only those potentates subservient to British interests survived.

The war ended on a particularly sour note in Europe. No one triumphed. Despite the treasure and lives expended on the campaigns in Germany, along the coast of France, and in the Mediterranean, almost nothing changed. The principal cause of the conflict on the Continent—Austria's desire for revenge against Prussia and the return of Silesia—came to naught. Frederick held Silesia, Austria got nothing, and France restored "all the countries belonging to the electorate of Hanover." France was also forced to dismantle the fortress at Dunkirk and return Minorca to England.

No peace, other than one that humiliated France, would ever satisfy Pitt. When he learned what had been agreed to in Paris, he turned on Bute and his colleagues with venom unusual even for him. Confined to his home by an attack of gout, Pitt read reports and listened to friends who brought him news of the debates in Commons. Although he knew that the "court had purchased an effective number of votes to ratify their treaty," he was determined to do all that he could to embarrass his opponents.[6] In the House of Lords the debate was furious. In answer to his critics Bute rose and declared that "he desired to have written on his tomb 'Here lies the Earl of Bute, who in concert with the King's ministers, made the Peace.' "[7] It was in Commons, however, that crowds packed the galleries to watch the spectacle.

Hoping that Pitt might recover in time to lead them in battle, opponents of the peace tried to delay a vote by referring it to committee. They were not disappointed. In the midst of the debate "the House was alarmed by a shout from without! The doors opened, and at the head of a large acclaiming concourse was seen Mr. Pitt, borne in the arms of his servants, who setting him down within the bar, he crawled by the help of a crutch, and with the assistance of some few friends, to his seat. . . . He was dressed in black velvet, his legs and thighs wrapped in flannel, his feet covered with buskins of black cloth, and his hands with thick gloves."[8] Pitt spoke for three and a half hours. "At intervals he obtained the permission of the House to speak sitting . . . ; supporting himself with cordials, and having the appearance of a man determined to die in that cause and at that hour."[9] Members gathered close to hear the faint voice. He lambasted Bute. Guadeloupe and Martinique should be taken, and the French ought to be excluded from any rights in India. He would not give them a rock on the Newfoundland shore, let alone two islands off the coast. Havana, so dearly bought, was the key to trade in the Caribbean and should be held. And most surprisingly for a politician who had so annoyed the present king's grandfather by his dismissal of German interests, he lamented that more had not been done for Prussia.

But Pitt's moment passed. To no one's surprise, Bute carried the day by a vote of 319–65. Despite Pitt's carping criticisms, Bute had done well. Had the government followed Pitt's advice and pushed for more concessions, the war would have been prolonged. If that had been the case, the Royal Navy could have controlled the situation overseas, but on the Continent affairs were doubtful. To be sure, France was financially exhausted, but it still possessed a powerful army, and its principal allies, Austria and Spain, were not without resources of their own.

American colonists celebrated the terms of the treaty. For more than a century North America had been embroiled in official and unofficial war. At virtually no time between the opening of King William's War (1689) until the collapse of the French in Canada was there real peace along the uncertain boundaries between the English and French in North America. Everywhere in the American colonies subjects of the king rejoiced that the French and Indian menace had been eliminated. Colonial legislators who had been so obstreperous and parsimonious when the king's commanders had laid their requests for men and money before them now fell over themselves rushing to offer proclamations of thanks to those who had delivered them. Aside from the soldiers in the field, America's chief hero was William Pitt. He had led the empire to victory.

In England, too, the crowds cheered the end of the war. Merchants rejoiced at the resumption of trade in an expanded empire. But while the bells rang out in joy, some in the government expressed concern. Victory had come at a huge financial cost. Pitt's strategic vision had exhausted Newcastle's purse. He had been lavish in his support to the colonies in both cash and promises. At the opening of the war the national debt had stood at a worrisome seventy-five million pounds. By the end of the conflict it had nearly doubled.[10] The price of conquered real estate had been high. Who would pay the mortgage? Surely, thought the men in London, the colonies ought to bear a fair share of the empire's expanded obligations. Thus far they had gained the most and paid the least.

Money was not the only worry in London. Although sentiment varied in intensity from colony to colony, for generations the people of British North America had shown a decided tendency toward defining themselves separately from their Old World relations. Central to this emerging "American" identity was the growth in power of the lower houses of the colonial assemblies. Often without notice, but sometimes in dramatic ways, local assemblies had been challenging and eroding the power of the royal government.

Most often this resulted from conflicts between the members of the colony's representative body and the royal governor. During the war these political encounters had grown more frequent and intense. At numerous times when Commanders in Chief Braddock, Loudoun, and Amherst sought support from colonial governments, they experienced firsthand the rising power of these bodies, which somehow managed to refuse and obey at the same time. Such behavior infuriated the generals and drew the ire of leaders in London, including the king and Lord Bute.

While the king's officers bristled at the boorish behavior of the colonials and their petty assemblies, Americans for their part grew increasingly resentful of what they viewed as the high-handed tactics of the men sent from England. Disputes over rank and command, the commandeering of supplies, wartime embargoes, and a host of other issues drove a deepening wedge between colonial authorities and the home government. Nonetheless, while the French remained in Canada and their Indian allies prowled the borderlands, the colonists were willing to suffer imperial indignities in return for imperial defense. After 1763, they would be less accommodating.

Amid the nation's exuberance, Bute's ally the duke of Bedford expressed a common concern among those closest to the king. He believed that England might have overextended itself; "we have too much already," Bedford noted. Taking Canada was a financial and strategic mistake. If these "few acres of snow" had been nothing but a drain to the French, of what use would they be to England? Even more important were the strategic implications. The duke noted presciently that Canada in French hands had been a monitor to the colonies. "The neighbourhood of the French to our North American colonies was the greatest security for their dependence on the mother-country, which I feel will be slighted by them when their apprehension of the French is removed."[11] Even as the duke spoke, disturbing news was arriving from the newly conquered west.

In the spring of 1763, after the French had officially withdrawn, English traders began to arrive, and the Indians discovered that life would be different. The French had been their partners. The English wanted to be their masters. The British would not sell rum. Instead they offered overpriced goods for which the Indians had little use. Native traders arriving at Detroit resented the new restrictions and complained to the fort's commander, Captain Donald Campbell.[12] The captain warned his superiors that "the French have a different manner of treating them from us." Perhaps it might be wise, he suggested, at least for a time, to follow the French traditions when dealing with the Indians.[13]

Campbell's concerns reached William Johnson, who shared his worries with Amherst. The general's reply was less than heartening. He told Johnson he did not agree with the custom of "bountifull" gift giving carried on by the French. Amherst did "not see why the Crown should be put to [the] Expense" of supporting the Indians. They should, he wrote, "be able to supply themselves." He continued, "as to purchasing the good behavior either of Indians, or any Others, is what I do not understand; when men of what race soever behave ill, they must be punished but not bribed."[14]

Having spent his entire career cajoling Indians with flattery and gifts, Johnson must have been taken aback, if not actually insulted, by Amherst's letter. It would be difficult to overstate Jeffrey Amherst's visceral dislike for Indians or his ignorance of their culture. For the Indians in the west who were already lamenting the departure of their French friends, Amherst's arrogance was frightening and inexplicable. Rumors began to travel that the British intended to seize their lands. Given previous British behavior in the Ohio country and elsewhere, such fears were hardly unfounded. In their dealings with the tribes the French had always been careful to behave as guests among them. No matter what their real intentions might have been, fur traders, Troupes de la Marine, and missionaries always gave the impression of being in Indian lands "temporarily." In that regard the French were cautious about building that most ominous symbol of occupation: the fort. When Amherst announced his intention of building a blockhouse at Sandusky, the Indians objected and complained to Johnson. Johnson understood their fears and suggested to Amherst that in light of these concerns he might wish to reconsider his decision. Amherst bluntly refused and dismissed the Indian objection as having "no manner of weight" with him.[15]

Defeated, disgraced, and dismissed, many Indians turned to spiritual sources for solace and the energy to fuel their resistance. Prophets arose. Among the most influential was Neolin, "the Enlightened." A Delaware, he rejected servile acceptance of English rule and preached resistance to the "dogs clothed in red."[16] Neolin inspired a native renaissance. Through him the Master of Life spoke:

> *This land where ye dwell I have made for you and not for others. Whence comes it that ye permit the Whites upon your lands? Can ye not live without them? I know that those whom ye call the children of your Great Father supply your needs, but if ye were not evil, as ye are, you could surely do without them. Ye could live as ye did before knowing them—before those whom ye call your brothers had come upon your lands. Did ye not live by the bow and arrow? Ye had no need of gun or powder, or anything else, and nevertheless ye caught animals to live upon and to dress yourselves with their skins. . . . I do not forbid you to permit among you the children of your [French] Father; I love them. They know me and pray to me, and I supply their wants and all they give you. But as to those who come to trouble your lands—drive them out, make war upon them.*[17]

Pontiac, an Ottawa chief, heard the teachings of Neolin. Robert Rogers had met Pontiac two years before when Amherst had sent him to accept the surrender of the French posts in the west. Rogers was impressed with the chief and described him as a man "greatly honored and revered by his subjects."[18] Pontiac was suspicious of the intentions of the British, and in the spring of 1763 he organized a meeting at Ecorse River a few miles south of Detroit. Ottawa, Chippewa, Pottawatomi, and Wyandot gathered. At the council Pontiac preached Neolin's fiery gospel of resistance. He told them that if they rose up their French brothers (the good whites) would return and help them. When the council ended, the warriors left carrying home the message of war and the promise of French help.

Within days of the meeting at the Ecorse Pontiac arranged with Detroit's commander, Major Henry Gladwin, to hold a council within the walls of the fort on May 7. Pontiac and more than three hundred warriors planned to walk into the fort with knives, tomahawks, and sawed-off muskets concealed beneath their clothes. When he gave the signal, the entire garrison would be massacred. The night before the council, an unidentified informant warned Gladwin. In the morning the major was ready. When Pontiac and the Ottawa paraded into the fort, they saw immediately that Gladwin

Pontiac, as he may have looked, in an unattributed portrait

had turned out the guard. Everywhere they looked, armed redcoats were standing ready. After some conversation, Pontiac gave up the plan and led his warriors out of the fort. For two days Pontiac remained nearby and made several more attempts to gain entrance. Gladwin would not allow it. Unable to take the fort from the inside, Pontiac threw aside the pretense and ordered attacks on the settlers around the fort. Detroit was under siege.[19]

News of the events at Detroit spread quickly through the west, and other tribes joined in the uprising. Thanks to Gladwin, Detroit held out. Other posts were not so fortunate. A band of Ottawa and Huron surprised and captured the garrison at Sandusky. In late May a relief force of ten bateaux sailing from the Niagara peninsula to Detroit was ambushed at Point Pelee on the western end of Lake Erie. Fort Miamis (near Fort Wayne, Indiana) surrendered, as did Fort Ouiatenon (Lafayette, Indiana). At the upper end of the lakes Fort Michilimackinac was taken by a classic ruse. One morning Chippewa warriors, who played lacrosse from morning to noon every day outside the fort, threw the ball inside the stockade. Pretending to retrieve the ball, the players ran through the gate. Indian spectators, mostly women, followed the men into the fort. Once inside, the women drew weapons from beneath their clothes and passed them to the men. In a matter of minutes they nearly annihilated the garrison.[20] In the Ohio area the old French posts at Venango and Le Boeuf surrendered. Fort St. Joseph on the southern edge of Lake Michigan and Presque Isle on Lake Erie also fell. Through the spring and summer the Indians mauled the British. Virtually every post in the west surrendered, with the exception of Niagara, Fort Pitt, and Detroit. Across the frontier, settlers and traders fled to escape attack.

Amherst was caught unawares and unprepared. Some of his regiments were still in the Caribbean and Cuba awaiting redeployment, while others that had returned to North America were recovering from tropical diseases and battle casualties. It would take considerable time to march these soldiers west. In the meantime "Pontiac's Rebellion" gained force. Pontiac understood that time was not on his side. The longer Niagara, Detroit, and Pitt held out, the more likely that Amherst would be able to marshal his forces for the counterattack. Vainly, the Ottawa and other tribes awaited word from their French brothers in Louisiana that they were coming to the rescue.

Amherst's reaction to the news from the west bordered on fury. He told Gladwin to put "every Indian in your Power to Death."[21] To Colonel Henry Bouquet, commanding a relief force marching west to Pitt in July, he wrote that the Indians should be infected with smallpox and hunted down with dogs. A few weeks later the general told Lieutenant Valentine Gardner that the Indians must be treated "as the vilest Race of Beings that ever Infested the Earth and whose Riddance from it must be esteemed a Meritorious Act, for the good of mankind."[22] Murdering prisoners, spreading smallpox, shooting women and children were all part of Amherst's plan to bring peace to the frontier.

In the case of smallpox, the general need not have worried. His men were ahead of him. When a group of Delaware chiefs arrived to parley at Fort Pitt in June 1763, the fort's commander, Captain Simeon Ecuyer, a Swiss mercenary, invited his guests in to negotiate. They talked, and then as a parting gift he presented them with two blankets and a handkerchief taken from the smallpox hospital. Captain William Trent, the Virginia officer who had built the first fort in 1753, was the man who supplied the "gifts." He noted, "I hope it will have the desired effect."[23] It did.

While Ecuyer held out, Bouquet assembled a relief force at Carlisle. He marched via Fort Loudoun, Bedford, and Ligonier. At Ligonier he abandoned his wagons and baggage and loaded four hundred packhorses with flour for the famished men at Fort Pitt. Three days later on August 5, 1763, about twenty-five miles east of the fort, his advance guard ran into a large force of Delaware, Shawnee, Mingo, and Huron who had come south from Sandusky. "The action became general . . . we were attacked on every side." The battle lasted into the night. Bouquet's men took a position on top of Edge Hill and fortified themselves with flour sacks. The Indians had the advantage and took a heavy toll on the British. The next day in a ploy to draw the Indians into a trap, Bouquet made a show of withdrawing some of his men from the perimeter. Believing that the British had left a hole in the line, the Indians poured through the gap only to be met by a fierce bayonet counterattack. As they retreated off the hill, other units pursued them. Bouquet's tactic worked, and on August 10 the battered column reached Fort Pitt.[24]

To the north Pontiac continued to press on Detroit. His coalition of tribes was fragile, and as it became increasingly apparent that the fort would not fall, individual chiefs struck deals with the British and headed home. In September the schooner *Huron* beat off a canoe attack and easily made its way safely to the fort with much needed supplies. Pontiac did all that he could to rally support, but on the evening of October 29 he received devastating news.

That night a young officer of the Troupes de la Marine, Cadet Dequindre, delivered a message from Major Pierre Joseph Neyon de Villiers, the French commander at Fort Chartres.[25]* It was addressed to the "French children." "The Master of Life," wrote Villiers, commanded peace. "What joy you will have in seeing the French and English smoke with the same pipe, and eating out of the same spoon and living like brethren."[26] The letter assured the tribes that the French king had not given away their lands to the English, only the lands he owned, and that the king "will never abandon [his] children and will always supply them from the far side of the Mississippi." The note ended "farewell. Live in Peace."[27]

Having lost so many of his own allies who had returned home for the winter, and now abandoned by his French brothers, Pontiac needed a respite. He dictated a note to Gladwin

---

*Near present-day Prairie de Rocher, Illinois.

My Brother

The word which my father has sent me to make peace I have accepted; all
my young men have buried their hatchets. I think you will forget the bad
things which have taken place for some time past. Likewise I forget what
you may have done to me, in order to think of nothing but good. I, the
Chippewas, the Hurons, we are ready to speak with you when you ask us.[28]

Gladwin was not ready to negotiate with the Indians. He would, he told
them, have to seek instructions from Amherst. The major, however, was a
reasonable and humane officer, more so than his general, and he wrote to
Amherst that while it was entirely possible to destroy the defeated tribes,
perhaps even as easily as providing them with free rum, it was not a good
policy. The natives were no longer a threat, and any prosecution of the war
would only harm the fur trade and lengthen the bill of costs.

Since Gladwin refused to speak to him, the Ottawa chief broke camp
and, accompanied by a few followers, headed south to see his French
brother Villiers. He reached Fort Chartres on April 12, 1764. The visit was
pointless; Villiers was packing for New Orleans—his war was over. After
several days of fruitless negotiation Pontiac returned north. Although his
power was waning, Pontiac's persistent preachings to resist British authority alarmed Thomas Gage. Gage, who had first come to America with
Braddock and remained to serve with Amherst, had succeeded Amherst
as commander in chief when the general returned to England in mid-
November.[29] Determined to crush the Indian uprising once and for all,
Gage assigned Bouquet and John Bradstreet the task. Bradstreet was to
strike from Niagara; Bouquet had orders to march from Fort Pitt.

Bradstreet planned to advance along the Lake Erie shore with a force of
twelve hundred men, mostly militia, to seek out Delaware, Shawnee, Ottawa, and others who had participated in the uprising. It took several weeks
for the militia to gather and for Bradstreet's carpenters to construct the
heavy boats (each forty-seven feet long) that would carry the force. While
work went forward, William Johnson arrived, and so too did nearly one
thousand Indians he had invited to Niagara to discuss peace. In July of the
previous year Johnson had hosted a similar meeting at his home for the Six
Nations. All but the Seneca had come to renew their pledge of friendship.
The absent Seneca instead took up the hatchet in sympathy with Pontiac. By

April, however, with Pontiac in flight and redcoats arriving, the Seneca had second thoughts. This time they too came to see Warraghiyagey, and on April 3, 1764, they signed a treaty repenting their transgressions and pledging friendship.

Johnson's oratory and the sight of Bradstreet's small army had the desired effect. The tribes pledged peace. On August 6 Bradstreet's flotilla, twelve hundred soldiers in large boats accompanied by three hundred Indians in canoes, set off for the south shore of Lake Erie. His mission was "to give peace to all such nations of Indians as would sue for it, and chastise those that continued in arms."[30]

Foul weather delayed Bradstreet's advance. On the twelfth he sought shelter in a small bay a few miles east of Presque Isle. It was there that a delegation of Shawnee, Delaware, Wyandot, and Mingo approached him. They blamed all the recent troubles on "some young men" and assured Bradstreet of their sincere desire for peace. Although he had no power to enter into any treaty—that authority was reserved to Johnson as Indian superintendent—Bradstreet drew up a "preliminary," which all the parties signed. Not only had Bradstreet exceeded his authority, a point that would not go unnoticed by Johnson, but he had also been deceived. Whoever the warriors were who met Bradstreet, they had no authority to negotiate for the tribes they claimed to represent. The agreement was meaningless. Johnson was furious at the trespass into his territory, and Gage was embarrassed that one of his senior officers had acted so foolishly. He told Johnson that Bradstreet's "Astonishing Treaty of Peace" did not contain "one Article whereby the least Satisfaction is given for many horrid Murders committed by those Barbarians, the sole Promoters and Contrivers of all our Troubles, and the Chief Actors in the Bloody Tragedy. . . . I disavow and Annull it."[31]

Unaware of what was going on behind him, Bradstreet continued his mission to Detroit. From Detroit he dispatched contingents to Michilimackinac and Green Bay to reestablish the king's authority. News of his arrival spread quickly, and within a few days Indian delegations began to visit. On September 7, 1764, Bradstreet convened a general congress. The Indians assured him that their eyes had been opened and that they desired peace. Bradstreet in return granted them amnesty, again without exacting any penalty. Bradstreet's peace-without-penalty policy ran counter to the

Crown's desire for revenge and won him few friends among his superiors. He returned along the lake to Sandusky, where he hoped to receive captives taken by the Indians. It was here that he learned that Delaware and Shawnee had attacked settlements to the south. Bradstreet made an attempt to move his men south, hoping to link with Bouquet, but low water in the creeks and long portages made it impossible. Instead he remained at Sandusky until October 18, when he and his army pushed off to return to Albany via Niagara and Oswego.

While Bradstreet was stranded at Sandusky, Bouquet was advancing in his direction from Fort Pitt. Bouquet had lost weeks of precious time trying to recruit Pennsylvania and Virginia militia. Not even the promise of bounties for Indian scalps and the guarantee that they could elect their own officers seemed to move these frontiersmen to sign up. Finally, by the end of September he had fifteen hundred men under arms, militia as well as the regulars. On October 1 the column set off from Fort Pitt and headed downstream to the Muskingum River and thence north into Shawnee territory, encountering only light opposition.

By the sixteenth Bouquet had reached the southern end of the portage between the Tuscarawas and Sandusky rivers. Here he met "Kiyaschuta, a chief of the Senecas, . . . Custaloga and Castor, chiefs of the Delawares and Keissenautchta, a chief of the Shawnee."[32] As a gesture of peace, the Delaware chiefs presented Bouquet with eighteen white captives. When the chiefs spoke, they echoed what their brothers had said to Bradstreet: All the troubles could be blamed on the young men. Bouquet took their measure and then retired for four days before making his response. He upbraided them and declared that their excuses were "frivolous to the last degree." He would, he said, accept their offer of peace only if they returned all captives. Two days later Bouquet moved his army to Wakatomica on the Muskingum to await delivery of the captives. He waited nearly two weeks until "on the 9th of November, the Indians brought in most of their prisoners, consisting of thirty-two Virginia men and fifty-eight women and children; forty-nine Pennsylvania men, and sixty-seven women and children." Having fulfilled their part of the bargain, that afternoon the chiefs sat with Bouquet and presented him with a wampum belt as a sign of peace. "With this belt we assemble and bury the bones of those who have been killed in this unhappy war, which the evil spirit excited us to kindle."[33]

Bouquet reported to Gage that he had "settled everything with the savages."[34] The following spring delegations arrived at Fort Pitt to sign formal treaties, and in June 1765 an expedition led by George Croghan made its way west to the Illinois country to talk with the western tribes and to find Pontiac. At Fort Ouiatenon Croghan deceived Pontiac by agreeing publicly to the chief's position that no matter what the French and English agreed between them they did not own the land but were tenants of the Indians. Not for a minute did Croghan, Gage, or the ministers in London doubt their absolute right to land claimed by the Crown and "deeded" by the Indians. Croghan's negotiations with Pontiac were only preliminary. Any final agreement needed the assent of William Johnson, and so Croghan invited Pontiac to travel with him first to Detroit and then later to Oswego for a meeting with Warraghiyagey. At Detroit the same promises of peace were exchanged. As the meeting adjourned, Pontiac agreed that he would come to Oswego for the grand peace in the summer.

True to his word, Pontiac came to Oswego on July 4, 1766. Chiefs of the Ottawa, Pottawatomie, Huron, and Chippewa accompanied him. Johnson, whose health had suffered considerably, did not arrive until the twenty-third, joined by chiefs of the Six Nations. According to Johnson, these people had lived in "a state of doubts and apprehensions" since the "reduction of Canada." They had been mistreated by the English, many of them had been murdered, and their land had been stolen. In desperation "their young men . . . quick of resentment . . . are ready to begin war without looking forward to its consequences."[35] The council lasted nine days, with one day lost for "bad weather." Johnson and the chiefs spoke and exchanged belts and gifts. The "Western Nations" embraced the "chain of Friendship" with their new father. On the thirty-first Pontiac bade Johnson farewell and asked him to keep open the "Road to Peace." Pontiac played his last important role at Oswego. Jealous of his power, perhaps angry that he had led them toward a war that they could not win, leaders of the western tribes turned on him. Shortly after Johnson left for home, Captain Norman McLeod, an officer at Fort Ontario, reported to him that a French trader from Detroit "offered to lay me a bet that Pontiac would be killed in less than a year."[36]

Pontiac returned to his home on the Maumee River. The west remained uneasy. Rumors of Indian uprisings and conspiracies spread unabated, fueled by the occasional kidnapping and murder. Pontiac's name was often linked to these incidents, but in truth his authority and influence had virtu-ally disappeared. On April 20, 1769, Pontiac entered the store of Baynton, Wharton, and Morgan in Cahokia. He engaged in friendly conversation with a Peoria Indian at the counter and left the store. The Peoria followed Pontiac into the street and without warning clubbed him from behind and then stabbed him.

News of Pontiac's assassination spread quickly, and so did the conspir-acy theories, most alleging some sort of British involvement. Nothing was proved, and to the surprise of nearly everyone, neither the Ottawa nor other western tribes made any attempt at revenge. For the first time in more than a decade, the frontier was relatively quiet as the British moved to consolidate their power and the Indians waited and watched.

Epilogue

Pontiac's concession to William Johnson at Oswego marked the completion of the Conquest. The great Ottawa chief had been the last obstacle to British victory. The French were defeated. The southern tribes had sued for peace, and the Iroquois were reconciled. Victory had come at a great cost. The forces of England, France, and their allies fought on virtually every continent. Thousands of soldiers had died in Europe, and many thousands more fell in America, Africa, and India. Never before had nations warred on such a vast scale. It was the first world war. England triumphed, and its war leaders laid at the feet of their sovereign vast new territories nearly twenty times the size of the British Isles. Not even Rome's legions had conquered so well and so quickly. A war that had began accidentally, and without a plan, ended with grand consequences.

In the aftermath of victory Britain faced several daunting challenges, particularly in North America. It needed to consolidate its gains, implement new governing structures, and find the financial resources to pay off a huge national debt as well as to support the ongoing costs of defending and administering its vastly expanded empire.

To consolidate and govern his new territory in North America, on October 7, 1763, the king issued a proclamation. In this hastily and carelessly drawn document he divided the new conquests into "four distinct and separate Governments, styled and called by the names of Quebec, East Florida, West Florida and Grenada." Bounds for each respected, for the most part, the historic lines long associated with them. Quebec's boundaries were defined as follows:

> Bounded on the Labrador Coast by the River St. John and from thence by a
> Line drawn from the Head of that River through the Lake St. John to the

south end of the Lake Nipissing; from whence the said Line, crossing the River St. Lawrence, and the Lake Champlain in 45 Degrees of North Latitude, passes along the High Lands which divide the Rivers that empty themselves into the said River St. Lawrence from those which fall into the Sea; and also along the North Coast of the Baye des Chaleurs, and the Coast of the Gulph of St. Lawrence by the West End of the Island of Anticosti, terminates at the aforesaid River of St. John.

The islands of St. Jean (Prince Edward Island) and Isle Royale (Cape Breton) were attached to Nova Scotia.

Of the four territories, Quebec was by far the largest and most heavily populated and virtually all French. The Treaty of Paris had guaranteed Quebecers their religion and lands. By the proclamation the king's new subjects were also promised "Royal Protection for the Enjoyment of the Benefit of the Laws of our Realm of England." They would have access to all "Courts of Judicature and public justice" and enjoy the right of appeal to the Privy Council.*

Having carved out these new colonies and dealt with their European inhabitants, the king proceeded to announce a new and far more controversial measure addressing land settlement and Indians. He ordered that "no Governor or Commander in Chief in any of our . . . Colonies or Plantations in America do presume for the present, and until our further Pleasure be known, to grant Warrants or Survey. or pass Patents for any Lands beyond the Heads or Sources of any of the Rivers which fall into the Atlantic Ocean from the West and North West, or upon any Lands whatever, which, not having been ceded to or purchased by Us aforesaid, are reserved to the said Indians, or any of them." By this order the king, for the moment at least, slammed the door on westward expansion.

Although Pontiac's rebellion added impetus to issuing this proclamation, it was not the sole cause. Since the surrender of Canada in 1760, British officials, particularly William Johnson, had been wrestling with the problem of how to manage Indian relations in these new lands. It was common knowledge, as the king himself wrote in the proclamation, that for

---

*English laws were not generally accepted in Quebec, especially in matters of "property and civil rights." The Quebec Act of 1774 reinstated French civil law to apply in respect to such matters.

King George III of England

years "great Frauds and Abuses have been committed in purchasing Lands of the Indians." Allowing settlers and speculators to cross into these new lands was certain to produce conflict. Pontiac's rebellion was simply a harbinger. Johnson helped convince the Board of Trade that, for reasons of justice and economy, closing these lands "for the present" was in everyone's best interest.

The proclamation line placed the imperial government in an impossible situation. The king's ministers in distant London stood as the guardians of Indian interests and the arbiter between those nations and an emerging American nation. Neither side trusted the other, and both were suspicious of the Crown. For colonial Americans, closing the west was tantamount to being shut out from the Garden of Eden. The war in America had begun over land. Like the Indians in the war who often found themselves prevented by their European allies from enjoying the spoils of battle, the colonials began to feel that they too were being denied their just desserts. How could the proclamation be reconciled with existing legal claims based upon colonial charters? Valid land titles existed beyond the line. Could they be extinguished without due process of law? What of the thousands of settlers, including hundreds of French, who already lived beyond the line? Confusion and controversy marked the issue of land claims before the war. The king's proclamation made a bad situation infinitely worse. It also antagonized a significant number of prominent men, among them George Washington and his fellow investors in the Ohio Company.

While the Lords of Trade struggled with the question of land, the exchequer was swimming in a sea of debt. In peacetime annual government expenditures ran in the neighborhood of £2.5 million. By 1761 that number had risen to more than £19 million. Along with a variety of other levies, the chief source of income, the land tax, had doubled to the extraordinarily high rate of 20 percent. Taxpayers, landowners in particular, pressed for relief. One possibility was to share the burden and levy taxes in America. Although there had been occasional discussions about such a policy, no one in government wished to face the political firestorm they knew it would ignite.

Despite the exchequer's best efforts, tax revenue could not keep pace with the war's rapacious appetite for money. The only alternative was to borrow, so that by the end of the war the national debt stood at a record £140 million. Through it all, however, thanks to the fiscal acumen of the men around Newcastle, the government's credit rating remained firm. Every loan was fully subscribed.

Peace brought hope to weary English taxpayers. As the burdens grew heavier during the war, they had been consoled by the belief that peace and victory would relieve them. The end of the war would mean a return to a more normal level of expenditures, and victory would bring the empire new lands and trade to tax. Landowners expected relief, and for this they looked to George Grenville, the new chancellor of the exchequer.

A seasoned politician, Grenville had once been an ally of Pitt's, but with the accession of George III and the rise of Bute he shifted his allegiance toward the Crown and Bute, "the Favorite." In April 1763, following the completion of the peace, Grenville took office as first lord of the treasury and chancellor of the exchequer. To him fell the enormous task of preparing the first postwar budget.

On March 9, 1764, Commons assembled to hear Grenville's fiscal plan. By then the chimera of a return to modest peacetime expenditures had evaporated. The issue was not how to reduce taxes but where to find new revenue. Grenville spoke "for two hours and forty minutes . . . with more art than sincerity."[1] He proposed a series of duties, which for the first time aimed at raising revenue in America. These included levying new or higher duties on textiles, coffee, and Madeira wine, as well as doubling duties on foreign goods entering via England. His program provided for a reduction in the sugar duty but at the same time put in place new legal mechanisms to ensure that the duty would in fact be collected. The next day Parliament approved Grenville's proposals, but fearing that even these measures might not answer the need for more revenue, the members added a resolution declaring that "it may be proper to charge certain stamp duties in the said colonies and plantations."[2]

Parliament was setting off on a new and dangerous course. Nonetheless, few in the body dissented. Having witnessed the disagreeable behavior of the colonials during the war, and now facing the ongoing costs incurred in defending them, most agreed with an anonymous adviser to the ministry who wrote that "it may be time (not to oppress or injure them in any shape) but to exact a due deference to the just and equitable demands of a British parliament."[3]

By insisting on collecting American revenue and at the same time denying America access to the west, the government in London had managed to take a broad swipe at a significant number of interests, including land speculators, settlers, traders, merchants, and seafarers. These, of course, were only the first of many "obnoxious" measures that succeeding governments would take, eventually rising to a mass critical enough to cause revolution. British attempts at evenhandedness, that is, asking colonials to contribute to the costs of empire and protecting the Indians from land-hungry whites, did not go over well in America.

For the Indians, however, the concentration of power in the hands of imperial authority provided a semblance of hope. Whatever their own racial biases, John Stuart and William Johnson were far more interested in the well-being of the native peoples under their charge than were local officials in New York, Pennsylvania, Virginia, and the Carolinas. Their offices answered to a distant king and his ministers whose sympathies were often with the native peoples. When Johnson wrote to the Board of Trade suggesting that Pontiac's rebellion was a result of General Amherst's policy of treating the Indians with "indifference and neglect," they responded, "We do entirely agree with you in opinion as to the causes of this unhappy defection [Pontiac's rebellion] of the Indians and are convinced that nothing but the speedy establishment of some well digested and general plan for the regulation of our Commercial and political concerns with them can effectually reconcile their esteem and affections."[4]

Any "general plan" that gained Indian "esteem and affections" was virtually certain to challenge colonial interests. England's attempt to regulate land settlement, manage trade with the Indians, and raise an American revenue stream all required that the government in London exercise greater authority in the colonies. Their aims were rational and just, but in the face of a growing sense of self-identity and separateness within the colonies, what the ministers in London sought to achieve was both impossible and incendiary. The loud clamor of the victory bells drowned out the voices from America urging caution and restraint. For a dozen more years, king and Parliament struggled to find a solution to the problems heaped upon them in 1763. During those years ministries came and went with an alarming frequency as they tried to deal with the consequences of 1763. Relations with the American colonies deteriorated as demands from London for an American revenue met resistance. Dispatch of troops to enforce unpopular laws sparked violence. Barely a dozen years after Englishmen and Americans had rejoiced together in victory, they were at war with one another.

By their revolution Americans succeeded in gaining independence and forming a new nation. In Canada, too, independence was eventually achieved and a new nation emerged, albeit more slowly and without a war. Indians were less fortunate. By the time of Pontiac's assassination Indian power east of the Mississippi was crumbling. To be sure both the Cherokee and the Iroquois, the two principal nations, remained; nonetheless, their future depended squarely upon the sufferance of a new imperial/colonial dynamic.

The scene of surrender played out at Montreal in 1760 between Amherst and the Iroquois was repeated, with a different cast, again and again in the west as the British war machine crushed any warrior rebellion. Abandoned by their French allies, the natives had no choice but to yield, comforted by the promise that as long as they submitted to the king's authority they could remain on their lands. Even that small concession, however, was only temporary. Peace lasted for barely a decade, shattered by a revolution that gave birth to a new nation whose citizens hungered for land and cared little for native rights of ownership. Americans advanced quickly westward across the Appalachian barrier into lands previously guaranteed to the natives by the Crown. By every means, fair and foul, the new republican rulers took their homes. In less than a half century after the creation of the United States, Indians east of the Mississippi were nearly all gone—"removed" to land across the river where they might stay forever and be forgotten.

The French and Indian War marked the beginning of a long decline for the native peoples in Canada and the United States. Their decisive role in that war has often been ignored, as shown on a fall morning in 2001 when a reporter for the *Montreal Gazette* described a moving ceremony. On that day the Marquis de Montcalm's "simple brown casket" was removed from its resting place in the chapel of the Ursuline convent. It was draped with the French flag under which he served and then placed on a carriage. "The Montcalm honour guard flanked the carriage on both sides. Soldiers bearing flags with the crest of each regiment Montcalm commanded followed." The cortege wound its way through the narrow streets of old Quebec as citizens and tourists stood silently watching. The procession entered the cemetery of the General Hospital and there, with proper ceremony, Montcalm was buried among his soldiers. Standing nearby, a British regiment, Fraser's Highlanders, played a musical tribute. The report did not mention any native peoples present. They were, once again, invisible.[5]

Notes

CA   Canadian Achives
DCB   *Dictionary of Canadian Biography*
DNB   *Dictionary of National Biography*
JR   *Jesuit Relations*
MHS   Massachusetts Historical Society
NYCD   *New York Colonial Documents*
PCR   *Pennsylvania Colonial Records*

Prologue

1. Carl Brasseaux, *The Founding of New Acadia* (Baton Rouge: Louisiana State University Press, 1987), passim; John Bartlett Brebner, *New England's Outpost: Acadia Before the Conquest of Canada* (New York: Columbia University Press, 1927), pp. 166–202.

2. John C. Webster, *The Career of the Abbé Le Loutre in Nova Scotia* (Shediac: Privately printed, 1933), pp. 1–2; *DCB*, 4:455.

3. Ibid., p. 1.

4. In the early 1720s the Tuscarora migrated north and joined the Iroquois Confederation, becoming the sixth nation. Daniel K. Richter, *The Ordeal of the Longhouse* (Chapel Hill: University of North Carolina Press, 1992), pp. 238–39.

5. Charles de Reymond to Phillippe Thomas Chabert de Joncaire, May 22, 1750, quoted in Theodore C. Pease, ed., *Anglo-French Boundary Disputes in the West, 1749–1763* (Springfield: Illinois State Library, 1936), p. xv.

1. Lining Up Allies

Epigraph. Wisconsin Historical Society *Collections* 18 (1908), p. 57.

1. *DCB*, 3:29.

2. Ralph M. Sargent, ed., *Travels into North America by Peter Kalm* (Barre: Imprint Society, 1972), pp. 361–62; *DCB*, 3:29; James Pritchard, *Louis XV's Navy, 1748–1762* (Kingston: Queens University Press, 1987), p. 7.

3. *JR*, 69:161.

4. Quoted in Norman W. Caldwell, *The French in the Mississippi Valley* (Urbana: University of Illinois Press, 1941), p. 97.

5. "Céloron's Expedition," Wisconsin Historical Society *Collections* 18 (1908), p. 57.

6. Galissonière's long memo may be found in Theodore C. Pease, *Anglo-French Boundary Disputes* (Springfield, Ill.: Illinois State Historical Library, 1936), pp. 5–22. For Shirley's views, see Shirley to Duke of Bedford April 24, 1749, Charles Henry Lincoln, ed., *Correspondence of William Shirley*, 2 vols. (New York: Macmillan, 1912), 1:478–80.

7. Shirley to Duke of Bedford April 24, 1749, Lincoln, *Correspondence of William Shirley*, 1:478.

8. François-Marie de Voltaire, *Candide ou l'optimisme* (Amsterdam, 1759). Reprinted in *Les Oeuvres completes de Voltaire*, edition critique par René Pomeau (Oxford: Oxford University Press, 1980), 48:223.

9. Patrice Higgonet, "The Origins of the Seven Years War," *Journal of Modern History* 40 (1968): 57–90.

10. Shirley to Duke of Newcastle, Paris, September 1, 1750, Lincoln, *Correspondence of William Shirley*, 1:508–9; John A. Schutz, *William Shirley, King's Governor of Massachusetts* (Chapel Hill: University of North Carolina Press, 1961), p. 166.

11. Paul Langford, *The Eighteenth Century: 1688–1815* (Oxford: Oxford University Press, 2002), pp. 129–30. For an analysis of the importance of fiscal management to British power, see John Brewer, *Sinews of Power: War, Money and the English State* (New York: Alfred Knopf, 1988).

12. Ralph Davis, "English Foreign Trade, 1700–1774," in W. E. Minchinton, ed., *The Growth of English Overseas Trade in the Seventeenth and Eighteenth Centuries* (London: Methuen, 1969), pp. 105–6, 118; Linda Colley, *Forging the Nation, 1707–1837* (New Haven: Yale University Press, 1992), pp. 62–69.

13. Quoted in Zenab E. Rashed, *The Peace of Paris* (Liverpool: University Press, 1951), p. 5.

14. Corelli D. Barnett, *Britain and Her Army, 1509–1970* (New York: William Morrow, 1970), pp. 179–80; Steven Ross, *From Flintlock to Rifle: Infantry Tactics, 1740–1866* (London: Frank Cass, 1966), p. 25.

15. For the French army, see Lee Kennett, *The French Armies in the Seven Years War* (Durham: Duke University Press, 1967), particularly pp. 72–87.

16. Quoted in Herbert W. Richmond, "The Influence of Seapower in the Struggle with France in North America and India," *National Review* 75 (1920): 400.

17. Quoted in Jeremy Black, *A System of Ambition? British Foreign Policy, 1660–1793* (London: Longmans, 1991), p. 43.

18. Langford, *The Eighteenth Century*, p. 129.

19. Duke of Newcastle to Horace Walpole May 14, 1754, quoted in Lawrence Henry Gipson, "A French Project for Victory Short of a Declaration of War," *Canadian Historical Review* 26 (1945): 362; Duke of Newcastle to Joseph Yorke, January 15, 1755, quoted in T. R. Clayton, "The Earl of Halifax and the American Origins of the Seven Years War," *Historical Journal* 24 (1981): 527.

20. Earl of Holderness to the governors in America, Whitehall, August 28, 1753, *NYCD*, 6:794–95.

21. Schutz, *William Shirley*, pp. 174–75.

2. George Washington Helps Start a War

Epigraph. (Williamsburg, January 1754), *The Papers of George Washington*, Colonial Series, ed. W. W. Abbot (Charlottesville: University of Virginia Press, 1983), 1:65.

1. *DCB*, 3:611.

2. Charles Le Moyne de Longueil to M. Rouille (minister of marine), April 21, 1752, *NYCD*, 10:245–51. The letter also summarizes the situation in Canada.

3. "Minute of Instructions to Be Given to M. Duquesne," April 1752, *NYCD*, 10:243, 220–31.

4. Charles A. Hanna, *The Wilderness Trail*, 2 vols. (New York: G. P. Putnam's Sons, 1911), 2:289–90.

5. Duquesne to Rouille, October 25, 1752, *Wisconsin Historical Society Collections* 18 (1908): 128.

6. *DCB*, 3:431–32; Duquesne to Rouille, August 20, 1753, *NYCD*, 10:256.

7. *DCB*, 3:613–15; Donald H. Kent, *The French Invasion of Western Pennsylvania, 1753* (Harrisburg: Pennsylvania Historical and Museum Commission, 1954), pp. 46–50.

8. William Johnson to George Clinton, April 20, 1753, *NYCD*, 6:778–79; James Thomas Flexner, *Lord of the Mohawks: A Biography of Sir William Johnson* (Boston: Little, Brown, 1979), p. 114.

9. "Minutes of Meeting Between His Excellency the Honble George Clinton and Seventeen Mohawk Indians, June 12–16, 1753," *NYCD*, 6:782, 788.

10. Thomas Lee to Hamilton Stratford, November 22, 1749. Minutes of the Provincial Council of Pennsylvania. *PCR* (Harrisburg: Theo Fenn, 1851), 5:423. For a sympathetic account of Dinwiddie, see Louis L. Koontz, *Robert Dinwiddie* (Glendale: Arthur H. Clark, 1941), pp. 157–72. John R. Alden is more critical in *Robert Dinwiddie Servant of the Crown* (Williamsburg: Colonial Williamsburg, 1973); Donald Jackson, ed., *The Diaries of George Washington*, 6 vols. (Charlottesville: University of Virginia Press, 1976), 1:118–29.

11. Washington's commission and instructions, both dated October 30, 1753, are in W. W. Abbot, ed., *The Papers of George Washington*, Colonial Series (Charlottesville: University of Virginia Press, 1983), 1:56–62; Dinwiddie to M. St. de Pierre, October 31, 1753, *NYCD*, 10:258.

12. Washington's own account of his journey may be found in Jackson, *Diaries*, 1:118–61. Secondary accounts abound, including Douglas Southall Freeman, *George Washington: A Biography*, 7 vols. (New York: Charles Scribner's Sons, 1948–57), 1:274–326.

13. Jackson, *Diaries*, 1:148.

14. Ibid., 1:151n.

15. Ibid., 1:160–61n.

16. Lawrence Henry Gipson, *The British Empire Before the American Revolution*, 15 vols. (New York: Alfred Knopf, 1958–70), 4:300; Koontz, *Dinwiddie*, pp. 249–52.

17. *DCB*, 4:616–18; J. C. B., an anonymous officer of la Marine, kept a journal of the expedition. Sylvester K. Stevens, Donald H. Kent, and Emma E. Woods, eds., *Travels in New France by J. C. B.* (Harrisburg: Pennsylvania Historical Commission, 1941), pp. 5–64.

18. Stevens, et al., *Travels in New France by J. C. B.*, p. 56; Koontz, *Dinwiddie*, pp. 307–9.

19. "Instructions to be Observ'd by Major Geo. Washington on the Expeditn to the Ohio," Abbot, *Papers of George Washington*, 1:65. Washington kept a journal on this mission. The original was taken by the French when Washington surrendered at Fort Necessity and has since disappeared. A translated version (apparently from the original) was published in Paris in 1756. An English version appeared in New York the following year.

20. Washington to Dinwiddie, March 9, 1754, Abbot, *Papers of George Washington*, 1:73–74.

21. Stobo had a remarkable career in the war. Robert C. Alberts, *The Most Extraordinary Adventures of Major Robert Stobo* (Boston: Houghton Mifflin, 1965).

22. Jackson, *Diaries*, 1:177.

23. Ibid., 1:180; Washington to James Hamilton, April 24, 1754, Abbot, *Papers of George Washington*, 1:83–84.

24. Jackson, *Diaries*, 1:180.

25. While a prisoner of the French at Duquesne, Robert Stobo drew a plan of the fort. Robert Stobo, *Memoirs of Robert Stobo* (Pittsburgh: J. S. Davidson, 1854); Freeman, *Washington*, 1: unnumbered pages between pp. 437–38.

26. Washington's account is in both Jackson, *Diaries*, 1:191–99 and Abbot, *Papers of George Washington*, 1:104–19.

27. Jackson, *Diaries*, 1:195–97, n. 59. Robert C. Alberts, *A Charming Field for an Encounter*. (Washington: National Park Service, 1975), p. 62; Fred Anderson, *Crucible of War* (New York: Alfred A. Knopf, 2000), pp. 50–59.

28. Washington to John Augustine Washington, May 31, 1754, Abbot, *Papers of George Washington* 1:118.

29. Washington to Dinwiddie, May 29, 1754, ibid., 1:111.

30. Quoted in Alberts, *A Charming Field*, p. 20.

31. Washington to Dinwiddie, Great Meadows, May 27, 1754, Abbot, *Papers of George Washington*, 1:105.

32. Washington to Dinwiddie, Great Meadows, June 3, 1754, ibid., 1:124. Sometime before June 25 Washington named the place Fort Necessity.

33. Stevens, et al., *Travels in New France by J. C. B.*, pp. 59–60; *DCB*, 3:148–49; M. Varin to M. Bigot, July 24, 1754, *NYCD*, 10:260–61; extract from M. de Villiers journal, *NYCD*, 10:261–62.

34. For an account of the surrender of the fort and the Articles of Capitulation, see Abbot, *Papers of George Washington*, 1:157–73.

35. Quoted in Alberts, *A Charming Field*, p. 35.

36. *PCR*, 6:156.

3. Braddock's March

Epigraph. Stanley M. Pargellis, ed., *Military Affairs in North America, 1748–1765* (New York: D. Appleton Century, 1936), p. 85.

1. After a war ending in 1713, the Tuscarora, an Iroquoian-speaking tribe, were displaced from their homelands in the Carolinas. Remnants of the tribe migrated north and joined their Iroquois cousins to become the sixth nation.

2. Lords of Trade to the governors in America, September 18, 1753, *NYCD*, 6:802; Timothy Shannon, *Indians and Colonists at the Crossroads of Empire: The Albany Congress of 1754* (Ithaca: Cornell University Press, 2000), passim.

3. James Delancey to Lords of Trade, October 15, 1753, *NYCD*, 6:803–4.

4. Roger R. Trask, "Pennsylvania and the Albany Congress, 1754," *Pennsylvania History* 27 (1966): 273–75.

5. Hendrick's speech is recorded in the minutes of the meeting. *NYCD*, 6:870; James H. Merrill, *Into the American Woods* (New York: Norton, 1999), p. 300.

6. The historiography concerning the Albany Congress is considerable. See Verner W. Crane and Lawrence Henry Gipson, "On the Drafting of the Albany Plan of Union," *Pennsylvania History* 27 (1960): 126–36; John A. Schutz, *William Shirley, King's Governor of Massachusetts* (Chapel Hill: University of North Carolina Press, 1961), p. 184; John R. Alden, "The Albany Congress and the Creation of the Indian Superintendencies," *Mississippi Valley Historical Review* 27 (1940): 193–210; Francis Jennings, *Empire of Fortune* (New York: Norton, 1988), pp. 72–108. The Plan of Union may be found in *NYCD*, 6:903–6.

7. Quoted in Elizabeth Malcolm-Smith, *British Diplomacy in the Eighteenth Century, 1700–1789* (London: Williams and Norgate, 1937), p. 133.

8. Harvey E. Fisk, *English Public Finance from the Revolution of 1688*. (New York: Bankers Trust, 1920), p. 122.

9. Newcastle to Walpole, May 14, 1754, quoted in Lawrence Henry Gipson, "A French Project for Victory Short of a Declaration of War, 1755," *Canadian Historical Review* 26 (1945): 362. Paul Langford suggests that the death of Henry Pelham began an era of instability that was not to end until the establishment of the administration of Lord North in the early 1770s; see Langford, *The Eighteenth Century* (London: A and C Black, 1976), p. 135. Patrice Louis-Rene Higgonnet, "The Origins of the Seven Years War," *Journal of Modern History* 40 (1968): 69.

10. Sketch of regulations and orders, November 16, 1754, Pargellis, *Military Affairs*, pp. 34–36.

11. Lee McCardell, *Ill-Starred General Braddock of the Coldstream Guards* (Pittsburgh: University of Pittsburgh Press, 1958), pp. 3–134.

12. Higgonnet, "Origins," pp. 79–81; Machault to Duquesne, October 6, 1754, *NYCD*, 10:270; Ian Steele, *Guerrillas and Grenadiers* (Toronto: Ryerson Press, 1969), p. 57; Max Savelle, *The Diplo-*

matic History of the Canadian Boundary, 1749–1763 (New Haven: Yale University Press, 1940), pp. 58–60.

13. Sketch for the operations in North America, November 16, 1754, Pargellis, *Military Affairs*, pp. 45–48.

14. For the role of the commander in chief, see Clarence E. Carter, "The Office of the Commander in Chief a Phase of Imperial Unity on the Eve of the American Revolution," in Richard B. Morris, ed., *Studies Inscribed to Evarts B. Greene* (New York: Columbia University Press, 1939), pp. 170–213; Henry P. Beers, "The Papers of the British Commanders in Chief in North America, 1754–1783," *Military Affairs* 13 (1949): 79–81; Alan Rogers, *Empire and Liberty: American Resistance to British Authority, 1755–1763* (Berkeley: University of California Press, 1974), pp. 52–53, 76, 90–91. Braddock's Instructions are in Winthrop Sargent, ed., *The History of an Expedition Against Fort Duquesne in 1755* (Philadelphia: Lippincott, Granbo, 1855), pp. 393–400.

15. Captain Orme's journal, in Sargent, *History of an Expedition Against Fort Duquesne*, pp. 281–357. Winthrop's *History* contains much more than Orme's journal, and it is the single most useful collection of sources on Braddock's march.

16. For a description of the regiments posted to North America, see Charles H. Stewart, comp., *The Service of British Regiments in Canada and North America* (Ottawa: Department of National Defense Library, 1962).

17. John St. Clair to Braddock, n.d., Pargellis, *Military Affairs*, p. 64.

18. Orme's journal, pp. 290–91; McCardell, *Ill-Starred General*, p. 166.

19. Different routes in North America, Pargellis, *Military Affairs*, pp. 31–33; Colonel Henry Bouquet to General John Stanwix, April 26, 1760, "The Aspinwall Papers," *Collections* of the MHS, 4th series, 9:243–45.

20. Orme's journal, pp. 296–97. Across level country the army marched at a rate of slightly less than two miles per hour. Ten miles was a good march for a single day. H. C. B. Rogers, *The British Army of the Eighteenth Century* (London: George Allen and Unwin, 1977), p. 77.

21. "A Proportion of Brass Ordnance, Howitzers and Stores . . . ," Pargellis, *Military Affairs*, pp. 479–87; Harold L. Peterson, *Round Shot and Rammers* (South Bend: South Bend Replicas, 1969), pp. 38–48; Rogers, *British Army*, pp. 80–81. Braddock estimated that in total he needed, 2,500 horses. Braddock to Napier, June 8, 1755, Pargellis, *Military Affairs*, p. 85.

22. Robert Orme to Washington, Williamsburg, March 2, 1755, Abbot, *Papers of George Washington*, 1:241.

23. Quoted in McCardell, *Ill-Starred General*, p. 185.

24. Quoted in ibid., p. 184.

25. Braddock to Napier, June 8, 1755, Pargellis, *Military Affairs*, pp. 84–92.

26. James R. Tootle, "Anglo-Indian Relations in the Northern Theater of the French and Indian War, 1748–1761," Ph.D. diss., Ohio State University, p. 253; *PCR*, 6:397, 589.

27. Braddock to Napier, June 8, 1755, Pargellis, *Military Affairs*, p. 85.

28. Ibid., p. 92.

29. Washington to John Augustine Washington, June 28, 1755, Abbot, *Papers of George Washington*, 1:323.

30. Ibid., 1:322.

4. French Victory, English Defeat

Epigraph. Quoted in Julian S. Corbett, *England in the Seven Years War*, 2 vols. (London: Longmans, Green, 1907), 1:58.

1. "French Account of the Action Near the River Ohio on the 9th of July 1755," Stanley M. Pargellis, ed., *Military Affairs in North America, 1748–1765* (New York: D. Appleton Century, 1936), p. 129.

2. Duquesne to Marquis de Vaudreuil, July 6, 1755, *NYCD*, 10:300; *DCB*, 3:401; John Gilmary Shea, "Daniel Hyacinth Marie Lienard de Beaujeu," *Pennsylvania Magazine* 8 (1884): 123–24; Malcolm MacLeod, "Daniel-Marie Lienard de Beaujeu, 1711–1755," *Dalhousie Review* (1973): 296–309.

3. Shea, "Daniel Hyacinth," p. 124.

4. Ibid., p. 125.

5. James Smith, *An Account of the Remarkable Occurrences in the Life and Travels of Colonel James Smith* (Cincinnati: Robert Clarke, 1870), pp. 10–11.

6. Descriptions of the events leading to the battle abound, and they are sometimes contradictory. See Lee McCardell, *Ill-Starred General Braddock of the Coldstream Guards* (Pittsburgh: University of Pittsburgh Press, 1986), pp. 209–65; Winthrop Sargent, *The History of an Expedition Against Fort Duquesne in 1755* (Philadelphia: Lippincott, Grambo, 1855), passim.

7. "The Journal of Captain Robert Cholmley's Batman," in Charles Hamilton, ed., *Braddock's Defeat* (Norman: University of Oklahoma Press, 1959), p. 28.

8. Ibid., p. 30.

9. McCardell, *Ill-Starred General*, p. 250.

10. "The Journal of a British Officer," in Hamilton, *Braddock's Defeat*, p. 51.

11. Ibid., p. 52.

12. Washington to Mary Ball Washington, July 18, 1755, W. W. Abbot, ed., *The Papers of George Washington* (Charlottesville: University of Virginia Press, 1983), 1:336.

13. "The Journal of a British Officer," p. 52.

14. Sylvester K. Stevens, Donald H. Kent, and Emma E. Woods, eds., *Travels in New France by J. C. B.* (Harrisburg: Pennsylvania Historical Commission, 1961), pp. 82–85.

15. "Journal of Proceedings from Wills Creek to the Monongahela," Harry Gordon to [?], July 23, 1755, Pargellis, *Military Affairs*, p. 107.

16. Biographical memoranda, John C. Fitzpatrick, ed., *The Writings of George Washington*, 39 vols. (Washington: U.S. Government Printing Office, 1939), 29:45; see also King L. Parker, "Anglo-American Wilderness Campaigning, 1754–1764," Ph.D. diss., Columbia University, 1970, p. 180.

17. Geoffrey J. Marcus, *Quiberon Bay: The Campaign in Home Waters, 1759* (London: Hollis and Carter, 1960), p. 2.

18. Quoted in Corbett, *England in the Seven Years*, 1:42–43.

19. Journal of M. de Vaudreuil's voyage to Canada, *NYCD*, 10:297–99; Boscawen's letter to his wife is quoted in N. A. M. Rodger, *The Wooden World: An Anatomy of the Georgian Navy* (London: Collins, 1986), p. 44; Hardwicke's comment is quoted in Corbett, *England in the Seven Years War*, 1:58.

20. *NYCD*, 10:292.

21. Sketch of regulations, Pargellis, *Military Affairs*, p. 35; commission from Edward Braddock, Alexandria, April 15, 1755, James Sullivan, ed., *The Papers of Sir William Johnson*, 14 vols. (Albany: University of the State of New York, 1921–65), 1:465–66; James Thomas Flexner, *Lord of the Mohawks: A Biography of Sir William Johnson* (Boston: Little, Brown, 1959), pp. 124–25.

22. Baron de Dieskau to Count d'Argenson (minister of war), September 14, 1755, *NYCD*, 10:316–18.

23. Johnson to Edward Braddock, June 27, 1755, *Johnson Papers*, 1:663.

24. [Minutes of] Conference Between Major General Johnson and the Indians, 21 June–4 July 1755, ibid., 6:964–89; Flexner, *Lord of the Mohawks*, pp. 129–33.

25. Flexner, *Land of the Mohawks*, 133.

26. Johnson to the Lords of Trade, September 3, 1755, *NYCD*, 6:994.

27. Ibid.

28. Gerald E. Bradfield, *Fort William Henry: Digging in History* (n.p.: privately printed, 2001), pp. 24–25; David R. Starbuck, *The Great Warpath: British Military Sites from Albany to Crown Point* (Hanover: University Press of New England, 1999), pp. 54–82; Noel St. John Williams, *Redcoats Along the Hudson:*

The Struggle for North America (London: Brassey's, 1997), pp. 82–83; Parker, "Anglo-American Wilderness Campaigning," pp. 188–98.

29. Quoted in Flexner, *Lord of the Mohawks*, p. 139.

30. Johnson to the Lords of Trade, September 3, 1755, *NYCD*, 6:997.

31. Johnson to DeLancey, September 4, 1755, Sullivan, *Johnson Papers*, 2:8–9.

32. Quoted in Fred Anderson, *A People's Army: Massachusetts Soldiers and Society in the Seven Years War* (Chapel Hill: University of North Carolina Press, 1984), p. 96.

33. Dieskau to Count d'Argenson, September 7, 1755, *NYCD*, 10:317.

34. Ibid.

35. For British descriptions of the battle, see *NYCD*, 6:1002–6; for French, see *NYCD*, 10:335–45.

36. For a visual depiction of the battle, see "A Prospective Plan of the Battle Fought Near Lake George on the 8th September 1755." Drawn by Samuel Blodgett, engraving by Thomas Johnston, Boston, 1755.

37. *NYCD*, 10:339.

38. Starbuck, *The Great Warpath*, pp. 112–13.

39. Quoted in Geoffrey Plank, *An Unsettled Conquest: The British Campaign Against the People of Acadia* (Philadelphia: University of Pennsylvania Press, 2001), p. 145; for a decidedly pro-British point of view, see James P. Baxter, "What Caused the Deportation of the Acadians?" *Proceedings of the American Antiquarian Society* 13 (April 1899):74–100.

40. John Brewse to the Board of Ordnance, October 18, 1755. Pargellis, *Military Affairs*, pp. 146–48; Dominick Graham, "The Planning of the Beausejour Operation and the Approaches to War in 1755," *New England Quarterly* 41 (1968):558–66; John C. Webster, *The Forts of Chignecto: A Study of the Eighteenth Century Conflict Between France and Great Britain in Acadia* (St. John: Rapid Grip, 1930).

41. *DCB*, 4:250.

42. Horace Walpole, *Memoirs of the Reign of King George the Second*, ed. Lord Holland, 3 vols. (London: Henry Colburn, 1846), 1:396.

43. Vaudreuil to Machault, October 30, 1755, *NYCD*, 10:375.

5. Montcalm and Loudoun

Epigraph. Henri-Raymond Casgrain, ed., *Lettres du Marquis de Montcalm* (Quebec: L. J. Demere and Frère, 1894), p. 35. *Collection des manuscrits du marchal de Lévis* (Montreal: C. O. Beauchemin, 1889–1895). This book is one of the volumes in Casgrain's invaluable collection. It consists of the following volumes: *Journal Des Campagnes Du Chevalier De Lévis, Lettres Du Chevalier De Lévis, Lettres De La Cour De Versailles, Lettres et Pièces Militaires, Lettres De M. De Bourlamaque au Chevalier De Lévis, Lettres Du Marquis De Montcalm au Chevalier De Lévis, Journal Du Marquis De Montcalm, Lettres Du Marquis De Vaudreuil au Chevalier De Lévis, Lettres De l'Intendant Bigot au Chevalier De Lévis, Lettres De Divers Particuliers au Chevalier De Lévis, Relations et Journeaux De Différentes Expeditions,* and *Table Analytique.*

1. Quoted in Julian S. Corbett, *England in the Seven Years War*, 2 vols. (London: Longmans, Green, 1907), 1:61.

2. A. C. Carter, "Transfer of Certain Public Debt Stocks in the London Money Market from 1 January to 31 March 1755," *Bulletin of the Institute of Historical Research* 28 (November 1955):208–9.

3. William Shirley to Thomas Dunbar, August 12, 1755, Charles Henry Lincoln, ed., *The Correspondence of William Shirley*, 2 vols. (New York: Macmillan, 1912), 2:231–34.

4. Arthur L. Perry, *Origins in Williamstown* (New York: Charles Scribners Sons, 1896), p. 326.

5. Johnson to Shirley, July 29, 1755, James Sullivan, ed., *The Papers of Sir William Johnson*, 14 vols. (Albany: University of the State of New York, 1921–65), 1:790.

6. John F. Luzader, *Fort Stanwix Construction and Military History* (Fort Washington: Eastern National, 2001), pp. 1–2.

7. Elkanah Watson, *History of Western Canals in the State of New York* (Albany: D. Steele, 1820), pp. 31–34.

8. William Livingston, "A Review of the Military Operations in North America," *Collections of the Massachusetts Historical Society* 1ST Series, 7 (Boston: MHS, 1800), p. 95.

9. Gilbert Hagerty, *Massacre at Fort Bull* (Providence: Mowbray, 1971), pp. 21–29.

10. Shirley's movements can be followed in Lincoln, *Correspondence of William Shirley*, 2:261–325; John A. Schutz, *William Shirley: King's Governor of Massachusetts* (Chapel Hill: University of North Carolina Press, 1961), pp. 205–24.

11. Journal of occurrences in Canada, *NYCD*, 10:403; Hagerty, *Massacre at Fort Bull*, p. 32.

12. Ibid., 10:404.

13. Abstracts of dispatches from Canada, *NYCD*, 10:423.

14. Susan Wright Henderson, "The French Regular Officer Corps in Canada, 1755–1760: A Group Portrait," Ph.D. diss., University of Maine, 1975, pp. 67–89. For the relationship between Vaudreuil and Montcalm, see Roger Michalon, "Vaudreuil et Montcalm, les hommes leurs relations influence de ces relations sur la conduite de la guerre, 1756–1759," in Jean Delmas, ed., *Conflicts des societes au Canada français pendant las Guerre de Sept Ans* (Vincennes, France: Service historique armee de terre, 1978), pp. 41–176; *DCB*, 3:458–69; *DCB*, 4:660–74.

15. *DCB*, 4:477. Lévis's service in Canada is documented in Casgrain, *Collection*. See "Notice Historique sur la Maison De Lévis," *Journal Du Chevalier De Lévis*, pp. 19–31.

16. *DCB*, 3:84–87.

17. Henderson, "The French Regular Officer Corps," passim; Guy Fregault, *Canada: The War of the Conquest* (Toronto: Oxford University Press, 1969), pp. 60–65.

18. Montcalm to Lévis, August 17, 1756, Casgrain, *Lettres Du Marquis De Montcalm*, p. 35.

19. Montcalm to Count d'Argenson (minister of war), June 12, 1756, *NYCD*, 10:414.

20. Among Shirley's most persistent and potent critics was the ambitious Thomas Pownall, who sought Shirley's post as governor of Massachusetts. Pownall's brother was secretary to the lords of trade and was quick to use his influence on Thomas's behalf against Shirley. Schutz, *Thomas Pownall* (Glendale: Arthur H. Clark, 1951), pp. 20–21, 59–67.

21. Stanley M. Pargellis, *Lord Loudoun in North America* (New Haven: Yale University Press, 1933), pp. 39–40.

22. Ibid., p. 41.

23. Daniel P. Marston, "Swift and Bold: The 60th Regiment and Warfare in North America, 1755–1765." M.A. thesis, McGill University, 1997, pp. 23–27.

24. Loudoun's formal title was "His Excellency John Earl of Loudoun Lord Machline and Tarrinzean etc etc etc, one of the Sixteen Peers of Scotland; Governor and Captain General of Virginia, and Vice Admiral of the same; Colonel in chief of the Thirtieth Regiment of Foot; Colonel in Chief of the Royal American Regiment; Major General; and Commander in Chief of all His Majesty's Forces Raised or to be raised in North America." Pargellis, *Lord Loudoun*, 43n.

25. John Shy, "James Abercromby and the Campaign of 1758," M.A. thesis, University of Vermont, 1957, pp. 1–25.

26. Pargellis, *Lord Loudoun*, pp. 83–86.

27. Loudoun to Henry Fox, August 19, 1756, Loudoun Papers, Huntington Library, San Marino, Calif.

28. Abstracts of dispatches from Canada, *NYCD*, 10:423.

29. The *Bulletin of the Fort Ticonderoga Museum*, published since 1927, chronicles the history of the fort. Of particular importance for this period are the documents edited by Nicholas Westbrook and Ian McCulloch in vol. 16 (1998):16–107.

30. Norreys O'Conor, *A Servant of the Crown in England and North America, 1756–1761: Based Upon the Papers of John Appy* (New York: D. Appleton, 1938), pp. 75–77.

31. *DNB*, 3:828.

32. King L. Parker, "Anglo-American Wilderness Campaigning, 1754–1764: Logistical and Tactical Developments," Ph.D. diss., Columbia University, 1970, p. 165. Bradstreet's bateaux were built locally, and so they differed in design and construction from similar craft laid down elsewhere. His boats were sharp at both ends and capable of carrying about twelve hundred pounds. In shallow water men moved the boats by poling. French bateaux tended to be larger and stable enough that men could fire from a standing position. English boats were less stable and likely to capsize under similar circumstances.

33. Loudoun to Duke of Cumberland, October 2, 1756, Pargellis, ed., *Military Affairs*, p. 235.

34. Edward P. Hamilton, ed., *Adventure in the Wilderness: The American Journals of Louis Antoine Bougainville, 1756–1760* (Norman: University of Oklahoma Press, 1964), p. 11; documents describing the Oswego campaign may be found in *NYCD*, 10:440–75.

35. Quoted in D. Peter MacLeod, *The Canadian Iroquois and the Seven Years War* (Toronto: Dundurn Press, 1996), p. 79.

36. The British view may be found in "A Journal of the Transactions at Oswego . . . by Patrick Mackellar," Pargellis, *Military Affairs*, pp. 187–221.

37. M. de Vaudreuil to Count d'Argenson, August 20, 1756, *NYCD*, 10:473.

38. M de Montcalm to Count d'Argenson, August 28, 1756, ibid., 10:464.

39. Ibid.

6. A Failure and a "Massacre"

Epigraph. Quoted in Ian Steele, *Betrayals: Fort William Henry and the "Massacre"* (New York: Oxford University Press, 1990), p. 100.

1. E. Malcolm-Smith, *British Diplomacy in the Eighteenth Century* (London: Williams and Norgate, 1937), pp. 142–43.

2. Arthur George Doughty and George William Parmalee, eds., *The Siege of Quebec and the Battle of the Plains of Abraham*, 6 vols. (Quebec: Dussault and Proulx, 1901), 1:xxi–xxx.

3. Horace Walpole, *Memoirs of the Reign of King George the Second*, 3 vols. (London: Henry Colburn, 1846), 2:68–69; O. A. Sherrard, *Lord Chatham: Pitt and the Seven Years War* (London: Bodley Head, 1956), p. 92.

4. Quoted in Sherrard, *Lord Chatham*, p. 131.

5. The literature on William Pitt the Elder is considerable. See Karl W. Schweizer, *William Pitt, Earl of Chatham, 1708–1778: A Bibliography* (Westport, Conn.: Greenwood, 1993).

6. Stanley Ayling, *The Elder Pitt* (New York: David McKay, 1976), p. 181.

7. Sherrard, *Lord Chatham*, p. 142.

8. Walpole, *Memoirs of the Reign of George the Second*, 3:84.

9. For an analysis of the problems faced by Loudoun, see Alan Rogers, *Empire and Liberty: American Resistance to British Authority, 1755–1763* (Berkeley: University of California Press, 1974), passim.

10. Fred Anderson, *A People's Army: Massachusetts Soldiers and Society in the Seven Years War* (Chapel Hill: University of North Carolina Press, 1984), p. 12.

11. Stanley M. Pargellis, *Lord Loudoun in North America* (New Haven: Yale University Press, 1933), pp. 90–91.

12. Anderson, *People's Army*, pp. 172–73; Pargellis, *Lord Loudoun*, p. 91.

13. Loudoun to Henry Fox, August 19, 1756, Loudoun Papers, Huntington Library, San Marino, Calif.

14. Louis E. DeForest, ed., *The Journals and Papers of Seth Pomeroy* (New York: Society of Colonial Wars, 1926), pp. 152–53; Pargellis, *Lord Loudoun*, p. 91.

15. Loudoun to Henry Fox, August 19, 1756, Loudoun Papers.

16. Loudoun to Denny, September 22, 1756, *Minutes of the Provincial Council of Pennsylvania* (Harrisburg: Theo Penn, 1851), 7:270.

17. Loudoun to Cumberland, August 20, 1756, Stanley M. Pargellis, ed., *Military Affairs in North America, 1748–1765* (New York: D. Appleton Century, 1936), p. 224.

18. J. R. Trumbull, *History of Northampton, Massachusetts,* 2 vols. (Northampton: Gazette Printing, 1902), 2:288.

19. Loudoun to Cumberland, November 22, 1756, Pargellis, *Military Affairs,* p. 269.

20. The standard biography is John R. Cuneo, *Robert Rogers of the Rangers* (New York: Oxford University Press, 1959). Rogers's journals have been most recently edited by Timothy J. Todish, in *The Annotated and Illustrated Journals of Major Robert Rogers* (Fleischmanns, N.Y.: Purple Mountain Press, 2002).

21. Loudoun to Cumberland, November 22, 1756, Pargellis, *Military Affairs,* p. 269. A modern historian, William Foote, "American Units of the British Regular Army, 1664–1772," M.A. thesis, Texas Western University, 1959, describes rangers as "expensive and unreliable," p. 215.

22. Cuneo, *Robert Rogers,* pp. 45–51; Todish, *Journals of Major Robert Rogers,* pp. 58–62.

23. Gerald E. Bradfield, *Fort William Henry: Digging Up History* (n.p.: French and Indian War Society, 2001), pp. 1–25; David R. Starbuck, *The Great Warpath: British Military Sites from Albany to Crown Point* (Hanover: University Press of New England, 1999), pp. 12–14; and Noel St. John Williams, *Redcoats Along the Hudson* (London: Brassey, 1997), p. 118.

24. Remarks on Forts William Henry and Edward by Henry Gordon. Pargellis, *Military Affairs,* p. 180.

25. Bradfield, *Fort William Henry,* p. 39.

26. Ian Steele, *Guerrillas and Grenadiers* (Toronto: Ryerson Press, 1969), p. 69. For a view more sympathetic to Bigot, see *DCB,* 4:59–71.

27. F. W. Burton, "The Wheat Supply of New France," *Transactions of the Royal Society of Canada,* 3rd series, vol. 30, section 2 (May 1936): 142; Edward P. Hamilton, ed., *Adventure in the Wilderness, The American Journals of Louis Antoine Bougainville, 1756–1760* (Norman: University of Oklahoma Press, 1964), pp. 86–87.

28. Hamilton, *Adventure in the Wilderness,* p. 86.

29. M. de Vaudreuil to the keeper of the seals, April 22, 1757, *NYCD,* 10:542–43; attack on Fort William Henry, 1757, *NYCD,* 10:544–46; M. de Montcalm to Count d'Argenson, April 24, 1757, *NYCD,* 10:547–50; Guy Fregault, *Canada: The War of the Conquest,* trans. Margaret M. Cameron (Toronto: Oxford University Press, 1969), p. 151; Steele, *Betrayals,* pp. 75–77.

30. Hamilton, *Adventure in the Wilderness,* p. 5.

31. Loudoun to Cumberland, August 29, 1756, Pargellis, *Military Affairs,* p. 233; Cumberland to Loudoun, December 2, 1756, Pargellis, *Military Affairs,* pp. 253–57; Loudoun to Cumberland, November 22, 1756, concluded at New York, December 26, 1756, Pargellis, *Military Affairs,* pp. 263–80; Evan Charteris, *William Augustus, Duke of Cumberland and the Seven Years War* (London: Hutchinson, 1925), p. 205.

32. *NYCD,* 10:555.

33. "Considerations Offered by [?] Upon a Scheme for Attacking Louisbourg and Quebec, 1757," Pargellis, *Military Affairs,* pp. 294–98, n. 1; quoted in Pargellis, *Lord Loudoun in North America,* p. 232.

34. Sherrard, *Lord Chatham,* p. 194; Walpole, *Memoirs of the Reign of King George the Second,* 3:20; Richard Middleton, *The Bells of Victory: Pitt-Newcastle Ministry and the Conduct of the Seven Years War, 1757–1762* (Cambridge: Cambridge University Press, 1985), pp. 14–15.

35. Rogers, *Empire and Liberty,* pp. 94–97.

36. Thomas Mante, *The History of the Late War in North America* (London: W. Strahan and T. Cadell, 1772), p. 101.

37. Pargellis, *Lord Loudoun in North America*, p. 240.

38. Loudoun to Cumberland, August 6, 1757, Pargellis, *Military Affairs*, pp. 391–92.

39. *DNB*, 9:253.

40. Pargellis, *Lord Loudoun in North America*, p. 242n; J. S. McLennan, *Louisbourg from Its Foundation to Its Fall, 1713–1758* (Halifax: Book Room, 1959), pp. 203–4.

41. The failure to take Louisbourg was compounded when en route home Holbourne's fleet ran into a hurricane. Half of his ships suffered serious damage, and one was lost.

42. Loudoun to Cumberland, October 2, 1756, Pargellis, *Military Affairs*, p. 235; Cumberland to Loudoun, December 2, 1756, Pargellis, *Military Affairs*, p. 254.

43. Notebook of French siege of Fort William Henry, July 1, 2, 9, 10, 11, 1757. Microfilm reel A573, CA.

44. Hamilton, *Adventure in the Wilderness*, p. 104; D. Peter MacLeod, *The Canadian Iroquois and the Seven Years War* (Toronto: Oxford University Press, 1996), pp. 97–98.

45. M. de Vaudreuil to M. de Moras, June 1, 1757, *NYCD*, 10:565–66.

46. Hamilton, *Adventure in the Wilderness*, pp. 142–43. MacLeod, *Canadian Iroquois*, pp. 98–113; Steele, *Betrayals*, pp. 87–90; *JR* 70:119–29. For a discussion about torture, see Nathaniel Knowles, "The Torture of Captives by the Indians of Eastern North America," *Proceedings of the American Antiquarian Society* 82 (1940):151–225;

47. *JR* 70:113–27; Hamilton, *Adventure in the Wilderness*, p. 155.

48. Journal of Joseph Fry (transcript), Francis Parkman Papers, 43:137–53, MHS; Fry to Thomas Hubbard, Albany, August 16, 1757, Parkman Papers, 42:154–56.

49. Steele, *Betrayals*, p. 99.

50. Montcalm to Monro, August 7, 1757, Parkman Papers, 42:140–41.

51. Hamilton, *Adventure in the Wilderness*, pp. 159–60.

52. Quoted in Steele, *Betrayals*, p. 100.

53. G. Bartman, aide-de-camp, to Monro, August 4, 1757 (transcript), Parkman Papers, 42:143–44.

54. Hamilton, *Adventure in the Wilderness*, pp. 166–67.

55. Ibid., p. 170; Steele, *Betrayals*, p. 108.

56. "Articles of Capitulation," (transcript), Parkman Papers, 42:148–50.

57. Hamilton, *Adventure in the Wilderness*, p. 170.

58. *JR* 70:179.

59. Quoted in Steele, *Betrayals*, p. 122.

60. Montcalm to Brigadier General Webb, August 4, 1757, *NYCD*, 10:618.

7. Ticonderoga

Epigraph. Stanley M. Pargellis, ed., *Military Affairs in North America, 1748–1765* (New York: D. Appleton Century, 1936), p. 420.

1. Basil Williams, *The Life of William Pitt*, 2 vols. (London: Longmans, Green, 1913), 1:337.

2. Quoted in Evan Charteris, *William Augustus, Duke of Cumberland and the Seven Years War* (London: Hutchinson, n.d.), p. 253.

3. Ibid., p. 273.

4. Ibid., p. 283.

5. Ibid., pp. 274–317; Richard Middleton, "A Reinforcement for North America, Summer 1757," *Bulletin of the Institute for Historical Research* 41 (1960): 58.

6. Quoted in Geoffrey Marcus, *Quiberon Bay: The Campaign in Home Waters* (London: Hollis and Carter, 1960), p. 17.

7. *DNB*, 11:1121.

8. Ibid., 5o3–8; O. A. Sherrard, *Lord Chatham: Pitt and the Seven Years War* (London: Bodley Head, 1955), p. 210.

9. Stephen F. Gradish, *The Manning of the British Navy During the Seven Years War* (London: Royal Historical Society, 1980), 7n; Herbert W. Richmond, "The Influence of Seapower on the Struggle with France in North America and India," *National Review* 75 (1920): 397–411. Although much respected for his prowess as a seaman, Anson had a reputation for political naïveté. His contemporary remarked that "Lord Anson [was] so ignorant of the world that he had been round it, but never in it." Horace Walpole, *Memoirs of the Reign of King George the Second*, 3 vols. (London: Henry Colburn, 1846), 1:194.

10. Walpole, *Memoirs of the Reign of King George the Second*, 2:263.

11. H. C. B. Rogers, *The British Army of the Eighteenth Century* (London: George Allen and Unwin, 1977), pp. 129–3o.

12. Although it is published somewhat later, Israel Mauduit, *Considerations on the Present German War* (London: J. Wilkie, 1760) provides a summary and critique of Pitt's strategy.

13. Jeremy Black and Philip Woodfine, eds., *The British Navy and the Use of British Naval Power in the Eighteenth Century* (Atlantic Highlands, N.J.: Humanities Press, 1989), p. 139; Rogers, *British Army*, p. 13o.

14. Rogers, *British Army*, p. 13o.

15. Marcus, *Quiberon Bay*, p. 21.

16. Julian S. Corbett, *England in the Seven Years War*, 2 vols. (London: Longmans, Green, 1907), 1:192; David Syrett, "The Methodology of British Amphibious Operations During the Seven Years and American Wars," *Mariner's Mirror* 58 (1972): 270–71.

17. Corbett, *England in the Seven Years War*, 1:200.

18. Walpole, *Memoirs of the Reign of King George the Second*, 3:46.

19. Middleton, "A Reinforcement for North America," p. 59.

20. James Wolfe to Henrietta Wolfe, September 17, 1757, CA microfilm reel A-575.

21. Wolfe to Edward Wolfe, September 21, 1757, Robert Wright, *The Life of Maj-Gen James Wolfe*, 2 vols. (London: Chapman and Hall, 1864), 2:382.

22. Wolfe to William Rickson, Blackheath, November 5, 1757, ibid., 2:396–97.

23. *DNB*, 13:856.

24. Stanley Ayling, *The Elder Pitt* (New York: David McKay, 1976), p. 215; Walpole, *Memoirs of the Reign of King George the Second*, 3:74–79.

25. Pitt to the governors of Massachusetts Bay, New Hampshire, Connecticut, Rhode Island, New York, New Jersey, December 3o, 1757, Gertrude Selwyn Kimball, ed., *Correspondence of William Pitt with Colonial Governors and Naval Commissioners in North America*, 2 vols. (New York: Macmillan, 1906), 1:136.

26. Francois Mario Arouet Voltaire, *Candide*. (Boston: Bedford/St. Martin, 1999), Chapter xxiii.

27. Quoted in Guy Fregault, *War of the Conquest* (Toronto: Oxford University Press, 1989), p. 161.

28. Mère la Grange de St. Louis to Père de Lounay, S.J., Quebec, October 10, 1757, Gerald Kelly, "Thy Hand Shall Lead Me: The Story of Esther Wheelwright," Gerald Kelly Research Materials, MHS; M. Montcalm to M. de Paulmy (minister of war), September 18, 1757, *NYCD*, 10:635–4o; Guy Fregault, *François Bigot*, 2 vols. (Montreal: Guerin, 1948), 2:226–33.

29. D. Peter MacLeod, "Microbes and Muskets: Smallpox and the Participation of the Amerindian Allies of New France in the Seven Years War," *Ethnohistory* 39 (winter 1992): 42–52.

3o. Quoted in D. Peter MacLeod, *The Canadian Iroquois and the Seven Years War* (Toronto: Dundurn Press, 1996), p. 117.

31. Edward P. Hamilton, ed., *Adventure in the Wilderness: The American Journal of Louis Antoine Bougainville, 1756–6o* (Norman: University of Oklahoma Press, 1964), p. 192.

32. M. de Montcalm to M. de Moras, Quebec, February 19, 1758, *NYCD*, 10:686.

33. In a coded message to Paulmy, February 23, 1758, Montreal, ibid., 10:691, Montcalm confided, "Notwithstanding our success, peace is desirable for New France or Canada, which must be reduced in the long run, considering the number of English and the difficulty of transporting provisions and reinforcements."

34. Quoted in Fregault, *War of the Conquest*, p. 228.

35. Quoted in Stanley M. Pargellis, *Lord Loudoun in North America* (New Haven: Yale University Press, 1933), p. 344.

36. Pitt to Loudoun, December 30, 1757, Kimball, ed., *Correspondence of William Pitt*, 1:133–34; Pitt to Abercromby, Whitehall, December 30, 1757, ibid., 1:134–35; John Shy, "James Abercromby and the Campaign of 1758," M.A. thesis, University of Vermont, 1957, pp. 6–11.

37. Loudoun to Cumberland, October 2, 1756, Pargellis, *Military Affairs*, p. 235.

38. Kimball, *Correspondence of William Pitt*, 1:133–53.

39. Captain Hugh Arnot to Loudoun, August 1, 1758, Nicholas Westbrook, ed., " 'Like Roaring Lions Breaking from Their Chains,' The Highland Regiment at Ticonderoga," *Bulletin of the Fort Ticonderoga Museum* 16 (1998): 28.

40. Daniel P. Marston, "Swift and Bold: The 60th Regiment and Warfare in North America," M.A. thesis, McGill University, 1997, pp. 28–37; King L. Parker, "The Influence of Warfare in Colonial America on the Development of British Light Infantry," Anglo-American Wilderness Campaigning, 1754–1764: Logistical and Tactical Developments," Ph.D. diss., Columbia University, 1970, pp. 171–72 and Rogers, *The British Army*, pp. 71–72.

41. Loudoun to Pitt, February 14, 1758, Parkman Papers, MHS, 42:212–20.

42. James is sometimes confused with his son John, who also served in North America.

43. William Eyre to Robert Napier, Lake George, 10 July 1758, Pargellis, *Military Affairs in North America*, p. 420.

44. Joshua Loring to James Rivers May 31, 1758, quoted in Shy, "Abercromby," pp. 74–75.

45. Arnot to Loudoun, August 1, 1758, Westbrook, "Like Roaring Lions," pp. 34–35; "Extracts from Captain Montgomery's Orderly Book, *Bulletin of the Fort Ticonderoga Museum* 12 (1970): 328–57, 439–40.

46. *DCB*, 3:399–400.

47. The *Bulletin of the Fort Ticonderoga Museum* is an indispensable source for the history surrounding Fort Ticonderoga. For the battle, see also: *NYCD*, 10:719–817; William Eyre to Robert Napier, Lake George, July 10, 1758, Pargellis, *Military Affairs*, pp. 418–22; Hamilton, *Adventure in the Wilderness*, pp. 228–35; "Montcalm's Correspondence," Dominion of Canada, *Report of the Public Archives for the Year 1929* (Ottawa: F. A. Acland, 1930), pp. 72–77; Timothy Todish, ed., *Journals of Major Robert Rogers*. (Fleishmanns, N.Y.: Purple Mountain Press, 2002), pp. 117–29; Rene Chartrand, *Ticonderoga* (London: Osprey, 2000); Ian McCulloch, " 'Like Roaring Lions Breaking from Their Chains': The Battle of Ticonderoga." Donald E. Graves, ed., *Fighting for Canada Seven Battles, 1758–1945* (Toronto: Robin Brass, 2000), pp. 23–80; Marston, "Swift and Bold," pp. 47–52.

48. Captain Alexander Monypenny to John Calcraft, July 11, 1758, in McCulloch, "Like Roaring Lions," p. 41; Frank B. Wickes, "Lord Howe," *New York State Historical Association Proceedings* 10 (1911): 238.

49. Eyre to Napier, Lake George, July 10, 1758, Pargellis, *Military Affairs*, p. 418.

50. Lawrence W. Lande, *Montcalm Before and During the Siege of Quebec: A Monograph* (Montreal: M. Lande, 1986), p. 56.

51. List and composition of the French army, July 8, 1758, Hamilton, *Adventure in the Wilderness*, pp. 231–32.

52. Abercromby to Pitt July 12, 1758; Kimball, *Correspondence of William Pitt* 1:299–300.

53. Eyre to Napier July 10, 1758, Pargellis, *Military Affairs*, p. 420.

54. Westbrook, "Like Roaring Lions," p. 41.

55. Journal of Abiel Spicer, Russell P. Bellico, ed., *Chronicles of Lake George: Journeys in War and Peace* (Fleischmanns, N.Y.: Purple Mountain Press, 1995), p. 101.

56. Anonymous to Dr. Peter Middleton, July 10, 1758, Charles E. Lart, ed., "Eyewitness Accounts of the British Repulse at Ticonderoga," *Canadian Historical Review* 2 (1921): 361–62.

57. Loudoun to Cumberland, November 22, 1756, December 26, 1756, Pargellis, *Military Affairs*, p. 264.

58. Westbrook, "Like Roaring Lions," p. 45.

59. H. R. Casgrain, ed., *Journal Du Marquis De Montcalm* (Quebec: L. J. Demers and Frère, 1895), p. 462.

60. Quoted in Francis Parkman, *Montcalm and Wolfe* (Boston: Little, Brown, 1897), p. 186.

61. Gilbert Parker and Claude G. Bryan, *Old Quebec* (New York: Macmillan, 1903), p. 261.

62. McCulloch, "Like Roaring Lions," p. 75.

8. Duquesne and Louisbourg

Epigraph. Alfred P. James, ed., *Writings of General John Forbes* (Menasha, Wisc.: Collegiate Press, 1938), p. 262.

1. Montcalm to Madame la Marquise de St. Veran at Montpelier, Carillon, July 14, 1758. Dominion of Canada, *Report of the Public Archives for the Year 1929* (Ottawa: F. A. Acland, 1930), p. 72.

2. M. Doreil to Marshal de Belle Isle, August 31, 1758. *NYCD*, 10:819–20.

3. Abercromby to Pitt, July 12, 1758, Gertrude S. Kimball, ed., *Correspondence of William Pitt*, 2 vols. (New York: Macmillan, 1906), 1:300.

4. Ian McCulloch, " 'Believe Us, Sir, This Will Impress Few People!' Spin-Doctoring, 18th Century Style," *Bulletin of the Fort Ticonderoga Museum* 16 (1998):92–107.

5. Eyre to Robert Napier, July 10, 1758, Stanley M. Pargellis, ed., *Military Affairs in North America, 1748–1765* (New York: D. Appleton Century, 1936), pp. 418–22.

6. Frederick A. Rahmer, *Dash to Frontenac* (Albany: Holland Patent, 1973), p. 14.

7. John Bradstreet, *An Impartial Account of Lieut. Col. Bradstreet's Expedition to Fort Frontenac* (London: Printed for T. Wilcox, 1759), p. 2.

8. Abercromby to Pitt, August 19, 1758, Kimball, *Correspondence of William Pitt*, 1:323–24; Francis Parkman Papers, 42:253–71, MHS.

9. Bradstreet, *An Impartial Account*, p. 128.

10. "A Journal of the Expedition Against Fort Frontenac in 1758 by Lieut. Benjamin Bass," *Quarterly Journal of the New York State Historical Association* 16 (1935):450.

11. Lieutenant Archibald McCauley to Captain Horatio Gates, Frontenac, August 30, 1758 (transcript), Parkman Papers, 42:272–73; Bradstreet to Abercromby, Frontenac, September 10, 1758 (transcript), ibid., 42:274–75. Fred Anderson, *A People's Army: Massachusetts Soldiers and Society in the Seven Years War* (Chapel Hill: University of North Carolina Press, 1984), pp. 157–58. Guy Fregault, *Canada: The War of the Conquest* (Toronto: Oxford University Press, 1969), p. 222.

12. Vaudreuil to Massiac, September 2, 1758, *NYCD*, 10:822.

13. Sylvester K. Stevens, Donald H. Kent, and Emma E. Woods, eds., *Travels in New France by J. C. B.* (Harrisburg: Pennsylvania Historical Commission, 1941), p. 103.

14. Forbes to Abercromby, April 20, 1758, Alfred P. James, *Writings of General John Forbes*, p. 65; King L. Parker, "Anglo-American Wilderness Campaigning, 1754–1764: Logistical and Tactical Developments." Ph.D. diss., Columbia University, 1970, pp. 252–65.

15. Forbes to Abercromby, May 21, 1758, James, *Writings of General John Forbes*, p. 69.

16. Forbes to John Stanwix, May 29, 1758, ibid., p. 102.

17. Helen Jackson, ed., "Selections from the Correspondence of Colonel Henry Bouquet,

1757–1764," *Pennsylvania Magazine of History and Biography* 32 (1908): 433; George Washington to John Stanwix, Fort Loudoun, April 10, 1758, W. W. Abbot, ed., *The Papers of George Washington* (Charlottesville: University of Virginia Press, 1988), 5:117–20; Douglas S. Freeman, *George Washington: A Biography*, 7 vols. (New York: Charles Scribners's Sons, 1948), 2:305–21.

18. Quoted in Freeman, *George Washington*, 2:327.

19. Washington to Francis Halkett, August 2, 1758, Abbot, *Papers of George Washington*, 5:361.

20. John Forbes to William Pitt, September 6, 1758, Parkman Papers, 42:276–81.

21. Forbes to Peters, August 28, 1758, Alfred P. James, ed., "Letters of John Forbes," *Pennsylvania Magazine of History and Biography* 32 (1908):90.

22. For a description and analysis of the complicated negotiating patterns in Pennsylvania, see James H. Merrill, *Into the American Woods: Negotiators on the Pennsylvania Frontier*, passim (New York: Norton, 1999); Francis Jennings, *Empire of Fortune: Crowns, Colonies and Tribes in the Seven Years War in America* (New York: Norton), pp. 249–348, is, as usual, very direct in his opinions.

23. Jennings, *Empire of Fortune*, p. 384.

24. Anthony F. C. Wallace, *King of the Delawares: Teedyuscung, 1700–1763* (Philadelphia: University of Pennsylvania Press, 1949).

25. Ibid., pp. 18–30.

26. Forbes to Pitt, September 6, 1758, Kimball, *Correspondence of William Pitt*, 1:338–43; Forbes to Pitt, October 20, 1758, ibid., 1:370–75; Jennings, *Empire of Fortune*, pp. 396–403.

27. Bouquet's activities can be followed in Sylvester K. Stevens, Donald H. Kent, and Emma E. Wood, eds., *The Papers of Colonel Henry Bouquet*, Series 21643, 21652, 21653 (Harrisburg: Pennsylvania Historical Commission, 1940). Parker, "Logistical and Tactical Developments," p. 277.

28. Washington to Francis Fauquier, September 28, 1758, Abbot, *Papers of George Washington*, 6:52–53; Forbes to Richard Peters (n.d), *Pennsylvania Magazine of History and Biography* 33 (1909):91–94; Forbes to Bouquet, September 23, 1758, James, *Writings of General John Forbes*, p. 220.

29. Colonel Adam Stephen to Colonel Henry Bouquet, September 15, 1758, Stevens and Kent, *Papers of Colonel Henry Bouquet*, series 21643, p. 173.

30. James Grant to John Forbes, September 14, 1758, Stevens, Kent, and Woods, *Papers of Colonel Henry Bouquet*, series 21652, pp. 130–35; Thomas Mante, *The History of the Late War in North America* (London: W. Strahan, 1772), pp. 156–57.

31. Colonel James Burd to Colonel Henry Bouquet, October 12, 1758, Stevens, Kent, and Woods, *Papers of Colonel Henry Bouquet*, series 21643, p. 189; Burd to Bouquet, October 13, 1758, ibid, p. 190.

32. Orderly book, Loyal Hannon, October 31, 1758, Abbot, *Papers of George Washington*, 6:101n; Forbes to Abercromby, Loyal Hanning, November 17, 1758, James, *Writings of General John Forbes*, pp. 255–56.

33. Initially, Forbes renamed Loyal Hannon Pittsburgh, but after the fall of Duquesne he used the minister's name for that post. Abbot, *Papers of George Washington*, 6:137n.

34. Questions and answers about Fort Ligonier, November 16, 1758, Stevens, Kent, and Woods, *Papers of Colonel Bouquet*, series 21643, pp. 196–97.

35. Forbes to Abercromby and Amherst, Fort Duquesne, November 26, 1758, James, *Writings of General John Forbes*, pp. 262–64; Bouquet to the duke of Portland, December 3, 1758, Stevens, Kent, and Woods, *Papers of Colonel Henry Bouquet*, series 21652, pp. 143–44.

36. Lawrence Shaw Mayo, *Jeffrey Amherst, a Biography* (London: Longmans, Green, 1916), pp. 12–14.

37. Pitt to Abercromby, January 27, 1758, Kimball, *Correspondence of William Pitt*, 1:167–69; Pitt to General Lawrence, January 27, 1758, Kimball, ibid., 1:169–170; Pitt to Admiral Boscawen, February 2, 1758, ibid., 1:176; Pitt to Boscawen, February 3, 1758, ibid., 1:180.

38. Mayo, *Amherst*, p. 55.

39. Wolfe to Lord George Sackville, February 7, 1758, Beckles Willson, *The Life and Letters of James Wolfe* (New York: Dodd Mead, 1909), p. 358.

40. John B. Brebner, *New England's Outpost Acadia Before the Conquest of Canada* (New York: Columbia University Press, 1927), p. 209.

41. J. S. McLennan, *Louisbourg, from Its Foundation to Its Fall* (Halifax: Book Room, 1979), p. 236. For a general overview, see Andrew Peter Podolsky, "Site of Imagination: The Fortress at Louisbourg and Stories of Empire," Ph.D. diss., Northwestern University, 1998.

42. *DCB*, 3; 71–74.

43. Estimates vary. See: Rene Chartrand, *Louisbourg, 1758* (Oxford: Osprey, 2000), pp. 39–42; William Wood, ed., *Logs of the Conquest of Canada* (Toronto: Champlain Society, 1909), pp. 64–65; McLennan, *Louisbourg*, p. 279n.

44. Julian S. Corbett, *England in the Seven Years War*, 2 vols. (London: Longmans, Green, 1907), 1:256–60; Richard Middleton, *The Bells of Victory: The Pitt-Newcastle Ministry and the Conduct of the Seven Years War* (Cambridge: Cambridge University Press, 1985), pp. 66–67.

45. McLennan, *Louisbourg*, p. 267.

46. Clarence Webster, ed., *The Journal of Jeffrey Amherst* (Toronto: Ryerson Press, 1931), pp. 33–46; Amherst to Pitt, March 30, 1758, Kimball, *Correspondence of William Pitt*, 1:219.

47. Journal of David Gordon, CA microfilm A-575; "Log of HMS *Namur*," Wood, *The Logs of the Conquest*, p. 167; Arthur G. Doughty, ed., *Historical Journal of the Campaigns in North America by Captain John Knox*, 3 vols. (Toronto: Champlain Society, 1914), 1:179; Webster, *Journal of Jeffrey Amherst*, pp. 43–44.

48. "Journal of an Expedition Against Louisbourg," *The Northcliffe Collection* (Ottawa: F. A. Acland, 1926), p. 90.

49. Ibid., p. 91. Webster, *Journal of Jeffrey Amherst*, pp. 47–48.

50. McLennan, *Louisbourg*, p. 247.

51. The daily operations of the siege can be followed in "Journal of an Expedition Against Louisbourg" and Webster, *Journal of Jeffrey Amherst*.

52. McLennan, *Louisbourg*, p. 276.

53. "Articles of Capitulation," *Northcliffe Collection*, pp. 87–88.

54. Amherst to Wolfe, August 6, 1758, William Stanhope Taylor and Captain John Henry Pringle, eds., *Correspondence of William Pitt*, 4 vols. (London; John Murray, 1840), 1:330–32; Webster, *Journal of Jeffrey Amherst*, p. 74.

55. Captain Thomas Bell, "Journal of the Gaspée Expedition and Other Matters," CA microfilm A 573; Journal of George Williamson, CA microfilm A 573; Wolfe to Edward Wolfe, August 21, 1758, Robert Wright, *The Life of Maj-Gen James Wolfe*, 2 vols. (London: Chapman and Hall, 1864), 2:455; Wolfe to Amherst, September 30, 1758, ibid., 2:456–58. Amherst ordered a similar expedition to ravage the St. John River area. "Nova Scotia Maj. Morris Report," Aspinwall Papers, *Collections* of the MHS, 4th series (Boston: MHS, 1871), 9:222–38.

56. Bell, "Journal."

57. Wolfe to Amherst, September 30, 1758, CA add. ms. copy 12845.

9. Quebec Besieged

Epigraph: Beckles Willson, *Life and Letters of James Wolfe* (New York: Dodd Mead, 1909), p. 453.

1. Wolfe to William Rickson, December 1, 1758. Robert Wright, *The Life of Maj-Gen James Wolfe*, 2 vols. (London: Chapman and Hall, 1864), 1:466. During the summer of 1758 Pitt had decided to dispatch additional troops, including cavalry, to Germany. Richard Middleton, *The Bells of Victory: The*

Pitt-Newcastle Ministry and the Conduct of the Seven Years War, 1757–1762 (Cambridge: Cambridge University Press, 1985), pp. 74–75.

2. This is the distance from Cap de la Madeleine to Quebec City.

3. In April Quebec's average high temperature is fifty-one degrees Fahrenheit; the average low is thirty-five degrees. In October the average high is fifty-four degrees Fahrenheit; the average low is thirty-nine degrees.

4. Gerald S. Graham, ed., *The Walker Expedition to Quebec, 1711* (Toronto: Champlain Society, 1953).

5. Reed Browning, "The Duke of Newcastle and the Financing of the Seven Years War," *Journal of Economic History* 321 (1971):362, 371, 374–77.

6. Wolfe to Pitt, November 22, 1758, William Stanhope Taylor and Captain John Pringle, eds., *Correspondence of William Pitt,* 4 vols. (London: John Murray, 1840), 1:370.

7. Wolfe to Amherst, December 29, 1758, Richard Middleton, ed., *Amherst and the Conquest of Canada.* (London: Army Records Society, 2003), pp. 9–10.

8. Wolfe to Pitt, December 24, 1758, Willson, *Life and Letters of James Wolfe,* p. 407.

9. Horace Walpole, *Memoirs of the Reign of King George the Second,* 3 vols. (London: Henry Colburn, 1846), 3:231.

10. Wolfe to Henrietta Wolfe, January 25, 1759, Wright, *Life of Maj-Gen James Wolfe,* 2:414; A. G. Bradley, *Sir Guy Carleton (Lord Dorchester)* (Toronto: University of Toronto Press, 1966), pp. 29–32.

11. Quoted in Stuart Reid, *Quebec, 1759* (Oxford: Osprey, 2003), p. 10.

12. Quoted in Willson, *Life and Letters of James Wolfe,* p. 411.

13. Wright, *Life of Maj-Gen James Wolfe,* 2:614; Ian McCulloch, "Pratfalls on the Paths to Glory," *Beaver* (December 1993–January 1994):14–19; Richard Middleton, *The Bells of Victory,* p. 103; Walpole, *Memoirs of the Reign of King George the Second,* 3:230.

14. *DCB,* 4:569–70.

15. Ibid., 4:772–73.

16. Willson, *Life and Letters of James Wolfe,* p. 359.

17. Whitworth A. Porter, *A History of the Corps of Royal Engineers,* 2 vols. (London: Longmans, Green, 1899), 1:190; report on Quebec by Major Patrick Mackellar, Arthur G. Doughty, ed., *An Historical Journal of the Campaigns in North America by Captain John Knox,* 3 vols. (Toronto: Champlain Society, 1914–16), 3:151–60.

18. "Secret Instructions of George II to General Wolfe with Respect to the Conduct of the Expedition, February 5, 1759," *Northcliffe Collection* (Ottawa: F. A. Acland, 1926), pp. 131–32; Arthur G. Doughty, ed., *Siege of Quebec and the Battle of the Plains of Abraham,* 6 vols. (Quebec: Dussault and Proulx, 1901–2), 1:95, 97, 99.

19. Wolfe to Amherst, March 6, 1759, Middleton, *Amherst and the Conquest of Canada,* pp. 27–28.

20. Murray to Amherst, March 18, 1759, CA add. ms. copy 12845.

21. Wolfe to Amherst, May 1, 1759, CA add. ms. copy 12845; Wolfe to Amherst, May 11, 1759, ibid.

22. J. C. Beaglehole, *The Life of Captain James Cook* (Stanford: Stanford University Press, 1974), pp. 40–51.

23. Wolfe to Amherst, May 1, 1759, CA add. ms. copy 12845.

24. Edward P. Hamilton, ed., *Adventure in the Wilderness: The American Journals of Louis Antoine Bougainville, 1756–1760* (Norman: University of Oklahoma Press, 1964), p. 324.

25. Tabular transcription of Wolfe's journal, CA MG 18, L5, vol. 5; Doughty, *An Historical Journal,* 1:349–50.

26. Wolfe to Pitt, May 1, 1759, Taylor and Pringle, eds., *Correspondence of William Pitt,* 1:406.

27. Doughty, *An Historical Journal,* 1:349–50.

28. Ibid., 1:353.

29. Log of HMS *Lowestoft*, William Wood, ed., *The Logs of the Conquest of Canada* (Toronto: Champlain Society, 1909), p. 233.

30. H. R. Casgrain, ed., *Journal du Marquis De Montcalm* (Quebec: L. J. Demers and Frères, 1895), p. 558.

31. "Minute Respecting the Promotion of M. de Montcalm, January 25, 1759," *NYCD*, 10:940.

32. Narrative of the siege of Quebec, ibid., 10:993–1001; Colin G. Calloway, *The Western Abenakis of Vermont, 1600–1800*. (Norman: University of Oklahoma Press, 1990), p. 172; *Northcliffe Collection*, p. 135; D. Peter MacLeod, *The Canadian Iroquis and the Seven Years War* (Toronto: Dundurn Press, 1996), p. 131; Mémoires sur la defense de Québec par le Marquis de Montcalm," Doughty, *An Historical Journal*, 3:179–83.

33. Hamilton, *Adventure in the Wilderness*, p. 323.

34. *An Authentic Plan of the River St. Lawrence* (London: Thomas Jeffreys, 1759) and *A Plan of Quebec* (London: E. Oakley, 1759); Sylvester K. Stevens, Donald H. Kent, and Emma E. Wood, *Travels in New France by J. C. B.* (Harrisburg: Pennsylvania Historical Commission, 1941), pp. 9–14.

35. *Northcliffe Collection*, pp. 209–14; Rene Chartrand, *Quebec, 1759* (Oxford: Osprey, 1999), pp. 65–74; W. J. Eccles and Susan L. Laskin, "The Battles for Quebec, 1759 and 1760," *Historical Atlas of Canada*, 3 vols. (Toronto: University of Toronto Press, 1987), 1: plate 43.

36. Journal of the Siege of Quebec, *Northcliffe Collection*, pp. 223–27.

37. Wolfe to Edward Wolfe, September 4, 1756, Wright, *Life of Maj-Gen James Wolfe*, 2:324.

38. Order, July 5, 1759, Doughty, *An Historical Journal*, 1:398–438; orders, July 27, 1759, CA microfilm A-575.

39. Quoted in Guy Fregault, *Canada: The War of the Conquest*, trans. Margaret M. Cameron (Toronto: Oxford University Press, 1969), p. 250.

40. Wood, *Logs of the Conquest of Canada*, pp. 147–48.

41. Wolfe to Montcalm, July 28, 1759, Willson, *Life and Letters of James Wolfe*, p. 453.

42. Reid, *Quebec*, p. 34.

43. Wolfe to Pitt, September 2, 1759, Gertrude S. Kimball, ed., *Correspondence of William Pitt*, 2 vols. (New York: Macmillan, 1906), 2:153.

44. Doughty, *An Historical Journal*, 1:451–52.

45. Wolfe's journal of the Quebec expedition, July 31, 1759 CA MG 18, L5, vol. 5.

46. Quoted in Willson, *Life and Letters of James Wolfe*, p. 459.

47. Wolfe to mother, August 31, 1759, Wright, *The Life of Maj-Gen James Wolfe*, 2:553.

48. Order to Murray, August 4, 1759, Doughty, ed., *An Historical Journal*, 2:9–10.

49. Journal of the siege of Fort Niagara, *NYCD*, 10:979.

50. Quoted in Brian L. Dunnigan, "Vauban in the Wilderness, the Siege of Fort Niagara," *Niagara Frontier*, 21 (1974):42; Dunnigan, *Siege–The 1759 Campaign Against Niagara* (Youngstown: Old Fort Niagara Association, 1996), pp. 11–22; M. Pouchot, *Memoir Upon the Late War in North America*, translated and edited by Franklin B. Hough, 2 vols. (Roxbury: W. Elliot Woodward, 1866), 2:160–206.

10. The Fall of Quebec

Epigraphs. W. J. Eccles and Susan L. Laskin, "The Battle of Quebec September 13, 1759," *Historical Atlas of Canada*, 3 vols. (Toronto: University of Toronto, 1987), vol. 1, plate 43.

Beckles Willson, *The Life and Letters of James Wolfe* (New York: Dodd Mead, 1909), p. 469.

1. Montcalm to Bougainville, July 21, 1759, Lawrence Lande, *Montcalm Before and During the Siege of Quebec* (Montreal: L. M. Lande, 1986), p. 28; H. R. Casgrain, ed., *Journal du Marquis De Montcalm* (Quebec: L. J. Demers et Frère, 1895), pp. 579–80.

2. Saunders's movements are detailed in William Wood, ed., *The Logs of the Conquest of Canada* (Toronto: Champlain Society, 1909), pp. 203–322.

3. Wolfe to brigadiers, August 29, 1759, CA add. ms copy 32895; Arthur G. Doughty, ed., *An Historical Journal of the Campaigns in North America*, 3 vols. (Toronto: Champlain Society, 1914), 2:3.

4. Nathaniel Cotton to George Grenville, August 27, 1759, CA MG 18, L5, vol. 4; *Northcliffe Collection* (Ottawa: F. A. Acland, 1926), pp. 140–41.

5. Casgrain, *Journal du Marquis De Montcalm*, p. 598.

6. Willson, *Life and Letters of James Wolfe*, p. 464.

7. Wolfe to Saunders, September 2, 1759, Robert Wright, *The Life of Maj-Gen James Wolfe*. 2 vols. (London: Chapman and Hall, 1864), 2:549.

8. Orders, Camp at Montmorency, August 1, 1759, Doughty, *An Historical Journal of the Campaigns in North America*, 2:47n; Wright, *Life of Maj-Gen James Wolfe*, 2:544–45.

9. Brigadiers to Wolfe, August 29, 1759, Wright, *Life of Maj-Gen James Wolfe*, 2:545–46.

10. Quoted in Stuart Reid, *Quebec, 1759* (Oxford: Osprey, 2003), p. 48.

11. Wolfe to Henrietta Wolfe, August 13, 1759, Willson, *Life and Letters of James Wolfe*, pp. 468–69.

12. David Syrett, "The Methodology of British Amphibious Operations During the Seven Years War," *Mariner's Mirror* 58 (1972):269.

13. Montcalm to Bougainville, September 5, 1759, *Northcliffe Collection*, p. 433.

14. Nathaniel Cotton to George Grenville, August 27, 1759, Wood, *Logs of the Conquest of Canada*, p. 230.

15. History and folklore have conspired to produce numerous stories about how Wolfe "discovered" this path. In fact, after weeks of reconnaissance, the path was obvious; the French had posted a guard at the top of the path. W. J. Eccles, "The Battle of Quebec: A Reappraisal," *French Colonial Historical Society Proceedings* 3 (1978): 72–73.

16. *Northcliffe Collection*, p. 143.

17. Brigadiers Monckton, Townshend, and Murray to Wolfe, September 12, 1759, CA add. ms. copy 32895.

18. Wolfe to Monckton, September 12, 1759, ibid.

19. Wolfe to Townshend, September 12, 1759, ibid.

20. Daniel W. Olson et al, "Perfect Tide, Ideal Moon: An Unappreciated Aspect of Wolfe's Generalship at Quebec, 1759," *William and Mary Quarterly*, 3rd Series, 59 (2002): 957–74.

21. He was also the brother of Captain Richard Howe, the commander of *Dunkirk*.

22. A number of quotes have been attributed to Wolfe and his officers before and during the battle. This particular version is in Christopher Hibbert, *Wolfe at Quebec* (New York: Cooper Square Press, 1987), pp. 135–36. Simon Schama, *Dead Certainties* (New York: Alfred A. Knopf, 1991), pp. 17–39.

23. Doughty, *An Historical Journal*, 2:96.

24. *DCB*, 4:249.

25. Quoted in René Chartrand, *Quebec 1759* (Oxford: Osprey, 1999), p. 86.

26. Chartrand, *Quebec, 1759*, pp. 86–87.

27. Quotes from the battlefield abound in a wide variety of sources. For a summary of them see Simon Schama, *Dead Certainties*, pp. 328-331.

28. "Colonel George Williamson to Lt. Gen Commander Ordnance [n.d.]," CA MG 18, L5, vol. 5.

29. The details and ceremony surrounding the surrender are described in Doughty, *An Historical Journal of the Campaigns in North America*, 2:123–134.

11. The Year of Great Victories

Epigraphs. Gazette de France, quoted in Guy Fregault, *Canada: The War of the Conquest* (Toronto: Oxford University Press, 1969), p. 257.

CA add. ms. copy 12845.

1. Quoted in Fregault, *Canada*, p. 257.

2. "Notes Sur le Fort Jacques-Cartier," *Bulletin des Recherches Historiques* 17 (1911): 290–92.

3. Townsend to Amherst, October 7, 1759, Richard Middleton, ed., *Amherst and the Fall of Canada* (London: Army Records Society, 2003), pp. 121–22.

4. Oliver Warner, *With Wolfe to Quebec* (London: History Book Club, 1972), pp. 185–98.

5. Horace Walpole, *Memoirs of the Reign of King George the Second*, 3 vols. (London: Henry Colburn, 1846), 3:229.

6. "Operations of the Army Under M. Montcalm Before Quebec," *NYCD*, 10:1033; Colin G. Calloway, *The Western Abnakis of Vermont, 1600–1800* (Norman: University of Oklahoma Press, 1990), p. 175; Timothy J. Todish, ed., *Annotated and Illustrated Journals of Robert Rogers* (Fleischmans, N.Y.: Purple Mountain Press, 2002), p. 171.

7. Amherst to Rogers, September 13, 1759, Todish, *Journals of Robert Rogers*, pp. 170–71; J. Clarence Webster, ed., *The Journal of Jeffrey Amherst* (Toronto: Ryerson Press, 1931), p. 168; Lawrence Shaw Mayo, *Jeffrey Amherst: A Biography* (New York: Longmans, Green, 1916), p. 158.

8. Sources differ on the actual date of the attack. Todish, *Journals of Major Robert Rogers*, p. 172.

9. Ibid., pp. 172–73.

10. Ibid., p. 186.

11. Ibid., 187.

12. Thomas Mante, *The History of the Late War in North America* (London: W. Strahan, 1772), p. 223.

13. T. D. Seymour Bassett, ed., "A Ballad of Rogers' Retreat, 1759," *Vermont History* 46 (1978): 22.

14. See, for example, M. de Vaudreuil to M. Berryer, September 21, 1759, *NYCD*, 10:1010–11.

15. Richard Pares, "American Versus Continental Warfare, 1739–1763," *English Historical Review* 51 (1936): 453; Herbert W. Richmond, "The Influence of Sea-Power on the Struggle with France in North America and India," *National Review* 75 (1920): 410; Julian S. Corbett, *England in the Seven Years War*, 2 vols. (London: Longmans, Green, 1907), 2:31–70; Geoffrey Marcus, *Quiberon Bay Campaign in Home Waters, 1759* (London: Hill and Carter, 1960), passim.

16. Corbett, *England in the Seven Years War*, 2:53.

17. *Gentlemen's Magazine*, December 1759, p. 557.

18. Quoted in Corbett, *England in the Seven Years War*, 2:64–65.

19. Quoted in ibid., 2:69.

20. *Gentlemen's Magazine*, December 1759, p. 557.

21. Horace Walpole to George Montagu, October 21, 1759, W. S. Lewis, ed., *Horace Walpole's Correspondence with George Montagu*, 2 vols. (New Haven: Yale University Press, 1941), 2:251.

22. H. C. Wylly, *History of the King's Own Yorkshire Light Infantry*, 6 vols. (London: P. Lund, Humphries, 1926), 1:48–49.

23. John Zephaniah Holwell, *A Genuine Narrative of the Deplorable Deaths of the English Gentlemen, and Others, Who Were Suffocated in the Black Hole in Fort William at Calcutta . . .* (London: A Millar, 1758); J. H. Little, "The Black Hole—The Question of Holwell's Veracity," in *Bengal: Past and Present: Journal of the Calcutta Historical Society*, 12 (1916), part 1, serial 23: 32–42, 136–171.

24. *Gentlemen's Magazine*, 1758, p. 262.

25. James L. A. Webb, Jr., "The Mid Eighteenth Century Gum Arabic Trade and the Conquest of Saint-Louis Senegal, 1758," *Journal of Imperial and Commonwealth History* 25 (1997): 37–58; Kate Hotblack, *Chatham's Colonial Policy* (London: Routledge, 1917), pp. 32–35.

26. Pitt to Cumming, February 9, 1757, William Stanhope Taylor and Captain John Henry Pringle, eds., *Correspondence of William Pitt*, 4 vols. (London: John Murray, 1838), 1:221–222.

27. Early in 1759 a British squadron under Commodore Augustus Keppel succeeded in taking the island.

28. The standard work on this subject remains Richard Pares, *War Trade in the West Indies, 1739–1763* (Oxford: Clarendon Press, 1936).

29. Mante, *History of the Late War in North America*, pp. 163–70; Marshall Smelser, *The Campaign for the Sugar Islands* (Chapel Hill: University of North Carolina Press, 1955), p. 19.

30. Mante, *History of the Late War in North America*, p. 164.

31. Smelser, *Campaign for the Sugar Islands*, p. 52.

32. Ibid., pp. 52, 56, 65.

33. Smelser, *Campaign for the Sugar Islands*, p. 86.

34. Mante, *History of the Late War in North America*, p. 175.

35. Ibid., p. 177; Smelser, *Campaign for the Sugar Islands*, pp. 96–97.

36. Arthur G. Doughty, ed., *An Historical Journal of the Campaigns in North America*, 3 vols. (Toronto: Champlain Society, 1914), 2:248.

37. J. Desbruyeres to Amherst, May 20, 1760, *The Northcliffe Collection* (Ottawa: F. A. Acland, 1926), pp. 426–29; Reginald H. Mahon, *Life of General the Hon James Murray* (London: John Murray, 1921), pp. 206–15.

38. Fregault, *Canada*, p. 272.

39. The events of spring 1760 are well chronicled in a to-date unpublished essay by Ian McCulloch, " 'From April Battles and Murrays Generals, Good Lord deliever me!': The Battle of Sillery, 28 April 1760." I thank him for sharing this essay with me.

40. Doughty, *An Historical Journal of the Campaigns in North America*, 2:352.

41. Ibid., 384.

42. Ibid., 386.

43. Murray to Pitt, May 25, 1760, Gertrude S. Kimball, ed., *Correspondence of William Pitt, When Secretary of State, With Colonial Governors and Military and Naval Commissioners in America*, 2 vols. (New York: Macmillan, 1906), p. 294.

44. Ibid.

45. Lawrence to Pitt, May 11, 1760, ibid., 2:284.

46. Journal of the Battle of Sillery and siege of Quebec, *NYCD*, 10:1088.

47. Murray to Amherst, May 19, 1760, CA add. ms. copy 12638.

48. Edward P. Hamilton, ed., *Adventure in the Wilderness: The American Journals of Louis Antoine de Bougainville, 1756–1760* (Norman: University of Oklahoma Press, 1964), p. 326.

49. Pierre Pouchot, *Memoires sur la derniere guerre de l'Amerique septentrionale, entre la France et l'Angleterre*, 3 vols. (Yverdon: n.p., 1781), 1:238, 2:105.

50. Amherst to Pitt, July 13, 1759, CA add. ms. copy 12845.

51. William Johnson to Pitt, Fort Johnson, October 24, 1760, James Sullivan, ed., *The Papers of Sir William Johnson*, 14 vols. (Albany: University of the State of New York, 1921–65), 3:269–75.

52. Amherst to Monckton, August 26, 1760. *Collections* of the MHS, 4th series, 9:307; Webster, *The Journal of Jeffrey Amherst*, pp. 231–32.

53. Pouchot, *Memoires*, 2:28.

54. Mante, *History of the Late War in North America*, p. 306.

55. Webster, *Journal of Jeffrey Amherst*, pp. 242–45.

56. Amherst to Pitt, September 8, 1760, Kimball, *Correspondence of William Pitt*, 2:329–33.

57. Doughty, *An Historical Journal*, 2:561; Webster, *Journal of Jeffrey Amherst*, pp. 245–46.

58. Amherst to Haldimand, September 9, 1760, *Report of the Public Archives of Canada* (1884), p. 7.

59. Webster, *Journal of Jeffrey Amherst*, p. 247.

12. Pitt Departs, the War Expands

Epigraph. *English Historical Review* 21 (1906): 132.

1. Indian Conference, Montreal, September 16, 1760, James Sullivan, ed., *The Papers of Sir William Johnson*, 14 vols. (Albany: University of the State of New York, 1921–65), 13:163–66.

2. Ibid.

3. Julian P. Boyd, ed., *Susquehanna Company Papers*, 11 vols. (Ithaca: Cornell University Press, 1930–71), 2:138–39.

4. Meeting at Easton with Delawares, *Papers of Sir William Johnson*, 3:771.

5. Ibid., 3:786.

6. Anthony F. C. Wallace, *King of the Delawares: Teedyuscung, 1700–1763* (Philadelphia: University of Pennsylvania Press, 1949).

7. Henry Timberlake, *The Memoirs of Lt. Henry Timberlake* (London; Printed for the author, 1765), p. 74.

8. David H. Corkran, *The Cherokee Frontier: Conflict and Survival, 1740–62* (Norman: University of Oklahoma Press, 1962), p. 174.

9. Muskogean people of the southeast included a number of tribes. The largest were Choctaw, Chickasaw, Cherokee, Creek, and Seminole.

10. The site of the fort and the Indian village is now covered by Lake Keowee, part of the Keowee Toxaway hydroelectric project.

11. Edward McCrady, *History of South Carolina* (New York: Macmillan, 1899), pp. 330–33.

12. Governor William Henry Lyttleton to William Pitt, December 29, 1759, Gertrude S. Kimball, ed., *Correspondence of William Pitt*, 2 vols. (New York: Macmillan), 2:230.

13. James C. Kelley, "Attakullakulla," *Journal of Cherokee Studies* 3 (winter 1978): 2–34.

14. John Pearson to Lyttleton, February 8, 1760, William L. McDowell, ed., *Documents Relating to Indian Affairs* (Columbia: University of South Carolina Press, 1970), pp. 495–96.

15. Alexander Miln to Lyttleton, February 24, 1760, ibid., p. 499.

16. Corkran, *Cherokee Frontier*, pp. 207–8; Charles H. Stewart, comp., *The Service of British Regiments in Canada and North America* (Ottawa: Department of National Defense Library, 1962), pp. 77, 322.

17. McDowell, *Documents Relating to Indian Affairs*, pp. xxxiii–xxxiv; John R. Maas, "'All the Poor Province Could do': North Carolina and the Seven Years War, 1757–1762," *North Carolina Historical Review* 79 (2002): 75.

18. *Gentlemen's Magazine* 30 (1760), p. 442.

19. Corkran, *Cherokee Frontier*, p. 245.

20. Journal of an expedition to South Carolina by Captain Christopher French, *Journal of Cherokee Studies* (1977): 275–301.

21. Pitt to Amherst, January 7, 1761, Kimball, *Correspondence of William Pitt*, 2:384.

22. Lawrence Shaw Mayo, *Jeffrey Amherst: A Biography* (New York: Longmans, Green, 1916), p. 197.

23. Pitt to Amherst, January 7, 1761, Kimball, *Correspondence of William Pitt*, 2:385.

24. By then, there had emerged a certain Louisbourg fellowship: Amherst, Wolfe, Murray, Monckton, Rollo, Holmes, and many junior officers.

25. Rollo to Pitt, June 8, 1761, Kimball, *Correspondence of William Pitt*, 2:440–43.

26. Horace Walpole, *Memoirs of the Reign of King George the Second*, 3 vols. (London: Henry Colburn, 1846), 3:302.

27. Adam Williamson notebook, CA roll A 573.

28. Julian S. Corbett, *England in the Seven Years War*, 2 vols. (London: Longmans, Green, 1907), 2:222; David Syrett, "The Methodology of British Amphibious Operations During the Seven Years War and American Wars," *Mariners Mirror* 58 (1922): 269–80.

29. Mante, *History of the Late War in North America* (London: Printed for W. Strahan, 1772), p. 356.

30. Corbett, *England in the Seven Years War*, 2:283n.

31. Geo. Fred. de Martens, comp., *Recueil de Traites d'Alliance, de Paix, de Treve . . .* (Gottingue: Librairie de Dieterich, 1817), 1:16–28.

32. Minutes of cabinet meeting, October 2, 1761, *English Historical Review* 21 (1906): 130–32.

33. Stanley Ayling, *The Elder Pitt, Earl of Chatham* (New York: David McKay, 1971), p. 291.

34. Mante, *History of the Late War in North America*, p. 392.

35. Wolfe to Henrietta Wolfe, November 6, 1751, Robert Wright, *The Life of Maj-Gen James Wolfe*, 2 vols. (London: Chapman and Hall, 1864), 1:165.

36. Pocock's journal, March 5, 1760, David Syrett, ed., *The Siege and Capture of Havana, 1762* (London: Navy Records Society, 1970), p. 57.

37. Rodney to Pocock, April 27, 1762, ibid., p. 98.

38. *An Authentic Journal of the Siege of Havana by an Officer* (London: T. Jeffreys, 1762), pp. 6–7.

39. Richard Pares, *War and Trade in the West Indies, 1739–1763* (Oxford: Clarendon Press, 1936), pp. 592–93.

40. *An Authentic Journal*, pp. 9–10.

41. Captain Augustus Hervey to Pocock, July 1, 1762, Syrett, *Siege and Capture of Havana, 1762*, p. 217; journal of Lieutenant Colonel Patrick Mackellar, ibid., pp. 221, 223, 233.

42. The average monthly temperatures in Havana during the summer are: June, eighty degrees Fahrenheit; July, eighty-two degrees; and August, 82 degrees.

43. While eighteenth-century British troops may have been expected to get along with less, U.S. Army Field Manual *FM 10–52*, pp. 3–4, stipulates a requirement of 4.7 gallons of water per day per man. By this standard Albemarle would have been transporting at least 660 barrels (32 gallons each) every day.

44. Syrett, *Siege and Capture of Havana, 1762*, p. xxix.

45. Mante, *History of the Late War in North America*, p. 429–30.

46. Ibid., p. 431; *An Authentic Journal*, p. 24.

47. Mante, *History of the Late War in North America*, p. 447.

48. King L. Parker, "Anglo American Wilderness Campaigning, 1754–1764: Logistical and Tactical Developments," Ph.D. diss., Columbia University, 1970, p. 295. When Israel Putnam's Connecticut Company arrived at Havana, they numbered 109 men. At the fall of the city, only 20 men were fit for duty. Thirteen had deserted, and the rest were dead, mostly from disease. Albert C. Bates, ed., *Rolls of Connecticut Men in the French and Indian War, 1755–1762*, 2 vols. (Hartford, 1905), 2:299–301.

49. *Colonel Draper's Answer to the Spanish Arguments* (London: J. Dodsley, 1764), p. 21.

50. William Amherst to Jeffrey Amherst, September 20, 1762. CA add. ms. copy 12839.

13. The End, the Beginning

Epigraph. *Memoirs of the Reign of King George the Third*, 4 vols. (London: Richard Bentley, 1845), 1:136–37.

1. Quoted in Stanley Ayling, *The Elder Pitt* (New York: David McKay, 1976), p. 299; Walpole, *Memoirs of the Reign of King George the Third*, 1:136–37.

2. Quoted in Ayling, *The Elder Pitt*, p. 301.

3. Quoted in Julian S. Corbett, *England in the Seven Years War*, 2 vols. (London: Longmans, Green, 1907), 2:358.

4. Full text of the treaty may be found in ibid., 2:377–390. A classic analysis of the treaty is presented by Richard Pares, *War and Trade in the West Indies, 1739–1763* (Oxford: Clarendon Press, 1936), pp. 596–612.

5. Pares, *War and Trade in the West Indies*, pp. 216–26.

6. Walpole, *Memoirs of the Reign of King George the Third*, 1:223.

7. Ibid., 1:222.

8. Ibid., 1:223–24.

9. Ibid., 1:226.

10. John Brewer, *The Sinews of Power: War, Money and the English State, 1689–1783* (London: Unwin, 1989).

11. Quoted in Basil Williams, *The Life of William Pitt Earl of Chatham*, 2 vols. (London: Longmans, Green, 1913), 2:85.

12. Howard H. Peckham, *Pontiac and the Indian Uprising* (Princeton: Princeton University Press, 1947), p. 70.

13. Campbell to Colonel Henry Bouquet, March 10, 1761, Sylvester K. Stevens and Donald H. Kent, eds., *The Papers of Colonel Henry Bouquet*, series 21646 (Harrisburg: Pennsylvania Historical Commission, 1941), pp. 62–63.

14. Amherst to Johnson, February 22, 1761, James Sullivan, ed., *The Papers of Sir William Johnson*, 14 vols. (Albany: University of the State of New York, 1921–65), 3:345.

15. Amherst to Johnson, August 9, 1761, ibid., 3:515.

16. Quoted in Francis Jennings, *Empire of Fortune: Crowns, Colonies and Tribes in the Seven Years War in America* (New York: Norton, 1988), p. 442.

17. Quoted in Daniel K. Richter, *Facing East From Indian Country* (Cambridge: Harvard University Press, 2001), p. 196.

18. Timothy J. Todish, ed., *The Annotated and Illustrated Journals of Major Robert Rogers* (Fleischmanns, N.Y.: Purple Mountain Press, 2002), p. 217.

19. Major Henry Gladwin to Amherst, May 14, 1763, in Francis Parkman Papers, MHS, 22:37–40.

20. Captain Etherington to Major Henry Gladwin, Michilimackinac, June 12, 1763, ibid., 22:101–5.

21. Amherst to Gladwin, June 22, 1763, ibid., 22:190.

22. Amherst to Captain Lieutenant Valentine Gardner, August 10, 1763, ibid., 22:413–14.

23. Jennings, *Empire of Fortune*, p. 447.

24. Bouquet to Amherst, August 5, 1763, Stevens and Kent, *Papers of Colonel Henry Bouquet*, Series 21653, p. 208.

25. Clarence W. Alvord, *The Illinois Country, 1673–1818* (Springfield: Illinois Centennial Commission, 1920), p. 241.

26. Peckham, *Pontiac and the Indian Uprising*, p. 236.

27. Ibid.

28. Ibid., pp. 237–38.

29. John R. Alden, *General Gage in America* (Baton Rouge: Louisiana State University Press, 1948), pp. 89–94.

30. Thomas Mante, *The History of the Late War in North America* (London: W. Strahan, 1772), p. 510.

31. Gage to William Johnson, September 2, 1764, Sullivan, *Papers of Sir William Johnson*, 11:344.

32. Mante, *History of the Late War in North America*, p. 536.

33. Ibid., p. 539.

34. Bouquet to Gage, November 15, 1764, Stevens and Kent, *Papers of Colonel Henry Bouquet*, Series 21653, p. 326.

35. Johnson to Lords of Trade, August 20, 1766, *NYCD*, 7:851.

36. Peckham, *Pontiac and the Indian Uprising*, p. 297.

Epilogue

1. *DNB*, 8:558.

2. DNB, 8:558.

3. John Shy, *Towards Lexington: The Role of the British Army in the Coming of the American Revolution* (Princeton: Princeton University Press, 1965), p. 64.

4. Lords of Trade to William Johnson, September 29, 1763, *NYCD*, 7:567.

5. *Montreal Gazette*, October 12, 2001.

A Note on Sources

Material for the Seven Years' War is as vast as the subject itself. Online catalog searches yield a mountain of titles, which can be overwhelming. For a more manageable point of entry, see the somewhat dated but still useful bibliographic guide by James G. Lydon, *Struggle for Empire: A Bibliography of the French and Indian War* (New York: Garland Publishing, 1986). A bit older than Lydon, but still very useful, are the two volumes by Lawrence Henry Gipson, *A Bibliographic Guide to the History of the British Empire, 1748–1776* (New York: Alfred Knopf, 1969), and *A Guide to Manuscripts Relating to the History of the British Empire* (New York: Alfred A. Knopf, 1970). These are volumes 14 and 15 of his monumental *A History of the British Empire Before the American Revolution* (vols. 1–3, Caldwell: Caxton Printers, 1935; vols. 4–15, New York: Alfred A. Knopf, 1939–70).

Although frequent targets for modern critics, Francis Parkman's *France and England in North America*, 9 vols. (Boston: Little, Brown, 1865–92), and *The Conspiracy of Pontiac*, 2 vols. (Boston: Little, Brown, 1851), remain important sources for this period. Of particular note are the two volumes, *Montcalm and Wolfe*, which despite its flaws, continues to hold its place as a piece of magisterial history and an American literary classic. Parkman's work on these two figures looms so large as to apparently prevent others from engaging them. Both Montcalm and Wolfe need modern biographies. Julian S. Corbett, *England in the Seven Years War: A Study in Combined Strategy*, 2 vols. (London: Longmans, Green, 1907), provides a strategic overview. England's domestic political issues are considered in Richard Middleton, *The Bells of Victory: The Pitt-Newcastle Ministry and the Conduct of the Seven Years War* (London: Cambridge University Press, 1985). A comprehensive contemporary view of the war from the British perspective is the very useful Thomas Mante, *The History of the Late War in North America and the Islands of the West Indies* (London: Printed for W. Strahan, 1772). The *Gentlemen's Magazine* and Horace Walpole, *Memoirs of the Reign of King George the Second*, 3 vols. (London: Henry Colburn, 1846), as well as his *Memoirs of the Reign of King George the Third*, 4 vols. (London: Richard Bentley, 1845), provide insight into the domestic reactions to news from abroad and a sampling of political gossip.

Military information can be found in: Andrew Gallup and Donald F. Shaffer, *La Marine: The French Colonial Soldier in Canada* (Bowie, Md.: Heritage Books, 1992); Lee Kennett, *The French Armies in the Seven Years War* (Durham: Duke University Press, 1967); and H. C. B. Rogers, *The British Army of the Eighteenth Century* (London: George Allen and Unwin, 1977). For the French navy, see James Pritchard, *Louis XV's Navy, 1748–1762: A Study of Organization and Administration* (Montreal: McGill-Queens University Press, 1987). The standard source for the Royal Navy remains William Laird Clowes, *The Royal Navy: A History from the Earliest Times to the Present*, 7 vols. (London: S. Low, Marston, 1897–1903).

The most recent analysis of the war is the fine work by Fred Anderson, *Crucible of War: The Seven Years War and the Fate of Empire in British North America, 1754–1766* (New York: Alfred A. Knopf, 2000). On the French side, Richard Waddington, *La Guerre de Sept Ans: Histoire diplomatique et militaire*, 5 vols.

(Paris: Firmin-Didot, 1899–1914) is comprehensive but old. Guy Fregault, *Canada: The War of the Conquest*, translated by Margaret M. Cameron (Toronto: Oxford University Press, 1969), provides the Canadian view. Beyond these standard general overviews, specific topics are covered in a dense thicket of monographic, secondary, and journal literature. One journal deserves special mention: The *Bulletin of the Fort Ticonderoga Museum*, published since 1927, is a treasure of information both primary and secondary. The multivolume *Dictionary of Canadian Biography* ought also to be counted an important source of information as well as *The Atlas of Canadian History*, 3 vols., edited by R. Cole Harris, with maps by Geoffrey J. Matthews (Toronto: University of Toronto Press, 1987–93).

Manuscript sources are important as well. British North America was a literate society, and its soldiers were wont to keep journals and diaries, and to write letters home. Many major historical societies and repositories, particularly those connected to the original colonies, have relevant collections. The papers of Francis Parkman, containing thousands of pages of transcripts, at the Massachusetts Historical Society are particularly rich and should be used in connection with the society's collection of diaries and journals from the war. The papers of Lord Loudoun are at the Huntington Library, and the Canadian Archives possesses originals and copies of a great number of papers relating to the principal officers, including Jeffrey Amherst and James Wolfe. Some of these original materials have been published and appear in a variety of colonial records series. Among the most important of these, despite certain questions about translation, is Edmund B. O'Callaghan, ed., *Documents Relative to the Colonial History of the State of New York*, 10 vols. (Albany: Weed, Parsons, 1853–58). The published colonial records of Virginia, South Carolina, and Pennsylvania are also useful, as are the variety of materials appearing in the *Collections* of the Massachusetts Historical Society. Published manuscript sources are more limited on the Canadian side. Parkman's contemporary and correspondent H. R. Casgrain was a prodigious collector, author, and editor. He oversaw the transcription and editing of *Collection des Manuscrits du Marechal de Lévis*, 12 vols. (Quebec: L. J. Demers and Frère, 1889–95). Arthur G. Doughty and George W. Parmelee, eds., *The Siege of Quebec and the Battle of the Plains of Abraham*, 6 vols. (Quebec: Dussault and Proulx, 1901), is a comprehensive collection of documents. Arthur G. Doughty also edited *John Knox, An Historical Account of the Campaigns in North America for the Years 1757, 1758, 1759 and 1760*, 3 vols. (Toronto: Champlain Society, 1914–16). *Reports of the Public Archives* (Ottawa: F. A. Acland, various dates), are also valuable.

Papers of several of the key players in the struggle have been published. These include: Clarence Webster, ed., *The Journal of Jeffrey Amherst, Recording the Military Career of General Amherst in America from 1758 to 1763* (Toronto: Ryerson Press, 1931); Richard Middleton, ed., *Amherst and the Conquest of Canada* (London: Army Records Society, 2003); Edward P. Hamilton, ed., *Adventure in the Wilderness: The American Journals of Louis Antoine de Bougainville, 1756–1760* (Norman: University of Oklahoma Press, 1964); Sylvester K. Stevens, Donald H. Kent, and Emma E. Woods, eds., *The Papers of Henry Bouquet*, series 21631, 21632, 20 vols. (Harrisburg: Pennsylvania Historical Commission, 1940–43); Stanley M. Pargellis, ed., *Military Affairs in North America, 1748–1765: Selected Documents from the Cumberland Papers in Windsor Castle* (New York: D. Appleton Century, 1936); David Syrett, comp., *The Siege and Capture of Havana* (London: Naval Records Society, 1970); James Sullivan, ed., *The Papers of Sir William Johnson*, 14 vols. (Albany: University of the State of New York, 1921–65); Gertrude S. Kimball, ed., *The Correspondence of William Pitt, When Secretary of State, with Colonial Governors and Military and Naval Commissioners in America*, 2 vols. (New York: Macmillan, 1906); Timothy J. Todish, ed., *The Annotated and Illustrated Journals of Major Robert Rogers* (Fleischmanns, N.Y.: Purple Mountain Press, 2002); Charles Henry Lincoln, ed., *The Correspondence of William Shirley, Governor of Massachusetts and Military Commander in America, 1731–1760*, 2 vols. (New York: Macmillan, 1912); W. W. Abbot, ed., *The Papers of George Washington*, Colonial Series, 10 vols. (Charlottesville: University Press of Virginia, 1983–1995). For documents on the diplomatic controversies in North America, see Theodore Calvin Pease, *Anglo-French Boundary Disputes in the West, 1749–1763* (Springfield: Illinois State Historical Library, 1936).

In recent years considerable attention has been directed toward examining the role of Native Americans in the struggle for North America. The task is difficult since virtually all the written materials arrive through European eyes. The various published colonial sources cited above contain reports, correspondence, and minutes of various meetings, as well as the texts of numerous treaties. For French relations with the Indians, Reuben G. Thwaites, ed., *The Jesuit Relations and Related Documents: Travels and Explorations of the Jesuit Missionaries in New France, 1610–1791*, 73 vols. (Cleveland: Burrows Brothers, 1896–1901) is essential. A fundamental beginning point remains William G. Sturtevant, general editor, *The Handbook of North American Indians*, 17 vols. (Washington: Smithsonian Institution, 1978–   ). Volume 15 of that work, edited by Bruce Trigger, *The Northeast*, is particularly important. Other scholarship includes: James Axtell, *The Invasion Within: The Contest of Cultures in Colonial North America* (New York: Oxford University Press, 1985); Colin G. Calloway, *The Western Abenakis of Vermont, 1600–1800: War, Migration, and the Survival of an Indian People* (Norman: University of Oklahoma Press, 1990); David H. Corkran, *The Cherokee Frontier: Conflict and Survival, 1740–1762* (Norman: University of Oklahoma Press, 1962); Gregory Evans Dowd, *War Under Heaven: Pontiac, the Indian Nations and the British Empire* (Baltimore: Johns Hopkins University Press, 2002); Francis Jennings, *Empire of Fortune: Colonies and Tribes in the Seven Years War in America* (New York: Norton, 1988); and D. Peter MacLeod, *The Canadian Iroquois and the Seven Years War* (Toronto: Dundurn Press, 1996); James H. Merrell, *Into the American Woods: Negotiators on the Pennsylvania Frontier* (New York: Norton, 1999); Daniel Richter, *The Ordeal of the Longhouse: The Peoples of the Iroquois League in the Era of European Colonization* (Chapel Hill: University of North Carolina Press, 1992); Richard White, *The Middle Ground: Empires and Republics in the Great Lakes Region, 1650–1815* (New York: Cambridge University Press, 1991).

Since many of the North American sites associated with the war evidence physical remains, archaeological studies can be useful. Two I found particularly useful are: Gerald E. Bradfield, *Fort William Henry: Digging Up History* (n.p.: French and Indian War Society, 2001) and David R. Starbuck, *The Great Warpath: British Military Sites from Albany to Crown Point* (Hanover: University Press of New England, 1999).

Twenty-first-century scholarship requires acknowledgment of electronic sources. A "google" search under almost any term associated with the French and Indian War (people, places, events) yields a long list of "hits." Some of these sites are nothing more than advertisements for tourist attractions, but many, particularly those associated with Parks Canada, the National Park Service, libraries, and the various states and provinces, are reliable. Increasingly, library and archival sources are online as well. Both the *Jesuit Relations* and the *Dictionary of Canadian Biography*, for example, are available electronically. The Canadian National Library and Archives presents a very impressive array of electronic sources, which is being added to almost daily.

Index

Page numbers in *italics* refer to illustrations.